THEORIES
OF THE MIXED ECONOMY

THEORIES
OF
THE MIXED ECONOMY

Edited by
DAVID REISMAN

VOLUME V

EVAN DURBIN

The Politics of Democratic Socialism

LONDON
WILLIAM PICKERING
1994

Published by Pickering & Chatto (Publishers) Limited
17 Pall Mall, London, SW1Y 5NB

© Pickering & Chatto (Publishers) Limited
Introduction © David Reisman

All rights reserved. No part of this publication may be
reproduced, stored in a retrieval system, or transmitted in
any form or by any means, electronic, mechanical,
photocopying, recording, or otherwise without prior permission
of the publisher.

British Library Cataloguing in Publication Data
Theories of the Mixed Economy. – Vol. V:
Politics of Democratic Socialism. – New
ed
   I. Reisman, David   II. Durbin, Evan
   330.126
Set ISBN 1 85196 213 1
This volume ISBN 1 85196 218 2

Printed and bound in Great Britain by
Antony Rowe Limited
Chippenham

CONTENTS

EVAN DURBIN

Evan Frank Mottram Durbin was born at Bideford, Devon, on 1 March 1906. His father, the Reverend F Durbin was (like his father before him) a Baptist minister: a man of strict principles, he was a pacifist in the First World War. His mother, also from a clerical background, was a committed Christian, an advocate of temperance and an opponent of theatre-going. She was deeply disappointed when Evan (whose first experience of public speaking had been as an occasional preacher) decided not to continue the family tradition of mission through ordination. Evan may not have become a clergyman, but he retained from his non-conformist childhood a belief in morality of intent and in personal responsibility which help to explain his distaste in later life for the inevitabilities of the determinists and the short-termism of the technocrats who would put expediency before ethics. He also retained a conviction that politics is about conscience. His parents had been Gladstonian Liberals but had come to support Asquith and Lloyd George in their campaign for progressive taxation and a national insurance safety-net. Durbin's parents were never much in sympathy with the unions and the planners. The Welfare State in the spirit of the Good Samaritan was, however, a cause with which they could identify themselves.

Evan Durbin was educated at Taunton School and then at New College, Oxford. He obtained a First Class Honours degree in Politics, Philosophy and Economics (after first obtaining a degree in Zoology, in which he had developed an interest at school). Lionel Robbins, at New College from 1926–9 (the short period in which he managed to tutor not only Durbin but also Douglas Jay, Hugh Gaitskell, Colin Clark, Frank Packenham and his College successor, E H Phelps Brown, who had been at Taunton with Evan) recognised Durbin's potential. First helping him to secure the one-year Ricardo Fellowship at University College, London, Robbins, made Professor at the London School of Economics following the sudden death of Allyn Young, invited Durbin to join the LSE as Lecturer in

Economics in 1930. Durbin was to become Senior Lecturer but was denied the Department's Readership when Hugh Dalton re-entered the House of Commons in 1935. Durbin attributed the decision to the fact that the senior economists (Robbins, Friedrich von Hayek, Arnold Plant) were opposed to government intervention and public works whereas he (with Brinley Thomas) was one of only two active socialists in Economics at the School.

Determined to convert his ideas into realities, Durbin lectured once a week in the 1930s for the Workers' Educational Association in the Potteries, as Hugh Gaitskell had done (full-time) in the Nottingham area. Like Gaitskell, Durbin stood, unsuccessfully, for Parliament – for East Grinstead (Sussex) in 1931 and for Gillingham (Kent) in 1935. With Gaitskell, Durbin in 1934 joined the secretive XYZ Club, founded in 1932 by Labour sympathisers in the City in order to advise politicians on economic issues. With Gaitskell, Durbin in the 1930s was active in the New Fabian Research Bureau (amalgamated into the Fabian Society in 1939) and in 1936 went on to the Labour Party's Finance and Trade Subcommittee. Gaitskell was lecturing in economics at University College when Durbin was at the LSE. At Oxford Gaitskell has not been above describing the intense young moralist ('Have you ever been hungry, man?', Durbin once asked Lord Longford) as 'a bit of a prig and a puritan'. In London they became close friends. Durbin's wife, Marjorie (whom he married in 1932) had been Gaitskell's student at UCL. Evan was best man when Hugh and Dora were married in 1937 at Hampstead Town Hall. After Evan's death Hugh was instrumental in setting up and administering the Durbin Trust Fund that paid for the education of Durbin's children. In the 1930s it was the common cause of Durbin and Gaitskell to chart a middle course between the syndicalists and the Marxists on the Left, the liberals and the Fascists on the Right. In the institutionalised role-plays that began in the Oxford University Labour Club and continued in London, Hugh would often take the part of a future Prime Minister, Evan that of a future Labour Chancellor.

As war in Europe approached, Durbin made no secret of his belief (by no means popular with Labour's internationalists) that appeasement and concessions could be justified if the abdication of the Sudetenland to Hitler's Germany might in the end prevent the sacrifice of British lives: 'I am not one of those persons who is prepared to die in order to extend the principle of self-government to other nations', he states on p 329 of his *Democratic Socialism*. Britain drawn despite Munich inexorably into the conflict, Durbin in a Labour pamphlet of 1942 was able at last to find a satisfactory answer to his question *What Have We to Defend?* – 'The meadows of the Thames, the wooded downs of Sussex, the ancient stones of Purbeck, the grey, grass-crowned bastions of Cornwall'. In the War Durbin was in the civil service, initially employed in the Economic Section of the War Cabinet and later as Personal Assistant to the Deputy Prime Minister, Clement Atlee. Peace restored, Atlee at No 10, Durbin was a beneficiary from the 1945 landslide when he finally entered the House of Commons as the Labour Member for Edmonton. In 1947 he was made Parliamentary Secretary in the Ministry of Works. Then disaster struck. On 3 September 1948 Evan Durbin was drowned while rescuing two children in a swimming accident, aged only 42.

Durbin's life was short and his intellectual contribution confined essentially to the 1930s. The context was the world depression and the prolonged unemployment; the General Strike of 1926 that had been triggered by wage-cuts and the *General Theory* of 1936 that looked to fiscal policy for reflation of demand; Ramsay MacDonald's coalition government of 1931 that pushed Labour out of power and the Continental dictatorships that saw little value in democracy. Durbin's writings address some of the central concerns of a troubled interregnum that had lost the gold standard and the invisible hand but was still to gain the deficit spending and the legitimation of pragmatism.

Money, cycles and unemployment are the theme of Durbin's *Purchasing Power and Trade Depression* (1933), his *Socialist Credit Policy* (1933), and his *The Problem of Credit Policy* (1935). Durbin had probably attended Hayek's 1930 lectures that later became *Prices and Production* (1931). Disagreeing with Hayek on the case for State-sponsored reflation (it was apparently Meade who persuaded Durbin that expansionary policies could succeed in an underemployed economy), Durbin shared with Hayek a continuing belief that more savings (and more investment) were the better means to produce an upswing than would be more consumption such as could all-too-easily transform a recovery into a recession by means of the accelerated inflation that excessive demand could release. In contrast to Hayek, Durbin looked to the State to solve the problem of intersectoral imbalance through central co-ordination – and supported the nationalisation of the Bank of England with the macroeconomic argument that the money supply is always and everywhere a political responsibility.

The relationship between political direction and economic prosperity was further explored by Durbin in a series of scholarly contributions to the debate between the market automaticity of the libertarians represented in Hayek's *Collectivist Economic Planning* and the centralised regulation that was championed by the Webbs in *Soviet Communism* and by Cole in *The Principles of Economic Planning*, all of 1935. Durbin was adamant that consumer sovereignty must be respected and that workers must be free to chose their employments: planning to him was never legitimate where the ends of the leadership took precedence over the goals of the citizenry. Durbin's target was market failure first and foremost. Where the competitive equilibrium is sub-optimal in public goods such as 'the enjoyment of equality', where the 'profiteering landlord' and the 'speculative builder' are licensed by liberty to impose Pigovian social costs such as the despoliation of the countryside, where small businesses are unable to forecast long-term trends and giant monopolies are empowered by economies of size to make a Marshallian decreasing cost into a Marxian increasing price, there, Durbin argued, it is democracy and not exchange that provides the better guarantee of the individual's welfare. Durbin forcefully made his case for mix in papers such as 'The Importance of Planning' (in G Catlin, ed, *New Trends in Socialism*, 1935), 'Democracy and Socialism in Great Britain', (*Political Quarterly*, 1935), 'The Social Significance of the Theory of Value', (*Economic Journal*, 1935), 'Economic Calculus in a Planned Economy', (*Economic Journal*, 1936) that, reprinted in the posthumous volume *Problems of Economic Planning* (1949), served as an eloquent reminder to Labour's revisionists in the following decade that orthodox microeconomics, centralised guidance and personal freedom ought best to be seen as complements and not as rivals.

Durbin's most influential work was his last. *The Politics of Democratic Socialism* was published in the dark days of 1940, at a time when persecution, dictatorship and struggle seemed to support the thesis of *Personal Aggressiveness and War* that Durbin had written in 1938 with the psychoanalyst John Bowlby – that the herd instinct, jealous possessiveness, displaced hatreds and repressed desires are bound to ride roughshod over any model of man that begins and ends with the Enlightenment economist's calculative rationality. Durbin's *Politics* was read in manuscript by Gaitskell and Tawney and clearly shows the influence of Bowlby (then staff psychologist at the London Child Guidance Clinic) and of the LSE moderate Reginald Bassett (whose *The Essentials of Parliamentary Democracy* of 1935 was the catalyst for much of Durbin's Part IV). Durbin's message was the need for a responsible State that would curb cyclical oscillations, control (and, exceptionally, nationalise) industry, ensure social security, guarantee equal opportunity, level unwarranted disparities; but that would also leave to private enterprise the freedom of manoeuvre that is the *sine qua non* for growth and upgrading, fellowship and *embourgeoisement*. Durbin died before he was able to write his companion-volume on *The Economics of Democratic Socialism*. Hugh Gaitskell, then Minister of Fuel and Power, drew heavily on Durbin's notes (these are now kept in the Durbin Papers, British Library of Political and Economic Science) for a talk he gave in April 1949 to a conference of London student organisations. Gaitskell, in the years before the publication of Crosland's *Future*, knew that there was no better exposition of the moderate's case than Durbin's *Politics*. When Malenkov, Deputy Premier of the Soviet Union, visited Britain in 1956, Gaitskell saw to it that he did not return home without a copy.

FURTHER READING

Primary

Purchasing Power and Trade Depression (London: Chapman and Hall, 1933)
Problems of Economic Planning (London: Routledge and Kegan Paul, 1949)

Secondary

Durbin, Elizabeth, *New Jerusalems: The Labour Party and the Economics of Democratic Socialism* (London: Routledge and Kegan Paul, 1985)

Gaitskell, H, 'The Ideological Development of Democratic Socialism in Great Britain', *Socialist International Information*, Vol 5,
1955
Phelps Brown, E H, 'Evan Durbin 1906–1948', *Economica*, Vol 18,
1951

THE POLITICS OF DEMOCRATIC SOCIALISM

THE POLITICS
of
DEMOCRATIC
SOCIALISM

An Essay on
Social Policy

BY

E. F. M. DURBIN

LONDON
GEORGE ROUTLEDGE & SONS LTD.
BROADWAY HOUSE : 68–74 CARTER LANE, E.C.4

CONTENTS

APPENDICES

LIST OF SECTION HEADINGS

7

SECTION HEADINGS

SECTION HEADINGS

PREFACE

THE intellectual debts I have incurred in the course of writing this book are too great ever to be repaid. My friends have written this book for me. Without their help my task would have been unmanageable and each Part of the book is the result of an invaluable collaboration with someone else.

I am particularly indebted to a continuous co-operation with Dr. Bowlby for the subject matter of Part I, to Professor Postan for setting my feet firmly on the paths of investigation that I have pursued in Part II, to Mr. Reginald Bassett for all the guiding principles of Part IV and to Professor Tawney and Mr. Robert Fraser for their essential contributions to the discussions out of which the substance of Part V emerged. Only Part III of the book is, in any important sense, my own.

I have a further debt to acknowledge to the various research assistants, whose voluntary labour made my own work possible. Miss Nadine Hambourg (now Mrs. T. H. Marshall) helped me with the historical sections of Part III; Miss Richenda Payne and Miss Eileen Simpson compiled between them most of the Tables contained in the Statistical Appendix to Part II; and without the long and generous help afforded to me by Miss Jane Samuel (now Mrs. Tom Page) the book would never have been finished. She helped me at all stages in the preparation of the material for Parts II, III and IV, she has contributed an important appendix (Appendix I), and she has helped to see the book through the Press.

Finally I must thank Mr. Reginald Bassett, Mr. Hugh Gaitskell and Professor Tawney for reading the book for me and for making criticisms and suggestions, most of which are embodied in the present text of the book.

It is only necessary to add that none of these persons is necessarily in agreement with, or responsible for, any particular thing that I have written. My debt to them all is none the less for that.

E. F. M. DURBIN

Nov. 1939

13

TO MY FRIENDS

E. J. M. B.
M. M. P.
R. B.
R. F.
R. H. T.
H. T. N. G.

NOTE. I am indebted to the publishers of this book for permission to reproduce certain passages from my article in *Personal Aggressiveness and War*, also published by them (contained in Part I of this book), and to the editor and proprietors of the *Economic Journal* for permission to reprint a few paragraphs from my article *Methods of Research* published in that journal in 1938 and embodied in the Introduction to this book.

E. F. M. D.

INTRODUCTION

THE conclusion which the argument of this book suggests is the entirely unoriginal one that democratic socialism, properly understood, is the best cure for poverty and the best method of furthering the happiness of the human race . . .

DOUGLAS JAY — *The Socialist Case*

INTRODUCTION

§ 1

Apology

It is not easy to justify the writing of this book. There is an immense literature dealing with 'socialism' already in existence. How can the writing of another book upon such a hackneyed subject be defended?

To make matters worse, I propose in this book to cover a number of subjects usually treated in separate books by different specialists. I intend to touch upon social psychology, economic history, Marxist doctrine and the academic subject of politics within the covers of this present volume, and I hope to write a second volume dealing with the economic aspects of socialism in the future. And this I propose to do, despite the fact that I have no technical competence in any of those fields, except the last. I am no psychologist. I can pretend to no scholarship in the vast literature of Marxian thought, and I have no more knowledge of political philosophy at my command than the ordinary student of the Honours School of Philosophy, Politics and Economics in the University of Oxford may be expected to possess. It will not be surprising if I fail in the self-appointed task of presenting systematically the case, as I understand it, for the maintenance and extension in our society of the twin principles of democracy and socialism.

The only reason for attempting to write this book, and the only justification that I can offer for doing so, is that I could not help myself. I write under compulsion — the compulsion to explain and defend the views about social and economic policy that I believe to be true — and I can only hope that to some readers the justification will seem adequate.

The compulsion to write a systematic treatise on democracy and socialism arises, in my mind, from two sources — first the collapse of the social hopes in which, as a young man, I grew up, and secondly, the growing certainty that the problems of social policy can only be solved by the combination, in some form, of the many social studies at present separated from each other.

I propose to say a word about each of these reasons in turn, since an account of them will do a great deal to explain the purpose and structure of this book.

§ 2

The Historical Background

The world in which I grew up was the 'post war' world of the 1920's. At the time it seemed an age of complex maladjustment. In Europe the heritage of the war and of the Treaty of Versailles had left us with the baffling international problems of reparations and disarmament. In Great Britain we were faced by a contracted export market, a 'hard core' of permanent unemployment, a greatly strengthened and militant Labour Movement, and a marked weakness in the foreign exchange market. These matters seemed grave at the time, and they came to a head in the serious crisis of the General Strike in 1926. Happily we survived that dangerous experience without social disaster.

Looking back upon this period now, late in the thirties, it seems to have been an idyllic pause for rest and recuperation sandwiched between two horrible nightmares. It was, as we now see, characterized by the existence of the two fundamental bulwarks of our social happiness — democracy and peace. Democracy was not in serious danger, and peace was not in serious danger — at least in Europe. The area of Europe governed under constitutions providing for some responsibility to the people had been greatly extended by the revolutions immediately following the war, and the dissatisfied powers in Europe were either surrounded, or disarmed, or both. It was then still reasonable to believe that the League of Nations could, and to hope that it would, be used to restrain the aggressive nations from obtaining their ends by force.

Since 1929 that order of things, and the hopes that sprang up within it, has slowly, but surely, fallen to pieces.

The story of the collapse of the 'European order' as we saw it during the 1920's is familiar and dismal. It begins with the 'Great Depression' of 1929. In the closing months of the decade there came the first serious break on the New York Stock Exchange. Spreading out from that centre in successive and expanding waves of disaster, the processes of a Trade Cycle depression, normal but severe, shook the political foundations of the world. Prices declined sharply, money incomes fell catastrophically, and every capitalist country was faced by a rising tide of unemployment. In three short years the volume of world unemployment had reached a staggering total — estimated to have exceeded thirty million persons. By 1932, however, the bottom of the depression had been reached, and in 1934 substantial recovery had occurred, particularly in the countries, like Great Britain, that had abandoned the Gold Standard. But recovery came to a greatly changed world. The economic hurricane that blew itself out in those three disastrous years left behind it a devastated Europe to face a dreary political dawn, heavy with pressing and bitter problems of social reconstruction.

The political consequences of the Great Depression were revolutionary. The world, for good or ill, will never be the same again. In traditional and stable democracies, like Great Britain and America, the governments of the day, regardless of party name or outlook on policy, were swept away. Conservative administrations and groups were driven into the political wilderness in America, France, the Scandinavian countries and New Zealand. The Labour Party was swept out of office in this country and in Australia. In every democratic country the Party or groups that were in power during the fatal period of the depression were ruthlessly, and in most cases irrationally, condemned and destroyed.

In some countries the democratic system itself was uprooted, and this political consequence was, in one case, more important than all the other results of the depression put together. In the election of 1928 the National Socialist Party in Germany received only sufficient votes to give them fourteen seats in the Reichstag. In 1932, only four and a half years later, the Party was the largest in the state, and together with its political allies (the Nationalists) secured a clear majority of the votes cast in one of the last free elections held in Germany. With his assumption of the Chancellorship at the end of January 1933, Hitler began the congenial task of liquidating the remnants of democracy in that country.

Overwhelmingly important as was the re-establishment of authoritarian government in Germany, it was, during this period, only part of a more general movement that extended and intensified the hold of absolute government upon the peoples of Europe. In Austria, in Poland, in Jugo-Slavia and in Bulgaria, the story was the same in kind, if not in degree.

The same tide of depression that swept parties out of power in the democracies, and destroyed democracy where it was not firmly established, also released waves of military aggression all over the world. Japan invaded Manchuria. Italy invaded Abyssinia. Japan invaded China. A group of generals rebelled against the Spanish Republic and were aided from abroad. Germany invaded Austria. Germany prepared to invade Czecho-Slovakia, and the great nations of Europe mobilized their forces against one another.

War was avoided at Munich by the cession of the Sudetenland, but in the spring of 1939 the remainder of Czecho-Slovakia was incorporated in the Reich, and finally the invasion of Poland precipitated the war.

The world has changed, and changed out of recognition, in the ten years since I and my friends spoke in small village halls up and down the country in favour of disarmament and the League of Nations. A 'brave new world' has been brought to birth through the travail of economic depression! Living in this quiet island, still cut off from the trends of European feeling, it is difficult to believe in the cruelty and irrationality of the world about us. We are becoming hardened to its horrors. Over a large area of Europe, torture has been restored as a normal instrument of government. In Russia men and women are made to stand packed together in specially heated rooms, with lice crawling over them, for days at a time until they die or go mad or confess to anything with which they are charged.[1] Or they are kept without sleep for weeks in tiny cells with blinding lights suffering from incessant noise until their will is broken and their personality

---

[1] See Appendix I.

destroyed. In Germany men are beaten with thin steel rods until they die. They are kicked to death without any charges being preferred against them.[1]

It is calculated that in Russia nearly 4,000,000 wretched 'kulaks' were driven out of their homes and occupations to die of starvation or to work in prison camps.[2] The estimates of the numbers in concentration camps, forced labour camps, and the hideous works projects of the G.P.U., vary from 1,500,000 to 2,000,000. The conditions in these camps are indescribable and the mortality shamefully high.[3] In Germany there are fewer persons persecuted in proportion to the population, but nevertheless, between 30,000 and 70,000 in concentration camps, and the community of Jews, numbering half a million, is slowly being squeezed to death.[4] Such large-scale brutality has rarely been witnessed, I am thankful to say, in the previous history of the world.

Imprisonment without trial, torture without trial, execution without trial, and the punishment of the perfectly innocent friends and relatives of mere suspects, are regular practices in Russia and Germany alike. In the purges of 1937 and 1938, 2000 executions were published in the Russian national newspapers alone. Many more were published in local papers. All these executions were preceded by nothing that we should regard as a judicial process — merely by the public registration of a 'confession' obtained by threats and torture. It is interesting to note in passing that this list of executions contained all but one of the Presidents and Prime Ministers of the constituent Republics, most of the general officers in the army, all the admirals, and nearly all the remaining Old Guard of the Revolution. Apart from the blood purge of 1934, the German regime has been guilty of nothing as bad as this, but its record is bad enough.[5]

And over half the earth the threat of war is actual or imminent.

---

[1] See Appendix I.
[2] For the casual process by which a 'kulak' was defined, see CALVIN HOOVER: *Economic Life of Soviet Russia*, Chap. *Agriculture*.
[3] See Appendix I.   [4] Ibid..
[5] Even in this quiet country our hands are not wholly clean. We still lash convicts, suffering from neuroses over which they have no control, until they faint. We still submit them to solitary confinement and punish children with the birch rod and the cane. Nevertheless, our cruelty is to the cruelty of the Russians and the Germans as a grain of sand to the whole seashore.

INTRODUCTION

Thousands of civilians have been killed in Spain, tens of thousands in China. Every device in the destructive hand of man — machine-guns, tanks, high-powered artillery and the bombing aeroplane—has been let loose upon the world to maim and murder men, women and children. In the parks and squares of London we must dig unsightly trenches, reminiscent and prophetic of the grave, into which we shall crawl like animals, to escape the destructive fury, the unleashed insanity, of our fellow human beings.

And to what rational end is the outpouring of all this blood, the infliction of all this pain? The answer is — for nothing, to no rational end whatever.

There can, therefore, be no question that the foundations of my personal hopes for the future — the extension and consolidation of democracy in the internal affairs of the great nations of the earth, and the regulation of the relations between them by an organ of collective authority powerful enough to prevent aggression — have been destroyed for a time, and probably for my lifetime.

I am not concerned here with the political issues involved in these events, nor to distribute praise and blame for their occurrence between groups or between persons. It is difficult to believe that the second of these two hopes was unreasonable. I cannot help feeling that with a little more wisdom, or a little more courage, the democracies could have established the authority of the League of Nations, at least in Europe, for an indefinite period. But I am not concerned to argue the question of foreign policy in this book.

I am concerned chiefly with a wholly different subject — with the scientific problem — *why have these things happened?* What are the sources of political freedom and what are the causes of human aggressiveness? In what kind of society can the ideals of freedom and peace and friendliness be realized together? It is against the background of world catastrophe, and the nightmares of cruelty and destruction through which we are still living, that I wish to raise these questions. They derive their urgency for me from the fact that my old hopes are dead. It is necessary for me to think out the problems of politics again, and to base a policy for the future upon a realism, more sober and careful than that of my youth.

§3

The Problem of Method in the Social Sciences

This brings me to the second introductory point. By what method is it possible to make the study of these matters more realistic?

I am a social scientist by profession and I begin by the assumption, common to the civilization of Europe since the eighteenth century, that the methods of science must be used if our studies are to throw light upon social behaviour, but few people who have given any considerable part of their time and energy to the pursuit of the existing social studies feel confident that many of them meet this need. Our subjects are too specialized. We spend all our energies in discussing and investigating, not separable sections of the social field, but 'aspects' of social behaviour. It is difficult not to feel that the complex reality of human society — the thing that we ought to understand — is lost between these different aspects of it.

Perhaps I might be allowed to quote a few paragraphs from an article of mine dealing with this problem in a different context. Discussing in the *Economic Journal*[1] the problems of method in research facing the social scientist in general, economist in particular, I wrote as follows:

> ... it is necessary to make (another) adverse criticism of the present state of the social sciences. They do not, as it seems to me, achieve a proper sub-division of the field of study.
>
> Sub-division is, of course, desirable and inevitable. The natural sciences would have got nowhere if all scientists had studied the whole of the natural world. The social sciences would have got nowhere if we had all studied the whole of society. But the fact remains that, unlike the natural sciences, our sub-divisions are largely (though not entirely) *abstractions from* reality rather than *sections of* reality.
>
> Botany is a study of a group of organisms — plants.

[1] E. F. M. DURBIN: *Methods of Research – A Plea for Co-operation in the Social Sciences* (*Economic Journal*, June 1938).

Zoology is a study of a different group of organisms — animals. Colloidal chemistry is a study of a group of substances — colloids. Crystallography is a study of a group of objects — crystals. In all these cases the objects of study are real and independent objects and groups. They are not objects of something complex. They are real things. But are most of our subjects so distinguished? Are they not mostly aspects of, abstractions from, social reality? Is economics not a study of the *economic aspect* of social behaviour? Is the academic subject of law not a study of the *legal aspects* of social behaviour? Is political history not a study of the *political aspects* of general history? And economic history a study of the *economic aspects* of general history? That is to say, our sub-divisions turn, once more, upon the definition of terms: economic, legal, political — and not upon sub-divisions in-hering in the objects of study.

And of course most social scientists recognize this . . . (No) economist would deny that (economic) behaviour is influ-enced by political ideas, laws and historical traditions. Lawyers increasingly recognize that law and the development of law is influenced by 'economic' and 'political' forces. The course of 'political' history cannot seriously be supposed to be independent of 'economic' events — and so forth. These considerations should force us to ask whether our present subjects do correspond to any real divisions in our object of study. Reality may escape between our 'aspects' of it . . . Let us take a few random examples:

(i) Suppose we wished to understand the legal institution of *property*; its nature, origin, present significance and probable future. How many of our existing subjects can, indeed should, contribute to our study? Almost all. With-out the aid of law we cannot understand what the institu-tion is. Without general history we cannot say how it came into existence or what are the forces likely to change it. Without economics we cannot understand its consequences. Many of its implications are brought to light by psychology. General sociology and anthropology have an important contribution to offer. Without the aid of all or most of these existing subjects we cannot say that we are studying this institution in its real social existence, or putting ourselves in a position to make prophecies about its future.

(ii) Or suppose that we wished to study *war* — a concrete, tragically concrete, social phenomenon. History is essential. Psychology is essential. Anthropology is essential. Economics and general sociology have valuable contributions to make.

Thus it would seem that the study of reality cuts across, or rather embraces, all our existing specialisms. United we might stand. Divided we certainly fall. How are we, then, to stand together?

I feel convinced that the solution of this problem can only be found, in the long run, through the organized co-operation of the existing specialists: economists with historians, historians with sociologists, sociologists with psychologists.

But it will be a long time indeed before such co-operation is wisely organized, and a longer time still before the results of it become available for the guidance of social policy. Is it impossible to do anything in the meantime, or to discuss fruitfully the course of social action?

This book is written in the hope that purely negative answers are not the right answers to these questions.

A discussion of the problem of method does, however, go some way to explain, if not to excuse, the peculiar form that this book will take. I have attempted to cover a wide field, and to say something about so many subjects, because I believe that all of them are essential to a proper understanding of economic policy. I propose to touch upon the academic subjects of psychology, economic history, political theory, and economics because the society in which we live, and whose form we must seek to improve, is composed of individuals whose motives and institutions and whose nature are never exclusively economic, or political, or personal; but compounded of all three types of motive, and intelligible only to those who will study men as they really are, complex and various in their nature.

With this word of introduction, to explain the motive and method of my project, I must now describe and justify the plan of it in somewhat greater detail.

§ 4

The Plan of the Book

The present book is divided into five Parts. These Parts are more distinct from each other than are the chapters of most books, but at the same time they are all concerned with one central theme — the theory and practice of democratic socialism.

The first Part is concerned, perhaps unexpectedly, with certain psychological and anthropological problems. It may be worth saying a word in explanation of this fact.

The necessity to begin with psychological and anthropological material springs from the fact that society is composed of individual human beings. No man can dispute the atomistic nature of society. The material world may or may not be composed of large numbers of small uniform particles, different in their properties from the objects we feel and see. The particulate theory of matter is, at least, open to doubt. The same thing cannot be said of society. It is atomistic through and through. We can see with our eyes and touch with our hands the different and separable units of which human society is everywhere and necessarily composed.

The study of individual psychology must, therefore, be relevant to the understanding of social behaviour. If a macrocosm is made up of many microcosms, light upon the nature of the microcosms must also illuminate the nature of the macrocosm. If a building is to be made of bricks, the architect must understand, among other things, the physical properties of bricks. It is, therefore, unnecessary to apologize for beginning this book with a Part concerned with individual psychology.

The purpose of Part I is to examine the evidence for believing that human beings are continuously divided between the desire to co-operate with, and the desire to destroy, each other; and that a large part of social behaviour, and therefore of history, can be understood by an examination of the circumstances favouring the dominance of either the one or the other type of impulse. It also emerges, in the course of considering this fundamental question, that the real motives guiding people are often hidden from them, and that, in general, human behaviour is far less rational than at first sight it may appear to be, and than most people think it is.

But let me hasten at once to say that I have no desire whatever to minimize or reduce the importance of institutional studies. After Part I we shall be almost wholly concerned with a discussion of economic and political institutions — and rightly so, because society is far more than the individuals composing it. A material body is not an unorganized heap or collection of atoms, even if the atomic theory of the constitution of matter is shown to be true. A table is an organized and differentiated group of atoms, and comes to possess, in virtue of its organization, qualities and powers that are wholly lacking in the atoms that make it up. A pile of bricks is not a building. In the same way a mere aggregate of human beings is not a society. They are bound together, and organized in complex patterns of relationship, to form a society. The study of these relationships, the uniformities they exhibit, and the sequences of cause and effect peculiar to the uniformities or institutions, is just as essential to the understanding of society as the study of the units between which the relationships exist. The nature of society is to be a system of relations between human beings. Both the relations and the human beings are the proper study of the social scientist.[1]

Part II of the book is concerned, therefore, with the pattern of economic institutions upon which the material life of society depends, a system of institutions that is normally designated by the term *capitalism*. I propose to discuss briefly the sense in which that term is used, and to describe in somewhat greater detail the most significant recent changes in the basic principles of its organization. From the examination of these trends of change the conclusion can be safely established that a number of reforms in the method

---

[1] Nor must the social scientist exclude either thought or feeling from his inquiry. It is necessary to understand both, if we are to understand either of these faculties of the human soul. The life of the individual and of society is quite unintelligible in terms of emotion or thought alone. Human beings cannot act unless they have some motive for doing so. Motives are nothing else but feelings and judgments of value. But neither can they act without some theory or intellectual view about the nature of the world in which they live and the means by which their ends can be achieved. Hence the study of human thought and feeling, mind and heart, intellectual and emotional faculty, must be combined in any comprehensive survey of social policy.

of its management are urgently desirable. At the same time it also appears that many of the gloomier prophecies about the imminent collapse of the economic order are exaggerated.

The conclusions established in Part II raise at once the question of political method. If certain important changes in economic organization are desired, by what method should those changes be brought about? The answer to this question occupies the next two Parts of the book.

Part III is concerned with the Marxist and Communist thesis that alterations in the distribution of economic power and social privilege, desirable from the standpoint of efficiency and justice, can be brought about only by the 'dictatorship of the proletariat'. The conclusion suggested by my examination of the Marxist argument is that it is not supported either by the principles of reason or by the weight of historical evidence. This, needless to say, is a controversial matter. Part IV carries the discussion a stage further by examining and defending the thesis that changes in the economic order, compatible with both efficiency and justice, are only realizable in a democratic state, and through the democratic method of persuasion and compromise. An attempt is made to relate this conclusion to, indeed to establish it from, the psychological conclusions to Part I.

Finally in Part V an attempt is made to make more practical and more precise the broad conclusion of Part IV. If it is true that greater efficiency and greater justice in our economic and social arrangements can be secured, and only secured, by the exercise of political liberty, what strategy and what programme will unify these principles? The last Part is concerned, therefore, with the construction of a programme for a socialist party that is democratic.

It may be worth adding the remark that throughout this book I use the term *democracy* to denote the political institution of government responsible to, and replaceable by, the people; and that by the term *socialism* in the narrow sense I mean the belief that greater equality in the distribution of income and property can be combined with economic efficiency only in an industrial system that is centrally controlled. By socialism in a broader sense I shall mean the more complex conception of social justice. It will, of course, be one of the main purposes of this book to make these terms and conceptions more precise and more detailed.

Finally, I may add that it is my hope and intention to publish at some later date a work concerned with the economic organization of a democratic and socialist economy. If and when it is written it will be entitled *The Economics of Democratic Socialism.*

CO-OPERATION AND CONFLICT

*An account of Recent Investigations into
the Causes of Warfare*

A SOCIAL structure is a nexus of present relationships. It lives only
as it is maintained by the will of social beings in the present. . . . It
is like a web that exists only as it is newly spun. If it seems to persist through time, it is because the attitudes and interests of social
beings persist, so that they will its continuous existence. The most
sacrosanct and seeming-permanent institutions exist by no other
right and in no other strength than that which they derive from
the social beings who think and act in accord with them. . . .

R. M. MacIver — *Society, its Structure and Changes*

CO-OPERATION AND CONFLICT

§ 1

Introduction — The Problem

THE greatest single achievement of science in the twentieth century consists, or so it appears to me, in the light that has been thrown upon the formation of personal character. As a result of the observations and reflections of the analytical psychologists, we are now in a position to understand in a way that was quite impossible before this work had been done the nature of the causes that determine the behaviour of individual human beings.[1]

For reasons that I have just discussed, it is highly probable that an increasing knowledge of the individual will also throw light upon the nature of society. This *a priori* expectation is borne out in practice.

But I am faced by an immediate practical problem. I think it obvious that psychological and anthropological studies contribute enormously to our understanding of every important social institution: the family, property, law, the distribution of authority and power in society, loyalty to the State, religion, co-operation, political conflict and war. Indeed, I would go further and affirm that it is impossible to understand these things as fully as we might without some knowledge of the light thrown upon them by the most recent addition to the armoury of the humane sciences. Those who still think that it is possible to study society without the aid of individual psychology stand in the intellectual position of the doctors who refused to modify their views of human physiology and pathology for a generation after the discovery of the circulation of the blood or the existence of microscopic parasites.

---

[1] The related studies of animal psychology and social anthropology have also made important contributions to the subject, as the remainder of this Part will show.

Intellectual conservatism is one of the most obstinate of vested interests.

Yet it is clearly impossible in this book, which is concerned primarily with the principles of economic and social policy, to attempt even the briefest *systematic* outline of the significance for the social sciences of the developments of character-psychology. Not only would such an attempt occupy the rest of the book, but I am not in the least competent to make the attempt. Only a person with a technical knowledge of analytical psychology and of comparative social institutions would be in a position to undertake such a task. On the other hand it would cast an atmosphere of unreality over my whole discussion of social policy if I neglected completely the contributions of psychology and anthropology to the origin and development of social institutions. What then am I to do?

The only possible solution to this problem lies in selection. All that I can hope to do is to lay before the reader an elementary account of the contributions made by these subjects to some *one* central social problem that has an important bearing upon the choice of social policy. That is what I propose to do in this Part.

For my purpose I have selected the problem indicated by the title of the Part. I propose to consider the light thrown by psychological evidence upon *the causes of co-operation and conflict between individuals and groups in human society.* I have selected this particular problem for two reasons:

In the *first* place it is a central problem. All other questions of policy and history are subordinate to it. No society can continue to exist unless peaceful co-operation can be maintained within it. War is the negation of both community and society, at least between the groups taking part in it. In one important sense the maintenance of society is the maintenance of co-operation, and the dissolution of co-operative habits into conflict is the dissolution of society itself.[1]

The over-riding importance of the decision between co-opera-

---

[1] Within the fighting group the feeling of unity and common purpose may be strengthened, but a wider society embracing the contending parties is unquestionably destroyed.

tion and war in the case of nations needs no emphasis from me. Our very lives depend upon it.

It is certain, therefore, that this is a central problem for the scientific study of society. For the same reason it is a central problem for the study of social policy. Few questions of policy, raised within or between the nation states that compose the modern world, do not involve at some stage in their development the choice between these two fundamentally different methods of achieving the purposes of individuals and of groups. The choice between individual and group co-operation on the one hand, or conflict on the other, is the first question that has to be decided in every discussion of political method. It is, therefore, of the very greatest importance to understand the light that has been thrown by the recent advances in psychology and anthropology upon the forces that determine this choice.

In the *second* place this is a practicable task, since a great deal of work has been done by anthropologists and psychologists upon the causes of peacefulness and aggressiveness. It is also practicable for me, since it is the one broad psychological problem that I have done something to study, in co-operation with a practising psycho-analyst, Dr. Bowlby.[1]

The work to which I refer is very scattered and unsystematic. Four groups of persons and four methods of study have made their contributions to our common pool of knowledge. The *animal psychologists*, and particularly Dr. Zuckerman in *The Social Life of Monkeys and Apes*, have thrown much light upon the primitive sources of aggressiveness and fighting in the animals most nearly related to the common ancestor of men and other animal species. *Child psychologists*, and particularly Professor Susan Isaacs, in her *Social Development in Young Children*, have discussed at length the growth of co-operation and the sources of conflict among children. The *anthropologists* have between them accumulated a great store of information on the subject of primitive warfare, and the

---

[1] As I have mentioned in the Preface, Dr. Bowlby and I have published our work under the title *Personal Aggressiveness and War*. This book was published by Messrs. Kegan Paul, Trench, Trubner & Co. The passages taken have been slightly altered in expression but not in meaning, to suit the needs of this book. §§ 2-7 of this Part consist largely of quotations from this book and those who have read that work should turn at once to the beginning of § 8.

analytical psychologists have made an intensive study of the origins of love and hatred in the civilized adult. There is therefore a considerable body of evidence in existence—scattered, but accessible.

Does this evidence, when it is brought together and analysed, throw any light upon the factors predisposing human beings to struggle or combine? Are there any distinguishable causes of social peace or warfare in this sense? Dr. Bowlby and I were led, by a survey of the evidence, to believe that there are such general factors. The rest of this Part will be taken up by a discussion of them.

§ 2

The Distribution of Co-operation and Conflict

The first point that emerges clearly from the evidence is the wide distribution in society of both these fundamental types of human behaviour.

The extreme form of conflict between persons and between groups is that of *fighting* — conflicts in which force is used. Now fighting is plainly a common, indeed a universal, form of human behaviour. It occurs in all periods of history and in the time before history — to judge by the behaviour of primitive peoples. It occurs in all types of social group, from the wars between civilized nations, through a descending order of civil war, riot, and public disorder to the personal fighting of adults and children. It is everywhere present, and cannot therefore be traced to the conditions created by certain forms of society, like those of capitalism and the nation state, whose distribution in space and time is much more limited than the distribution of fighting. The simple causes of fighting must lie in the character of human beings common to all periods of history and all types of society — that is, to the qualities of human nature itself.

The same is true of the practice of peaceful co-operation. Fighting, or the extreme form of conflict, while universal in distribution, is not continuous in time. The most warlike groups and the most aggressive individuals spend considerable periods in peaceful toleration of, and positive co-operation with, other animals or persons. Most organized communities have enjoyed longer periods of peace than of war. The greater part of human activity — of man-hours — is spent, not in war, but in peaceful co-operation. The scientific problem is, therefore, twofold — why is there peaceful co-operation? And why does peaceful co-operation sometimes break down into fighting? The practical problem — at least, for lovers of peace — is how peaceful co-operation is to be preserved against the universal tendency exhibited in history for it to degenerate into war.

§ 3

The Causes of Peaceful Co-operation

What then, does the evidence suggest, are the simplest causes of peaceful co-operation? Here it is necessary to distinguish between groups with and without 'government' — that is, an apparatus of force constructed with the conscious and explicit purpose of preserving peace within the group. Clearly the existence of a powerful organization taking action to preserve peace constitutes in itself a strong and immediate cause for the appearance of peace.[1] With the consequence of this obvious point we shall be concerned at the end of this Part. For the moment, however, we are interested in a prior and more fundamental question. What are the causes of peace in a group without government or any effective machinery for the restraint of fighting? Why do animals co-operate in the absence of any agent powerful enough to prevent them from fighting?

Now a survey of the life of mammals in general, and of apes and men in particular,[2] suggests that the causes of peace in the absence

---

[1] I feel unable to accept Dr. Glover's rather casual rejection of instruments of government and collective security as a means of preserving peace; see GLOVER: *The Dangers of being Human.* I feel that he does not appreciate the strength of the will to co-operate expressed in them.

[2] For a more detailed statement and analysis of the evidence see *Personal Aggressiveness and War*, Part I, Appendix *passim.*

of government are, for the extra-familial group,[1] of three main kinds:

1. The obvious, most important, and overwhelming advantage to be derived from peace lies in the division of labour and the possibility of thus achieving purposes desired by the individual, but obtainable only by active co-operation with others. This is so plain in the case of adult human society that the point is scarcely worth elaborating. The whole of the difference in the variety of satisfactions open to the individual in isolation and the same person in the active membership of a peaceful society, measures the advantages to be derived from continuous co-operation between adults. The extent of co-operation in any groups other than adult human societies is, of course, much more limited. But groups of children co-operate in simple tasks, and in games that require a specialization of function between the individual members of the group. And there is some evidence to suggest that apes exhibit still simpler forms of co-operation, and that even mammals who hunt and live in herds develop simple differentiation of function for various common purposes of defence or attack.[2]

Co-operation extends enormously the opportunities for life and satisfaction within groups that have developed it. It is reasonable to presume that these advantages are also *causes* of co-operation, since many of the results of co-operation are of survival value. In any case, few persons would wish to deny that the sovereign advantages of co-operation are for adult human beings one of the main causes of voluntary peace.

2. In the case of apes, there is also evidence that satisfaction is found in the mere presence of others of the same species.[3] Whether this satisfaction is exclusively sexual — i.e. whether the advantage lies in the possibility of varied relations with the opposite sex — there is not sufficient evidence to determine. In so far as it is

---

[1] I have not concerned myself with the reasons for peace within the family (a) because it leads at once to the rather different question of the nature of sexual and familial ties; (b) because the family usually exhibits the phenomenon of patriarchal and matriarchal authority.

[2] This last point is not universally conceded by the students of animal behaviour. Apes appear to scratch each other, and some herds of herbivores seem to maintain a system of outposts and sentries. But it has been denied that these phenomena can be compared with the purposive co-operation found in human society. The conflict of view could only be resolved by further investigation.

[3] *Personal Aggressiveness and War*, pp. 52-55.

sexual, such gregariousness may easily become a source of conflict within the group. This we shall see in a moment. But in so far as pleasure is felt in the mere presence of other members of the group, there is a force binding those members together in peace.

The counterpart of the primitive sociability of the apes in children and adult human beings is obvious. Its relationship to sexual promiscuity remains as obscure in human beings as in apes, but the existence of a pleasure felt in the presence of human company could scarcely be denied. Sociability is therefore an independent cause for the existence and stability of society.[1]

3. The reasons for co-operation so far mentioned are all self-regarding advantages. They derive their importance from the existence of kinds of individual satisfaction that can only be obtained with the aid of others. It is not, however, to be supposed that self-regarding ends are the sole causes of peaceful co-operation. It is obvious that in the development of the child there is to be traced the emergence of an interest in others for their own sakes, a gradual but growing recognition of the rights of others to the kinds of advantage desired by oneself; and finally in the fully developed personal relationships of friendship and love, the positive desire for the loved one's happiness as a good for oneself. From reflection and logic this care for the good of others can make the common good a personal end. The existence of a general desire for the common good is clearly a force making for peace in adult society. But its power will only extend as far as the idea of the common good extends.[2] If the common good is only felt to reach to the limits of a racial, or a geographic, or a social group, there will be no force in this recognition of the limited common good within the group to prevent the use of force outside and on behalf of it.

All this is very important, but it is also very obvious. It is indeed the commonplace of pacifist literature. It is never difficult to find reasons for peaceful co-operation. And with such overwhelming advantages in its favour, the real problem is why peace so frequently degenerates into fighting. It is consequently much

[1] I feel it unnecessary to argue the obscure and rather formal controversy as to whether there is a specific 'herd instinct'.
[2] Op. cit., pp. 107-112.

more in the study of the actual breakdown of peaceful co-operation among apes and children and grown-up people that recent
descriptive work has brought new light. The work that we, that is,
Dr. Bowlby and I, think to be of greatest interest on this point
falls into two parts. There is first the careful work of observation
that has been carried out by Dr. Zuckerman on apes, and on
children by Dr. Susan Isaacs. This work does much to throw
into clear perspective the simplest causes for aggression and fighting in the absence of government. The second clue to the puzzle
is to be found, in our opinion, in the mass of descriptive material
laid bare by the anthropologist, and in the case-papers of patients
treated by the therapeutic technique of psycho-analysis. I propose,
therefore, to distinguish in this brief survey between the simple
causes and forms of aggressive behaviour common to apes and to
human beings on the one hand, and the more complicated forms
exhibited by human beings alone, on the other. For an account
of the complications added by the faculties of the adult human
mind, we shall offer a brief and necessarily controversial
interpretation of the significance of the anthropological and
psycho-analytical evidence as to the origins of personal and
group-aggressiveness.

§4

The Simpler Causes of Fighting

The evidence taken from the observation of the behaviour of
apes and children suggests that there are three clearly separable
groups of simple causes for the outbreak of fighting and the ex-
hibition of aggressiveness by individuals.

1. One of the most common causes of fighting among both
children and apes was over the *possession* of external objects. The
disputed ownership of any desired object — food, clothes, toys,
females, and the affection of others — was sufficient ground for an
appeal to force. On Monkey Hill disputes over females were
responsible for the deaths of thirty out of thirty-three females in

a short period of time.[1] Two points are of particular interest to notice about these fights for possession.

In the *first* place they are often carried to such an extreme that they end in the complete destruction of the objects of common desire. Toys are torn to pieces. Females are literally torn limb from limb. So over-riding is the aggression once it has begun that it not only overflows all reasonable boundaries of selfishness but utterly destroys the object for which the struggle began and even the self for whose advantage the struggle was undertaken.

In the *second* place it is observable, at least in children, that the object for whose possession aggression is started may sometimes be desired by one person only, or may be desired by him merely because it is desired by someone else. There were many cases observed by Dr. Isaacs where toys and other objects which had been discarded as useless were violently defended by their owners when they became the object of some other child's desire.[2] The grounds of possessiveness may therefore be irrational in the sense that they are derived from inconsistent judgments of value.

Whether sensible or irrational, contests over possession are commonly the occasion for the most ruthless use of force among children and apes.

One of the commonest kinds of object arousing possessive desire is the notice, goodwill, affection, and service of other members of the group. Among children one of the commonest causes of quarrelling was 'jealousy' — the desire for the exclusive possession of the interest and affection of someone else, particularly the adults in charge of the children. This form of behaviour is sometimes classified as a separate cause of conflict under the name of 'rivalry' or 'jealousy'. But, in point of fact, it seems to us that it is only one variety of possessiveness. The object of desire is not a material object — that is the only difference. The object is the interest and affection of other persons. What is wanted, however, is the exclusive right to that interest and affection — a property

---

[1] Op. cit., p. 57.

[2] This finds an interesting echo in the greater world of politics. Nations will often maintain that certain colonial territories are of no advantage to them, and yet bitterly resist any proposal to hand them over to other countries; or rich people arguing that riches do not bless the rich, angrily resent any suggestion that they should be transferred to the poor.

in emotions instead of in things. As subjective emotions and as causes of conflict, jealousy and rivalry are fundamentally similar to the desire for the uninterrupted possession of toys or food. Indeed, very often the persons, property in whom is desired, are the sources of toys and food.

Possessiveness is then, in all its forms, a common cause of fighting. If we are to look behind the mere facts of behaviour for an explanation of this phenomenon, a teleological cause is not far to seek. The exclusive right to objects of desire is a clear and simple advantage to the possessor of it. It carries with it the certainty and continuity of satisfaction. Where there is only one claimant to a good, frustration and the possibility of loss is reduced to a minimum. It is, therefore, obvious that, if the ends of the self are the only recognized ends, the whole powers of the agent, including the fullest use of his available force, will be used to establish and defend exclusive rights to possession.[1]

2. Another cause of aggression closely allied to possessiveness is the tendency for children and apes greatly to resent the *intrusion of a stranger* into their group. A new child in the class may be laughed at, isolated and disliked, and even set upon and pinched and bullied. A new monkey may be poked and bitten to death. It is interesting to note that it is only strangeness within a similarity of species that is resented. Monkeys do not mind being joined by a goat or a rat. Children do not object when animals are introduced to the group. Indeed, such novelties are often welcomed. But when monkeys meet a new monkey, or children a strange child, aggression often occurs. This suggests strongly that the reason for the aggression is fundamentally possessiveness. The competition of the newcomers is feared. The present members of the group feel that there will be more rivals for the food or the attention of the adults.

3. Finally, another common source of fighting among children is a failure or *frustration* in their own activity. A child will be pre-

---

[1] This teleological rationalism does not explain the phenomenon of what we have termed irrational possessiveness. Dr. Bowlby's and my explanation of the fact that a child will fight merely to possess objects because they are wanted by others is that the child in question begins to suspect that, just because someone else wants the discarded object, he must have been mistaken in supposing that it was worthless. But evidence on this point is not available.

vented either by natural causes such as bad weather, or illness, or by the opposition of some adult, from doing something he wishes to do at a given moment — sail his boat or ride the bicycle. The child may also frustrate itself by failing, through lack of skill or strength, to complete successfully some desired activity. Such a child will then in the ordinary sense become 'naughty'. He will be in a bad or surly temper. And, what is of interest from our point of view, the child will indulge in aggression — attacking and fighting other children or adults. Sometimes the object of aggression will simply be the cause of frustration, a straight-forward reaction. The child will kick or hit the nurse who forbids the sailing of his boat. But sometimes — indeed, frequently — the person or thing that suffers the aggression is quite irrelevant and innocent of offence. The angry child will stamp the ground or box the ears of another child, when neither the ground nor the child attacked is even remotely connected with the irritation of frustration.

Of course, this kind of behaviour is so common that everyone feels it to be obvious and to constitute no serious scientific problem. That a small boy should pull his sister's hair because it is raining does not appeal to the ordinary unreflecting person to be an occasion for solemn scientific inquiry. He is, as we should all say, 'in a bad temper'. Yet it is not, in fact, really obvious either why revenge should be taken on entirely innocent objects since no good to the aggressor can come of it, nor why children being miserable should seek to make others miserable also. It is just a fact of human behaviour that cannot really be deduced from any general principle of reason. But it is, as we shall see, of very great importance for our purpose. It shows how it is possible, at the simplest and most primitive level, for aggression and fighting to spring from an entirely irrelevant and partially hidden cause. Fighting to possess a desired object is straightforward and rational, however disastrous its consequences, compared with fighting that occurs because, in a different and unrelated activity, some frustration has barred the road to pleasure. The importance of this possibility for an understanding of group conflict must already be obvious.

These are the three simplest separate categories of cause we are able to observe in the evidence. One further point, however, remains to be made about the character of the fighting that occurs among apes. It is a marked characteristic of this fighting that, once it has broken out anywhere, it spreads with great rapidity throughout the group, and draws into conflict individuals who had no part in the first quarrel and appear to have no immediate interest whatever in the outcome of the original dispute. Fighting is *infectious* in the highest degree. Why? It is not easy to find an answer. Whether it is that the apes who are not immediately involved feel that some advantage for themselves can be snatched from the confusion following upon the rupture of social equilibrium, or whether real advantages are involved that escape the observation of the onlooker, is not at present determined. Or it may be that the infectiousness of fighting is irrational in the same way that the irrelevant expression of aggression due to frustration is irrational. Whatever the explanation, the fact remains that fighting spreads without apparent cause or justification — that 'every dog joins a fight', in other and older words. This excitability, and the attraction which fighting may possess for its own sake, is likely to be a source of great instability in any society. It is one of the most dangerous parts of our animal inheritance.

So much for the simpler forms of aggression. It is now time to consider the light thrown by anthropological and psycho-analytic evidence upon the behaviour of adult human beings.

§ 5

The Further Causes of Aggressive Behaviour

So far the material from which we have sought illumination has been derived from the simple behaviour of children and apes. We must now consider more complicated behaviour. There are, as we have already pointed out, at least two relevant studies — anthropology and the case histories recorded by psycho-analysts. It is impossible to survey the vast mass of anthropological material in detail, but even such a slight study as we have been able to make suffices to show the very great importance of other causes of fighting among primitive peoples.

CAUSES OF AGGRESSIVE BEHAVIOUR

Before we begin this task it is necessary to make one preliminary and simple observation about the nature of adult aggression in general. It is of first importance to realize that, as far as aggressiveness and fighting is concerned, there is no noticeable improvement in the *behaviour* of adults compared with that of the most savage animals and children. If anything, it is more ruthless. The recent history of Europe establishes this conclusion with horrible insistence. There is no form of behaviour too ruthless, too brutal, too cruel for adult men and women to use against each other. As I have pointed out in the introduction to this book, torture is becoming normal again; the knuckle-duster and the whip, other more refined instruments of flagellation, and the armoury of mental pain, are the commonplace instruments of prisons and concentration camps from Japan to Spain. Men and women have been shot down without trial, soaked in petrol and burned to death, beaten to unrecognizable masses of flesh and bone, hanged by the hair and hands until they die, starved and tortured with fear and hope during the 'Reigns of Terror' that have accompanied and succeeded the civil wars in Russia, Italy, Poland, Austria, Germany and Spain. Cruelty knows no boundary of party or creed. It wears every kind of shirt. And over all of us there hangs, perpetual and menacing, the fear of war. No group of animals could be more aggressive or more ruthless in their aggression than the adult members of the human race.

Are there then no differences between the aggression of more primitive beings and that of adult men? We suggest that there are only two differences. In the *first* place the physical aggression of adults is normally a group activity. Murder and assault are restricted to a small criminal minority. Adults kill and torture each other only when organized into political parties, or economic classes, or religious denominations, or nation states. A moral distinction is always made between the individual killing for himself and the same individual killing for some real or supposed group interest.[1] In the *second* place, the adult powers of imagination and reason are brought to the service of the aggressive intention. Apes and children when they fight, simply fight. Men and women first construct towering systems of theology and religion, complex

[1] Op. cit., pp. 107-112.

49

analyses of racial character and class structure, or moralities of group life and virility before they kill one another. Thus they fight for Protestantism or Mohammedanism, for the emancipation of the world proletariat or for the salvation of the Nordic culture, for nation or for kind. Men will die like flies for theories and exterminate each other with every instrument of destruction for abstractions.

The differences of *behaviour* are therefore not substantial. The form is the same, the results are the same. Group fighting is even more destructive than individual fighting. A machine-gun or a bomb is no less lethal because its use can be shown to be a necessity of the Class War, or more noble because it brings the light of Italian civilization to the Abyssinian peoples. Now it might be argued that there is no continuity of character between the wars of civilized people and fighting of the simpler orders. We cannot, however, see any reason for supposing so. Indeed, the only question of interest appears to us to lie in the matter of causation. Are the causes exactly the same? Or are they changed in any important way by the greater powers and complexity of the adult human mind?

We are therefore brought back to the question: What are the causes of aggressiveness in adult human beings? I would maintain that anthropology and psycho-analysis suggest a number of ways in which the powers of the human mind change and add to the causes of aggression. There appear to be at least three different mechanisms discernible in the material of these two sciences.

§ 6

Animism — or False Theories of Causal Will[1]

The first and most obvious of these mechanisms is the cause of war revealed so very plainly by the study of primitive inter-group conflict. It consists in the universal tendency to attribute all

---

[1] It is difficult to find the right term for the kind of intellectual habit we have in mind. For a more detailed discussion of the evidence, see *Personal Aggressiveness and War*, pp. 94-103 and pp. 117-126.

events in the world to the deliberate activity of human or para-human *will*. All happenings, whether natural and inevitable, or human and voluntary, are attributed to the will of some being either human or anthropomorphically divine. If a thunderstorm occurs, or a hurricane visits a village, or a man is killed by a tiger, the evil is attributed either to the magic of a neighbouring tribe or to the ill-will of demons and gods. In the same way, good fortune, however natural, is attributed to the deliberate intention of some other being. This universal tendency in the human mind is termed *animism*.

It is certain that this imaginative tendency on the part of human beings leads to war. It is obvious why it should. If evil is attributed to the direct malice of neighbouring and opposing groups, the only possible protection against further evil lies in the destruction of the source of ill-will. It is, however, of great importance whether the supposed enemy is human or supernatural. If it is spiritual, the natural reply will be placatory sacrifices or the harmless ritual of beating or burning or making war upon the evil spirit. The evidence shows many amusing examples of ritual warfare against the spirits, undertaken by primitive peoples after some natural disaster. But if the supposed author of evil is not supernatural, but human, the results are neither harmless nor amusing. If the typhoon is attributed to the magic of neighbouring peoples, or of dissident minorities within the tribe, then the destruction of the enemy, root and branch, is the only safe course. Hence, after a thunderstorm or an accident, the restless fears and hatred of the tribe will find expression in a primitive war against neighbouring tribes, or the stamping out of some hapless group of victims within it. Enemies without and traitors within must be exterminated.

It is difficult to exaggerate the frequency and importance of this cause of fighting in human societies of all degrees of civilization. It is a universal tendency among the simpler people of all nations to attribute evil to some person or group of persons. It is present everywhere in party politics. Every evil is loaded upon political opponents. Socialists attribute all disasters, whether economic or political, to 'capitalists' or 'the capitalist class'. Conservatives think it obvious that the last uncontrollable and world-wide depression in trade was due to the 'bad government' of the Socialists in this country. Other movements find different and more peculiar scapegoats in 'the bankers' or 'the Jews' or 'the Russians'. In each case what is noticeable and dangerous is that a vast power and a deep malignity is attributed to the inimical group. The supposed malignity is often purely illusory. The attributed power transcends all reality. When the open conflict of party politics is suppressed by an authoritarian regime the tendency is exaggerated rather than reduced. Some unfortunate minority within the group — 'the Jews' or 'the kulaks' — become the source of all evil, the scapegoat of all disaster. Or an overwhelming hatred is conceived for another nation. Out of these real terrors and derivative hatreds merciless persecutions and international wars are likely to spring.

I shall go on to show that the sources of aggression among human beings are much more complicated than either the simple causes operating in animals or this common habit of attributing everything to some human agency. Yet it should be obvious that much of the behaviour of large groups can be explained by the categories of cause we have already discussed. Possessiveness, frustration, animism are potent causes of conflict between groups, whether parties, classes or states. After we have discussed the complex history of aggression within the individual we shall have reason to revert to these simpler forms of behaviour. The behaviour of the group is in an important sense simpler and more direct than the behaviour of the individual. It seems probable that the complex character of the civilized individual undergoes a degeneration or simplification when he is caught up into, and expresses himself through, the unity of the group. But in the meantime we must consider the light thrown by psycho-analysis upon the history and development of aggressive impulses in the civilized adult.

§7

The Transformation of Aggressive Impulses — Displacement and Projection

What light does psycho-analytic evidence throw upon the problem of adult aggression? It is, of course, impossible to consider at all adequately the mass of material and theory comprised in the work of this school of psychology. All that I can attempt at this point is a brief account of the main conclusions — as they appear to me — to be drawn from the evidence. It is scarcely necessary to point out that these views are only one interpretation of the data, and although I think this interpretation to be the most accurate, it could only be verified by an empirical investigation designed to show the existence of certain emotional mechanisms widely distributed in civilized societies.

I suggest tentatively, therefore, that the evidence of psycho-analysis[1] justifies the following conclusions:

1. That the *primary* causes of aggression (and of peaceful co-oper-ation) are identical among adult men with those of children and apes. The character of the *id* — or complex of instinctive impulses— does not change materially as the individual grows older. The same sources of satisfaction — food, warmth, love, society — are desired and the same sources of conflict — desire for exclusive possession of the sources of satisfaction, or aggression arising from a sense of frustration — are present. But in the life of most children there is a controlling or warping influence present in a varying degree — that of *authority*. The child is denied for various reasons — good or bad — an open and uninterrupted access to the means of its satisfaction. It is denied the breast or bottle, the toy or the company of adults, at the time or to the extent that it wishes. The evidence seems overwhelming that such frustration leads to a violent reaction of fear, hatred and aggression. The child cries or screams or bites or kicks. We are not for the moment concerned with the question whether this frustration is desirable or not. We are simply concerned with its results. The result is 'bad temper' or 'naughtiness' — a resentment of frustration. This original resent-ment and the aggression to which it leads we would call *simple aggression.*

Further development turns, in my view, upon the way in which this simple aggression is treated. The statistically normal method of treatment is, we suggest, further frustration or *punishment*. The child is slapped or beaten or subjected to moral instruction — taught that its behaviour is wrong or wicked. Again I am not concerned with the question of the rightness or wrongness of this

[1] Op. cit., pp. 73-94.

procedure, but only with its consequences. I suggest that the result of punishment is to present the child with a radical conflict — either he must control the expression of his simple aggression or suffer the punishment and the loss of love that simple aggression in a regime of discipline necessarily entails.[1]

This conflict in the child is in our view an important source of aggressiveness in the adult. The conflict itself is a conflict between a fundamental tendency to resent frustration and the fear of punishment or, what is just as important, the fear of loss of love. To the child the parent[2] is both the source of satisfactions and the source of frustrations. To express aggression is to endanger the life of the goose that lays the golden eggs. Not to express simple aggression towards original objects is the task that faces the child. Now one result of the child's attempt to resolve the conflict is called *repression*.[3] Much has been written about the nature and consequences of repression. The hypothesis of the existence and independent functioning of an unconscious mind has been elaborated to explain the analytical evidence, and a whole litera-ture of theory has been built upon this idea. I am not here primarily concerned with psycho-analytic theory, but I am sure that the main contributions of the evidence to an understanding of the sources of aggressiveness can be explained quite simply. The overwhelming fact established by the evidence is that aggres-sion, however deeply hidden or disguised, does not disappear. It appears later and in other forms. It is not destroyed. It is safe to conclude from the evidence that it cannot be destroyed. Whether we conceive simple aggression stimulated by frustration as a quantity of energy that has to be released somewhere, or whether we imagine that a secret and unconscious character is formed that is aggressive, although the superficial character is peaceful, or whether we simply suppose that a certain kind of character is

---

[1] Op. cit., pp. 73-76.

[2] Throughout this Part I use the term 'parent' to refer to the person or persons, whoever it may be, who are responsible for looking after the child – whether they are in fact parents or nurses or aunts or teachers.

[3] The tendency to aggression is not the only thing that may be repressed. Certain other impulses that are punished or condemned by adults or repudiated by the child himself may also be repressed. Much psycho-analytic evidence and theory is concerned with the repression of these other impulses, particularly the sexual impulses.

formed, peaceful in certain directions and aggressive in others — is a matter of comparative indifference and mainly, indeed, of terminology. The fundamental fact is that the punishment of simple aggression results in the appearance of aggression in other forms. The boy, instead of striking his father whom he fears, strikes a smaller boy whom he does not fear. Disguised aggression has made the boy into a bully. The girl who dares not scream at her mother grows up to hate other women. Again a character has been formed by a simple aggressiveness that has been controlled but not destroyed. And in the same way, revolutionaries who hate ordered government; nationalists who hate foreign peoples; individuals who hate bankers, Jews, or their political opponents, may be exhibiting characteristics that have been formed by the suppression of simple aggression in their childhood education.[1] These aggressive aspects of adult character and the aggressiveness to which they lead we call *transformed aggression*. It is the displaced and unrecognized fruit of suppressed simple aggression.

2. The second great contribution of psycho-analytic evidence is to show the kind of transformations that simple aggression undergoes as the adult faculties develop. The fundamental problem of the child is, as we have seen, a double one: that of self-control and of *ambivalence*. In order to escape punishment the child must prevent its aggressive impulses from appearing — it must control its natural aggression. But this is not the whole of the problem. The parent has become for the child the object of two incompatible emotions — love and hatred. As a source of satisfaction and companionship, the parent is greatly beloved. As a source of frustration and punishment, the parent is greatly feared and hated. The evidence demonstrates overwhelmingly that such a double attitude to one person puts a terrible emotional strain upon the child. In the growth and development of character a number of imaginative and intellectual efforts are made to alleviate or avoid the severity of this internal conflict.

[1] I am not for a moment suggesting either (a) that logical and objective cases cannot be argued in favour of revolutions, wars, and persecutions, or (b) that the positive valuation of such things as justice, liberty and other social values may not reasonably involve a hatred of their opposites. I am only suggesting that the repression of simple aggression may result in these forms of hatred. Objective arguments are, in every case, different in kind from the personal motives of those who advance them.

One other aspect of the subjective life must be mentioned before we examine the processes by which internal strain or anxiety is reduced to a minimum — and that is the question of *moral judgment*. I am not at this juncture concerned with the theories of the origin of what the moralist calls the conscience and the psychoanalyst the *super-ego*. It is obvious that persons are deeply influenced in their behaviour and their feelings by what they think they ought to do and ought to be — their 'sense of duty'. I think it also clear from the evidence of psycho-analysis that the content of this moral sense — the total of the things a man feels to be his duty — is made up partly of objective moral judgments and partly of compulsions arising from the teaching and discipline of childhood.[1] The moral sense is neither wholly rational nor wholly subjective and irrational. It is partly the one and partly the other. But, whatever the origin of the moral sense, there is conclusive evidence that it can become the source of immense burdens of shame and guilt, both to the child and to the adult. Again I think that the available evidence demonstrates beyond question that such guilt in the adult is composed partly of a sensible consciousness of moral failure, partly of an irrational fear of punishment derived from the experiences and wild imagination of childhood, and partly of a half-conscious recognition of the dangerous aggressive impulses within himself. All these elements combine to make a considerable burden of guilt — acknowledged or unacknowledged — for most individuals, a burden that rises to intolerable levels for depressed and suicidal subjects.

There is, then, much support in the empirical work of character psychology for the theological doctrine of a 'man divided against himself'. Not only do we both love and hate the same people, but we are divided into an impulsive and appetitive character, only part of which we acknowledge, on the one hand, and a stern and inescapable sense of duty, often partially unrecognized, on the other. These divisions of our being are at war with each other and are responsible for much of the unhappiness of individual life. They are the direct source of the universal phenomenon of *morbid anxiety*.

[1] And partly of the remnants of the exaggerated and fantastic moral judgments of the child.

It is to reduce anxiety and guilt to a minimum, and to resolve the conflict of ambivalence, that the major psychological mechanisms are developed. These are of two kinds — *displacement* and *projection*: both of them are frequently used for the expression of transformed aggression.

(a) *Displacement.*[1] This is perhaps the simplest mechanism of all. Several examples of it have already been cited. It is extremely common in political and social affairs. It consists in the transference of fear, or hatred, or love from the true historical object to a secondary object. The secondary object may be loved or hated for its own sake, but to the sensible degree of feeling is added an intensity derived from the transference to it of irrelevant passion. The child is thwarted by its father and then bullies a smaller child. The father is reprimanded by his employer, of whom he is afraid, and then is angry with his son. A girl both loves and feels jealous of her mother. To deal with this situation she may direct her loving feelings towards her schoolmistress, and thus feel free to hate her mother more completely. A boy may hate his father through familial discipline and grow up to hate all authority and government. He would be a revolutionary under any regime. Children who both love and hate their parents grow up to love their own country blindly and uncritically, and to hate foreign countries with equal blindness and unreason. They have succeeded in displacing their opposite emotions to different objects.

The tendency to identify the self with the community is so. common as to be obvious.[2] The transference of the predominant feelings of childhood from parents to the organs of political life — to the State and the parties in it — is almost universal. Hence the importance of symbolical figureheads and governors, Kings and Führers. Hence the fanaticism and violence of political life. Hence the comparative weakness of reason and moderation in political affairs.

The advantage to the individual of these displacements or transferences of emotion from their historically relevant objects

[1] Op. cit., pp. 84-87.
[2] Nor is such an identification by any means wholly unreasonable. After all, the communities in which we are brought up have entered into us and made us what we are. It is natural that we should feel that what happens to them happens also to us more personally than it really does.

should be obvious. In the *first* place the confusion and strain of the ambivalent relation is often resolved. Instead of both loving and hating the mother, it is possible to love the schoolmistress and to hate more freely — however secretly — the person who was originally both loved and hated with equal intensity. Instead of both loving and hating the same adults, it is possible to love the nation or the Communist Party with pure devotion, and hate the Germans or the 'Capitalist Class' with frenzy. In either case the world of emotional objects is redeemed from its original chaos; simplicity and order are restored to it.. Action and purposive life is possible again.[1] In the *second* place the displacement is often, indeed usually, towards a safer object. It is safer to kick a smaller boy than to kick one's father. It is safer for the individual to hate the capitalists than to hate his wife, or to hate the Russians than to hate his employers. Thus fear and anxiety — though not banished — are reduced. Happiness is increased. Of course greater safety is not always reached in any objective sense. To join the Communist Party, instead of divorcing one's wife, may result in some countries in imprisonment and even death. To become a patriot may mean early enlistment and a premature grave, when the alternative was objectively less dangerous. But, unless we are to deny the teleological interpretation of human affairs altogether, it seems obvious that the internal conflicts of fear and guilt are alleviated by displacement. And there is ample direct evidence to support this view.[2]

From our present point of view the importance of this mechanism can scarcely be exaggerated. Adult aggression, as we have seen, is normally carried out in group activity. Political parties

[1] When a suitable division of emotion and transference is carried out suddenly the phenomenon of 'conversion' often appears. Persons suddenly decide to give all their devotion to the Church or Party, and all their hatred to the 'world' or the Party's enemies. Conflicts suddenly disappear and a frustrated and unhappy individual becomes a confident and happy Christian or Communist or National Socialist. Of course, which of these things he becomes is determined by other forces – including the social and historical environment.

[2] It is also important to realize that the displacement may be temporary. Certain displacements of hatred or love involve further conflict and guilt. Thus the boy who transfers his hatred to his father into bullying may feel, after a time, extremely guilty about his cruelty. Members of extreme parties may find themselves involved in blood guilt. Thus displacement, always bringing temporary relief, may lead in vicious circles more and more deeply into conflict towards final breakdown or suicide.

make civil war. Churches make religious war. States make international war. These various kinds of groups can attract absolute loyalty, and canalize torrents of hatred and murder, through the mechanism of displacement. Individuals can throw themselves into the life and work of groups, because they find a solution to their own conflicts in them. The stores of explosive violence in the human atom are released by and expressed in group organization. The power of the group for aggression is derived partly from the sensible and objective judgments of men, but chiefly, in our view, by their power to attract to themselves the displaced hatred and destructiveness of their members. Displacement, though not the ultimate cause, is a direct channel for the ultimate causes of social conflict.

(b) *Projection.*[1] A second group of mechanisms that are of the greatest importance in understanding individual and social behaviour are those of projection. It is not so simple a mechanism as that of displacement, but the psycho-analytic evidence demonstrates that it is of frequent occurrence in social life. The mechanism consists in imagining that other individuals are really like our own unrecognized and unaccepted selves. It is the projection of our own characters upon others.

There are two parts of subjective character that the individual 'projects upon' others in this way — two kinds of unrecognized motives of his own that he imagines are animating other people: first, his real but unrecognized impulses, and secondly, his unrecognized conscience. In the first case we suppose others to be wicked in ways wherein we do not admit ourselves to be wicked; in the second we suppose them to be censorious and restrictive, in ways wherein we do not recognize our own super-ego to criticize and restrain us.

(i) *The Projection of Impulse.* Examples of the way in which people project upon others the evil that is really in themselves are not far to seek. There are men and women who imagine that everyone's hand is against them; persons who are mean and parsimonious, and who assume that everyone else is seeking to swindle them. Persecution manias or *paranoia* contain, as well as simple animism, an element of this mechanism. In all these cases

[1] Op. cit., pp. 89-93.

it seems obvious to us that the individual is either assuming that people will treat him as he wishes to treat them, or that he imagines them to be animated by the motives and impulses that are really his own. The miser attributes to others his own impulse to swindle. The paranoiac imagines the object of his fears to be animated by his own wicked and destructive passions.

Most cases of political persecution appear to be of this kind. We have already seen that much of this behaviour can be explained in terms of the simplest animism — the tendency to blame some human will for all disasters. But the existence of such a tendency does not explain why persecution continues when no disaster is present or threatening. And yet it does continue after all reasonable occasion has passed. Almost all authoritarian regimes treasure a pet object of persecution indefinitely. The National Socialists persecute the Communists and the Jews; the Bolsheviks persecute the Trotskyists and the *kulaks*. It is commonly said that regimes 'need a scapegoat'. We suggest that over and above any objective reasons for persecution — the need for an excuse in case of failure or the desire to crush opposition by fear — and explaining the continuation of persecution long after the objective reasons have lost their force, there is an element of pure projection. The persecuted minorities are made to carry the projected wickedness of the dominant masses. They are truly the scapegoat of the people, not only in the sense that they are hated and despised, but also that they are made literally to bear the 'sins of the people'. We think it important to realize that the National Socialists seriously believe that the Jews are responsible for national degradation — that the Communists seriously believe that the *kulaks* threatened the regime — and that they believe these things against all evidence, because they have successfully projected upon these groups so much of the disruptive elements within themselves. The hated minorities are genuinely thought to be the cause of disruption, because they have become the external symbol of internal wickedness.

The advantage of this mechanism is again obvious. It reduces anxiety to force the enemy out of the gate of one's soul. It is better to hate other people for meanness, and to bear the fear of their ill-will, than to hate oneself for being miserly. To see wickedness in others, though terrifying, is better than to be divided against oneself. It avoids the terrible burden of guilt.

The importance of projection for the understanding of group aggressiveness is also plain. If it is possible to project upon other groups all the evil within a group, then, as in the case of simple animism, the forces of hatred and fear against the external group will grow more and more intense. If Communists can persuade themselves that all aggressiveness and cruelty is with the Fascists, and Fascists that all treachery and destructiveness is with the Communists, then civil war can be fought with better will and greater ferocity on both sides. If Englishmen owning a quarter of the world can feel that all ruthless imperialism is exhibited by Germany, and Germany with the most powerful army in Europe can feel herself threatened by Russia, then the selfishness of the one group and the aggressiveness of the other can be justified without being reduced. Projection is an admirable mechanism for turning the other man into the aggressor, for making hatred appear as a passion for righteousness, for purifying the hate-tormented soul. By this means all war is made into religious war — a crusade for truth and virtue.

(ii) *The Projection of Conscience.* Finally, to complete the story, there is the projection of the conscience. In order to escape the pains of self-condemnation, the individual projects upon others the moral judgments and condemnation of his own heart. This leads to a particular form of paranoia or persecution mania, in which persons resent, not only the real, but also purely imaginary, moral judgments and legal restraints imposed by the State. It is particularly common among the revolutionary opponents of an existing order. Communists exaggerate enormously the degree and deliberateness of capitalist repression. National Socialists in opposition exaggerated absurdly the oppressions of *das System.* Both parties, all the while, intended to create a far more repressive system themselves. This projection of internal moral censorship, while of great interest in explaining many of the phenomena of political life, is not of central importance in understanding the causes of international war. Displacement and the projection of impulse are the great channels of transformed aggression. The projection of the super-ego is chiefly a cause of revolution and civil war.[1]

I have now completed my survey of the causes of aggression in human beings. I have suggested that there is no substantial difference in behaviour between civilized men and other animals, that adults are just as cruel — or more so — just as aggressive, just as destructive as any group of animals or monkeys. The only difference in our view is one of psychological and intellectual mechanism. The causes of simple aggression — possessiveness, strangeness, frustration — are common to adults and simpler creatures. But a repressive discipline drives simple aggression underground — to speak in metaphors — and it appears in disguised forms. These transformations are chiefly those of displacement and projection. These mechanisms have as their immediate motive the reduction of anxiety and the resolution of the conflicts of ambivalence and guilt. They result in the typical form of adult aggressiveness — aggressive personal relations of all kinds — but above all in group aggression: party conflict, civil war, wars of religion, and international war. The group life gives sanction to personal aggressiveness. The mobilization of transformed aggression gives destructive power to groups. Aggression takes on its social form. And to justify it — to explain the group aggression to the outside world and to the group itself in terms that make it morally acceptable to the members of the group — great structures of intellectual reasoning — theories of history and religion and race — are built up. The impulses are rationalized. The hatred is justified. And it is typical of the complexity of human affairs that something in these theories is always true. But most of it is false — most of it a mere justification of hatred — a sickening and hypocritical defence of cruelty. This is particularly true of the political persecutions of dictatorships. We must now try to apply the conclusions of this evidence to the main subject of this book.

[1] The projection of the super-ego is a reason for hating and attacking any form of government. If, therefore, the League of Nations or any collective security system became strong, there would then arise, if our theory be true, aggressive revolutionary minorities within the collective system. This is an important point made by Dr. Glover.

§8

Three Conclusions

There are, I think, three important conclusions relevant to my purpose that can be derived from this brief survey of the causes of co-operation and conflict among human beings.

The *first* of these is the ancient and obvious conclusion of political theory that the social institution of *government* is a potent cause of peace in society and therefore of incalculable benefit to mankind.

The evidence taken from the life of anarchical animal and human groups bears out the common thought of political philosophers. The absence of government means the absence of order. The alternative to efficient government is a brutal chaos of arbitrary power and gross injustice. In the hackneyed words of Hobbes 'the life of man would be solitary, poor, nasty, brutish and short'. This conclusion is, I am sure, sustained by the evidence.

Whatever our theory of the state may be, it cannot be denied that most of its labour is devoted to the organization of peaceful activities and to defining, without the use of force, the framework of laws and institutions within which individuals and smaller groups can work together in tranquillity. But the state has another and vitally important task. In all modern societies — whether democratic or dictatorial, capitalist or communist — the government and the apparatus of force that it controls, seeks to prevent the breakdown of social equilibrium into civil war. One of the worst crimes in any state is treason against it, and the vast and increasing power of the state is built up, primarily in order to crush the various aggressive minorities who propose to resort to force in defiance of the law.

There is no pacifism within the state. If members of the criminal minority resort to force, force will be used against them. If larger groups threaten the peace by rioting, first the police and then the more heavily armed forces at the disposal of the government will be used against them. The theory and practice of government is, in part, the theory and practice of mobilizing an overwhelming force against anyone or any group that will not keep the law in peace. In my view it is therefore not surprising that the area of the strong nation state has been predominantly the area of peace. Of course, this is not always so. Civil war has broken out more than once in the strongest modern states. But almost all wars and all the largest wars have been between nations — that is, in the realm of anarchy outside the rule of law supported by force.

No doubt there exists another great force making for peace within the state — that is, the spontaneous acceptance of law, and the moral sanction that law *qua* law therefore possesses. Peaceful co-operation is preserved and the law obeyed, in the vast majority of cases, without the direct intervention or supervision of the police. Yet force, nevertheless, is present in the background. People may often obey the law because they wish to do so. But they must obey it whether they wish to or not — or go to prison. And, in fact, there is always a criminal minority who do not obey the law, and against whom force always is and must be used. There is always a disruptive tendency present in society — a tendency to form aggressive and revolutionary minorities — and, in so far as they are allowed to grow without the opposition of force, society draws nearer and nearer to civil war. The recent history of Europe offers many examples of such a development. Moreover, it seems easy to us to exaggerate the strength of the feeling for the moral authority of the law. It seems straining the use of terms to say that the dissident minorities of authoritarian governments 'accept the law'. It seems plainly untrue that peasants admit the moral sanctity of oppressive systems of agrarian law, or that the organized proletariat of a capitalist system really *accept* the justice of the present laws of property. It may be that they feel that an unjust law is better than no law at all; but few dictators, at any rate, would willingly divorce themselves from the use of force or would expect internal peace to be preserved by the strength of moral sentiment alone.[1]

[1] Although it is well outside the subject of this Part and constitutes an altogether larger question, I cannot help feeling that the existing evidence largely supports the view that, while there is no unbreakable link between peace and justice, there is such a connection between peace and force. In my view, peace has often existed in the past, and exists in many places now, where the general condition of society is not accepted as just. It is tolerated because the alternative to it – the appeal to force – has been made a less eligible alternative. I believe that some persons and groups are so aggressive that, in the absence of force to restrain them,

The application of this view to international affairs and the problem of international war is obvious. Article XVI of the Covenant of the League of Nations was and is, in my view, the only hope for the *peace* of the world.[1] Until law is backed by force there seems to me no hope for law or peace. Law is not justice, but neither is war. Aggressive minorities will make international war and civil war, but they will not make justice. And while the achievement of justice will greatly aid the establishment of peace, the handing over of the world to the will of the minority of aggressive states, or of the state to the aggressive minorities within it, will secure neither justice nor peace. Thus, while the struggle for justice and for a system of law that is sufficiently just to be accepted freely by all men is one of the central tasks before this generation, the evidence suggests to the present writer most strongly that the organization of international force for the preservation of international peace and the fulfilment of international law is the most urgent task of all.

Of course, force will not cure the impulses of aggression. Some psychologists, impressed by this fact and also by the consideration that government is a symbol to most people of their own projected conscience, have concluded that the organization of force is not favourable to peace. We should agree that force is not a therapeutic agent. A policeman will not cure a murderer of the desire to kill. An international air force will not cure Hitler or Mussolini of the desire to kill. But that, I feel, is not the point. The immediate problem is not to cure the aggressor, but to prevent the aggression, or to see that, if the aggression takes place, it can only lead to one outcome — the vindication of the law. That is the vital point. The problem is to see that the great majority of human beings who are peaceful, and the great part of human activity that is constructive, should be protected from the savage

[1] It is arguable that Article XVI needs strengthening; but, as any kind of collective action is permissible within its terms, the efficiency of it would seem more a matter of will than of machinery. But I am not concerned in this book with the technical problems of international relations.

they will break the peace and compel everyone else, reluctantly but sensibly, to arm themselves in order to resist force with force, and thus escape arbitrary and unscrupulous evil thrust upon them by unjust means. Peace can only triumph with a sword in its hand. Such is the commonplace view of all intelligent supporters of international law.

and destructive violence of the aggressive minorities. It is only if the lovers of peace and social reconstruction will use force to protect themselves that peace within and without the nation can be preserved.

To accept this gloomy, but in my submission fundamentally realistic, view of the necessity for government does not in the least mean that it is impossible to alleviate the pressure of aggressiveness within the social group. This brings me to the *second* of my relevant conclusions. The psychological and anthropological evidence suggests very strongly that one of the most important institutions determining the behaviour of any social group is to be found in the type of *emotional education* characteristic of the group. The character of this institution determines the amount of aggressiveness generated within the group.

Transformed aggression is due, in my view, to the repression both by the self and by parental authority of simple aggression. Simple aggression, in its turn, I have argued, is due to the frustration of impulse. It would seem upon this analysis that adult aggressiveness could be diminished either by a reduction in the extent to which impulse is frustrated or by a diminution in the extent to which primary aggression is punished. If children could be frustrated less frequently by being given more open access to the means of their satisfaction, or if they were punished less severely when they resented frustration; if, in short, they were allowed to express desire and anger more freely, it should follow, contrary to common expectation, that they would make more happy, more peaceful, and more social adults. The evidence shows overwhelmingly, as we have already seen, that the suppression of simple aggression does not kill it. It drives it underground and makes it far more horrible and destructive. It is only in the expression of it that it becomes diminished. It is only within the circumstances of freedom that social habits and a spontaneous desire to co-operate can flourish and abound. 'Spare the rod and spoil the child' — as a quiet and convenient member of the familial group. Spare the rod and make a free, independent, friendly, and generous adult human being.

There are three points to be made in amplification of this suggestion:

1. A certain amount of frustration is inevitable and a certain amount of external repression is almost equally so. A child cannot have all that it wants. In the first place, the parents may not be rich enough to supply it even with enough to eat. In the second place, some of its desires — though we suspect they would be few except in the first few years of life — are contradictory and dangerous. A baby must be denied the fire that it wishes to reach, or the bright but poisonous berry that it wishes to suck. In the third place the satisfaction of some of its desires may make social life impossible or intolerable. The child cannot rampage when its parents are tired or ill. It cannot be taken for a walk when its mother must get the tea. Upon a thousand occasions frustration is inevitable. But I suggest that, even if frustration is inevitable, it should be reduced to a minimum and could be reduced enormously below its present level. The restraint of impulse is far too frequently carried out upon principle — as a desirable form of 'discipline'. Parents believe that children ought not to have what they want — that denial of impulse will make a good character. I hold that the opposite of this is the truth.

Nevertheless, some frustration is inevitable. What then can be done to alleviate its ill effects? I suggest that much more can be done by refusing to suppress and punish the natural resentment that frustration calls forth. This I feel to be the essential point. Take the child away from the fire, refuse to take it for a walk, deny it a second piece of cake; but avoid being angry or hurt or disapproving if a scream of rage or a kick on the shins is the immediate consequence of thwarting the child's will to happiness. To permit children to express their *feelings* of aggression, whilst preventing *acts* of irremediable destruction is, I suggest, one of the greatest gifts that parents can give to their children.

2. I believe the evidence suggests that such methods of education will have consequences precisely the opposite of those expected by the parent unaware of the evidence of modern analytical psychology. People greatly under-estimate the rapidity and strength with which the social and affectionate impulses of the free child develop. And yet it is blindness to do so. After all, enormous advantages accrue to the child from co-operation. It is, as I have emphasized *ad nauseam*, the overwhelming impulse of

67

human life. And I suggest that the child, freed from frustration and unsympathetic discipline, will in fact become the very opposite of the popular picture of the 'spoiled child'. Instead of violent and ungovernable anger, inordinate selfishness and vanity, the child who is not afraid to express feeling is likely to exhibit affection, independence, sociability, and courage more rapidly and more naturally than a repressed child. Such children, the evidence suggests, become reasonable and sociable at a surprisingly early age. Family life with them is not a nightmare of disorder, or the false calm of strong discipline, but a moderately peaceful and very lively society of free, equal, and willing co-operation.

3. At the same time I do not wish to over-draw the picture. There are certain inevitable conflicts and sources of disturbance in individual and family life. Sexual jealousy, for one thing, is unavoidable. It seems unlikely that the strain between father and son, mother and daughter, can be wholly avoided. Nor does the reduction of external repression remove internal conflict. Self-repression — the fear that anger felt towards the source of satisfaction will 'kill the goose that lays the golden eggs' — will still remain. Hence the reduction of repression is not a panacea. It will not produce heaven within the family or a race of perfect adults in a generation. Neurosis and aggressiveness will still be there. Social friction and the threat to peace will not be wholly eliminated. I only suggest that these things will be greatly reduced.

This doctrine is somewhat more speculative than the analysis of the causes of aggressiveness. It is not established by the existing evidence with the same degree of certainty. The number of children educated more freely is still small. No society has embarked upon the experiment of a wide and rapid change in the technique of parental control. No generation has yet grown up that has been influenced by the spread of these ideas. It is, therefore, too soon to say whether a change in the educational environment can bring about a substantial reduction in the aggressiveness of adults. I personally feel that the evidence gathered from the treatment of children is overwhelmingly on one side. I believe it to be almost certain that if children were actually brought up more freely they would be much happier, much more reasonable, and much more sociable.[1] It is obvious that social and international relations would greatly benefit if people were happier, more reasonable and more sociable. But this belief is still in the realm of probability rather than fact. It is, of course, a purely empirical question. Will a certain form of education make human adults less aggressive without making them less strong? It is the combination of strength with reasonableness, of power with affection, that I think desirable. I have no faith in, nor desire to educate, a pacifist generation. I believe the rejection of force, and the passive acceptance of other people's aggression, to be as profoundly neurotic as the manifestation of transformed aggression itself. But with the subject of pacifism we are not concerned. I only wish to emphasize that I do not expect to arise from a better form of emotional education a generation of persons unable or unwilling to protect themselves, who kneel down before the aggressor and fling wide their gates to his attack; but a generation of men and women who will defend their rights and yet willingly concede equal rights to others; who will accept the judgment of third parties in the resolution of disputes; who will neither bully nor eat humble pie; who will fight, but only in defence of law; who are willing and friendly members of a positive and just society.

Unfortunately this hope is not for us but only for a posterity that shall come long after us. We have not the time nor the opportunity to do these things. It would take decades to affect the course of political relations by emotional education. And, in any case, there is not the remotest possibility of beginning now. Half the nations of the world are in the grip of regimes in which this type of education, so far from being encouraged, is being destroyed. Even in democratic communities there is no widespread belief in the kind of argument we have been advancing; much less is there any serious attempt to reform family practice in this direction. Even if there were, the successful execution of a new technique of parental guidance requires a new and less neurotic generation to carry it through. Improvement in the emotional atmosphere that surrounds the representative child can only be

[1] The evidence of the therapeutic value of analysing aggressive children – a process consisting amongst other things of treating them more sympathetically and without punishment – is particularly convincing on this point.

brought about slowly, and from generation to generation, as each group of parents brings to its children a less warped and aggressive personality. It is possible to begin, but not to proceed rapidly, with this basic social therapy. In the meantime, if this is all the hope there is, we shall have perished by half a dozen wars. And each war, by strengthening the fears and hatreds inside national groups, will make the task of better education more difficult. What therapy cannot cure, government must restrain.

Thus, as I see it, there are two ways, and only two, in which social conflict can be reduced in its frequency and violence — one slow, curative, and peaceful, aimed at the removal of the ultimate causes of war in human character by a new type of emotional education; the other immediate, coercive, and aimed at symptoms, the restraint of the aggressive minority by force.

Finally, there is a *third* conclusion, more general than the other two, that stands out clearly from the evidence. It is the importance of the *irrational* and the *unconscious* in social life. We are not what we seem to be and think we are. We do not even want the things we say we want, nor seek the ends we seem to seek. No theory of human society or history based upon a doctrine of rational or conscious purpose can contain the whole truth. To understand why people behave as they do, we must remember the things that they have forgotten, the motives they dare not confess, the springs of action they cannot admit. The ideology of any movement or of any society is only half the story. The other half, and for us the most important half, lies below the surface.

The result of accepting this part of the evidence of analytical psychology is most important for my purpose. It introduces a new perspective into social study and political reflection. Nothing is quite the same as it was before. Those who come to see themselves, their friends, and the societies in which they live, through the categories of modern psychology experience the same kind of shock as those who look for the first time at some common object through a microscope, or at the moon through a telescope. In one sense everything is the same, in another sense everything is changed. What appeared to be simple is shown to be complex, and yet things that were previously unintelligible now become simple and clear. Floating unsuspected in the blood are the essential animalculae of life and death, and the mysterious markings upon the face of the moon are seen to be the shadows of great mountains.

The social scientist must look through the psychological microscope; so must the politician. They will then see the real, but macroscopic, institutions of government and property, party and revolution, with which they deal and must continue to deal, dissolve into a thousand fragments of personal ambition and patriotism, of secret love and hatred, unconscious purpose and need. Systems of thought can then be traced to secret emotional roots, and great institutions, rich in dignity, to the primitive fears of childhood and the jungle. Ideas will lose a little of their importance; but the structure and laws of our emotional life, previously mysterious and unintelligible, will be flooded with light.

The most important conclusion of this Part is, therefore, a negative one.

Nothing that men say of their purposes can be accepted at its face value. This is so because men and women do not even know what they are doing, nor are they conscious of the ends that guide their action. Many of the paradoxes of history disappear in the light of this simple but revealing principle. Some of the most outstanding mysteries of the relation between thought and action exhibited in history become far less unintelligible.

The Christian Churches, founded upon a doctrine of love and preaching a gospel of mercy, have nevertheless used every refinement of torture and every instrument of pain — from the rack to the stake — in order to break and crush opposition to their interests or dogmas. Communists, with the high words of human equality and human brotherhood upon their lips, have shot and tortured, imprisoned and starved, the powerless masses that they have controlled. Democracies, paying solemn lip-service to the cause of equality between the nations and of government over them, have nevertheless divided the world as they chose while their enemies were weak, and have betrayed the doctrine of collective security when their enemies became strong.

All these things, the crude and often horrible paradoxes of history, become intelligible as soon as we realize that the conscious purpose and the real purpose of individuals and of groups need bear no direct relationship to one another. Human beings may say that they want one thing and really want its opposite, and do this, not because they are rogues or hypocrites, but because the human mind possesses a dangerous power to disguise even from the thinking and willing agent the clear purposes of its own thought and action. We do not know ourselves. We are not the simple creatures of rational purpose that we think we are. The springs of our action lie hidden, like corpuscles and phagocytes, secret but dominant, in our spiritual blood.

It is therefore necessary to assess ideas and theories in the light of the emotional life of the 'ideologists', and to judge every institution and system of thought by the emotions that are involved in it and justified by it. 'By their fruits ye shall know them.' — 'Do men gather grapes of thorns, or figs of thistles?'

For the purpose of this book we can go forward, therefore, with a knowledge of some of the forces that make for co-operation and conflict in social life, with an appreciation of the advantages of the institution of government and the importance of the form of emotional education in any group; and with the knowledge that the categories of rational thought and conscious purpose are not sufficient by themselves to make social behaviour intelligible or the choice of policy well grounded. These are simple ideas in themselves, but they are of considerable value, and bearing them in mind we must now turn to the study of economic and political institutions. Such is the kind of people that we are. Among what institutions do we live in the contemporary world?

PART II

CAPITALISM IN TRANSITION

An analysis of recent trends in the development of the British economic system

... my critic ... feels himself obliged to metamorphose my historical sketch of the genesis of capitalism in Western Europe into an historico-philosophic theory of the *marche générale* imposed by fate upon every people, whatever the historic circumstances in which it finds itself.

But I beg his pardon . . . He is both honouring and shaming me too much . . .

. . . events strikingly analogous but taking place in different historic surroundings led to totally different results. By studying each of these forms of evolution separately and then comparing them one can easily find the clue to this phenomenon, but one will never arrive there by the universal passport of a general historico-philosophical theory, the supreme virtue of which consists in being super-historical.

KARL MARX, 1877 — Letter to the Editor
of the *Otyec est vennige Zofisky*

CAPITALISM IN TRANSITION

§ 1

Introduction

WE must now turn from the study of the hereditary and individual to the institutional and social element in contemporary human behaviour.

Let me begin by emphasizing briefly the attitude to institutional studies that I have already explained in the Introduction. I have begun this book with a brief consideration of individual psychology because it is obvious that society is an atomic structure, whose atoms are individual human beings. From a study of them it is possible to arrive at certain broad ideas that throw light upon the behaviour of societies. But this is not in the least to decry or diminish the importance of studying social institutions. The rest of this book will be given up to a consideration of them. And this is reasonable because the behaviour of adult human beings is not determined solely by the hereditary propensities of their common human nature, but by the reaction between these propensities and the social system in which they were brought up and by which they were, from the first moments of their being, influenced and formed. We are not only parts of a society, but society is part of us. Hence, in order to understand and prescribe a policy for society, we must understand the 'institutions' and institutional 'systems' of which society is composed. To do so we must consider the kind of economic and social order characteristic of our time.[1]

[1] It may be as well, in order to avoid misunderstanding, to specify the sense in which the term 'economic and social system' is used. Do such things as 'economic systems' exist? From one point of view they plainly do not. All periods of history are complex, all events isolated, and all instances particular. Many economists and historians concentrating upon the particularity of events have been led to suppose that no such entities as the 'capitalist system' or a 'democratic period of history' could be thought to exist. (*Continued over page.*)

Now, in order to make such a task possible, it is first necessary to define more strictly the limits of my present inquiry. The social system is an exceedingly complex thing. It includes not only the institutions particularly associated with economic processes — like money, exchange, forms of productive enterprise, property and inheritance — but also, political and psychological uniformities — like representative government, family, forms of punishment and codes of sexual ethics. It is impossible, both for reasons of space and from the limitations of knowledge, to deal with

There is, in my view, a true element and a false element in this contention. The true element lies in the complexity of a society at any moment of time. The institutions and forces that have been typical in the past remain alive in the present, and what is to become typical of the future has already come into existence in the present. There is no simplicity and no uniformity. Economic and social systems do not succeed one another as cards in a pack but as one picture 'dissolves into' another in a cinematographic film.

Let me take an example. Suppose we hold that there was such a thing as a 'medieval economic system', that this system was gradually replaced by a 'capitalist economic system' during the seventeenth and eighteenth centuries, and that the 'capitalist system' became dominant in the nineteenth century. To hold that all these statements mean something is not to impose a false simplicity upon the complexity of history. It is obvious that at no time does 'a system' exist in a pure form. Even in the purest periods of capitalist domination – the seventies or eighties of the last century in the British economy – there are important relics of the medieval economy left in it, particularly in agriculture and trade, and institutions were already present at that time that were destined to grow towards a new collectivist economy. Neither here, nor in any period, is there any simplicity of economic form.

But this is not to say that the term 'system' has no meaning. The false element in the doctrine of the economists and historians to which I have referred consists in any exclusive concentration upon the particularity of events. No progress in understanding can possibly be made in the field of historical and social studies – just as in the studies of the physical world – unless the common element in varied instances is discovered by comparison and reflection. And it is ridiculous in the highest degree to suppose, when we survey the total economic and social life of a tribe of hunters and collectors in a jungle, a developed peasant agriculture in India or China, and an industrialized urban community in Lancashire or New York State, that the differences between what is typical or common in the actions of these three social groups is not sufficiently marked to enable us to speak of a primitive, a medieval and a post-medieval type of economy and society. There are so many patterns of behaviour typical within each of these societies, but rare or absent in either of the others, that the differences are as significant as or more significant than the similarities.

These uniformities or patterns of behaviour may properly be called *institutions*. And if there is a unity and harmony – however crude and interrupted – between the sets of institutions, then the relations between the institutions and the institutions themselves may properly be called a *system*. It is in this sense that these terms will be used throughout this book. Hence by an institution I shall mean a pattern or uniformity of behaviour common to many individuals within the group, and by a system a loose integration of such institutions to form a working machine that functions at least sufficiently well to preserve life within itself.

76

anything like the total list of these institutions in one book. At the same time it is impossible to know *a priori* which of the institutions are really important in determining the course of history. As will be seen from the first Part of this book, I am certain that many of our most important institutions have scarcely been studied at all. Under the guidance of false or over-simple doctrines of history and human society the social sciences have hitherto concentrated upon economical and political arrangements and have neglected the institutions more closely related to the formation of individual character.[1] This is, I am sure, a false emphasis. I have already argued that one institution, the form of emotional education typical of a society, is as important as any other single institution and more important than most that have been studied in the past. Hence, if the truth is to be faced, we are really in the dark as to the institutional studies that are important for the understanding of political history. Only the kind of empirical work described in the Introduction could resolve the urgent problems of selection and emphasis that face the social sciences.

The only thing to be done at the moment is therefore to pursue a conservative course of inquiry and to make use of institutional studies in so far as they are available, adding to them as much as a simple interpretation of individual psychology can offer. I should be the last to pretend that this is a satisfactory procedure, but no other appears to be practicable. At some time in the future it may be possible, by an extension of co-operative studies, to do something better than this. In the meantime we must concentrate upon the results of the contemporary study of political and economic institutions.

In this book I am chiefly concerned with the future of the great capitalist democracies, in particular Great Britain and America. As the title that I have given to them implies, these are societies founded upon the union of the political system of *representative democracy* with the economic system of *capitalism*. It is therefore to the study of these two systems or sets of institutions that we must now turn. I propose to discuss the nature of the democratic

[1] See Part I, § 8.

tradition in Part IV. In this present Part I shall examine the structure and development of the capitalist system.

I must begin by asking what the term capitalist system should be taken to mean.

§ 2

The Institutional Basis of Capitalism[1]

What do we or ought we to mean when we use the phrase 'the capitalist system' as a technical term in political discussion?

Leaving on one side the cruder definitions of capitalism, which identify it with the darker side of human nature, we can consider the answer given by economic historians. They suggest that the capitalist system consists in an economic order possessing three typical characteristics or common forms of behaviour:

> a rational technique of production in industry, trade and finance;
> unlimited acquisitiveness as a motive in individual life;
> a steady and rapid expansion of output.

Let me say a word in brief explanation of each of these characteristics.

A *rational technique* in an economy stands in contrast to the habits and institutions of *traditionalism*.

The typical condition of technical processes in a pre-capitalist economy is that of irrational tradition. The processes of sowing, gathering and reaping in agriculture; of spinning, weaving and dyeing in the textile industries; of mining, smelting and refining in the metallurgical industries; are not determined by scientific experiment and discovery, or by the rational adjustment of means to ends, but by the compulsion of slowly acquired traditions and criteria of excellence established through the accident of local memory. It is said, for example, by economic historians that towards the end of the medieval period in this country every technical detail in the manufacture of woollen

---

[1] I am concerned here only with the *industrial* capitalism characteristic of the last century and a half of economic development.

cloth was legally prescribed by Parliament. This may be an extreme case, but even in cases where the technique of production was not protected by the severe sanctions of the law, the idea of 'appropriate technique' was that of 'the good way in which our fathers worked' rather than the economizing of means or the maximizing of output. The grip of tradition was everywhere strong, and no one who knows the technical 'conservatism' of a pre-capitalist peasantry to-day — in India or China or Russia — will doubt the predominance of such forces in a medieval economy.[1]

What is new in the Industrial Revolution, at the time when the capitalist order is brought into existence, is not the *discovery* of mechanical principles and mechanical devices. On the contrary, the knowledge of many of them existed long before any Industrial Revolution occurred. The machinery used in a medieval clock or the sideshows of a medieval fair was far more complicated than the simple mechanical devices employed in the first machines of an Arkwright or a Watt. The new principle is the idea that processes of reason, science and mechanics should be applied to the technique of industrial production; that machines could and should be used to raise output. A medieval society looks upon machines as *toys*. A capitalist society looks upon them as instruments of production. What has changed is not knowledge, but a habit of thought. What has really altered is an emotional judgment.[2]

Unlimited acquisitiveness is another, and equally important, aspect of the same fundamental break with traditionalism. The conception of a proper ideal of personal life, which is typical of a medieval society, is that of *status* or *caste*. A man or a woman is born into a certain place or order in society, with traditional duties, traditional privileges, traditional functions and traditional stages of personal development. Spiritual guidance as to these duties is provided by

---

[1] It is scarcely necessary to point out that the term *rational* applies only to the technique of production and not to the objects of production or the form of society within which the technique is used.

[2] And what is true of capitalism in its European origin is also true of the relation between capitalist and medieval economies to-day. What is absent in the industry and agriculture of India and China is not knowledge, but the habit of mind that regards the application of rational and mechanical principles and devices to production as possible and right. It is a habit of mind – an intellectual institution – that is missing.

the Church. Ghostly comfort, and the certain assurance of eternal compensation for the transient sufferings of time, is available for everyone in the unshaken conviction of personal immortality. It would of course be ridiculous to suppose that men and women were ever, in any society, devoid of ambition and the impulses of acquisitiveness, but there is, nevertheless, a real sense in which contentment was and is easier to find in a pre-capitalist society. Ambition is more limited; the sense of personal achievement satisfied by status and the knowledge of traditional forms faithfully observed.

In marked opposition to this stand the accepted and respectable acquisitive ideals of capitalism, based upon the judgment that men should go as far in terms of wealth and prestige as their abilities will permit them to do. This change of outlook about the true purpose of individual life is one of the most difficult to establish in an emergent capitalist system. It is the basis of all the complaints about the 'stupidity', the 'irrationality', the 'untrustworthiness' of the peasantry made by the new and revolutionary class of industrial technicians, whether in eighteenth-century England or twentieth-century Russia. It is a process of education and adaptation that has been studied in detail by economic historians under the general title of 'the adaptation of labour to the needs of the capitalist system'. It is a psychological and spiritual change that is of vital importance to the growing system. It is the basis of industrial discipline, factory technique and the specialization of function. Without it men will not work hard enough, nor long enough; sometimes they will not work for wages at all. It is equally necessary for the development of the willingness to save, without which industrial expansion is impossible. It is the vital counterpart in emotional life of rational science in the intellectual life of mankind.

Finally, *rapid expansion* is an historical characteristic of the new capitalist system. Under its auspices the area of the world brought within the circle of economic exchange is enormously expanded. The population of the capitalist societies rises by leaps and bounds. The increase of physical production outstrips them both, and the world is brought into an era of unprecedented, almost unbelievable, economic growth. The history of this expansion we shall have to consider in greater detail before this Part is finished.[1]

About this historical analysis of the institutional basis of capitalism, two things must be noticed.

1. In the *first* place, the last characteristic — that of *expansion*— is not really similar in institutional nature to the other two. It is not causal in the sense that they are. As any economist knows, the immense growth of physical output is a simple result of the application of science to industry, and of the willingness to work harder and save more. It is a consequence, and not a part, of the institutional basis of the system. We shall only consider it, therefore, as an economic consequence — of great social importance — due to the co-existence in the society of the two basic institutions of rational technique and unlimited acquisitiveness.

2. In the second place, it is very important for our purpose to note that the historian's list of basic institutions is not complete. Emphasis falls, naturally enough, upon what was new, what was unprecedented, in the historical development of the capitalist economy. But to understand its contemporary working, it is not enough to understand what is novel in it. There are at least two further institutions that are of fundamental importance to it.

The *first* of these is *property*. As a legal institution property existed long before capitalism. Indeed, the group of legal rights comprised within the institution, and the types of object in which property is legally possible, are both restricted, rather than extended, during the period of capitalist development. It is an age of a reduction of the power of property rather than an age of its aggrandizement. Hence the historians do not treat it fully in their analysis of institutional origins. Nevertheless, property is a vital part of the institutional system. By it the government of industry is determined. The right to the exclusive use of instruments of production is guaranteed by law, and the disposal of them between different technical employments is vested in the owner or proprietor of them. As the machines are the new factor of production in the early stages of capitalist development, and as the other factors must be persuaded and forced unwillingly into co-operation with them, it is the owner of the machine — the entrepreneur —

---

[1] See Part II § 8 and the Statistical Appendix §§ 7-8.

who becomes the natural organizer of production. Hence the organization of industry is entrusted by society to the institution of property, and the distribution of property comes to determine, in the early stages of capitalism, the distribution of executive control. The legal institution of property is therefore an essential part of the institutional basis of capitalism itself.

And, as we shall see, the continuous retention of the right of *inheritance* within the ever-changing bundle of property rights is of the greatest importance in determining the kind of social hierarchy compatible with a developing capitalist economy.

The *second* institution not fully treated in the historian's definition of capitalism is the *relation between the political authority of the State and the economic authority of the proprietor*. Capitalism is a genus with several species and it is the form of this relationship that divides national capitalisms more than anything else into two broad types. In the first of these the relationship is paternalist and authoritarian. The State is one of the chief agents in bringing the capitalist system into existence within the national economy, and it continues to superintend and control the activities of the industries it has created. This form of state fostered and *state controlled capitalism* was and is typical of Germany, and was also exemplified in pre-revolutionary Russia. In both those countries heavy industry and the means of communication were aided and controlled in their development by the State. The opposite is the case with the capitalism to be found in Great Britain and America. In their origins, these capitalisms were *laisser-faire* capitalisms. The State was passive and permissive in its attitude to the 'new industry', or even hostile to it, and this tradition of independence — a lack of control by or responsibility to any central authority — is a vital element in their constitution and one of the most important determinants of their historical development.

Hence by 'capitalism' in this discussion of its contemporary processes of change I shall mean an economy founded upon four basic institutions: (*a*) rational technique, (*b*) unlimited acquisitiveness, (*c*) property in the material means of production, and (*d*) a *laisser-faire* relationship between the State and industry. It is with the modern developments of this system that we are chiefly concerned in this Part, but before we can turn to them we must briefly consider the record of this system in the days of its emergence and dominance.

§ 3

Historical Assessment

Two very different historical prophecies were made about the future of this great experiment. The prognosis of the Classical economists was optimistic, while that of the Marxists was dramatically gloomy. As we shall see in § 5, this clear opposition of hypotheses can now be tested by the historical evidence at our disposal.

The optimistic forecast of the apostles of *laisser-faire* was based upon the belief that the process of capital accumulation, resulting from the acquisitive impulses of the 'rational' capitalist, brings into operation a powerful 'virtuous circle' of cumulative expansion. The argument is familiar. Saving and the construction of capital increases the productive capacity of the industrial system, and so raises the level of real income. Out of larger real incomes it is natural to suppose that more will be saved. The rate of capital construction is therefore increased; real income rises still faster, and a cumulative expansion begins. Nor is there any reason, according to this doctrine, why the process should ever stop. It will lead, ever more rapidly, to an economic Utopia.

The Marxist gloom rests, as we shall see, upon the view that the increasing power of the capitalist bourgeoisie will be used by them to intensify the inequality in the distribution of wealth. Rising inequality will bring with it two self-destructive developments. In the first place, the rate of saving will become too large to permit the successful marketing of the rising output of consumptive goods — the dilemma of under-consumption. In the second place, the Marxists, perhaps failing to distinguish sufficiently clearly between relative and absolute movements in the standard of living, believed that the intensification of inequality would mean a progressive reduction in the real wages of the proletariat. The 'increasing misery' of the working classes spelled, in their judgment, an inevitable political catastrophe.

Now, whatever may be thought of these two hypothetical prophecies in their pure form — and we shall return to discuss them in
§ 5 — there are several simple historical judgments that are
commonly passed upon the capitalist system by almost all students
of it. The most important of these judgments are not, I think, in
dispute and they are three in number:

First, it is plain that, judged by material standards, industrial
capitalism was unquestionably superior to any form of economy
that preceded it. Its record of immense, almost explosive, growth
proves that. It is calculated that real wages doubled in this
country during the first half of the nineteenth century and doubled
again in the second half. This was at a time when the working
population roughly quadrupled. There was therefore something
like a 1600% increase in the physical production and consumption
of wage goods alone in one hundred years. It is doubtful whether
a similar increase could be found before the advent of capitalism
in any previous period ten times as long. Whatever set of figures
is studied, the same conclusion emerges — the new system exhibited a previously unthinkable power of expansion.

We shall discuss whether this headlong pace has been maintained in recent times, before this Part of the book is finished. But
it is certain that the institutional discoveries made in the sixteenth
and seventeenth centuries released for a hundred and fifty years
immense stores of productive energy. The explanation of this
phenomenon is not difficult to find. It lies in the immense
superiority of rational over traditional techniques of production,
and in the material power released by the emancipation from
social restraint of the acquisitive impulses of mankind.

The *second* undoubted fact about the social system established
upon the basis of property and inheritance is the continuation in
it, and the enhancement by it, of *economic inequality*. This is the
common ethical indictment brought against it. In this matter it
is necessary, however, to preserve some sense of proportion. The
critics of capitalism sometimes write as though the system had
created social and economic inequality. Such an assertion is
absurd. Not only did inequality of a severe kind exist long before
the capitalist system came into existence, but in many ways the
same forces that created capitalism also modified the degrees of

inequality that were permitted by the law. Legal privilege was greatly reduced. Political equality was greatly increased. Slavery was abolished. Gradually higher taxation began to modify the absolute claims of property. In all these ways capitalism reduced the forces making for inequality.

But there is plain evidence that the growth of capitalism did greatly increase the inequality in the distribution of the national income. While total real wages increased by approximately 100 % in the second half of the nineteenth century, the increase in real incomes from property was much greater than this. As the large incomes are provided by property, these relative growths imply an increase of the degree of inequality. In any case, the degree of inequality existing at present is known to be extreme. The facts are familiar. In Great Britain it is roughly true to say that 10% of the population receive appreciably more than one-half of the national income — that the other 90% must live upon less than half of the national income. The distribution of property is even more unequal: 10% of the adult population own more than 90% of the property; 1% of the population own something like 60% of the property. The figures are simply extraordinary, and yet they are well authenticated. Again we shall have to ask whether the degree of inequality is growing greater or smaller. There is no doubt, however, that it is now very great.

Finally, it is a familiar generalization that the departure from a quiet and traditionally ordered economy and society while it reduced some sources of *insecurity* introduced others. Not only has the economic system been dominated since its beginning by wide swings of industrial activity — the phenomenon known to the economist as the 'Trade Cycle' — but the very principle of adjusting means to ends involves a high degree of mobility and insecurity when the means and the ends both vary. In a self-supporting peasant economy, governed by a traditional agricultural technique, a traditional programme of consumption and an hereditary form of tenure, the sources of economic insecurity are restricted to the climate and to disease. The main causes of economic disaster are famines and plagues. In a developed capitalist economy these evils are much reduced, but they are replaced by all the adaptations required by the free market to alterations in technical conditions, consumers' preferences, the quality of the factors of production, and the ceaseless ebb and flow of the monetary circulation. Change, uncertainty, insecurity, and unemployment must result.[1]

Expansion is then the great virtue of capitalism; inequality and insecurity are its greatest vices.

It will be noticed that, in this brief and familiar assessment of the system, I have made no mention of two charges that are commonly preferred against it — that capitalism must suffer from a constant or periodical deficiency of consumers' purchasing power; and that it must for this, or some other reason peculiar to it, lead to international war. I have not set down these charges because I do not believe that they are true. The first of them I have examined elsewhere[2] and I shall return to it in a future volume.

I think it is generally agreed by economists that the institutions of rationalism, acquisitiveness and property do not necessarily involve any marked degree of income deficiency. Of course it is arguable, and I shall argue, that the institution of *laisser-faire* in the money market is largely responsible for the fluctuations of the Trade Cycle.[3] But that is not the same thing as supposing that capitalism is inherently incapable of providing an adequate monetary income to consumers. With the second false charge I have already dealt, at least by implication, in the first Part of this book. Since warfare occurred long before capitalism came into existence, it is difficult to see that there can be any interesting sense in which capitalism can be regarded as '*the* cause of war'. An effect cannot precede its cause, and the causes of warfare and fighting are more widespread in space and time than the institutions of capitalism. It is not my intention, therefore, to pursue these false trails any further in this book.[4]

[1] For a fuller discussion of some aspects of this problem see PROF. FISHER: *Clash of Progress and Security.*
[2] Cf. *Purchasing Power and Trade Depression*, Chaps. I-III.
[3] This is one of the subjects that it would be relevant to treat in my projected work *The Economics of Democratic Socialism.*
[4] It will be familiar to students of economics that a certain school of economists – the Classics and the 'neo-Classics' – have constructed a rational account of the capitalist system, and have gone on to argue that it (the system) is the best or the only practicable method of organizing the economy. I have discussed these views in Appendix II, *The Classical Defence of the Capitalist System.*

§4

The Recent Institutional Changes in Capitalism

Up to this point the ideas that I have set down in this Part — the institutional analysis of capitalism and the historical assessment of its achievement — are very familiar. They are the stock-in-trade of all past controversy. To them little has been added. I now want to go on to suggest that an examination of contemporary changes in our economic system will show many of these old arguments to be irrelevant, and many of the institutional assumptions upon which they were based to be out of date. The economic system has developed so far, and new forms of organization within it have become quantitatively so important, that it is really necessary to think of a new variant — a sub-type of capitalism — as coming into existence under our eyes. We live in a period in which the basic institutions of the recent past have been so greatly modified that a new system is emerging. It is to the nature of this emerging system, and the forces that are causing it to appear, that we must now turn.

I propose to examine at least *eight* major changes in the institutional framework of capitalism, and that list is by no means an exhaustive one. It is necessary to select the most important in order to preserve proportion in the picture. But, before I seek to describe these changes in detail, it is perhaps worth discussing the possible classification of them according to their origin. What general social process has brought these changes about?

In Great Britain and America — both democracies in some real sense — the most fundamental description of the whole process of transformation is, I am convinced, that it represents a *short-sighted adaptation of the institutions of* laisser-faire *capitalism to the needs of ordinary men and women.* The process of development is short-sighted, because that is the way democracies work. Most men do not look far ahead. They cannot imagine a new heaven or a new earth, and they do not value a logical imagination in their leaders. The changes nevertheless represent a process of adaptation to the needs of common men, because therein lies the most important virtue of responsible government — that it gives to the great majority of people what they want. Government, in a slow and fumbling way characteristic of democracy, comes to express their will. By a series of small but sharp reactions against conditions and events that ordinary people plainly dislike, the course of history and the form of society is slowly moulded more nearly to their heart's desire. Just as an evenly dispersed cloud of animalculae will slowly congregate in that part of a containing vessel where food is present, merely by reacting negatively every time that they touch the limit of the foodless area, so the great mass of mankind will slowly mould their social order to suit themselves by reactions that appear, when they are made, to be a purely blind and negative response to external stimuli. The curious nature of this process goes far to explain the paradox that democracies, whose policy is so often confused and even contradictory, can yet build up societies that are more stable, freer and happier than authoritarian states of any kind whatever. To this general point we shall return in the next two Parts of the book.

To be more specific, I think it can be shown that the sources of change in British and American capitalism have been the reactions of common men and women to the main features of its growth — the rise in the standard of living, the extent of insecurity in economic life, and the degree of inequality in the distribution of wealth. To this list of causal forces must be added a shorter list of specific institutional and legal changes, or inventions, that have had most important social consequences. Of these the invention of money and credit, and the invention of Joint Stock enterprise in its limited liability form, are the most important. It is under those four heads that we shall consider the process of contemporary economic development, and it will be seen that the process is, in a very special sense, *inevitable*. It is inevitable in the sense that it could only be other than it was, if the emotional character and structure of values of common men and women had been different from what they were. The growth of rigidity, the growth of restriction, the decline of saving, that we are to trace, could only have been prevented if the general reactions to insecurity, inequality and growing wealth had been different. This is not to say that changes in the temper of a democratic electorate can never be induced by persuasion and reason; but nothing short of this, nothing short of the emotional and intellectual conversion of the common man, could have made the process of historical development other than it was. Mere legislative changes and mere intellectual discoveries would not have been enough to change the course of economic history. The significance of this point will be clear before we have gone much further.

We must now turn to consider in detail the consequences of common men's reaction to inequality, insecurity and a rising standard of living.

A   *The Institutional Consequences of Insecurity*

There can be no question that, quantitatively speaking, the most important changes have been bound up with the popular reaction against the growth of insecurity inherent in the life of *laisser-faire* economy. The growth of Trade Unions and the consequent rigidity in the labour market, the growth of the Social Services, and the recent extension of the social control of business, are all due to the search for safety in a precarious economy. We must look at these processes in turn.

(a) *Trade Unions and the Ossification of the Labour Market.* The facts here are familiar. Already in 1929 Professor Clay gave these figures of persons affected by forms of collective bargaining:

Trade Union Membership	4,900,000
Trade Boards	1,500,000
Joint Industrial Councils	1,000,000
Agricultural Wages Board	1,100,000

and he passed this judgment upon them:

> ... if we add together the numbers covered by Trade Boards, Agricultural Wages Boards, Joint Industrial Councils, and Unions in certain industries, which, like coal and cotton, have adopted none of these forms of organization, we get a total of *eight millions* out of a wage earning population which, excluding domestic service, numbers *something under fourteen millions.* When we remember that the influence of an agreement or a determination reached by a representative body tends to go beyond the limits of the membership of the organizations,

and even trades, directly represented, we may safely conclude that there are few important gaps left in the provision for the settlement of wages by collective bargaining in Great Britain.

These processes have gone further to-day.

There can be no question that this growth of collective bargaining, in one form and another, is a 'protective reaction' on the part of the great mass of the workers to the conditions imposed upon them by the insecurity of competition. By collective organization they protect themselves against arbitrary tyranny in the factory, against rapid downward movements of money wages, and through the insurance and benefit activities of the Unions, against the hazards of personal life. It is no accident that unions have emerged and grown to strength in every democracy that has undergone an Industrial Revolution. Ordinary men and women have been naturally impelled, by their acquisitive and self-protective impulses, to seek strength and safety in combination.

But the results of this combination are far-reaching — and not foreseen by the parties to it. The growth of combination means a loss of plasticity in wage rates and of much mobility between different employments. This effect has been beautifully demonstrated by Professor Isles in his *Wages Policy and the Price Level* — where he compares by means of graphs the relations between the movements of money wages and money prices before and after the war. The pre-war relationship is shown on p. 92. It will be seen that money wages then moved always in the same direction, and to a roughly proportionate extent, as prices rose and fell. The relationship in the later period is shown on p. 93. It will be seen that the close relationship between the two series has disappeared. Money wages have become relatively rigid. Prices can fluctuate as they please, but money wage rates remain relatively firm. In the recent Trade Cycle movement in this country the Board of Trade's General Price Index fell from a quarterly average of 81 in 1929 to a quarterly average of 60.6 in 1932 — a decline of over 25%. In the same period the average money wages fell from 99.5 to 95 — a decline of less than 5%. In the recovery movement the same relative stability was exhibited. Prices rose from 60.6 in 1932 to over 80 in the course of 1937 — a rise of nearly $33\frac{1}{3}\%$. In the same period money wages rose from 95 to

100 — less than 6% of their previous level. It is obvious that a high degree of rigidity has been created inside the market for labour.

The effect of this development on the smooth operation of the capitalist system is considerable. It means that the fluctuation of profits through the course of the Trade Cycle is accentuated. In combination with the provision of unemployment benefit, which we are to discuss in a moment, the incentive to the mobility of labour between employments is reduced.[1] It must result, as I have argued elsewhere, in the abandonment of fixed exchanges by all national capitalisms, since the maintenance of fixed exchanges in face of rigid wage rates produces unnecessary unemployment.[2] Hence the capitalist form of economic internationalism is doomed, or, at least, it can only be maintained at a heavy cost of dislocation and unnecessary poverty.

In general it is obvious that the free-moving, self-adjusting, perfectly sensitive competitive capitalism of the theoretical textbooks has disappeared for ever as long as one essential omnipresent market in it — the market for labour — is jammed and rigid. It would be as sensible to expect an internal combustion engine to work smoothly with an immovable distributor, as to expect an economy based on private enterprise to work properly when one essential part of its self-adjusting mechanism cannot move at all. There can be little doubt that the increase in the average level of unemployment in Great Britain through all phases of the Trade Cycle in the last fifteen years is largely due to the rigidity of money wages. And the evil consequences of wage rigidity (for the capitalist economy) are by no means fully revealed in the accentuation of unemployment. Mal-distribution of labour between employments, and the failure to utilize certain types of capital, will still further reduce the national income.[3]

[1] It must however be borne in mind that certain other agencies—cheaper travel, employment exchange, and literacy — have done something to increase the ease of movement.

[2] See my *Problem of Credit Policy*, Chap. VII.

[3] I am not of course arguing that wage 'rigidity' is a *social* evil. 'Rigidity' implies greater security for the majority who remain in employment and the movement of money wages by slow and easy stages may make the life of most people far more tolerable. It nevertheless remains a serious difficulty for the capitalist system.

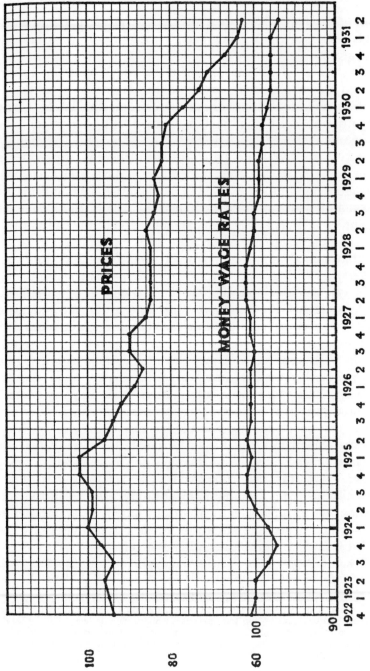

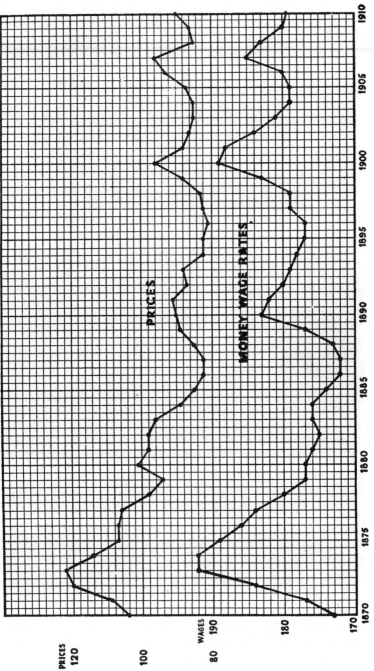

CAPITALISM IN TRANSITION

(b) *The Social Services and the Growth of Public Expenditure.* Another universal reaction in democracies to the insecurity of the economic system is the demand that the taxing power of the State should be used to protect the individual from the main economic dangers of personal life. The process begins with the creation of national schemes of elementary education. An educational system, partly financed out of public funds, is thought desirable and slowly secured by progressive governments. The movement does not end there. At a subsequent stage the large group partially emancipated by universal primary education presses for further protection, and in the period which might be called that of the 'liberal revolution' the protective functions of the state are extended to almost all the main hazards of physical life — childbirth, loss of employment, illness, old age. In the Lloyd George 'period' of English social history and in the Franklin Roosevelt 'period' of American social history, the basis of a comprehensive scheme of social security is laid down. Upon it is built an increasing structure of services — increasing in number and in the generosity of their provisions — Health Insurance, Unemployment Insurance, Unemployment Assistance, Old Age Pensions, Widows' Pensions, Maternity Benefit, educational services for children and adults. Nor is the process of growth likely to end. The establishment of national nutritional standards and of a Nutrition Service is already on the horizon of practical affairs, and the proposal to institute Family Allowances is growing in popularity under the pressure of a declining child-population.

We are not for the moment concerned with the social or political results of this growth in the social services, but with its economic and institutional consequences. There can be no doubt that the growth of these social forms of provision springs from the same demand for security as brought trade unions and collective bargaining into existence. Just as the latter institutions have unforeseen economic consequences, so do the social services. At least the measures necessary to finance them have such consequences.

The growth of the absolute size of British and American Budgets is a familiar cause of lamentations on the part of the rich in these two countries. The steady growth of the *relative proportion* between

94

budgetary expenditure and the national income would cause
even wider anxiety if it were appreciated. The following figures
give a rough picture of the situation in this country in the last
seventy-five years:[1]

	National Income £ millions	Budget £ millions	Rates £ millions	Total £ millions	%
1860-1	760	68.4	14.9	83	10.9
1868-9	814	71.7	25.3	97	11.9
1882-3	1274	83.6	38.1	122	9.5
1884-5	1274	72	44.1	116	9.1
1889-90	1285	91.2	48.1	139	10.8
1913-4	2300	197	93	290	12.6
1923-4	3800	690	162	852	22
1929-30	4384	748	185	933	21.2
1933-4	3962	778	179	957	24

It will be seen that public expenditure is taking a larger and larger
proportion of the total national income. It has risen in the course
of this period from under 10 % of the total income to nearly 25 %.
Taxation authorities are now claiming nearly one-quarter of the
national income.

Nor is there the slightest reason to suppose that this process
will stop. Indeed, it is certain that it will not. Further increases in
the social services are virtually certain to come soon. Larger
armament expenditure is already decreed. If and when the
national income declines in another depression, the fraction of the
total income used to meet governmental expenditure will, apart
from borrowing, rise to one-third or two-fifths of the total. If our
present public expenditure had to be financed out of our depression
money income it would be necessary to collect 30% of the national
income to do it.

Of course nothing like the whole of the increase is due to the cost
of the social services. Fifty per cent of our present budgetary expenditure arises out of the costs of previous wars and future wars.
But that is not my point. Two broad forces in democratic capitalism are continuously increasing the *proportionate* importance of
public expenditure. They are the costs of military defence and the
costs of economic security. The industrialization and the mechan-
ization of warfare — itself a consequence of capitalist technical
development — and the demand for economic protection on the

[1] The sources for these figures are to be found in the Statistical Appendix III
§ 2 (a).

part of the common people are the two main causes for the increase of public expenditure. But whatever the causes, the consequences are the same. The area of the economy directly controlled by the Government, the section of expenditure consumption and production that is already socialized, has grown enormously, is still growing, and is likely to grow still further.

This development is important in itself. When it is combined with another consequence of democracy — the form of taxation imposed by the people upon the taxing authorities — the consequences are even graver. We shall consider this point in a moment.

(c) *Depression Planning.* The third separable consequence of the search for security is somewhat different from the other two. It is not yet quantitatively measurable. It is none the less important. Indeed it is, in many ways, the most important of all the popular reactions to the insecurity of capitalism, because it is bringing slowly into existence the institutions of an economy different in kind from that now existing. It consists in a frontal attack upon the institution of *laisser-faire* itself. The causal connection between the search for security and the disappearance of *laisser-faire* is sometimes ignored and nearly always misunderstood.

The facts are familiar to, and widely lamented by, the defenders of the *ancien régime*. The essential point is as follows: Whatever the name of the government in power and whatever its theoretical principles may be, the central control of industry, trade and finance is everywhere extending at an amazing rate. Whether it is the Labour administration of Great Britain at the beginning of this decade, or the Democratic regime of President Roosevelt in America, or the British Conservative Government of more recent times, the business of enlarging the economic powers and functions of the State is ceaselessly pressed forward. The continuity and extent of the change is becoming revolutionary. The hastily improvised and partially abortive schemes of the American President are well known. In ambition they covered the greater part of American industry, finance and agriculture, and even after the collapse of the National Recovery Administration the proportion of the American economy controlled, or at least deeply influenced, by the organs of the Federal Government, is extraordinarily large.

In this country, the process of change has been less spectacular, less rapid, less improvised, but more stable and more remarkable for that reason. If one surveys what has happened in the last ten or fifteen years, the growth of the economic activities of the central government is extraordinary. In the course of that period the government has come to control or influence the foreign exchange market through the Exchange Equalization Fund, the foreign loan market through the informal machinery of control set up in 1931, the short-term money market as the supplier of Treasury Bills, and the long-term capital market through its control of credit policy, and of the short-term rate of interest. It has brought a large fraction of the agricultural industry within its sphere of influence by subsidies to, or marketing boards for, milk, pigs, bacon, hops, potatoes, beet, wheat and other cereals.. The list of industries now brought into some kind of subordinate relationship to the government is extraordinarily long — shipping, aviation, electricity, broadcasting, road transport, coal, iron and steel, railways and parts of the textile trades. This is apart altogether from the general functions of economic co-ordination and control implied by the provision of currency, power over means of communication, weights and measures, and all the other functions never surrendered, even at the height of the *laisser-faire* economy, by the State. A list of the economic activities undertaken or controlled by the State or its nominees now reads something like this:[1]

(*a*)   the activities of the Office of Works
(*b*)   the work of the Stationery Office
(*c*)   the Service Departments
(*d*)   the London Passenger Transport Board
(*e*)   the British Broadcasting Corporation
(*f*)   the Central Electricity Board
(*g*)   the Port of London Authority
(*h*)   the Forestry Commission
(*i*)   the Railway Rates Tribunal
(*j*)   the Railway and Canal Commission

[1] This list is taken from G. D. H. COLE: *Machinery of Socialist Planning*, Chap. II. The long list contains, it is scarcely necessary to point out, several very different categories and degrees of 'intervention' or control.

(*k*) the Import Duties Advisory Committee
(*l*) the Exchange Equalization Account
(*m*) the Bank of England Industrial Development Board
(*n*) the Export Credit Department
(*o*) the control of Local Government expenditure through:
      the Ministry of Health
      the Board of Education
      Treasury Minutes to Local Authorities
(*p*) Housing legislation
(*q*) the work of the Ministry of Transport
(*r*) the agricultural marketing schemes already mentioned
(*s*) the marketing and other cartelization schemes and subsidies to:
      coal
      iron and steel
      shipping   } already mentioned
      textiles
      aviation
(*t*) the Social Services
(*u*) the safety and other industrial assurance provisions of the law
(*v*) Trade Board and Minimum Wage Acts.

The immense growth of 'intervention' revealed by this list shows no sign of slackening. Not a year passes without some addition to it. Schemes for the further control of the coal industry, and for the first steps in the central organization of the textile industry are already items on the agenda of what is supposed to be a 'conservative' administration. The slow, steady and relentless extension of government and legislative control will, at its present pace, bring within a generation the greater part of industry and finance within the organized sector of the national economy. The pace of transition from one form of industrial control to another is more rapid than the movement towards *laisser-faire* which accompanied the Industrial Revolution itself.

Nor has this growth of legislative control been causally connected with the war or with preparation for war. It is a common mistake to suppose that this is so. The process has, of course, been accelerated by the approach of war; and it has been forced ahead at a revolutionary speed by the outbreak of war. But, in their origins, the changes have little to do with war. After the war of 1914-18 the object of legislation was a return to pre-war 'normality'; industries were handed back to private enterprise, controls were removed, rationing and price-fixing abandoned, even the gold standard was restored. In America the decade of the 1920's was a period of exceptionally rapid *laisser-faire* capitalist expansion. The change in the direction of legislation in the 1930's had taken place in Great Britain and America long before the threat of war had come to dominate the political and economic scene, and it has proceeded as far and with greater rapidity in America, where war is not yet an important factor, as it has in Great Britain. It is therefore nonsense to suppose that the movement towards a controlled economy is solely, or even chiefly, due to the experience or fear of war.

The real explanation is very different from this, but it is not very far to seek. It lies in the reaction of vigorous democracies to the recurrent phenomenon of Trade Cycle depression. Periodically the common man is made aware through declining income, rising unemployment and a general diminution of his prosperity that all is not well with the economic system upon which his livelihood depends. As this declension into relative poverty threatens his security, he makes a vigorous demand that 'something should be done' about it. This 'demand for action' is not clear-headed nor far-sighted. The electorate does not clearly know what it wants. It only knows quite certainly what it does not want. And this is a very natural and justifiable attitude. It is impossible that the common man should be equipped with the requisite imagination and technical knowledge to draft for himself the blue prints of a new economy. It is to meet this deficiency in him that the system of representative democracy has been devised. The representative proposes; the electorate disposes. And those of us who are paid by society to discover the processes of change and to meet the social needs of the day — economists, lawyers, and politicians — fail to earn the bread provided for us if we do not prepare the blue prints demanded from us.

Hence the common man makes a confused, but an irresistible, demand that action should be taken. He begins by turning out whatever party is in power during a major depression — Labour in Britain, Republican in America — and he returns other parties — Conservative or Democrat — pledged to 'deal with the problem'.

Now the Parties returned to power are in something of a dilemma. They must take action. They are committed to it by their own election promises and it is plainly in the interests of society that they should take it. In the long run it is the second reason that counts.

Yet they cannot take action in the relevant sphere — that of economic policy — without infringing the basic principles of a *laisser-faire* economy. It is precisely the principle of *laisser-faire* that must go if *anything* is to be done to the industrial system, since that principle implies the 'self-imposed impotence of government' in the sphere of trade and industry. Hence if they are to take action they can do so only by slowly destroying the basic institution of *laisser-faire* itself. This, we have seen, is what they do. The resulting legislation constitutes yet another way in which the democratic demand for security is incompatible with *laisser-faire* capitalism.

One comment remains to be made. The general character of the action taken to meet the democratic demand arising out of a Trade Cycle depression is always the same. It is *called* 'planning'. It actually consists in the substitution of monopoly control for competition in all the markets and industries that it touches. Whether it is described as 'agricultural adjustment' in America, or 'agricultural planning' in England; whether it consists of processing taxes and restricted output in America or milk marketing schemes in Britain; whether it applies to pigs or to coal; the policy is one of organized monopoly and restricted production. The power of the State is used not to oppose and limit monopoly, but to create it. We move at a bewildering pace into a regime of State organized monopoly.[1]

About this policy two things are to be noticed. First, it is in the interest of *all* the factors employed in the industries affected. It

---

[1] In addition to this trend of legislation there is no doubt a tendency for the technical causes of monopoly to predominate in recent years. The growth of large-scale standardized methods of production is an obvious case in point. Nevertheless see Prof. Robbins's survey of this problem in his paper *The 'Inevitability' of Monopoly* (published in his *Economic Basis of Class Conflict*).

benefits labour as well as property. The policy is therefore not difficult to initiate, though it may be difficult to reverse. Secondly, it benefits both those groups at the expense of the community. Industries live by strangling each other. Benefits are gained for a section by starving, not by feeding, the whole of society. As the number of monopolized sections increases, even the sectional benefits diminish, as all prices rise against everybody. We come to live, not by taking in each others' washing, but by each man garrotting his neighbour. It is a policy of slow, suicidal, sectional restrictionism.

To this aspect of the matter we shall return. For the moment we are only concerned with the historical process of change, not with its political implications or economic consequences, and we must turn to consider other matters.

B *The Institutional Consequences of Inequality*

Insecurity has not been the only ill consequence of the capitalist system. As every schoolboy knows, or ought to know, inequality is its second major evil.

If we look at the broad sweep of history, it is apparent that up to the present time the fact of social inequality has had important political consequences, but that insecurity has produced greater economic changes.

Inequality has certainly brought egalitarian political movements into existence. These movements are of two broad types — the egalitarian parties that repudiate democracy as the right method of political action, and those that do not. The Social Democratic Parties of Germany, France, and Scandinavia, and the Labour Parties of Great Britain, Australia, and New Zealand are typical examples of the latter category; and the Communist Parties of Russia and of most other countries are typical of the former.

Now these Parties, wherever they exist, constitute a direct threat to the institutions of *laisser-faire* capitalism. They all propose, though in different ways and at different speeds, to replace that system by institutions guaranteeing a central control of industry and a broad measure of social equality. As such they constitute the final stage of the democratic repudiation of capitalism. But in this country egalitarian parties have had, as yet, little opportunity to govern. Their influence has therefore been restricted, so far, to the field of ideas. This is even more true in the case of America. Consequently the direct reaction against inequality has not yet exerted anything like the same degree of influence as has the flight from insecurity. It is important for those who wish to understand political history to remember this.[1]

Nevertheless, the reaction against inequality has not been wholly without influence upon institutions, and in one important particular it has had disastrous consequences for the health of our traditional capitalism. This particular influence has been exerted through the institution of graduated taxation.

(a) *Graduated Taxation and the Rate of Saving.* As we have seen, one of the dominant characteristics of our society is the steady growth in the proportion of the national income absorbed by taxation and the expenditure of public authorities. Now this money has to be raised from somewhere. It is in the determination of the incidence of taxation that the democratic reaction to inequality has been important. Broadly speaking democratic governments have established the principle of *progressive* taxation — that is to say that a person with a larger income should pay a larger *fraction* of his larger income into the public treasury. Here is the position as quoted by the Colwyn Committee for the year 1925-6 — comparing the size of income with the percentage paid in taxation:

Income for Year	Income Wholly Earned	Income Half-Earned Half-Unearned
£100	11.9	13.0
£200	10.2	11.3
£500	6.2	8.4
£1000	11.0	14.4
£2000	15.2	19.3
£5000	23.2	29.5
£10,000	31.2	40.1
£50,000	44.4	57.7

It will be seen that after its low point, at the £500 a year level, the proportion of income paid in all types of taxation rises steeply. That this tendency is increasing as time passes is shown by a comparison between 1913-14 and 1925-6 given by the Committee:

[1] No doubt the general ideas of Parties in opposition to a government have exerted considerable influence upon the course of policy; but their effect upon the distribution of income is limited to the one described in the text.

Income £ a Year	Wholly Earned		Income Half Un-Earned	
	1913-14 %	1925-6 %	1913-14 %	1925-6 %
100	5.4	11.9	6.6	13.0
200	4.0	10.2	5.3	11.3
500	4.4	6.2	7.1	8.4
1000	5.2	11.0	8.3	14.4
2000	4.9	15.2	8.4	19.3
5000	6.7	23.2	9.6	29.5
10,000	8.0	31.2	11.8	40.1
50,000	8.4	44.4	13.6	57.7

From these figures, it will be seen that, whereas the increase in percentage paid on wholly earned income rose from 4.4 % to 8.4 % in the earlier period, it rises over the same range of income from 6.2% to 44.4 % in the latter. That is an immense increase in progressiveness. And the same is true for half-earned incomes. The proportion for them rose from 7.1 % to 13.6 % in 1913. In 1925 it rises from 8.4 % to 57.7 %.

This may be a good or a bad thing in itself, but unquestionably it has one peculiar, unforeseen and disastrous consequence. It strikes heavily at the funds available for capital accumulation and economic progress. As we have seen, the theory of inequality presupposes that the group of large incomes will provide society with most of its savings. They are supposed to be the mainspring of capitalist progress. But if they are seriously reduced by the burden of taxation falling upon them — cut in half for the upper income groups — then the volume of saving from this source will be disproportionately reduced. The democratic reaction to inequality will deprive inequality, through the institution of progressive taxation, of its sole suggested economic justification, and at the same time diminish the spectacular productive power of the economy.

That this is not a fanciful interpretation of the course of history is shown by an examination of the calculations made of our national Rate of Saving by Professor Bowley and Mr. Colin Clark. If we take their estimates of the proportion that saving bears to total money income we get the figures given overleaf. It will be seen that the Rate of Saving, which was over 17 % immediately before the war, had fallen to 11.4 % by 1924, and had declined still further to under 8 % in the quinquennium 1926-31.

	Total Income £ millions	Net Savings £ millions	Rate of Saving %
1911	2160	350	16.3 ⎫
1913	2200	400	18.2 ⎬ 17.25
1924	4165	475	11.4
1926	3680	247	6.7 ⎫
1927	3890	381	9.8
1928	3850	380	9.9 ⎬ 7.75
1929	4000	335	8.4
1930	3940	250	6.3
1931	3500	190	5.4 ⎭

The same result is obtained if we take Mr. Colin Clark's rather different estimate of the amount invested — on a new definition of investment that need not detain us here — over a longer period. Here is his estimate of the proportion such investment bears to total income.[1]

	Percentage %
1907	12.2
1924	8.1
1929	7.2
1935	6.9

Over the period the proportion declines from 12.2% to 6.9% — a reduction by nearly one-half of its earlier level. This is a long period tendency of the greatest importance. It means that the pace of capital accumulation has been halved.

The reason for the decline is brought out beautifully by Professor Bowley in his *Economic Consequences of the War*. By 1924 the real national income had been restored to almost exactly its 1911 level, when allowance for the rise in prices and the increase in population had been made. Professor Bowley shows how this comparable real income was distributed between public expenditure, private consumption and private saving. Here are the figures:[2]

	1911	1924
Total National Income	£4155m	£4165m
Saved	£ 675m	£ 475m
Paid in Rates and Taxes	£ 460m	£ 855m
Spent fully	£3020m	£2835m

It will be seen that the fundamental change is the increase in the amount paid in taxation which nearly doubled during the period — rising from £460m to £855m. Of the increase, approximately

[1] CLARK: *National Income and Outlay*, p. 185.
[2] BOWLEY: *Economic Consequences of the War*, p. 136.

one-half was taken from consumption expenditure, and one-half from saving. Consumption expenditure was reduced by nearly £200m. But the reduction of saving is a reduction from a smaller total and so the Rate of Saving is brought down from 17% to 11%. Nor, as we now know from subsequent figures, was the reduction of the Rate to stop there. Taxation was to rise still further and saving fall still further. This later change was not peculiarly associated with war finance. The cause lies deeper than that. Once again historical processes inhering in the relationship between democracy and capitalism are changing the institutional shape and economic life of the system. In this case it is touched upon a vital spot — its power of expansion.

The process of reducing the savings of the rich has gone extraordinarily far in very recent years. In the judgment of Mr. Clark it has now gone to the limit so that the rich, as a class, make *no* contribution to the national savings whatever. This is what he says:

> The outstanding fact of the situation is that three channels of saving — namely, the obligatory saving funds of local authorities, trading profits held back by company officials, and savings for security by the working and middle classes — provided enough to meet nearly the whole of investment requirements in recent years, and more than enough at the present time.[1] *Large private incomes have ceased to count as a source of saving. . . .*

These are the figures upon which he bases his conclusion:

	Total Savings in these three Classes £ millions	Total Investment and Losses £ millions
1924	330	357
1927	435	360
1928	390	390
1929	405	344
1930	530	279
1931	304	199
1932	337	169
1933	380	181
1934	461	274

[1] This statement of Mr. Clark's may suggest that the level of investment has been sufficient – in a social sense. This is not its meaning. It refers to the adequacy of these sources of saving to meet the current level of investment – not to the adequacy of the level of investment itself.

And he passes this final judgment:

> During the last four years it appears that the sources of savings specified have been adequate to account for the whole total of investment; in other words, that private saving has not recovered to the modest level which it occupied in the years prior to 1929, *and in fact private individuals are probably still on balance spending from their capital.*

If this judgment of Mr. Clark's is accurate, or even if anything approximating to it is true, the social significance of the inequality in the distribution of income has greatly changed in recent years. To this question we shall return.

We must now consider the institutional consequences of the third broad historical characteristic of the capitalist system. We have discussed the consequences of insecurity and inequality, and we must now investigate the consequences of expansion. As we shall see these consequences are of quite a different kind.

C. *The Institutional Consequences of Expansion: the Development of the Capitalist Social Classes*

The most important social consequence of the growth in productive power is the rise in the general standard of living that it makes possible. I have already mentioned the great rise in the level of real wages that took place in the nineteenth century, and we have also seen that the growth in real property incomes was even greater. I shall discuss the more recent history of the rate of expansion in the next section of this Part. For the moment I am concerned with the *effects* of this expansion upon the social and institutional basis of capitalism.

The most important of these effects is unquestionably the complacency with which the system came to be regarded during its period of rapid expansion. The social stability of capitalism in Britain during the nineteenth century, and in America during the twentieth, must surely be traced to the rapid rise in the standard of living made possible by the immense underlying growth of physical production. If this is so, then the future stability of the system is likely to depend partly upon its power to maintain its own historical rate of growth. This is all the more necessary in view of the growth of the expectation that it will do so. Persons and groups have become accustomed to a progressive economy. Mere stability at any given level of real income, however high, is not likely to satisfy them. Progress has become a constant expectation.

But apart from this general result of expansion, there are more specific consequences of the greatest interest for our present purpose. They consist in the changing class composition and changing class relationships engendered within capitalist society by a rising standard of living. Some of these consequences are familiar and some are not, but we must examine them all.

(a) *The Growth of the Intermediate Classes.* It will be remembered that Marx divided the social groups within the capitalist society into two main, historically important, classes — the upper bourgeoisie and the proletariat. The upper or *grand bourgeoisie* were the new emerging class of owner managers — owning the new instruments of production, the machines, and managing the business based upon them. The proletariat was composed of the great working masses — owning nothing but their labour and depending for their employment upon obtaining access to the new machines. The history of capitalism, according to Marx, would be determined by the struggle between these two fundamentally antagonistic groups. Now we shall be concerned with the broad theory that history is necessarily determined by the struggle of groups founded upon differing economic interest in the next Part of the book. We are only interested, for the moment, in the narrower thesis that the capitalist class system was based upon, and would more and more approach, this diarchy of social classes.

To maintain this view it was and is necessary to maintain two further historical hypotheses. It is first necessary to maintain that the pre-capitalist classes of medieval landlord and peasant were bound to disappear, or at least, that they were fated to lose their political importance. For the study of national capitalisms like those of France and Germany this is a vitally important thesis, and one that is scarcely borne out by the history of those nations. In both France and Germany the peasantry appear to have consolidated, and if anything improved, their position in the national economy; and that fact has made a vital difference to the political history of those two countries.

Peasantries have exhibited a remarkable and unexpected power of survival. They have refused to fade from the picture; instead they have often controlled the policy of the countries to which they belong, and used that power to preserve their own existence.

For the study of Great Britain and America, however, this thesis is of less importance, because of the disappearance, in both countries, of the peasantry. It is true that in America *agriculture* remains a quantitatively important occupation, but not in any pre-capitalist form. Agriculture has itself become capitalistic. It is also true that in Great Britain agriculture remains an important 'interest', and that the land-owning aristocracy, continuous in time with the pre-capitalist landlord, remains a most important section of the British Conservative Party; but the interests of the pre-capitalist aristocracy as a class have been so closely fused with those of the industrial bourgeoisie that the continuous importance of the landed interest, though of real significance for the understanding of our social history, need not detain us here.

The second necessary part of Marx's thesis, and the doctrine that is of vital importance for the interpretation of the history of Great Britain and America, is the view that the classes intermediate between the bourgeoisie and the proletariat were fated to be ground between the upper and nether millstones of the other two classes. This is the famous prophecy of the *Communist Manifesto:*

> The lower strata of the middle class — the small tradespeople, shopkeepers, and retired tradesmen generally, the handicraftsmen and the peasants — *all these sink gradually into the proletariat,* partly because their diminutive capital does not suffice for the scale on which modern industry is carried on, and is swamped in the competition with the large capitalists, partly because their specialized skill is rendered worthless by new methods of production. Thus the proletariat is recruited from all classes of the population.
>
> Further, as we have already seen, *entire sections of the ruling classes are, by the advance of industry, precipitated into the proletariat,* or at least threatened in their conditions of existence. . . .[1]

It is this essential part of Marx's thesis that has proved substantially wrong. It is no doubt possible to put various glosses

[1] *The Communist Manifesto.* Martin Lawrence, Authorized Edition 1934, pp. 16-18.

RECENT CHANGES IN CAPITALISM

upon the written words of the Master in order to bring their meaning nearer to the truth, but the broad fact is that the intermediate classes have not been ground in recent years between any millstones. On the contrary they have flourished and abounded. It is a fact familiar to all students of class structure that for various reasons: the technical development of industry, the growth of secondary education, the increase of government service, the increase in the demand for personal and distributive services — for these reasons and many others — the classes intermediate between the bourgeoisie proper (the owning and employing class) and the proletariat (the industrial employees), have grown both absolutely and in proportion to the total population. Shopkeepers, government officials, clerks, the employed professional class, school-teachers and typists — the 'black-coated workers' and the 'suburban householder' — are a growing and increasingly powerful group. It is difficult to exaggerate the social importance of this fact.

Let us look, for a moment, at the facts. First let us take the various estimates of the total *number of persons* in these occupational groups. This is Mr. Clark's estimate for 1931[1] of the occupational distribution of the population:

Managerial	1,180,000
Working on own account	1,272,000
Clerical, commercial and professional	3,698,000
	6,150,000
Agricultural and Fishing Operatives	936,000
Other manual workers	10,899,000
Unemployed	3,289,000
	15,124,000

It will be seen that, upon the assumption that the unemployed are restricted to the industrial proletariat, the intermediate groups now come to more than six millions out of a total employed population of twenty-one millions. When it is remembered that there is likely to be a larger proportion of females and dependent children without employment in the 'upper' group, it

[1] COLIN CLARK: *National Income and Outlay*, Table 10, p. 32 – males and females added together.

109

is obvious from this crude calculation that the intermediate classes come to something over 30 % of the population.

But what about historical trends of growth? Is this 30 % likely to increase or diminish? Here there are many estimates. They differ greatly in detail, because they proceed upon different occupational classifications, but they are nevertheless amazingly consistent in demonstrating the growth of the relative importance of the intermediate classes. Let us look at a few of them.

1.   Bowley and Stamp give this estimate of the growth of the 'middle class' since 1881:[1]

	Numbers	Percentage of Occupied Population
1881	1,600,000	19.0
1921	4,600,000	26.9
1931	4,483,000	29.1

This calculation shows a marked and steady increase in the proportionate importance of this class maintained over a period of fifty years.

2.   Klingender makes estimates over a longer period of the *professional* classes. These are his figures:

	Percentage of Total Employed				
	1851	1881	1901	1921	1931
Lower Professions	1.6	2.6	2.5	2.7	2.9
Higher Professions	1.0	1.2	1.3	1.5	1.5

They show an increase of nearly 100 % in the *relative* importance of the lower professions over a period of eighty years, and of 50 % in the relative importance of the higher professions.[2]

3.   Finally Colin Clark makes an estimate of the growth of the middle class in the decade of the twenties[3] — an estimate corresponding very closely to that of Bowley and Stamp.

		Percentage of Occupied Population
1921	4,745,000	27.6
1931	4,483,000	29.1

He estimates the actual number of salaried workers to have increased by nearly 800,000 in the decade 1921-31. There is clear evidence, therefore, both of the large absolute size of the intermediate classes and of their tendency to grow in relative importance.

[1] BOWLEY and STAMP: *Three Studies on the National Income.*
[2] KLINGENDER: *Conditions of Clerical Labour in Great Britain*, p. xxi.
[3] CLARK: *National Income and Outlay*, pp. 41 and 38.

4. This evidence as to numbers is borne out most emphatically by the evidence as to *income*. Calculations have been made by Colin Clark and Professor Carr-Saunders as to the proportion of the total national income paid in *salaries*. Both estimates show a great increase in this proportion:

	1911	1924	1929	1931	1935
Clark[1]	15.6	25.4	26.6	27.8	25.0
Carr-Saunders[2]	12.0	22.0		24.0	26.0

The two estimates show a slight discrepancy in the trend estimated since the war, but over the whole set of figures a very great increase in the relative importance of salaries is apparent. On one estimate they rise in importance by $66\frac{2}{3}$% in twenty years, while on the second estimate they double in relative importance. That is plainly the record of a growing economic group.

Now, as I have already said, it seems to me difficult to exaggerate the social and political importance of this development. We are living in a society whose class composition is shifting steadily against Marx's proletariat. Estimates of future political trends and the analysis of policy should be based upon this inescapable fact. Let us consider for a moment the political implications of this development. It is not unfair to consider the intermediate classes as predominantly 'conservative' in the political sense. The same is true of two further groups in the population — agricultural workers and personal servants — who are in many ways pre-capitalist in their social nature, and who are certainly not 'proletarian' in their outlook. Of course there are marked individual exceptions to any such generalization, but few would deny the predominantly conservative influence of all these groups in the political life of society. And yet these groups taken together constitute a very considerable proportion of the total electorate. Bringing together the estimates of these groups to which we have referred we get these results for 1931:

Managerial, independent and clerical	6,150,000
Agriculture	1,020,000
Domestic Service	1,540,000
	8,710,000

[1] CLARK: *National Income and Outlay*, p. 79.
[2] CARR-SAUNDERS: *Social Structure of England and Wales*.

From these figures it would appear that bourgeois and pre-capitalist groups between them account for nearly $8\frac{3}{4}$ millions out of 21 millions, or *over 40% of the whole employed population*. When we remember that these groups have a larger proportion of adult dependants without employment attached to them than has the group of wage-earners, it is obvious that the proportion of the electorate included within these categories is greater than 40 %. It is therefore certain that Marx's picture of the class structure of an advanced capitalist system, consisting of a small group of the true, or upper, bourgeoisie surrounded by a vastly greater proletariat, has proved completely false. Over 40% of the society has come to be included in non-proletarian groups, and the percentage is still rising. A society that is increasingly proletarian is a thing of the past. The society in which we live is an increasingly bourgeois society. That is an inescapable fact, whether we like it or not, and it is not the only thing to be said about the changing class composition of our contemporary society.

(b) *The Social Development of the Proletariat.* We have seen that the historical development of the capitalist system is making our society more bourgeois in the literal sense — that the proportion of the population belonging to the economic category of the bourgeoisie is steadily increasing. But even more important, per-haps, is the historical trend that is rapidly *adding bourgeois charac-teristics to the proletariat* itself. In all sorts of ways — through the slow growth of education, through the acquisition of higher professional qualifications by large groups within the proletariat, and above all, through the acquisition of small stocks of property — the proletariat of the Marxist textbook is rapidly disappearing. There is no single English word to describe the totality of this process. It amounts to the conversion of the people who now occupy the technical position of the proletariat (the persons employed to tend machines) into persons not fundamentally different from the Marxist category of the *petit bourgeoisie*. It is an old jibe made against the British Labour Movement by extremists coming from abroad that there is no socialist or working-class Party in Britain — but only a gathering of working-class 'shopkeepers' — with the mentality and habits and caution of the British grocer. The jibe is no doubt very near the truth, but it is un-Marxist of the Marxists not to smell out the historical and institutional explanation of this obvious fact.

It is not possible in a book of this description to trace out the detail of this *embourgeoisement* (to coin a horrible term) of the proletariat. Nor do I possess the knowledge to do so. But it is possible to select one important and highly characteristic aspect of it — in one sense a definitive aspect of it — and that is the growth of *small property*.

It will be remembered that the definition of the proletariat given by Marx is made with specific reference to the possession of property. The proletariat is the great class of industrial workers who own *nothing* but their labour, and who therefore, have 'nothing to lose but their chains' — to quote the peroration of the *Communist Manifesto*. It is the literal and sober truth to affirm that a class so defined is rapidly disappearing. In Great Britain it is disappearing. In America it has disappeared.

I must, of course, be careful not to overstate the case. There is no sense in which property *as a source of income* is becoming typical of our society. The percentage of the population that depends to any great extent on property as a normal source of income is still exceedingly small. Less than one-third of the population leave as much as £100 at death. Less than 10 per cent leave as much as £1000. Consequently property, as an important source of income, is still limited to a negligible fraction of the population.

But that is not the only form in which property can exist. It can be valued not as an important interest-yielding asset, but as a small *monetary reserve* held against periods of low income like illness or death, or high expenditure, like Christmas time. It is in this form that property has become extremely widespread. Now it is obvious that this type of monetary reserve is a very humble form of property. The sums of money involved seem very small to the class of person who examines these figures, and who is likely to possess immensely greater financial resources. It would be dangerous, however, to conclude that property as a monetary reserve is not psychologically, and therefore socially, almost as important as if it were a source of income. There is no evidence to show that the poor man who has spent a lifetime scraping together sixpences and shillings to build up a reserve of £50 or £100 is less attached to that sum, or less influenced by a desire to preserve and increase it, than the middle-class or professional man who has accumulated £5000 or £6000 by the time that he retires. There are good psychological reasons for supposing that the attachment to the small sum will be as great as to the large sum. The subjective importance of the accumulation is likely to depend more upon the emotional effort required to create it, and upon the character of the person owning it, than upon its absolute monetary size. The psychological and social consequences of a store of money are therefore likely to be largely independent of mere pecuniary value.

Now two things can be demonstrated plainly about property in this second sense — first, that it is now very widespread among the population; secondly that it has increased in recent years at an amazing rate. Let me make these points in turn.

The important avenues for the small savings of the working class are six in number — the Post Office and Trustee Saving Banks, National Savings Certificates, the acquisition of house property through the Building Societies, the Industrial and Provident Societies, the Friendly Societies, and the Retail Co-operative Societies. For one of these, the acquisition of house property, reliable figures are not available for various reasons; of which the most important is that it is quite impossible to tell how many people have failed to retain the houses once bought by them through the societies. But reliable figures are given for the other five categories in the *Statistical Abstract for the United Kingdom*. Let us consider the figures for 1935.

In 1935 the adult population was approximately 31 millions, and the number of census households shown in the census of 1931 was 12 millions. There were, therefore, very roughly, about 12 million separate 'consumption units' in Great Britain in 1935. In that year the numbers of persons holding balances in the various categories of society enumerated above and the balances standing to their credit were as follows:

	Members	Funds £	Average Holding £ s. d.
Industrial and Provident Societies	8,610,000	302,900,000	35 4 0
Friendly Societies	7,600,000	118,700,000	15 12 0
Retail Co-operative Societies	7,440,000	175,700,000	23 10 0
Post Office and Trustee Savings Banks	11,900,000	587,730.000	49 18 0
National Savings Certificates (approx.)	8,500,000	500,000,000	58 16 0

These figures are really striking — especially when they are examined as a group. They suggest that a very large proportion of the 12 million social and consumption units making up the nation have some sort of monetary reserve — some small holding of property. 12 million separate accounts in the Savings Banks contained an average holding of £50! That fact, in itself, is sufficiently striking. To it must be added memberships of nearly 9 millions for Industrial and Provident societies, 8½ millions for National Savings Certificates, 7½ millions each for the Friendly Societies and Co-operative Societies, with average holdings running from £15 to nearly £60. The picture becomes even more impressive.

Let me make plain at once that it is not possible to tell the total number of different persons involved in this huge total of separate memberships — because of the existence of multiple membership. A skilled workman is likely to belong to an industrial society and a retail co-operative society, and also to own a deposit in a savings bank. The 12 million members of the savings banks are, however, likely to represent the same number of different persons, since it would be unlikely for a substantial number of persons to have more than two separate bank accounts. Attempts have been made to assess the total number of different persons involved in all types of membership by those with access to special sources of information, such as the Chairman of the National Savings Committee (Lord Mottistone). This is what he said:

> With the information at present available I am afraid that no precise official estimate [of the number of British small investors] can be made. We know, for instance, that the number of depositors in the Post Office Savings Bank is about 10 millions. The number of depositors in the Trustee Savings Bank is over 2 millions. According to an estimate by the Money Order Department of the General Post Office there are roughly 8½ million holders of National Savings Certificates. In addition there are, perhaps, 1 million holders of Government stock purchased through the Post Office Savings Bank or through a Trustee Savings Bank.
>
> We do not know, however, what degree of overlap there is in these totals — for example, the number of holders of

National Savings Certificates who are also among the savings bank depositors. There are other possibilities of overlap which it would be very difficult to trace; *but making all allowance for overlap, there can be no doubt that Sir John is right in thinking* that the total standing to the credit of small investors is well over £3,000,000,000 and *that the number of investors is over* 15 millions.

It will be seen that the figure of 15 millions to which Lord Mottistone refers consists entirely of the group of persons owning Savings Bank deposits and National Savings Certificates. There must be a great number of persons who have no balances of this kind — whose only reserve is held in the form of a modest subscription to a Friendly society or a retail co-operative society. Hence the total number involved must be much greater than this 15 million. How much greater no one at present can say. But, if it lies somewhere between 15-20 millions of persons, it is remarkable enough, when that total is compared with 30 million adults and 12 million households existing during the same period.

Again it is important not to exaggerate the significance of these figures. Even if there are 20 million different persons involved in the total of 44 million separate memberships, it would not mean that every one of the 12 million households contained a membership. It would not mean this, because there is an unknown, but unquestionably important, degree of multiple membership within the family. For example, all the children of a middle-class family may have separate Post Office savings accounts, or wives may have accounts as well as their husbands. The certainty that multiple membership exists within the family on a large scale robs these figures of any simple and direct quantitative significance. Suppose, for example, that on the average two persons in each household with any accounts, had separate accounts. Our purely hypothetical total of 20 million *persons* would then be reduced to 10 million *households* — and only two-thirds of the existing households would possess any monetary reserve at all.[1]

It will therefore be seen that these figures must be interpreted with the greatest possible caution. And yet, when that has been said, it is impossible to escape the conclusion that a very large distribution of small property has taken place. *It seems virtually*

---

[1] Further investigations on this point are urgently needed.

ertain that more than half the households in the country now possess some kind of property other than their labour, have something 'to lose', as well as 'their chains'. Most of them are likely to have an accumulated co-op 'divvy', a balance in a Christmas club, a Savings Bank account, or part of a house to lose — in addition to their chains — and they are no more likely to want to lose these reserves than is their middle-class counterpart eager to lose his more substantial insurance policy or guaranteed annuity.

But in many ways the more important and the more interesting fact that emerges from the study of these figures is the nature of the *trend* in them. We are particularly concerned in this book with the broad ways in which capitalist society is changing, and the *growth* of small property in recent times is certainly one of them. The growth is out of all proportion to the growth of the population, and the growth in the last fifteen years has been more rapid than at any previous time. There is even evidence of a steady acceleration in the *rate of growth* over the last century, and we have now reached a point at which small saving is taking place at a rate sufficient to provide a substantial fraction of our total national savings — an unthinkable position even twenty years ago.

The figures from which these conclusions are derived are set forth in full in § 5 of the Statistical Appendix. It is only necessary to present the conclusions to be derived from that evidence here:

First, the growth in the absolute size of the funds at the disposal of small savers has been tremendous in the last forty years. The membership of the savings banks doubled between 1890 and 1930 — rising from 7,310,000 in 1890 to 15,070,000 in 1920. The funds standing to the credit of the depositors rose from £112 millions in 1890 to £587 millions in 1935 — an increase of 500 % in forty-five years. These figures are out of all proportion to the growth in population. The growth of the humbler types of property is even more remarkable. The membership of Industrial and Provident societies went up from 2,690,000 in 1910 to 8,610,000 in 1935 — a 300 % increase in twenty-five years. The funds rose from £36 millions to £300 millions in the same period — a 900 % rise in twenty-five years! And the same is true of retail co-operative societies. These are immense absolute rates of growth.

The rate of growth is now greater than it has ever been before —

at least in terms of deposits. Compare the general conspectus o small property in 1930 and in 1935 for the humblest types of sucl property. These are the *changes* over the period:

	Membership	Funds £
Retail Co-operative Societies	+1,100,000	+35,000,000
Industrial and Provident Societies	+1,100,000	+66,000,000
Friendly Societies	+80,000	+10,000,000
Savings Banks	—500,000	+154,000,000
	+1,780,000	+265,000,000

That is to say, during a period when population was growing ver slowly, total memberships went up by over 1¾ millions, or by 5.2 % of the total membership in the earlier period, while funds went u by £265 millions, or 22½ % of their total in an earlier period These large increases took place during a period of five years tha was also a period of phenomenal trade depression! That is to say during a half-decade containing one of the greatest depression ever recorded in our business history, the proportion of the adul population covered by the institution of small property wa increased by something like one-twentieth, and the average valu of all the small reserves was increased by one-fifth! That is a extraordinary tribute to the strength of the historical trend — i could not even be halted by the greatest depression of recent times

Secondly, it is possible to find clear evidence in the figures tha the pace at which the institution is spreading is itself increasing If we take successive periods of fourteen years in the longest se of figures that we have at our disposal — those of the *funds* held i savings bank deposits — we find that the rate of growth durin these periods itself increases. Here is the position of the total fund at the disposal of the depositors:

1846 1860	£32m £41m }	28% in 14 years
1896 1910	£108m £169m }	60% in 14 years
1921 1935	£356m £588m }	65% in 14 years

It will be seen that the *percentage* increase in funds over these thre equal periods has risen — and the last of them during a period i which general prices fell rapidly. If this acceleration in the rat of growth is maintained for long, it will produce quantitatively important changes in the distribution of property.

Finally, it is possible to show that small savings have now become an important fraction of our total national savings. A calculation of the total value of a comprehensive list of small savings was published in 1936 by a firm of stockbrokers (S. Maguire & Son). It corresponds very closely to other estimates of the same quantity, so that it is reasonably reliable. These are the figures given for total assets held by small savers:

1925	£1,670,000,000
1934	£2,480,000,000
1936	£2,800,000,000

These figures show an increase in total savings by small savers of £1100 millions in a period of eleven years — including both depression and recovery phases of the Trade Cycle — making an average of £100 millions a year. During the two years of boom 1934-6 the increase is over £300 millions — or a saving at the rate of £150 millions a year. Now this volume of saving made by small savers must be compared with an approximate total of national savings at the rate of £300 millions a year over the whole period, and of £450-500 millions during the years of prosperity. It will therefore be seen that, in depression and boom alike, the small saver has been providing nearly a *third* of our total national savings.

It is of interest to compare this with Mr. Colin Clark's estimate — already mentioned in this Section — that the rich have, as a class, ceased to make any contribution whatever to the national savings. If the relatively poor are now providing a third of the savings, and if their rate of saving is increasing at an accelerating rate, it is certain that the distribution of property will tend to become, slowly no doubt, but nevertheless surely, more equal. With the political importance of all this we shall be concerned in a moment. The historical implication of the figures seems inescapable.

I have sought to show two things from the examination of these figures — *first* that the economic and social character of the proletariat has not remained static. The proletariat has acquired many of the characteristics that were regarded, fifty years ago, as those typical of the *petit bourgeoisie*. It has acquired elementary education, and it — or a considerable fraction of it — has acquired a small reserve of property. A statistical study of the circulation of newspapers, of the attendance at cinemas, and of the numbers taking regular holidays, would all reveal, I suspect, the acquisition of other and not unimportant habits that were once regarded as typically and exclusively middle class.[1] The general increase in production, and the consequent rise in the standard of living, has attenuated to a marked degree the proletarian character of the proletariat. *Secondly,* I have attempted to argue that the possession of stocks of property is now widespread, is still increasing and, to judge by historical evidence, is likely to increase still faster in the future. The distribution of savings between classes has now so altered that the passage of time is likely to diminish, rather than to exacerbate, the inequality in the distribution of property. These may be surprising conclusions. They may be unwelcome conclusions to those who prefer revolution to reform. But, for those who respect historical evidence, there seems to be no escape from them.

D.   *The Institutional Consequences of Limited Liability*
    Last in the list of institutional changes that I am describing we must now consider the revolution that has taken place in the form and social function of *property*. This revolution has been brought about more by the legal inventions of limited liability and the device of the small participation or 'share' than by any broader historical force. The changes are none the less important for that, and we must consider their nature in some detail.
    The historical facts are familiar. After a prolonged legal and political struggle in the nineteenth century, two important principles were established late in the fifties, at any rate in this country:[2]

[1] Since writing these words I have seen the *Report on the Press* published by P.E.P.   That document records a total weekday sale of 10 million papers and a Sunday sale of 15 millions. These figures are to be compared with 12 million households. It is clear that almost every household takes a paper and almost every adult in the community reads one.
[2] For a history of the emergence of Limited Liability see EVANS: *British Corporation Finance, 1760-1840*; SHANNON: *The Coming of General Limited Liability* (*Economic History*, Supplement Vol. II); HUNT: *The Development of the Business Corporation in England, 1860-1867*. For the history of the small share see Evans.

(a)   that the right to limit the liability of the person subscribing capital, and participating in the profits of an undertaking, to the amount of money originally subscribed by that person should be granted to any corporation or joint-stock enterprise by the mere process of registration.

(b)   that no limit should be set by law to the smallness of the participation or 'share' in the enterprise that might be legally offered upon the market for capital.

The granting of these legal privileges upon so wide a scale completed the mobility of capital between occupations, and rendered possible an immense extension of the number of persons willing to enter the general capital market. The degree of risk involved in any single act of investment was enormously diminished, and the amount of knowledge about the enterprise necessary to justify anyone participating in it, was correspondingly reduced. These legal changes had immense quantitative consequences.

In the *first* place, the new form of financing industry swept through the whole industrial system. Messrs. Berle and Means — in their path-breaking book on the *Modern Corporation and Private Property* — calculate that by 1929, no less than 92 % of labour employed in the manufacturing industries of the United States was employed by limited liability joint-stock enterprise (p. 14). The domination of this form of property organization was nothing like as great in trade and agriculture. The corresponding figures are only 40 % for trade and 4 % for agriculture. But the figures demonstrate beyond question that limited liability joint-stock enterprise has become the dominant and typical form of *industrial* organization.

Similar figures are not, as far as I am aware, available for Great Britain, but they are certain to be comparable with those of the United States. The domination of industry by the joint-stock company may not have gone quite so far in this country, but the importance of agriculture to the British economy is much smaller than it is to the American, so that the importance of the corporation for the whole economic system is almost certainly restored to the American level. Hence the dominant form of industrial property is now that of the limited liability bond and share. There are very interesting legal and economic consequences for the capital market bound up with these changes in the typical form of the property claim upon which it would be interesting to dwell, but I must press on to the broader social results of the change.[1]

In the *second* place the direct consequence of reducing both the risk and the size of the minimum possible participation in an enterprise, combined with the rise in the standard of living, was to increase immensely the number of participators. The number of separate shareholders — who are the legal owners of the corporation and who are ultimately responsible for the administration of the undertaking — was greatly increased. These are a few of the figures of the number of shareholders in the largest American companies — quoted by Messrs. Berle and Means:

1931	American Telegraph and Telephone Company	642,080
	Pennsylvania Railroad	241,300
	United States Steel Corporation	174,500
1929	Consolidated Gas Co.	93,000
	General Electric Co.	60,000
	Atchison, Topeka and Santa Fé Rly. Co.	59,000

In this case, similar figures are available for Britain, with one difference. In the American figures the companies were selected because they were known to be the largest companies; but in the British group quoted below, the selection is random, so that the number of shareholders shown in it is typical and not maximal. It is therefore clear that the numbers involved in the companies of the two countries are more comparable than might be expected. Here are a few taken at random from recent company reports:

1936	London & North Eastern Railway	173,000
	Great Western Railway	93,000
1935	Imperial Chemical Industries	76,000
1936	Shell Transport and Trading	75,000
1935	Courtaulds Ltd.	42,000

In the American case Messrs. Berle and Means show the immense increase that these numbers have undergone in recent times. Here are the figures given by them for the three largest companies.[2]

	American Telephone & Telegraph Co.	Pennsylvania Railroad	United States Steel Corporation
1902	12,000	28,000	25,000
1920	139,000	133,000	95,000
1931	642,000	241,000	174,000

[1] Cf. PROFESSOR POSTAN: *Recent Trends in the Accumulation of Capital* (*Economic History Review*), 1935.
[2] See BERLE and MEANS, op. cit., p. 55.

RECENT CHANGES IN CAPITALISM

In each case it will be seen that there has been an immense increase in the number of legal owners participating in each enterprise during the last thirty years. The smallest increase — that of the Steel Corporation — shows a growth of over 600% in the course of a generation.

We shall discuss the administrative and social significance of these phenomena in a moment.

In the *third* place there is overwhelming evidence in the American case that Marx's prophecy about the 'concentration of capital' has been fulfilled in a particular way through the instrumentality of Limited Liability. In one sense it has plainly not been fulfilled. A concentration of *legal ownership* has not taken place. On the contrary, an immense dispersion of ownership has occurred. Quite apart from the increase in small property that we have just examined, and which does not greatly affect the ownership of industrial capital, it is clear that a considerable *dispersion* of ownership has occurred. The growth of the number of shareholders participating in the ownership of these large and representative industrial undertakings in America is immense.

But Marx's prophecy has been fulfilled — at least in America — through the growth of the large corporation. Messrs. Berle and Means calculate that the 200 largest corporations in America between them: (*a*) control 50% of the total corporate wealth of America; (*b*) control 80% of the assets traded in the New York Stock Exchange; and (*c*) made 66⅔% of the new capital offers in America between 1922 and 1927. They further calculate that, at the relative rates of growth shown by these 200 corporations, on the one hand and by all the rest, on the other (5% and 2% respectively in the 1920's), that *by 1950 the 200 corporations will control 70% of the corporate wealth of the United States.* Moreover, an examination of the directorates of these 200 companies shows that the nominal control of their affairs is vested in the hands of only 2000 different men, of whom a considerable proportion are inactive, so that the formal control of these vast capital resources has passed into the hands of a 'few hundreds' of separate individuals. If these trends continue, it is at least within the bounds of possibility that by 1950 70 % of the corporate wealth of America will have passed into the nominal control of less than 1000 men. This is 'concentration of control' with a vengeance!

Even in face of these startling figures it is necessary, however, to preserve some sense of proportion. To start with, the percentages in question only refer to the Corporation form of legal ownership. This form of wealth dominates only the industrial field. It only covers, as we have seen, 40% of trade and 4% of agriculture. These two forms of enterprise between them operate over half the area of the American economy. In fact the 200 Corporations, as Messrs. Berle and Means point out, control only 22% of the total wealth of the country (p. 22). Nor are the extrapolations wholly safe. There is some evidence contained in Berle and Means's figures, not properly emphasized by them, suggesting that 200 Corporations were not relatively strong financially during the period of high boom under examination. The Corporations owned 50% of the capital, but they only covered 43.2% of the new revenue (p. 29). That is not a good record. It suggests that the large corporation was not relatively profitable, and therefore not certain to grow with relative rapidity during a period of depression. We are now almost half-way between 1930 and 1950, and it would be interesting to know whether the trends have continued unabated, as Messrs. Berle and Means expected.

But, whether they have proceeded further or not, the broad fact of a concentration of power in the hands of the directorate of the large corporations in America cannot be denied. It is a factor of great social significance, which we must soon examine.

Has the same process occurred in Great Britain? Unfortunately no one is in a position to answer the question. Large corporations — the Imperial Chemicals Ltd. and Lever Brothers — have certainly emerged. But no one knows how large a fraction of our wealth is now controlled by the 'upper 200' of our companies, and that is a pity, because it is important to know. It is as important a piece of research as could be imagined; but it has not yet been done, and we can only go on upon some reasonable assumption. If we proceed, then, upon the assumption that the process has gone as far as it has in America when we are discussing the distribution of economic power, and not as far when we are thinking of the integration of the economy, we shall at least be facing the worst possibilities. As the agitation against monopolies has been so much less severe in this country it is difficult to believe that the process can have gone further.

These then are the facts about recent trends in the form of property and of industrial control within the capitalist system — that limited liability has swept the board, that ownership has been dispersed over groups of shareholders running into scores of thousands in the case of large enterprises, and that nominal control has been progressively concentrated into the hands of a small class of company directors. It is with the consequences of these trends that we are now concerned. It is, I think, plain that the important consequences have been two in number — one that is familiar and concerned with the social function of property, the other that is less familiar and is concerned with the internal structure of the upper bourgeoisie. To these two consequences — the seventh and eighth in our sequence of important institutional changes in capitalism — we must now turn.

(a) *The Dispersion of Ownership and the Divorce of Ownership and Control.* The increase in the number of legal owners of the representative capitalist enterprise was bound, for purely technical reasons, to bring about revolutionary changes in the relationship between property and industrial administration.

We have already seen that, according to the theory of capitalist institutions, the control of industrial resources is vested in the property owner. The function of the owner is to administer his property efficiently, and to change its employment from time to time in order to maximize his receipts from it. But this mechanism is quite unworkable when the number of owners passes a certain point. It is difficult for 20 persons to govern an enterprise directly and efficiently. It is almost impossible for 100 owners to do so. It is quite out of the question for 1000 to attempt it, and ridiculous for 10,000 or 100,000 to think of it. The subdivision of ownership, and the multiplication of shareholders, were bound to cause a major redistribution of power within the corporation. Power was bound to be delegated away from the legal owner. Power is certain to pass into the hands of a class of professional delegates — the directorate of modern company finance — as soon as the number of owners passes beyond the size of a workable committee. The divorce between ownership and control is then complete.

But the separation of privilege from responsibility has proceeded to an extreme degree in modern industrial practice. It is virtually true to say that most directors have lost *all* trace of their function as delegates; that most owners have lost all trace of the sovereignty theoretically vested in them by their property right. Directors have become all-powerful, shareholders all powerless, in the affairs of nine companies out of ten. And this has happened for a very simple reason. The same subdivision of shares that makes the number of owners in each enterprise so large produces a great subdivision in the property of the individual. A rich man, instead of sinking his fortune in two or three concerns, in each of whose government he will retain a lively interest, disperses his fortune over twenty, or thirty, or a hundred different companies. In the case of a small estate that came under my personal notice, the individual had dispersed a modest holding of £3000 over 48 different investments. Now it is quite out of the question that a busy man should take a serious participating interest in the administration of fifty or a hundred widely scattered and widely differing industrial enterprises. He will not be able to attend the statutory annual meetings. He may not even be able to read the annual reports that are sent to him. His interest is so small, his knowledge is so inadequate, that he could not play an efficient part in the government of 'his' companies, even if he had the time to attempt it. Hence the owner becomes a cipher, the shareholders' meeting a farce, and the directorate a dictatorship. It is only at the moment of bankruptcy or in the process of major reconstruction — once or twice in the lifetime of a company — that the legal owner occupies any important position in the scheme of things. He has a right to participate in the profits — that is all. The separation of ownership and control is complete, absolute, and irrevocable.

Now this extraordinary development of the institution of limited liability has brought a curious consequence in its train. It has placed the control of industry in the hands of an irresponsible, self-recruiting, nepotic oligarchy — the class of the *company director.* Consider the position of the ordinary company director. To whom is he responsible? The true answer is — to no one. He is plainly not responsible to society — the institution of *laisser-faire* guarantees his freedom from any general responsibility to the State. But neither is he responsible, in any real or enforceable sense, to the legal owner. Messrs. Berle and Means show the legal devices by which every vestige of control — even the power to retain a stable proportionate share in the profits of an enterprise — has been slowly filched from the theoretical owner, the shareholder. And, as we have seen, the shareholder is quite incompetent to exert any control over the directorate of his companies even if he wishes to do so, because he has neither the time nor the knowledge to make his criticisms wise or relevant. Thus the modern company director has established for himself a most enviable position. His word is law. He need brook neither offensive criticism nor galling restraint. He has achieved what Lord Baldwin once called the 'prerogative of the harlot — *power without responsibility*'.

Thus the consequences of the dispersion of the ownership of each undertaking over a large number of shareholders have been two. Dispersion has, as we have just seen, created an oligarchy in industry, working behind closed doors, responsible to no one, with a group interest that is different, or may be different, from that of the owners or employees of the enterprise, or from the broader interests of society. And the second direct consequence is a change in the status of, a loss of function by, the institution of property in industrial resources. The property holder is no longer an administrator. He contributes nothing to the government of industry. He has become wholly parasitic — receiving a share in the profits of the enterprise and a share in the income of society, without discharging any continuous administrative function whatever.[1]

It is true that the original subscriber to the loan, by which the enterprise was first financed, undertook a risk through venturing his wealth in a new concern. But, after the shares have been

---

[1] It is true that the director is normally also a shareholder in the companies of which he is a director – but his interest is rarely a predominant part of his income. His main source of income in the firm is normally the fees of direction rather than the interest on shares.

bought and sold a dozen times, and the market has placed a specialist's valuation upon them, the element of risk has been greatly diminished, and the shareholder is left as a functionless pensioner of the enterprise.[1]

If then the company director has become an irresponsible dictator, and the rentier a functionless parasite, what has happened to the internal structure and social position of the *grand bourgeoisie* as a class?

(b) *The Changing Structure of the Upper Bourgeoisie.* We have already seen that one of the two fundamental Marxist classes — the proletariat — has not remained a static social phenomenon. On the contrary it has divided and changed its nature — acquiring many of the most important characteristics of the *petit bourgeoisie*. We have now to consider the position of the other basic group — the *upper bourgeoisie*. Has that remained static in composition and in social form? It has not.

Let us begin with the critical question of administrative power. Has the power of this class over industrial administration increased or diminished? It will be remembered that Marx expected it to increase. At first sight, it may seem obvious that it has enormously increased. We have just been discussing two trends in the history of company finance that appear to press all the power into the hands of a willing and irresponsible minority. We have seen that the directorate of a modern company has acquired all the power

---

[1] Again it is true that the shareholders as a class prevent social decumulation by maintaining the value of shares, and so holding down the Rate of Interest. They are providing *gross* saving, although they are not providing *net* saving – to make use of a technical distinction. But this is a purely passive function. It associates property with no positive service to society. The maintenance of the market value of the shares does nothing directly to maintain the efficiency of the undertaking. The holding of stock is valuable to society only because the method of financing the construction of capital is by way of the acquisition of property rights, and, if capital accumulation were socially financed, then the necessity for this 'service' of gross saving would wholly disappear. As long as physical depreciation were offset, the capital would continue to exist without anyone owning it, or without the least necessity to pay anyone for its mere existence. This is not the case with the services of administration and management. These are necessary services in any society whether it is *laisser-faire* or collectivist, and it is reasonable to pay the persons who provide them. Hence, as long as property was associated with the function of direction, the payment of interest to the owners of capital at least possessed this justification – that it was one method of rewarding a necessary service; but with the separation of ownership and control the rentier becomes a .pure parasite, receiving a payment for no value received, discharging a function that is only necessary because his parasitism exists.

that used to be vested in the owner, and that in America, at least, the financial control has been concentrated into the hands of a very small number of persons.

Nevertheless I cannot help feeling that the reality is very different from the appearance. There can be no question that the *directorate* has increased its powers immensely as against, at the expense of, the *shareholder*. But it seems equally clear to me that it has lost as much, or more, real control over administration to a third group — the *management*.

It is this new class, which has come into existence as a result of the development of company finance — the class of *professional employed managers* — that is so greatly neglected in the Marxist discussion of the development of the upper bourgeoisie. The truth is that the early type of the bourgeois entrepreneur who was owner, director, and manager of an enterprise all in one, has disappeared in all the older industries. He still appears as a princely figure — a Lord Beaverbrook or a Lord Nuffield — in new industries like those of daily journalism or the cheap automobile. But over the great area of the old basic industries he has ceased to be typical. Instead, his functions have been subdivided, and each of them taken over separately by new types or classes of person —

> the pure director,
> the pure rentier,
> the pure manager.

The *director* is the person who is paid to occupy the position of final sovereignty, to take decisions on the broad strategic problems of the enterprise, and to choose the personnel in the upper ranks of the managing hierarchy. The pure *rentier* is the shareholder, whose position we have already discussed. He does nothing, he says nothing, he knows nothing. He is just paid an income. The *manager* is an employee of the company. He is paid a salary, he is liable to dismissal — and he administers the company's affairs from day to day. It is this new type of worker, who has little or no *rentier* interest in the concern in which he works, and no formal control over it, whose economic position and class interest has been neglected in the study of changing class structure.

Now it seems obvious to me that, broadly speaking, the power gained by the directorate from the shareholder has been lost in equal degree to the management.

This must be true of the large company and the large company director. The affairs of a large bank, a large railway, a large manufacturing combine are so complicated, so widely scattered in space, and so different in the type of technical competence required, that it is inconceivable that the directorate should discharge any important work of management in it. The structure of management must be largely independent of the directorate in the day-to-day government of the enterprise. In the same way, the large company director — with ten or twenty or fifty different directorships — cannot possibly undertake any detailed work of management within any one concern. The directorate must become increasingly concerned with questions of high policy, questions of finance, questions of the principles of production policy, and with the selection of high officials in the managerial hierarchy. These are certainly important functions. Yet the loss of the power to manage is, nevertheless, a loss of real economic power.

Let me illustrate what I mean by an example. If one thinks of a large modern railway, then the activity of production is the running of trains. The provision of this service implies an immensely complicated hierarchy of management — from the station master responsible for the co-ordination of local service, through the district, haulage, personnel, permanent way, goods and passenger managers to the paid officials at the head of the traffic, haulage, commercial, advertising, research and legal departments of the central organization. At the head of them all sits a curious, and slightly irrelevant, Board of Directors. Where, in such a hierarchy, is the real administrative power located? In one sense it is concentrated in the hands of the directors. They are in a *legal* position to dismiss any employee of the company; they alone can direct the investment of resources, and make general rules for the conduct of the business. And yet, in another sense, power has passed out of their hands entirely. Suppose, for example, that the whole board of directors disappeared overnight? Next morning the railway would continue to operate as though nothing had happened. Trains would run to time. Tickets would be sold. Funds would be invested.

Advertisements would be made. And these activities would continue for weeks and months, with no appreciable deterioration in the services provided. No doubt, after a relatively long period, there would be some deterioration in the adaptability of the railway to changes in the external world if the gentlemen in question were not replaced; but the decline would be slow and subtle, and by no means sure. Compare this slow loss of efficiency with the utter confusion that would immediately reign if the *management* were all destroyed in one night. It would be doubtful if the railway could operate for a single day if central, district and station managers were all removed at once — even though the physical equipment and the wage-earners remained unchanged in organization and efficiency. This is because the real activity of daily co-ordination and administration has passed into the hands of the managers — their services are indispensable in short and long periods alike.

If this rough and crude picture of the specialization of function within the bourgeois class is anywhere near the truth — and there is plainly something in it — two consequences follow:

First, it must be the case that the directorate, as a class, have lost the kind of political power that flows from economic power. If it came to a crisis they would find that power had gone from them. They possess formal powers greatly in excess of their real powers, and greatly in excess of the powers that they could retain in a period of rapid transition *if the management class were set against them*, and if they — the managers — were prepared to act upon their own responsibility. Loss of function carries with it a loss of power, and the power of the directorate is now founded upon legal right, and is no longer based upon overriding and inescapable social necessity — the continuous discharge of an essential productive service.

Second, a result follows, of particular importance for those who hold that class interests are the dominant force in history, and that social classes are defined by a possession of common economic interests. Those who accept this thesis can no longer hold that the *upper bourgeoisie constitutes one class*. It has become, through the technical development of company finance, subdivided into three classes. The subdivision of function brings into existence three separate functional groups with divergent economic interests — the rentier class, the class of directors, and the managerial class. There is no reason why the interests of these three groups should always be identical, and indeed it is obvious that they often are not. The interests of the directorate lie in the maintenance of the enterprises they control, the extension of their size and power, and the building up of their financial stability. The interest of the rentier class lies in high dividends. A struggle over the division of the product is likely to arise between these two groups. Indeed it plainly has arisen already. It comes to a head over the disbursement of dividend income. It is in the interest of the rentier to increase the distribution, and it is in the interest of the directorate to retain a large proportion in the form of undistributed profits. Mr. Clark calculates that over half the profits are, in fact, retained.

Now this is only one example of the kind of conflict that can arise within the ranks, and between the groups, of the upper bourgeoisie. For our present purpose the most important of these possible conflicts, because it is the conflict of greatest potential political significance, is the conflict of interest between the directorate and the management. There can be no question that this conflict is real. The managers are a class of employees, the directorate are a group of employers. Between two groups so related personal and group tension is inevitable. Interests conflict, forms of recruitment and education conflict, status within the organization conflicts. The relation of employer and employed is, for very good psychological reasons, one of the most difficult and ambivalent types of relationship in the world.

Nor is it any reply to this argument to contend that all the groups in the upper bourgeoisie have a common interest against the proletariat. That is perfectly true, but it does not meet my point. The fact remains that, in so far as class distinctions are based upon conflicts of pecuniary interest, the organization of modern joint stock enterprise exhibits a grouping of this kind:

> The Directorate
> The Rentier Class
> The Employed: The Management
>   The Clerical (petit bourgeois) Class
>   The Proletarian Workers

Conflicts of interest can, and will, spring up between any two of these groups. Who is to say that one of the many possible conflicts is a determining or overriding conflict, to which all the others are relative or subsidiary? If it is contended that the conflict between the upper four groups and the proletariat is different in kind from any other conflict, then the class distinctions that mark off the proletariat from the rest of society are not solely those of economic interest. Economic interest divides the other classes from each other equally deeply.

It may well be that a sense of solidarity exists between the director, the manager and the *rentier*, uniting them in irreconcilable opposition to the proletariat, but if there is such a unifying principle it cannot be one of pure economic interest. If, as one is led to suppose, the conflict of interests and of social groups is more complicated than the simple Marxist antinomy of bourgeoisie and proletariat, then it is at least possible that the groupings within the upper bourgeoisie can be used to divide the class as a class, and that other parties and other classes might, by dividing, govern. To the political implications of this possibility we shall return.

§ 5

The Present Position of Capitalism

I have now completed my survey of the main changes in the institutional structure of capitalism. I have drawn attention to *eight* important changes — the growth of collective bargaining and the stiffening of the labour market; the development of the social services and the increasing proportion of the national income consequently absorbed by taxation; the rapid spread of State control and of State organized monopolies; the reduction of the Rate of Saving by our progressive system of taxation; the rise to power of the intermediate classes; the conversion of the proletariat into a class with the mentality and interests of the *petit bourgeoisie*; the dispersion of shareholdings resulting in a divorce between legal ownership and administrative control; and the subdivision of the *grand bourgeoisie* into three distinct groups, by the technical necessities of the institution of limited liability.

Two things remain to be done in order to complete this account of historical development, and to introduce the problem of policy. The first of these is to survey the fate of the basic institutions upon which capitalism is based, and then to pass judgment upon the scientific hypotheses that professed, and still profess, to throw light upon its future.

(a) *The Fate of Capitalist Institutions*. It is obvious that these eight changes involve between them the break-down of certain parts of *laisser-faire* capitalism. It will be remembered that I defined *laisser-faire* capitalism by the possession of four fundamental institutions — 'rationality' of industrial technique, unlimited acquisitiveness, property in the material factors of production, and freedom of enterprise in industrial management.

Two of these institutions are unaffected by the developments I have just summarized. 'Rationality' in industry is quite untouched. There was never a time when scientific inquiry into methods of production was prosecuted more actively, when money was spent more lavishly upon technical research and physical science. We live in an age of organized and rapidly advancing industrial rationalism.[1] Nor is the capitalist form of acquisitiveness seriously changed or limited. It is true that the historians of the labour market notice a tendency for the rise in the standard of living to rob the acquisitive motive of its expansionist characteristics. There is an increasing pressure, so these observers contend, to take the increase in the real earnings of labour in the form of reduced hours of labour rather than in a rise of real physical consumption. But a reduction in the average hours of labour is an old story in an expanding economy, and in any case it only represents a change in the form, and not a diminution in the force, of the acquisitive motive. There is no evidence that men are less moved by the desire to better themselves, or return to a way of life controlled by status and tradition. Rationality and acquisitiveness are still dominant and fundamental.

---

[1] 'Rationalism' is, of course, used more in its relevant and limited technical sense – implying merely the application of science and reason to the problems of organizing production – in the search for profit.

It is not the same, however, with the other basic institutions of *laisser-faire* capitalism. Property and freedom of enterprise have been profoundly changed and deeply shaken by the eight historical trends I have enumerated. Let us take the case of *property*. Unless the analysis of the previous section is entirely mistaken, property in industrial capital has wholly lost the social functions supposed to be grounded in it. It has ceased to be the reward for management, and it has largely ceased to serve as a reward for personal saving. Property in capital has become the functionless claim to a share in the product of industry. The institution is worse than indefensible — it is useless.

This may seem an extreme statement, and yet there is a sense in which it is literally true. The divorce of ownership and control is also the divorce of property and management. In so far as enterprise passes into the control of limited liability companies, the small participator or shareholder ceases to be of any importance in the conduct of the business. Few companies are worried about the quality of the intelligence, or administrative capacity, of their shareholders. Ownership is a cipher. Rentier income is paid, collectively, for nothing. And, with the withering away of the savings of the rich, the only rational justification that has ever been suggested for an inequality in the distribution of property has finally disappeared. The propertied classes are now parasitic in the final sense that their income is purely a distributive share, and contributes nothing to the increase of production. Of course this is not all that there is to be said about the contemporary institution of property. As we shall see in a moment, there are inescapable political reasons why it will survive in some form as long as democratic constitutions prevail; but it is nevertheless most important to realize the extent to which the usefulness of property in capital has been undermined as an institution through losing the only unshakable basis for any institution — that of necessary function.

The state of the last of the four basic institutions of *laisser-faire* capitalism is even worse than that of property. Property may have lost its usefulness, but it does still exist. Freedom of enterprise is rapidly ceasing to exist. Whatever party is in power, the area of the economy brought, whether for good or for ill, within the supervision and control of the State is steadily and relentlessly increased. Freedom of enterprise is not only withering spontaneously away, but it is also being deliberately, consciously and carefully destroyed amid popular acclamation. In its place is appearing an ever-thickening jungle of uncoordinated government control, whose main purpose is restriction, and whose chief fruit is the substitution of monopoly for competition. Whatever may be the result of this legislation, it is not freedom of enterprise. It is something new — a system that deserves the clumsy and tangled name of 'State-organized, private-property, monopoly capitalism'. So much is the platitude of contemporary economic history.[1]

This is, I would suggest, the present institutional position of our British economy. Rationality and acquisitiveness are dominant and flourishing. Property is a whited sepulchre, healthy seeming without, rotten with loss of function within. Freedom of enterprise is dying. What then does the future hold? What is to be said of the emergent economic order, the new capitalism that is coming to life in our time?

(b) *The Classical and Marxist Hypotheses and the Future of Capitalism.* At the opening of §3 I stated, in their simplest form, two sharply opposed hypotheses about the future of the capitalist system. The Classical economists prophesied for it a glorious future: stability, rapid expansion, a utilitarian paradise. The Marxian critics prophesied disaster — increasing inequality, declining standards of living, revolution and apocalypse.

It will already be obvious to the reader that the historical facts scarcely justify either extreme hope or extreme despair. The classicists were wrong to presume stability in the basic institutions of the system; while the Marxists denied the possibility, and have subsequently closed their eyes to the results, of rapid material expansion. We may therefore look for a moment at the particular

---

[1] It is scarcely necessary to point out that I am using this phrase in rather a different sense from that in which Lenin used it when he spoke of 'monopoly capitalism'. He believed in the existence of a law of economic development, and thought that a growing incapacity to consume the products of industry would force national capitalist states into imperialist war. My account pre-supposes a fundamentally different origin and a different result. The movement to monopoly springs, in my view, from deliberate democratic will, and not from economic necessity or the wishes of monopolistic minorities. It does not result in any pressure for war.

ways in which these contrary prophecies have not been fulfilled, for there is no better nor more scientific method of throwing light upon the probable future.

The failure of the Classical hypothesis to account for all the facts may best be shown by stating those qualities of the emergent system of 'State organized monopoly capitalism' which make it fall far short of any reasonable pattern of economic institutions. It departs in two essential ways from the automatic, self-regulating and rapidly advancing economic order that was, and is, the ideal rational form of the capitalist system:

1. Monopoly capitalism brings with it a marked loss of elasticity. The commodity market is increasingly dominated by fixed prices, valuation and restriction schemes, proprietary goods and rigid quotas. The labour market is increasingly controlled by bilateral monopoly. The capital market is shrunken, dominated by the search for safety on the part of prudent savers, and jammed with fixed interest contracts. It is no wonder that such a system is overwhelmed by severe Trade Cycle depressions, and afflicted with a constant high percentage of unemployment. It is only remarkable that it is not more deeply affected by these things. Indeed, the powers of adaptability and growth still remaining in the system are the surprising feature of its recent history, as we shall see before we have completed our review of it.

2. The reduction in the rate of saving and investment is bound to reduce still further the future adaptability and expansion of the system. Even economists who commit themselves to extreme under-consumption explanations of the Trade Cycle — Mr. Keynes and Mr. Harrod for example — would scarcely deny that the willingness and ability to save is a determinant of long-period, historical growth. If the rate of net saving is reduced to nothing — as it will be one day if present trends are not reversed — it is impossible to believe that the past and present rate of expansion could be maintained. The economy would be reduced to a dependence upon capital saving inventions for the sinews of progress. It is difficult to think that such inventions would be sufficient to take the place of capital accumulation. Although, as we shall see in a moment, it is a false exaggeration to suppose that the capitalist system has yet lost all power of growth, it is nevertheless a serious

weakness of monopoly capitalism that the rate of saving set up within it is so low, and that it is still dwindling.

It might be thought that the growth of small savings set a strict limit to the probable future decline of the rate of saving. This is not so for the reason that the rich, as a class, may actually decumulate if the level of taxation increases still further. This can happen without any individual consuming his or her capital. As the levels of taxation, including inheritance duties, rise against the wealthy they may sell securities at the death of the legator to meet the calls of the tax collector. The savings of the poor would then be absorbed in the purchase of these legatee securities and the rate of saving in the community could be reduced to zero. And even apart from this possibility the rate of saving set up by the poor is likely to be very low.

There is no reason to suppose that the trends of historical development responsible for our present economic dilemmas will either change their direction or abate their strength. If people pin their faith to a natural or inevitable reversal of these trends, which of them do they expect to be reversed? One thing is reasonably certain: the trends will not change as long as political government is responsible to the people.[1]

The trends enforcing ossification and a high rate of consumption are all popular. They consist in the extension of the principle of collective bargaining, the growth of the social services, depression planning, the progressiveness of taxation and the growth of limited liability. It is difficult to suppose that any one of these trends is in the least likely to alter. There is not the slightest evidence that they are doing so. New groups of labour are continuously brought under some collective agreement. The popular demand for social services and governmental intervention in industry is stronger than ever. Limited liability shows no sign of diminishing the area of its control. The changes that I have listed will grow in importance rather than diminish. In so far as they are diseases of the body economic they will continue to weaken the patient more and more.

Just as the Classical hypothesis has been invalidated by the weaknesses developed during the maturity of the system, so has

[1] See Appendix II.

138

the Marxist hypothesis been modified by the strength it has exhibited.

It is in the highest degree improbable that the present trends of change will lead to an immediate collapse, or that economic and social policy is likely to become rapid or revolutionary. The emergent type of capitalism has much to recommend it to a short-sighted democracy, and it has developed loyalties and interests that are likely to stabilize, rather than to destroy, it. This is so for a number of reasons:

1. The new form of capitalism — monopoly capitalism — is *not* in a state of physical collapse. It is an illusion to suppose that it is. Let us consider for a moment the recent history of the *rate of expansion.*

It will be remembered that one of the most fundamental, if not the most fundamental, historical characteristic of *laisser-faire* capitalism is the immense rate of growth produced within and by it. Its social success was unquestionably built upon that secure foundation. What then has happened to the rate of physical growth as the form of capitalism has changed?[1]

The rate of physical expansion can be measured in two different ways — either by looking at general indices of physical production and their chief component commodities, or by examining the course of real wages. It is a striking and puzzling phenomenon of the period in which we are interested — the last two decades — that the two kinds of assessment give different results. Why that should be it is difficult to say, but nevertheless it is the case.

Let us begin with the general index of physical production and of some of its main constituent commodities. It is unfortunately impossible to obtain series that are continuous before and after the last war. A break must be recorded for those years, and a new series begun whose absolute height is not strictly comparable with the previous readings. What has been done — as will be clear from the text of the Appendix — is to divide the quinquennial averages of physical production by the estimated population of the

[1] It is the purpose of the last two sections of the Statistical Appendix to review the evidence on this point. It would take an immense time to survey the whole of the relevant evidence, but it is possible to look briefly at some of the most essential parts of it.

period. This has been done for pig iron, coal and the general index of physical production. The results are set forth in the Tables of § 8 of the Appendix and in the graphs facing this page.

It will be remembered that the figures separated by the war-time gap are not comparable in their absolute height. But even so, an examination of the movements shown in the figures before and after the war, considered separately, show a marked difference of form. In no case, except that of coal, does any equal length of time before the war show the same flat or downward course as do all the figures after the war. In the case of coal, the reduction in the absolute level of *per capita* production is so very great that it strengthens, rather than weakens, the view that *the pace of growth of physical production, measured in this way, has declined.*

But when we turn to the other index of the rate of expansion, and consider the course of *real consumption incomes* in more recent times, we get a very different picture. The figures are set forth in § 7 of the Statistical Appendix. This is Colin Clark's estimate of the course of the net national income at 1930 prices — read at four-yearly intervals:

	£ millions
1924	3679
1928	4117
1932	3995
1936	4960

This shows an immense pace of development — the National Income has risen from approximately £3680 millions to £4960 millions in twelve years — *an increase of over one-third during less than half a generation.* The same result is given if we examine Mr. Clark's estimates of real income per head of the population — both for those in full employment and on an average allowing for unemployment. He gives these figures for the same period:

	Full Employment	Including Unemployment
1924	202.4	185.0
1928	214.0	195.0
1932	220.4	183.4
1936	251.3	221.8

It will be seen that the average real income produced by our advanced capitalism has gone up from £200 to £250 per year in

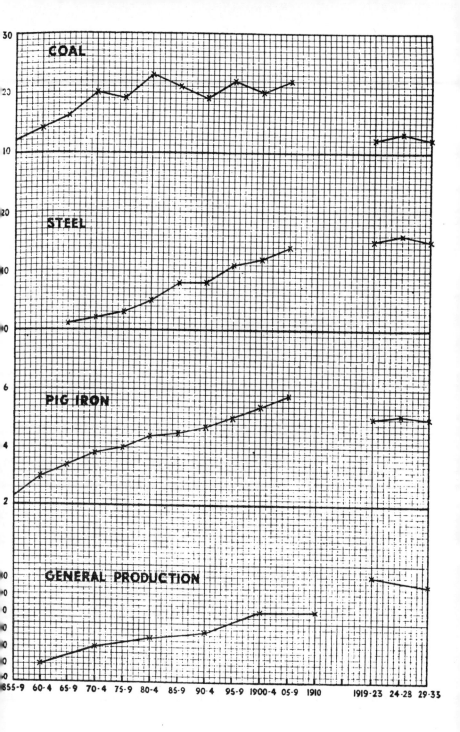

12 years — an increase of a quarter in real productivity — and allowing for unemployment from £185 to £222, a similar proportionate movement. That is a remarkable pace of growth. And a similar result is recorded in Layton and Crowther's estimate of the course of *real wages* over a slightly different period. They also make the distinction between full employment and the allowance to be made for unemployment, and the results they give are these:

	Real Wages Full Work	Real Wages Less Unemployment
1922	201	184
1925	195	180
1929	206	192
1933	233	202

It will be seen that, according to this set of figures, the real reward of the worker in full employment has gone up from 201 to 233 — an increase of over 16 % in eleven years. For the whole working population the corresponding figures are 184 and 202 — an increase of 10 % in eleven years.

These figures show beyond question that the power of the capitalist system to raise the level of consumption — to increase the production and consumption of consumption goods — has not wholly passed away. We live in a period of rapid expansion.

In the nineteenth century the standard of living rose steadily and quickly. In the period immediately before the war it was stationary or declining — at any rate for the wage-earner. Since the war we have resumed a steep upward trend. Indeed, there can have been few periods in the history of the British economy when the level of consumption has risen faster.

We are, therefore, faced by a paradox and a conclusion. The paradox lies in the conflict between the evidence derived from general physical indices and from the old staple commodities, on the one hand, and that derived from the level of physical consumption, on the other. The paradox need not delay us. It probably springs from a change in the physical constitution of capital, a movement away from the old staple materials and metals, a decline in the relative significance of the ferrous metals and coal in the physical constitution of the means of production. These commodities are heavily weighted in the general indices of physical production, and if, as appears probable, the capitalist system proceeds first to the construction of a great mass or skeleton of heavy metal machinery (railways, looms, machine tools, foundries and buildings); and then moves on to the manufacture of lighter machinery, requiring finer metals and materials (aluminium, fine steels, woods and chromium); the general indices based upon the earlier types of material will increasingly fall behind, in their rate of growth, the actual course of physical production. This is exactly what appears to have happened if we compare, as we have just done, indices based upon the production of finished commodities with those weighted with the old staple commodities.[1]

There is, then, a serious problem of contraction facing the old staple industries. It need not however delay us here, as it is a limited and relative problem, while we are concerned with the broader social consequences of the present trends in physical production.

There can be no doubt what those broader social consequences are likely to be. The trends in consumption are markedly upward, the rise in the standard of living is rapid. It is impossible to escape the conclusion that great strength and consequent stability remains in capitalism, even in its State controlled and monopolized form. In so far as expansion is a ground for social stability, monopoly capitalism continues to possess it. It may be that it will cease to possess it soon. Still further reductions in the rate of saving, and still greater impediments to mobility and adaptation, may bring the renewed upward movement to a halt before long. The cessation of expansion has not come yet, and in the meantime the enemies of capitalism must not presume upon internal stagnation or self-induced collapse, if they wish to see the institutions of capitalism reformed and superseded. It may not be pleasant to face these conclusions, but they must be

[1] If this theory is right, it makes explicit a most interesting historical trend, and one that will give rise to grave problems of policy in a progressive capitalism. For, if the relative importance of coal and iron are fated to decline in the same way that the relative importance of the old staple agricultural products (cereals, roots and meat) declined in an earlier period, then the old industries must face the same constant depression that agriculture has endured for the last seventy years. They will suffer a permanent relative depression, if no better method for reducing their absolute size is found than that of slowly squeezing them to death.

faced by anyone with a respect for historical evidence. The walls of Jericho will not fall at a shout nor crumble from within.

2. Nor is the pace of physical expansion the sole source of stability for the present variant of the capitalist order. At least three of the institutional trends that I enumerated in the last Section have a profound stabilizing influence as part of their total social results — the growth of the social services, the growth of the middle class, and the acquisition by the proletariat of the characteristics of the petit bourgeoisie. The stabilizing influence of the last two trends of development is obvious. A society in which the lower middle classes and the pre-capitalist classes — the clerk, the small shopkeeper, the waiter and the civil servant — are increasingly important as a group, is not likely, short of defeat in war, to be a revolutionary society. Neither is a working class that is acquiring property at a more rapid rate than ever before likely to become a more revolutionary class than it has been previously. It is perfectly true that there is no strict correlation in this country between poverty and political unrest, or between depression and the success of reforming and 'left wing' parties. If anything, the correlation is inverse — prosperity often moves the English electorate towards the left. The British people appear to feel more optimistic about reform, and less fearful of change, when they are doing well. Yet this is not inconsistent with what I am trying to say, because I am now discussing the pace of change, and not the direction it will take. And the pace, I suggest, is bound to be moderate in the hands of an increasingly middle-class electorate and an increasingly respectable proletariat.

Of even greater importance is the stabilizing influence of the social services. In discussing these humane activities in the last Section, I considered them as a source of economic change, as a growing fiscal burden and as one chief reason for the decline in the rate of saving. But they have another and even greater social consequence. They succeed in meeting the need that called them forth; they satisfy the demand for security from which they sprang. A society in which the individual receives a measure of support in the main crises of his life — a small income when he is unemployed, or ill, or aged — is infinitely more secure, and therefore more contented, than one in which the certain reward of any

nescapable disaster is shameful humiliation at the hands of the
Poor Law at the best, and death by starvation at the worst. There
may be discontent over the deficiencies in the security provided.
There may be agitation to improve the standards of payment or
treatment under one or all of the services made available, but the
central fact is that they exist. A society protected from the
shocking results that follow if there are no covenanted benefits to
meet these emergencies is bound to enjoy greater internal peace,
a deeper sense of corporate unity and milder impulses to reform.
The social services are, for all their deficiencies, a primitive
recognition of human solidarity, a crude realization of the
splendid idea of corporate responsibility for individual disaster,
of the profound social truth that we are members one of another.
In America these services are called 'social security' measures.
They are well named, for they are not only measures for the
security of men in society but measures for the security of social
relationships, of social order among men.

3. Finally, there is a less respectable, and yet not less powerful,
reason for stability in a slow rate of change. This last cause arises
from the obverse side of the institutional trend that I called the
trend towards restrictionist 'planning'. In the last section we
considered this movement as a source of change — as the destroyer
of a basic institution — free enterprise. But it also has a stabilizing
influence. For the supersession of competition in one industry
after another, and the calling into existence of unifying agencies
within these industries — cartels, marketing boards, crop control
boards, wages boards — create vested interests standing for the
maintenance of monopoly restrictions and the benefits derived
by the monopolist from them. These vested interests are not
unlikely to oppose measures of reform — whether from right or
left — which aim at taking from them the benefits of restriction.
It is unquestionably easier in a democracy to create a monopoly
by legislation than to destroy it. Moreover, it is a mistake to
suppose that the beneficiaries under these State organized
monopolies are exclusively the propertied interest or the rentier
class. A monopoly is likely to benefit all those — whether owners
or workers — who derive their income and employment from
the industry. Hence the resistance to measures of full social

control, and the new expansionist policies that could be enforced within a completely socialized industry, is just as likely to come from the employed, as it is to come from the propertied interests that are affected by the socialization proposals. Again let me repeat that I am not contending that this opposition will be successful. I am not discussing the direction of change but only its speed. And it seems clear to me that just as the rise in the standard of living, and the increase of security, is likely to abate the fury of revolutionary zeal and consequently the pace of change, so also is the growth of important minorities interested in the preservation of the *status quo*.[1]

The truth is that there is much to be said for 'State organized private property monopoly capitalism'.

§6

Policy and Conclusion

The antithesis between historical reality, and the two logical expectations about it, sets plainly before us the two broadest conditions within which the problem of economic policy must be solved. The capitalist economy is ossified, restrictionist and unjust; but it is expanding and stable. The society based upon the capitalist economy is unequal and restless; but it is democratic, middle class and conservative. What then ought to be done? What policy affecting its economy should a democratic capitalist society adopt? What are the limits within which change can take place? In so far as reason and foresight can play a part in influencing the choice of ends and the selection of means to those ends, what measures should a democrat and an egalitarian advocate?

The broadest division among the students of policy is between those who wish to *reverse* the institutional trends that we have

---

[1] I am indebted for the appreciation of this last point to conversation with Mr. Lees Smith, M.P.

considered and those who wish to move with the stream of democratic history, and thus deflect the institutional trends in it towards the construction of a new, more mobile and more consistent centralized or collectivist system.

I am not for the moment concerned with the first of these views. I have considered it in an Appendix to this Part.[1] It is the position of those of us who take the second alternative that I am here discussing.

We have no desire to restore the things that are gone — to recapture the first careless frenzies of capitalist production. We are prepared to work in harmony with the economic policies initiated and tolerated by democracies, and we seek to utilize them in order to construct the institutional basis for a wiser and juster form of society. We wish to use the power of the State to establish expansionist policies within the growing socialized sector of the economy; to restore and maintain a high level of active accumulation; to moderate insecurity still further; to curb the cyclical oscillations of economic activity by a control of the income and investment position of the community; and to secure much greater equality in the distribution of the product of industry. It is only possible to do this by the supersession of private property as the seat of industrial control, as distinct from property as a form of personal reserve. The institutional trends that have robbed property of its functions must be strengthened and developed until property is completely deprived of its power.

This then has been the double purpose of this Part. I have tried to establish from statistical evidence the main institutional trends of democratic capitalism. It seems clear to me that the evidence establishes beyond question the validity of the common-sense judgment that *laisser-faire* capitalism is passing away — strangled by democratic resentment of a curious and unconscious kind. In its place a new type of capitalism is coming into existence — State controlled, monopolistic, and still predominantly inegalitarian. The case against such an economy, and the weaknesses exhibited by it are obvious. Its virtues lie in the maintenance of a most substantial rate of expansion, and in the increase in the degree of security enjoyed within it. Its strength is based upon the size

[1] See Appendix II: The 'Classical' Defence of the Capitalist System.

and strength of the groups interested in the preservation of its restrictive monopolies.

The problem of policy can thus be defined as the search for a method whereby the virtues of capitalism — rationalism and mobility — can be combined with democratic needs — security and equality — by the extension of the activity of the State upon an ever-widening and consistent basis. This, at least, is the problem for those of us who reject the doctrine that the only economic hope of mankind must for ever lie in a competitive and free enterprise economy.[1] It is. then, to the problem of extended State control that we must now turn, equipped in part for the task with the psychological and economic evidence now at our disposal.

Immediately before us, challengingly, lies the contention of the Communists, that these changes can only be achieved, that property rights can only be superseded, by the use of force and through the suppression of responsible government.

[1] See Appendix II.

PART III

THE DICTATORSHIP OF THE
PROLETARIAT

A Critique *of Communist Political Theory*

He who recognizes *only* the class struggle is not yet a Marxist; he
may be found not to have gone beyond the boundaries of bourgeois
reasoning and politics. To limit Marxism to the teaching of the
class struggle means to curtail Marxism — to distort it, to reduce it
to something which is acceptable to the bourgeoisie. *A Marxist is
one who extends the acceptance of the class struggle to the acceptance of the
dictatorship of the proletariat.* In this is the main difference between
a Marxist and an ordinary bourgeois. On this touchstone it is
necessary to test a *real* understanding and acceptance of Marxism.

LENIN: *State and Revolution,* 1917

THE DICTATORSHIP OF THE PROLETARIAT

§ 1

Introduction

HATRED has been made into a religion by the two extreme political groups of our time. The social objectives of the Fascist and Communist movements may differ; their words and their social theories certainly are different; but the emotion upon which they both depend for their strength is the same — hatred — and the method of their government and the tone of their society is the same — terror. I have tried to lay bare the deep sources of these feelings in the first Part of this book. It is with the political theory of the second of these movements that I am now concerned.

Rationalization is a mental activity well known to the psycho-analyst. The victim of the uncontrollable hatreds and fears, many of them transformed in the ways that we have discussed; displaced and projected on to external objects and frequently upon social groups; is forced to offer to himself and to others a set of arguments in order to make intelligible and respectable his fundamentally irrational behaviour. It is for this reason that the extraordinary religions of the past and the extraordinary social theories of the present are taken seriously by intelligent persons, and are thus able to gain wide support. It is therefore necessary to ask about any body of political thought, especially if it is superficially unscientific, this question — what emotion or set of emotions does the acceptance of this doctrine justify? In almost all cases the answer, whatever it is, will throw light, not indeed upon the scientific or logical validity of the doctrine itself, but upon the hidden emotional character of the *doctrinaires*. It will be useful to bear this point in mind throughout the remainder of this book.

But let me say at once that the psychological origin of a doc-trine, or the nature of the emotional motives that lead people to accept it, does not disprove the validity of it. Darwin might have been impelled by the most neurotic of impulses to give his life to the severities of scientific inquiry, but that would not prove the theory of 'natural selection' to be false. Kant or Marx might have been insane, but the theory of the mind active in the determination of its own experience advanced by the former, and the materialist interpretation of history suggested by the latter, could not be invalidated by a psychiatrical examination of their authors. Both the theories must be discussed on their own merits. The dis-cussion of the second of them is the task of this present Part of the book.

§ 2

Statement of the Communist Thesis

Every student of politics is now familiar with the traditional thesis of the Communist movement on the sources of political change, and the necessities of political strategy. History is the epiphenomenon of an underlying struggle between economic classes. That is to say, the activities of political parties, and the conflict of political ideas, are simply the superficial and visible results of the invisible movements in the struggle of economic groups contending for power — just as in a different sphere, the colours and shapes of the visible world are due, if the atomic theory is true, to the movements and collisions of the fundamental, but invisible, atoms of material substance.

In this struggle, it is further supposed, no single economic group or class will give up its privileges, or the political power by which alone those privileges can be maintained, without offering the kind of resistance that makes continuous political democracy impossible. Thus capitalist democracy, the kind of democracy that has come into existence in Great Britain and America, is inherently unstable. The system of representative democracy was set up, according to this theory, by the capitalist bourgeoisie as one strategic move in the class struggle at a time when it served the double purpose of reducing the power of the landed interest and of deceiving and placating the proletariat. It will be swept aside, or amended out of recognition, by the class that created it, if at any time in the future a serious attempt is made to use it as an instrument of proletarian power for the purpose of destroying the political control, and curtailing the privileges, of the bourgeoisie. Hence equality and social justice — social ends that are in the *interests* of the proletariat alone — and the necessary means to that end, a Planned Economy, can only be set up by a proletarian party that will take to arms before the bourgeoisie, overthrow the opposing class by force, and set up a proletarian dictatorship during the last phase of the class war.[1] This party is the Communist Party. The Communist Party will lead the proletariat, and it will, after the liquidation of the class enemy, proceed to the creation of a free and equal society.[2]

This, in the very broadest outline, is the Marxist theory of history and the Communist theory of political strategy derived from that theory. We shall have to discuss, before this Part is finished, the extent to which these views are still held by the responsible political leaders of the international Communist movement; but this doctrine certainly has been held intermittently by leading exponents of Communist thought for nearly a century.[3] It has been immensely influential in the formation of

---

[1] As we shall see in the further Sections of this Part, the theory of Communism fluctuates between the view that the proletariat should first take up arms and the rather different conception that they will be forced to do so, after the acquisition of political power, by the counter-revolutionary and undemocratic action of the bourgeois parties. I shall consider the difference between these views in the following Sections and particularly in the Addendum to this Part.

[2] It will be noticed that I have passed somewhat lightly from the proposition that civil war is inevitable to the view that 'a dictatorship of the proletariat' should follow it and could be used to create a just society. I shall separate these very different propositions in my analysis of the thesis.

[3] There is, of course, no rigid uniformity in the position adopted by Marxists over so long a period as nearly a hundred years. Particularly on the nature and functions of the dictatorship of the proletariat there are very great fluctuations of opinion. I think, however, that I can show the revolutionary and dictatorial thesis to be one continuous thread of thought, accepted by particular groups and prominent persons throughout the whole period. The thesis was advanced by Marx in his earlier and more revolutionary days, was revised and re-stated by Lenin, and has been swallowed in its entirety by contemporary Marxists. Between the earlier Marx and the later Lenin lies a period of forty years (1860-1900) when democratic ideas were in the ascendant, even in Communist circles. As Borkenau says in his *History of the Third International* – 'it is difficult to realize the strength of the democratic conviction of pre-war revolutionary Marxists'.

working-class opinion (in all countries but this) and it is now the religion of large and increasing numbers of individuals, particularly intellectuals, on the left wing of democratic politics. I am chiefly concerned with it, in this book, as one method of justifying the political dictatorship of one party — the Communist Party — and I must now proceed to analyse and discuss the broad thesis I have just stated.

§ 3

Analysis of the Communist Thesis

It will be seen that the doctrine of history and politics that results in a defence of the 'dictatorship of the proletariat' is based upon four separable propositions, and must depend for its validity upon their validity. I wish first to show that these propositions have been consistently held in the history of Communist thought, and I then propose to discuss the relations between them before going on to assess their validity.

The four propositions, upon which the Communist theory of political strategy is based, arranged in a descending order of generality, are: that history is controlled by economic forces; that economic forces must take the form of group struggle; that group struggle must lead to civil war; and that a just society can be constructed by the dictatorship of one party. We must examine each of these propositions in turn.

I propose to quote passages from the earlier work of Marx and Engels at the beginning of the period, and from the writings of the most recent school of Marxist thought at the end of it. The common elements are striking.

1. The first and most fundamental of them is the famous *materialist interpretation of history*. It consists in the affirmation that historical development is controlled exclusively or predominantly by 'economic' motives or forces. This thesis is stated in the *Communist Manifesto* in opposition to any idealist or 'intellectual' theory of history:

> Does it require deep intuition to comprehend that man's ideas, views and conceptions, in one word, man's conscious-

ness changes with every change in the conditions of his material existence, in his social relations and in his social life?

What else does the history of ideas prove, than that intellectual production changes its character *in proportion as material production is changed*? The ruling ideas of each age have ever been the ideas of its ruling class.

When people speak of ideas that revolutionize society they do but express the fact, that within the old society the elements of a new one have been created, and that the dissolution of the old ideas keeps even pace with the dissolution of the old conditions of existence. [1]

Engels writing forty years later, [2] summarizing what was, to him, the central part of the argument contained in the *Manifesto*, says:

The *Manifesto* being our joint production, I consider myself bound to state that the *fundamental proposition* which forms its nucleus, belongs to Marx. The proposition is: *That in every historical epoch, the prevailing mode of economic production and exchange, and the social organization necessarily following from it, form the basis from which is built up, and from which alone can be explained, the political and intellectual history of that epoch. . . .*

It will be seen that the interpretation of history here described changes from the unexceptionable view that '. . . man's ideas, views and conceptions . . . *change*(s) with every change in the conditions of his material existence' — a statement that is little more than a truism — to the much more significant and challenging dogma that the '. . . prevailing mode of economic production . . . and exchange form the basis from which is built up, and from which *alone* can be explained, the . . . history of that epoch'. The first of these views implies no more than that economic forces and institutions are among a number of factors that can influence men's ideas and the course of history. It would be very odd indeed if this were not true and there is, as far as I am aware, no case against this form of the doctrine. But the second view gives pre-eminence, or exclusive power, to economic forces and interests in the determination of social life and therefore of history. Economic changes

---

[1] *Communist Manifesto*, Authorized Edition, Lawrence and Wishart, p. 26. All the page references for the *Manifesto* are to this edition of it.
[2] ENGELS: *Preface to the Manifesto*, Edition of 1888.

are not one cause of history, they are *the* cause of history. What precisely is meant by *economic* changes in this context we shall have to inquire in a moment. For the present it is only necessary to show that the second and significant form of the doctrine is a continuous element in Marxist thought right down to the present day.

This is how Professor Laski expresses it:

> The *basic* factor in any given society is the way in which it earns its living; all social relations are built upon provision for those primary material appetites without satisfying which life cannot endure. . . .
>
> *Changes in the methods of production appear to be the most vital factor in the making of change in all the other social patterns we know.* For changes in those methods determine the changes of social relationships; and these, in turn, are subtly interwoven with all the cultural habits of man . . .[1]

Here, in 1934, and not in 1848 or in 1888, we have the clear statement of the most extreme form that the materialist interpretation of history can take — that the whole course of human history is determined by the technical discoveries ('changes in the methods of production') in industry and trade through the class struggles to which they give rise.

And, of course, the same view is held by John Strachey. This is what he says, quoting Engels with approval:

> In conclusion it will be worth while to quote (two) precise definitions of the materialist conception of history. The first of these is by Engels:
>
> 'The materialist conception of history starts from the principle that production, and with production the exchange of its products, is the basis of every social order; that in every society which has appeared in history the distribution of products, and with it the division of society into classes or estates, is determined by what is produced and how it is produced and how the product is exchanged. *According to this conception, the ultimate cause of all social changes and political revolutions is to be sought,* not in the minds of men, in their increasing insight into eternal truth and justice, but in

[1] Laski: *The State in Theory and Practice*, p. 108.

changes in the modes of production and exchange; they are to be
sought not in the *philosophy* but in the *economics* of the age
(*Anti-Duhring*, p. 300).'[1]

These quotations demonstrate beyond doubt that the first of
the four basic contentions of the Marxist analysis — that history is
exclusively determined by 'economic' forces, and even exclusively by technical discoveries — has been seriously maintained by
Marxists from the dawn of Marxist thought in the forties of the
last century down to the most recent publications of the Left Book
Club.

2. The same thing is true of the second basic doctrine — the
'class struggle theory of historical change'. Marxist theory passes
on from the doctrine that the causal processes in history are
'economic' to the further view that such economic forces always
exercise their influence through the struggle of groups. These
groups are defined by the possession of a common economic
interest, and Marxists, by a process of thought natural to them,
identify such groups with the existing social classes. This doctrine
of the class struggle is the text of the *Communist Manifesto*, opening
as it does with ringing dogmatism:

> The history of all hitherto existing society is the history of
> class struggles.[2]

And this second proposition is referred to forty years later by
Engels in the same passage that I quoted a moment ago and that
can now be continued:

> ... That proposition (the fundamental proposition of the
> *Manifesto*) is: That in every historical epoch, the prevailing
> mode of economic production and exchange, and the social
> organization necessarily following from it, form the basis upon
> which is built up, and from which alone can be explained,
> the political and intellectual history of that epoch; *that con-*
> *sequently the whole history of mankind* (since the dissolution of
> primitive tribal society holding land in common ownership)
> *has been a history of class struggles, contests between exploiting and*
> *exploited, ruling and oppressed classes. ...*[3]

[1] JOHN STRACHEY: *The Theory and Practice of Socialism*, p. 365.
[2] *Communist Manifesto*, p. 10.   [3] ENGELS: *Preface of* 1888.

Needless to say it is to this proposition above all that the Marxist tradition has been faithful, and uncompromising statements of it are to be found in the recent works that we have already quoted. This is what Professor Laski says:

> *History, in a word, is the record of a struggle between groups whose purpose is to defend claims* to which they regard themselves as entitled by reason of the implications they see in the development of the productive process.[1]

That is plain enough, and so is Strachey's form of the same doctrine:

> The essential conclusion which can be drawn from the materialist conception of history is, then, that *the dynamic factor in history is the attempt of successive social classes*, themselves set in motion by technical and economic changes, *to remould society to suit themselves.*[2]

It may therefore be said that the doctrine that historical change is everywhere and always due to the assertion of group rights and the rational search for group gains has been strenuously held by the oldest and the newest schools of Marxist thought.

It is interesting to note in passing that this doctrine of historical change and social evolution bears a marked resemblance to the theory of natural selection proposed by Darwin as an explanation of biological change and the evolution of species. In both theories the dynamic element in the whole process is provided by *group struggle*. This similarity is commented on favourably by Engels. Immediately after his definition of the central proposition that I have already quoted twice, he makes this significant comment:

> *This proposition*, which, in my opinion, *is destined to do for history what Darwin's theory has done for biology*, we, both of us, had been gradually approaching for some years before 1845.

It would be interesting to know if the modern exponents of the doctrine accept the parallelism as willingly as Engels, and if so, what they make of the substantial modifications that the parallel

---

[1] LASKI: *The State in Theory and Practice*, p. 116.
[2] STRACHEY: *The Theory and Practice of Socialism*, p. 364.

conception has undergone with the further development of biological knowledge and theory.

3. We now come to the third element in the Marxist theory: the view that the *struggle* between classes must take the form of *force*, that the struggle (Kampf) must become war (Krieg). It is obvious that only this proposition will justify a transitional dictatorship of the proletariat, since, unless civil *war* is inevitable, it is at least conceivable that crises of economic and social evolution could be resolved by the methods of peaceful political *struggle* evolved within stable democracies. The inevitability of civil war is an essential proposition for the Marxist analysis. If civil war is inevitable in, for example, the process of attenuating the privileges now vested in property, then most of the Communist analysis of contemporary politics follows without argument. If civil war is not certain, however, much of it falls to the ground.

On this critical point there is some hesitation among Marxists.[1] Nevertheless, the main burden of their dogma is clear, and their whole position would be meaningless without it. This is the doctrine of the *Communist Manifesto*, recurring throughout it:

> In depicting the most general phases of the development of the proletariat, we traced the more or less *veiled civil war*, raging within existing society, up to the point where that war breaks out into *open revolution*, and where the *violent overthrow* of the bourgeoisie lays the foundation for the sway of the proletariat.[2]
> ... If the proletariat during its contest with the bourgeoisie is compelled, by the force of circumstances, to organize itself as a class; if, *by means of revolution*, it makes itself the ruling class, and as such sweeps away *by force* the old conditions of production, then it will, along with these conditions, have swept away

---

[1] See for example on this point the obscure passage in STRACHEY: *The Theory and Practice of Socialism*, p. 412, where he rather boggles over the matter. It is obvious from the whole passage that, being a fundamentally reasonable man, he does not himself feel sure what will happen, but he fails to see that this is an admission fatal for the structure and coherence of his whole argument. As we shall see in a moment, he gives such an extraordinary definition of the 'dictatorship of the proletariat' that he robs it of all meaning. He thus preserves a certain internal consistency in his own position, but only by robbing it of controversial importance and all revolutionary logic. Lord Baldwin and Sir John Simon would willingly support a dictatorship of the proletariat as defined by Strachey.

[2] *Communist Manifesto*, p. 20.

the conditions for the existence of class antagonism and of classes generally, and will thereby have abolished its own supremacy as a class.[1]

And finally, in commenting on 'bourgeois socialism' the dictum is repeated:

> ... By changes in the material conditions of existence, this form of Socialism, however, by no means understands the abolition of the bourgeois relations of production, *an abolition that can be effected only by a revolution*, but administrative reforms, based on the continued existence of these relations; etc. ....[2]

All this is pretty clear and the substance of it is still repeated by Professor Laski in 1934. This is what he says:

> The conclusion that we have reached is the grave one that in a society where the instruments of production are privately owned the main fact of significance is the struggle for the possession of the state-power between the class which owns those instruments and that which is denied access to the benefits of that ownership. The conclusion implies that the state is always biased in the interest of the former; *and those in whose interests its authority is exercised will not surrender their advantages unless they are compelled to do so. ...*[3]

This indeed is obvious. No one expects a voluntary surrender of privilege or the conquest of egalitarian ideas without a struggle against, and subsequent legal compulsion of, the dispossessed classes.

But what sort of struggle? What sort of compulsion? On this point Professor Laski is quite clear and quite dogmatic.

> What looms before us is a battle for the possession of the state power. *What is now clear is the vital fact that the class relations of our society have become incompatible with the maintenance of social peace* ... in the choice between peaceful transformation and the maintenance of privilege at the cost of conflict, *the owners of property now, as in an earlier day, are prepared to fight for their legal privileges rather than to give way.* That attitude is shown not merely by the barbaric overthrow of democratic institutions in Fascist countries. It is shown *even more clearly*

[1] *Communist Manifesto*, p. 28.   [2] Ibid., p. 34.
[3] LASKI: *The State in Theory and Practice*, p. 138.

[sic] *by the resistance to social reform in the United States and Great Britain,* by the overt hostility of the Right to democracy in France . . .[1]

It will be noticed that there is one subtle change of emphasis between Marx and Engels on the one hand, and Professor Laski on the other. In the view of the *Manifesto* it is the proletariat that is to be the active revolutionary class; it is the proletariat that is to overthrow bourgeois democracy, that is to refuse to tolerate the continued reign of law and constitution, that is to be the 'aggressor' in the legal sense. But in Professor Laski's picture of the future it is not the proletariat, but the bourgeoisie, that is to fill the revolutionary role. It is the bourgeoisie that will refuse to accept the arbitrament of the popular will, and prefer to overthrow the democratic constitution by force. The source of aggression has undergone a change and the revolutionary will of the proletariat a curious eclipse.[2] But there is a proposition common to both the *Manifesto* and the later writings of Professor Laski. It is the prophecy that the struggle between these two classes — or indeed any two classes — cannot be resolved by peaceful struggle, but only by force. Civil War is inevitable. It behoves all parties to the struggle to arm in preparation for the inevitable clash of arms. Democracy is doomed.

4. We now reach the final and apocalyptic stage of the Marxist prophecy. '. . . there shall be no more death, neither sorrow, nor crying, neither shall there be any more pain, for the former things are passed away'. After the destruction of the bourgeoisie the Class War is ended, and the reign of light will begin. We are to be purified by a bath of blood, but we are to be purified. Justice, and social peace, and 'true' liberty can only be bought, but can safely be bought, by violence and terror.

It is the essential conclusion of the Communist theory, that after the struggle is over, after the civil war to which it must lead has

---

[1] LASKI: *The State in Theory and Practice*, p. 274.
[2] I do not wish to exaggerate the importance of this supposed difference of emphasis. This is one of the points on which there has been a considerable fluctuation of view in the history of Marxist thought. Both Engels and Lenin tended at various times to stress the 'defensive' nature of the war to be waged by the proletariat. There is however a marked difference between the *Manifesto* and the later views of the Marxists. The failure of the proletariat to become revolutionary in the course of history is, of course, the explanation of the change.

been won, a free and equal society can be set up by the dictator-ship of the proletariat. It is true that Professor Laski is less hopeful on this point than other Marxist thinkers, but he is an exception to the rule. From the *Manifesto* onwards the apocalyptic hope and vision is inspiring and clear. Here is the prophecy of the *Manifesto*:

> The Communist revolution is the most radical rupture with traditional property relations; no wonder that its development involves the most radical rupture with traditional ideas.
>
> But let us have done with bourgeois objections to Communism.
>
> We have seen above, that the first step in the revolution by the working class, is to raise the proletariat to the position of ruling class, to win the battle of democracy.
>
> The proletariat will use its political supremacy, to wrest, by degrees, all capital from the bourgeoisie, to centralize all instruments of production in the hands of the state, i.e. of the proletariat organized as the ruling class, and to increase the total of productive resources as rapidly as possible.
>
> . . . . . .
>
> *In place of the old bourgeois society with its classes and class antagonisms, we shall have an association in which the free develop-ment of each is the condition for the free development of all.*[1]

This is a high hope indeed, and it echoes down the generations of Marxist literature. It is one of that great sequence of visions by which mankind has been inspired, and without which a gospel of hatred and suffering could not draw men to itself. Here is Strachey's statement of the same faith:

> And this confusion (over the necessity to suppress existing forms of liberty) will, paradoxically enough, necessitate a more considerable curtailment of the liberty of some sections of the population than would otherwise be necessary. If everyone could be relied upon to see clearly that, when the dispossessed capitalists cried out that they were the champions of the im-mortal cause of human freedom, they were merely crying for their lost dividends, then there would be little need to restrict their liberty to cry out; for they would be crying for the moon. *But if certain sections of the population are still confused enough to take them at their word, then it will become necessary to restrain the outcry.*

[1] *Communist Manifesto*, pp. 27-28.

Thus we must face the fact that, for a period, the British and American workers will almost certainly be compelled to restrict the civil liberties of the dispossessed classes to an extent that these classes will consider outrageous. *But even during that period the degree of liberty enjoyed by incomparably the greater part of the population will have been enormously extended. It will still be restricted and imperfect compared to the liberty which will be possible when a truly classless society will have emerged. But it will be incomparably fuller and wider than are those partial, if precious, liberties which we possess in Britain and America to-day.*[1]

If only we agree to set up a temporary dictatorship, if only we will begin by restricting liberty a little, if only we shed a little blood; then a new heaven and a new earth shall surely be our reward — 'for the former things are passed away'.

Here then is the Communist thesis, now held for nearly a century: It affirms that history is controlled by economic forces, that these forces take the form of class conflict, that class conflict must result in violence and civil war, that when a temporary period of violence is over the dictatorship of the proletariat can resolve all social conflict, and initiate a utopian age of justice and peace. It is this argument that I propose now to criticize.

§4

Criticism of the Communist Thesis

The first and most obvious criticism to be made on the doctrine outlined in the previous section is that it is not a single doctrine. The four separate propositions *are* separate propositions; they do not follow logically or necessarily from each other, and do not therefore justify each other. Communists often speak and write as though the steps of the foregoing argument were the stages of a consistent and necessary sequence of thought — that a belief in the materialist interpretation of history involved a faith in the validity of the class war theory of historical change — and so through all the stages of the Marxist analysis. Now this is simply not the case. Consistent these propositions may be,

[1] *The Theory and Practice of Socialism*, pp. 209-210.

to each other they are not. The acceptance of the
st interpretation of history in no way involves the
n that political change is due to class conflict. The
acceptance of the view that a civil war over the distribution of
property is inevitable in no way justifies the theory that a dictatorship of the proletariat can establish social justice. It would be as
sensible to argue that an acceptance of the laws of arithmetic
made it necessary to beat one's wife. The degree of necessary
connection between the four propositions making up the Communist thesis is scarcely greater than this ridiculous *non sequitur*.

Let me explain what I mean in each of the supposedly necessarily connected stages in the Communist thesis. In the *first*
place, it does not in the least follow from the proposition that the
course of history is determined by economic considerations alone,
that economic interests must necessarily manifest themselves in,
and operate through, group conflict. It may be so, but the second
statement does not follow from the first. It would be perfectly
possible to accept the materialist interpretation of history, and
yet to reject the class struggle theory of political change. It would
be reasonable to do this because it does not follow from the view
that economic interest is the dominant force in social life that
economic interest must always involve a conflict of interests.
The economic purposes of individuals and of groups may be
served more fully by co-operation than by conflict. I do not say
that this is so. I only say that it does not follow from the proposition that economic interests are omnipotent, that economic
interests are always in conflict. A second quite independent
assumption or proposition has been introduced into the argument,
and it must be justified in its own right by separate and convincing
evidence.

The *second non sequitur* is even more obvious. It does not follow
in the least from the doctrine that all historical change is the result
of group conflict, that this conflict must·necessarily result in the
use of force or an outbreak of civil war. There are many differing
types of struggle possible within a society, and most of them do not
involve fighting or the use of force. The struggles of commercial
competition, the conflicts of parties within a law-abiding democracy, the struggle of individuals for posts of leadership and

influence, are all types of struggle in which the rewards of success are real, in which one group must be victorious and the other defeated, in which there is no reconciliation of interest within the limits of the particular conflict, and yet in no one of which force or warfare is inevitable. Once again it would be consistent to accept the class *struggle* theory of political change without despairing about the preservation of social peace. It would be possible to hold, that is to say, that all history is a record of class struggle, and yet to hold that at certain times and in certain societies the struggle can be resolved, and victory can be gained by one party to it, without the use of physical violence. It may be impossible to avoid civil war, but the statement that it is impossible is a third and separable proposition, and the truth of it must again be established by separate evidence.

And, in the *third* place, the same lack of necessary connection is to be found in the last step of the analysis. It does not follow, most plainly does not follow, from the doctrine that civil war is inevitable, that the result of it will be social peace and justice. It might be held that this view follows logically from the belief that the dictatorship of the proletariat will be the dictatorship of the vast majority in the interests of the vast majority; but we have already seen that the industrial proletariat no longer constitutes a *vast* majority of the people, and we shall have reason to consider in a moment a radically different interpretation of the essential nature of a proletarian dictatorship. Be this as it may, it clearly does not follow from the doctrine that civil war is a necessity, that social justice will follow victory in it. It would be just as reasonable to argue that, if international war were inevitable, international justice must follow from it. The fallacy in the second case is now generally admitted. Necessity and justice are not certainly linked together in social affairs. There is, therefore, an element of unreasoning optimism about the last step in the Communist thesis.[1]

Leaving on one side for a moment the lack of necessary coherence in the Marxist system, we must now turn to consider

---

[1] Such untutored hope would be pathetic if it were not so clear, upon the psychological plane, that the hope is made an excuse for the pre-existing temper of ruthlessness. Men and women about to be cruel always exhibit a sickening conviction that they are only being 'cruel in order to be kind'. There is nothing more repulsive than conscientious brutality.

each of those propositions separately. In this book, concerned primarily with policy, I am chiefly interested in the last two propositions of the total thesis — the propositions that civil war between the bourgeoisie and the proletariat is inevitable, and that a dictatorship of one party to that struggle can establish, upon secure foundations, a just society.[1] But it will perhaps be permissible to say a word about the two broader theses from which these conclusions are supposed to follow. I shall therefore examine and criticize all four of these propositions separately.

A. *The Economic Interpretation of History*

It may seem ridiculous and presumptuous of me, who am no historian, to think that it is possible to write anything that is both valid and new about the materialist interpretation of history. A sea of controversial ink has been spilled in this discussion by men with far better qualifications to take part in it than any that I possess. And yet there are certain observations about it, particularly about the new form in which it has been re-stated by recent writers, that I feel called upon to offer.

A theory of history must also be a theory of society and a theory of human life. History is a record of the life of men in society. It must therefore embrace in its totality the forces that have controlled society and moved men in their social relations. An *economic* interpretation or theory of history must attribute a primary importance to economic influence — however *economic* influence may be defined. Indeed, it must attribute a determining or solitary influence to economic causes, for otherwise there is little interest in the theory. No one would be greatly moved by the doctrine that economic causes were one type of cause active in history — one among many such types — because who would wish to deny such a view? It is only when it is affirmed that economic causes and economic motives are the *sole* or *primary* set of causes and motives that anything is being said that is worth discussing.

---

[1] It may be as well to point out that it does not even follow *necessarily* that a civil war between bourgeoisie and proletariat must be followed by a *dictatorship* of either side. It is conceivable that either party, if victorious, might be willing to maintain a democracy in active life. But I do not wish to challenge the Marxist thesis at this point, as I do not believe that the history of civil war leaves much doubt on the matter.

But as we have just seen, prominent Marxists, from Marx onwards, have been prepared to say that — '. . . the *ultimate* cause of *all* social changes . . . is to be sought . . . in the economics of the age'.

It is perhaps difficult to believe that such a theory can be seriously held, and yet it has appealed to brilliant minds in all generations since it was first formulated. Nevertheless, it is impossible for me to see how it can be sustained in any intelligible form.

A theory of history must also be a theory of human life. It must account for St. Francis as well as Mr. Gradgrind, for St. Thomas Aquinas as well as Mr. Gladstone. All the forces that control men and women in their social life must have some place in a general theory of history. It is these forces that make men behave as they do, and their behaviour is the thing of which history is the record. Yet it seems inconceivable that there is any sense in which we can think of economic motives as the sole causes of the human behaviour we see about us. We know from our own experience that we are moved to action by the thought and appreciation of many things. We are influenced by our own self-regarding purposes, the affection that we bear to those we love, the traditions of our families, class, and racial groups, by the form of our intellectual education, by loyalties whose source we cannot remember, by the shapes of fields and trees, by lust and cricket and friendship. Where is the end to the catalogue of causes that can affect us as individuals and through us, the course of history? And, if we attempt to look below the surface of these conscious purposes, as we tried to do in the first Part of this book, we shall find the forces affecting us changed in degree and kind, but we shall discover no reduction in their number or variety. We find them changed, and distorted, and, above all, hidden from us by the displacing, projecting and rationalizing powers of the human intellect and imagination, but we find them multitudinous still. The adult mind changes the form, without diminishing the variety, of the factors that are capable of moving us to action. Unless, therefore, it is possible to describe all the members of this long list of causal factors as 'economic', and to do that would be to rob the term of all meaning — since there would be no members of the group of 'non-economic' causes — it is difficult to see in what form a truly 'economic' interpretation of history can be affirmed.

We must therefore turn aside for a moment to consider very briefly the precise meaning of the term *economic* in the phrase — the *economic interpretation* of history. What are economic, as distinct from non-economic, causes and motives?

Now it would obviously be possible to interpret the term so widely that the statement: 'history is determined wholly by economic causes'; would become a mere tautology. If by 'economic' causes, or 'economic' purposes, or 'economic' ends, we meant all the ends or conditions of the world that men have desired or have moved them to action, the economic interpretation of history would become a purely circular statement. It would consist merely in saying that historical change has been caused by the ends that have caused men to act, or that historical change was caused by the causes of historical change. In order to mean anything, the economic ends or purposes must be a *particular* kind of end or purpose, standing in opposition to certain other kinds of human motive. What then is the general character or feature that separates off economic ends from non-economic ends?

It is by no means easy to discover any clear definition of the term *economic* in Marxist literature. Something like a definition of the term is offered by Strachey when he says: 'It would be quite unrealistic to suggest, however, that men and women are responsive to nothing but considerations of *immediate individual self-interest.*' As this sentence occurs in a passage in which he is expressing the difference between the crude and the sophisticated versions of the economic interpretation of history, it seems probable that it contains some description of what is meant by 'economic'. Economic ends would therefore seem to mean the ends of 'self-interest,' and since action is supposed to be directed correctly towards these ends, it is clearly implied that economic motives and actions are those of *rational acquisitiveness*. If the term economic does not mean this to Marxists, I do not know what it does mean.

On this view, then, the 'economic interpretation of history' turns out to mean the view that history is determined, and the action of individuals and groups controlled, by rational acquisitive self-interest. 'Non-economic' ends as motives for action would then become either altruistic purposes or irrational purposes.

Even in a form as general as this the 'economic interpretation' of history has very little precise meaning, for two reasons. In the *first* place, there would be little left of the existing body of Marxist theory if it could be shown that the ends of rational acquisitiveness were very varied or liable to great change. Plainly the 'economic ends' must be still further limited to those with which the existing subject of economics deals — the objects of desire purchasable with money — if the kind of conclusion that Marxists wish to establish is to stand.

Let me try to explain this point carefully. If people desire a great variety of ends other than an increase in their standard of living, if they are just as interested in their bowling average at cricket or the victory of their local team at football, as they are in protecting or increasing their money or real wages, very little would remain of the imposing structure of Marxist thought. It is only if the ends for which people care are limited to the improvement of their economic position narrowly defined — the increase of the number of things that they can buy with money — that the view of history we are here examining could be sustained.

And it must be admitted that a casual inspection of the life of the British masses would tend to throw doubt upon the validity of any such psychological assumption. The relative attendance at football matches on the one hand, and political and trade union meetings on the other, would not lead one to suppose that the ends actively pursued by the British working class were exclusively 'economic'!

In the *second* place the mere nature of the end desired by any person cannot by itself lead to action or explain action by that person or group. There must also exist some kind of intellectual view about the means by which the end can be obtained. It is not enough for me to wish to drink water in order that I may act so as to achieve that end. I must also have some view, derived either from observation or scientific reasoning, as to how water can be obtained. It is not enough, in order to understand my action, to know that I wish to drink. It is also necessary to know what I think about the methods of obtaining water. There is therefore a purely intellectual or scientific element in every human action, and the state of the science of means must determine at every point the course of history.

The attitude to science of those who uphold the 'economic interpretation of history' is curious and paradoxical. They hate the doctrine that the discoveries of the human mind can play any part in the determination of events — 'the ultimate causes . . . are to be sought, *not in the minds of men*, . . . but in the economics of the epoch concerned'. Yet they make one curious exception to this view. A common form of the materialist interpretation of history lays immense emphasis — almost exclusive emphasis — upon one part of the science of means; namely that of technical invention. Now, apart altogether from the false historical theory of invention that is implied in Marxists' account of it, it is obvious that technical inventions are due to scientific work, and are to be found in some sense *in the minds* of men. Hence intellect and science are allowed to play a vital part in influencing the course of history, but only at one point — that of technical industrial invention. But what reason can there be for concentrating upon one small part of the science of means in this arbitrary and inexact way? The inventions of the Industrial Revolution, and indeed industrial invention in general, compose between them only one part of our scientific thought, and form only a small fraction of our total view about how our ends can be achieved. Why is a discovery about the smelting of iron different in kind from a discovery about the way to paint, the way to teach, the way to live together in peace, or even the way to be happy? If discoveries about industrial chemistry are relevant, why not those about law and ethics, psychology and philosophy? Plainly any discovery that influences our views as to the methods by which we can secure the things we desire will influence the actions we decide to take, and thus the course of history. It is ridiculous to attempt to exclude any of our scientific discoveries from the field of efficient causation in history.

The only account, then, of the economic interpretation of history that gives it both substance and intelligibility is the view that: (a) takes 'economic motive' to mean the rational desire to raise the standard of living narrowly defined, and (b) takes account of the changing knowledge of, and prevalent views about, the methods of achieving our ends, broadly defined. The interpretation of history that can be rationally sustained is the view that rational acquisitiveness so defined, guided by the state of knowledge, is the determining force in history. Is this view true?

We are now brought back, after this digression on terminology, to the question of substance. We have already seen that once we realize, as we must do, that a theory of history is also a theory of human life, it is almost inconceivable that the gamut of human passion, and the infinite variety of human life, can be constrained within the strait-jacket of one set of ends, however important. We are clearly influenced continuously by the thought of our material welfare. But are we influenced by nothing else? Do we order our whole lives and choose all our group loyalties by the thought of nothing but our real wages? It is almost inconceivable that this is so. Yet we make history what it is. It is only if we are moved by these considerations alone that a *purely* economic interpretation of history can be sustained.

It is the appreciation of something like that fact which has led some of the apostles of the materialist gospel to re-state the doctrine in a form that is less repellent to common sense. They have tried to do this by denying the *exclusiveness* of economic motive, while retaining its *primacy* in the causation of history. This is what Professor Laski writes:

> *It is no part of my case to argue, either, that all historical change is necessarily determined by the economic factors whose significance I have been discussing; I argue only that the economic factor is the predominant element in that determination. I fully admit the influence of personality, tradition, logic, as factors in the making of change . . .* It is not less true that tradition, personality and logic, while predominantly shaped by the economic factor, also shape it in their turn. There is a reciprocity of influence between the factors of social change which no serious observer can reasonably deny.
>
> *But the admission of pluralism in historic causation is not the same thing as a denial of the primacy of the economic factor. I am concerned only to insist that the part any other factor will play depends upon an environment the nature of which is determined by its system of economic relationships. . . .*[1]

[1] LASKI: *The State in Theory and Practice*, pp. 120-121.

Here it will be seen that Professor Laski is concerned to maintain a double proposition — that economic causes are not the sole category of causes in history, *and* that economic causes are the primary or fundamental type of cause. He wishes to maintain both a pluralist theory of causation and to preserve a 'primacy for the economic factor'. He states dogmatically that: '. . . the admission of pluralism . . . is not the same thing as a denial of the primacy of the economic factor.'

Strachey commits himself to exactly the same position. There are passages in which he recognizes with admirable clarity the power in history of forces that he does not wish to call economic.

> *It would be quite unrealistic to suggest, however, that men and women are responsive to nothing but considerations of immediate individual self-interest. The fact is that men often respond powerfully to the most various, the most idealistic and the most impersonal appeals.* Indeed, what tragedies have not been caused by the fact that they respond to such appeals as hastily and as uncritically as they do. Again and again it has been found possible to make men, not only work, but die for ideals and causes, good, bad and indifferent. Men have always been only too ready to fling themselves into every kind of impersonal enterprise or combat, and have helped to wreck civilization by so doing. Gibbon in a famous passage tells us how whole generations of the men of antiquity died for a diphthong. *Century after century, men have been willing to throw away their most substantial concerns, and to devote themselves body and soul to some cause which they believed to be sacred. The more we read history, the less we shall doubt men's idealism and the more we shall doubt their perspicacity.*[1]

This is an excellent statement of one of the many reasons for believing that rational acquisitiveness, or indeed any rational motive whatever, cannot be the sole cause at work in historical change. It is an excellent account, some people may be tempted to think, of the enthusiasm to be found in Communist and Fascist Parties alike.

And again the same author writes about the economic interpretation of history itself.

[1] STRACHEY: *Theory and Practice of Socialism*, pp. 130-131.

In fine, the materialist conception of history does not
assert that history is a one way street in which every political
change is caused by a social change, and every social change
by an economic change, and every economic change by a
technical change. It asserts, on the contrary, that history is a
complex of reciprocating interactions between technical,
economic, social and political events. . . .[1]

All this is very sensible. Yet he goes on to quote a few pages later[2]
with approval what he terms a 'precise definition of the materialist
conception of history' as we have already given it:

The materialist conception of history starts from the
principle that production, and with production the exchange
of its product, is the *basis* of every social order; that in
every society which has appeared in history the distribution
of the products, and with it the division of society into classes
or estates, is determined by what is produced and how it is
produced, and how the product is exchanged. *According to
this conception, the ultimate causes of all social changes and political
revolutions are to be sought, not in the minds of men, in their increasing insight into eternal truth and justice, but in changes in the
mode of production and exchange; they are to be sought, not in the
philosophy, but in the economics, of the epoch concerned.*

I contend that it is impossible logically to hold both these views
at the same time.

Modern Marxist thinkers are trying to maintain an odd and half-
hearted position. They are trying to retain the *primacy*, and to
abolish the *solitariness*, of economic causation. Economic causes
are not the only voice in history, but they have the last word.
That is the position, odd as it may seem, occupied by these
thinkers.

I feel sure it is wrong. I feel convinced that it is based upon a
confusion of thought, and I must attempt to demonstrate why I
think so.

There are surely two views, but only two views, that can be
consistently held, about the part played by economic motives, as
we have now defined them, in the course of history. The *first* of
these is the view that Mr. G. D. H. Cole now calls the 'realistic'

[1] STRACHEY: *Theory and Practice of Socialism*, p. 361.
[2] Ibid., pp. 365-366.

interpretation (as distinct from the materialist interpretation) of history. This view asserts that the motives of rational acquisitiveness constitute *one* important and omnipresent group of causes in history, but that this type of cause is not the only type. This form of the doctrine can and should be maintained as a healthy corrective to any simple idealist theories of history — such as those implied in the writings of Professor Robbins or Mr. Keynes[1] — or the more sophisticated, but not less fallacious, Hegelian forms of the same theory. It would assert, in opposition to the view that the course of history is wholly determined by intellectual discovery, that at every time and in every place the pursuit of self-interest by individuals and by groups is driving men to action and history to events. It would supplement this assertion by a detailed analysis of the part played by this force, and the group conflict to which it leads — in religious and constitutional struggles, in civil and international war. It would tear aside, as it has done, the seemly veil of intellectual rationalization, and show working beneath it the sordid ambitions of class and privilege. It would expose the hypocritical rationalization of group interest with which the history of political thought is filled. All this would be, and has been, to the good. It constitutes an essential contribution to any true theory of history. Much of the interpretation that Marxists have given to the actual course of events in history will stand. The emphasis upon the importance and the *omnipresence* of acquisitiveness in the affairs of men is a true emphasis, as long as it does not pass, openly or secretly, into the assertion that acquisitiveness is the *sole* force in any society at any time.

But this form of the theory — consisting in the analysis of the economic element in the determination of events — does not lead to the conclusions that Marxists wish to establish, and they are never contented with it. Common sense — or Mr. Cole's 'realism' — does not and cannot satisfy them. It does not lead to the view of history and politics desired by Marxists, because it leaves quite undecided the nature of the forces, other than those of an economic and acquisitive character, at work in history. Above all it leaves uncertain *the relative importance of the non-economic as opposed to the economic determinants in the story*. This is a position intolerable to the

[1] See Appendix II.

174

Marxist. We have already seen that an acquisitive theory of history simply cannot be stated intelligibly without some reference to the state of the science of means. If to this modification must be added all sorts of other determinants, such as altruism, a desire for group co-operation, local tradition, and the love of football; and most important of all, the secret and powerful movements of purely *irrational* impulses, then what is left of a rational 'economic interpretation' of history? Clearly nothing more than the common-sense view that acquisitive motives are an important and universal force in social behaviour and therefore in history.

With this form of the theory there is little need to quarrel, but not only does the acceptance of it involve abandoning many of the conclusions — such as the impotence of ideas — to which Marxists are committed, but they (the Marxists) show no willingness whatever to accept the more reasonable version of their own theory. As we have already seen Professor Laski says, immediately after admitting the importance of non-economic forces in history: 'But the admission of pluralism in historic causation *is not the same thing as a denial of the primacy of the economic factor.* I am concerned only to insist that the part any other factor will play depends upon an environment, the nature of which is *determined by its system of economic relationships.*'[1]

Strachey's view is precisely the same, since he quotes with approval the passage from Engels in which 'production . . . is the *basis* of every social order . . . *ultimate causes* of all changes . . . are to be sought in the *economics* of the age'.

They, and all who think with them, are therefore committed to the *second*, and much more challenging, view, that economic causes, though not solitary, are in some sense *basic* or *ultimate* or *fundamental*; that the influence of economic causes is different in kind from that of all other types of cause. It is this second form of the theory that appears to me to be wrong. And this for a number of reasons.

To begin with it is surely a mistake in the logic of causation to suppose that a group of causes *can* be determining or ultimate, and yet not be solitary.

It is not open to Professor Laski to accept a pluralist theory of

[1] LASKI: *State in Theory and Practice*, p. 121.

175

history, and to continue to maintain the 'primacy of the economic factor'. If there are two causes, each necessary before an event will occur, it is not possible to speak of one of them as being primary or ultimate. It would be as sensible to say that the left leg was the primary cause of walking, or that one end of a see-saw was the fundamental cause of its rhythmical movement. If there are two essential causes of an event, then there is no question of primacy between them; to say that there is a primary cause is either to mean that no other cause is necessary for the event to occur, or to mean nothing. The Marxists must choose between saying that economic causes or rational acquisitiveness is the sole force in history on the one hand, or abandoning the doctrine of the peculiar or basic nature of economic causes on the other.

Let me explain at once that I am not trying to argue that it is impossible to arrange types of causes in some order of importance or frequency of operation. To continue my previous analogy: it would be perfectly sensible to say that my right leg was more important to me than my left, even in walking; and it would plainly be sensible to say that economic acquisitiveness was a more important cause of my behaviour than, say, the desire to excel at the game of ludo. In such cases what I am saying is either that the cause is more significant for my happiness — I should suffer a greater loss of freedom or happiness by losing my right leg than I should by losing my left — or that the cause operates more frequently — I am more often moved by a desire to raise my standard of living than to win at ludo. But what I must not say is that my right leg is *the fundamental cause* of my walking, or that, when I am playing ludo the *ultimate* explanation of my behaviour lies in my desire to raise my wages. When two causes are present, two causes are present, and neither is more 'fundamental' than the other. A pluralist theory of the causes of historical development means that history would have been different if any one of the sets of causes had differed from what, in fact, it was.

This is made particularly obvious when we reflect upon the uniqueness of the course of events in history. Little things may have greater consequences. Even Marxists could not deny that the outcome of a battle may influence the course of history — and the outcome of a battle may turn upon very small things:

For the sake of a nail the shoe was lost
For the sake of the shoe the horse was lost
For the sake of the horse the rider was lost
For the sake of the rider the battle was lost
For the sake of the battle the war was lost
For the sake of the war the kingdom was lost
So all was lost for the loss of a nail

— is after all a true comment on one aspect of historical change.

In the case of history, a doctrine of plurality of causes is peculiarly and dramatically incompatible with the view that one set of causes is fundamental or basic. To maintain any form of the materialist conception of history it is necessary to affirm that economic causes are the sole set of causes at work in human life.

It is in this form that the theory is so precisely unacceptable. We know, both by the inspection of our consciousness and by the observation of others, that the character of the things that move us is not limited in this way. Men and women are impelled to social and personal action, not only by the ends of rational acquisitiveness narrowly defined, but by the emotions of family affection, by loyalty to groups founded upon geographical, racial, religious and cultural unity, by the pursuit of the non-economic pleasures to be found in artistic and athletic self-fulfilment; the whole of their activity is permeated through and through by the desire to co-operate peacefully with other human beings, and is guided by the state of human knowledge. That, or something much more complicated than that rather than something much more simple, is, we now know, the correct picture of human life.[1]

The numberless ways in which our real life differs from the determined activity of acquisitive automata must be of significance in history. The variety of human motive means that the account of human affairs based upon the analysis of economic interest alone must be incomplete, and it can only be by chance that prophecies based upon such an analysis prove correct. Let me take an example of what I mean. If there were two societies, with the same class structure and with the same pattern of conflicting economic interests between the groups, then the

[1] This is to say nothing of the possibility of free will and the certain occurrence of irrationality.

Marxist must contend that the history of these two societies woul
be identical. I maintain that it would be inconceivable that the
should be similar, except by chance, unless a great number c
other conditions were identical between them. If one of them ha
a democratic tradition and the other had not; or if one played foot
ball and the other did not; or if one was Protestant and the othe
Catholic; or if one had a Public School system and the other ha
not; or if one ate roast beef and the other pork — I believe the cours
of their respective histories would profoundly differ. They woul
differ because these other differences determine the nature of th
actions of large numbers of individuals and so determine the caus
of social action. And who, contemplating the immense variety o
the national types in the existing national capitalisms, can reall
deny that the evidence is on the side of variety, and not on the side
of uniformity, in their behaviour?[1]

Finally, let me mention yet another way in which the economic
interpretation of history is unrealistically simple. One of the most
important ways in which social reality differs from the Marxist
picture of it has already been emphasized in the first Part of this

[1] A simple example may help to illustrate this obvious, but frequently forgotten,
point. Compare Germany and the United States. From a consideration of
their technical economic structure a great similarity in their historical development
might be expected. Both these countries are capitalist systems of a similar age.
They both passed into their industrial revolutions at approximately the same time.
They both are divided into the three great group interests: the bourgeoisie, the
proletariat and the agricultural interest. They are both large, self-contained,
continental areas. On the economic interpretation of history, their histories should
have been approximately similar. In fact they could scarcely have been more
different. The reason is not far to seek. Indeed it is painfully obvious to all except
the wilfully blind. The history of these two great nations, *economically similar*, is
different because their racial composition is different, because their political
tradition is different, because their form of education is different, because one plays
football and the other does not. Who can gather the character of a nation into an
economic category, or express the intricate process of history in a Marxian syllogism?
The same would be true of a pair of colonial capitalisms – e.g. Australia and
Argentina. Both began as the commercial colonies of a great European power. Both
developed into capitalism by borrowing capital from Europe. Both retain an active
exporting agriculture and contain a group of the native population. Their economic
similarities are therefore most marked. Their histories, on the other hand, could
scarcely be more different.
It would be interesting to construct two groupings of the present national
societies - one on a basis of economic similarity and one on the basis of historical
or social similarity. Into one group would go 'old capitalisms', 'new capitalisms',
'colonial capitalisms', 'peasant economies', etc. Into the other would go 'peaceful
democracies', 'peaceful authoritarian states', 'imperial democracies', and so on.
I believe there would be extraordinary little parallelism between the two groupings.

book. 'Economic', as we have seen, must be taken to mean *'rationally acquisitive'*. But, as we saw in the first Part, whatever are the forces that control the course of history and the behaviour of society, they are not by any means exclusively rational. The things that move us—be they good or bad, constructive or destructive, towards love or towards hate—are both conscious and unconscious, rational and irrational. We are not simple products of conscious desire. In all our lives as individuals and societies we are moved, and deeply moved, by loves and hatreds we cannot remember, by loyalties and incidents long forgotten and angrily denied. We are not what we seem nor what we say we are. We are deeper and more complicated, and in many ways more terrible, than we seem.

For all these reasons it appears to me to be impossible to accept the 'economic interpretation of history', in its consistent form, as a true theory of history.

I shall be told, I know, that the theory cannot be refuted by simple arguments of this kind. It will be said that there is more in the controversy than I have supposed; that alternative forms of the theory are tenable; and that I have misinterpreted the authorities that I have quoted. This may, indeed, be true, and those of us who cannot accept any of the existing variants of this theory await any new forms of it with sustained and lively interest. But, in so far as I understand them, the present doctrines appear to be based upon a false simplication of human nature and on an incorrect interpretation of the theory of multiple causation.

Before I leave this question, it may be of interest to offer a tentative explanation of the method by which those who hold the incorrect doctrine have been led to adopt it.

I believe that the explanation is not difficult to find. It is yet another example of a most common source of error in the history of human thought. Philosophers and scientists, having found a *universal* aspect of something, are often led on to suppose that this aspect is the *sole* aspect, the sufficient explanation of the phenomenon they are studying. Thus natural scientists, having found an aspect of reality — the material aspect of it — that proved amenable, at any rate for a time, to processes of mechanical and mathematical explanation, were led on to suppose that material objects were in some sense *the* fundamental cause and sufficien explanation of the whole of our experience. This they did despit their immediate consciousness of processes of reason, judgment of value, and emotional experiences, all of which were plainly no material in their nature. They knew in every moment of thei conscious life that they were not themselves dead masses of matte. — that there was some important distinction between them and stone — and that the variety of human experience could not there fore be comprehended within, or in any important sense explainec by, the qualities of dead matter alone.[1]

It is to be noticed that the physical materialists did not make their mistake because they were wrong to assert that, in some sense, all experience is grounded in matter. There is a materia aspect to *all* human experience. All human beings are materia bodies. All human activities are associated with changes in the material world — if only in the movement of blood through the channels of the body or the chemical processes of metabolism in the brain. At every point, and in every experience, matter is present and the qualities of matter are active in making the sequence of events what it is. The mistake of the materialists is therefore not their insistence upon the *universality* of material causation. Their mistake lies in attributing to matter an *exclusive*, or determining, or funda-mental significance. Matter cannot possess this significance as long as the qualities of our experience differ from the qualities of material things. Matter is a universal, but not a *solitary*, deter-minant of things as they are.

Exactly the same mistake is made by those who have accepted the economic interpretation of history. They have found a uni-versal phenomenon in history, and they have supposed that it was a sufficient explanation of history.

Let me make clear what I mean by an example. Marxists assume that when it has been shown that economic interests are involved in wars of religion, or in great constitutional struggles, it has also been proved that those wars were caused by the economic interests involved in them, or that they were the consequence of

---

[1] For an illuminating discussion of the mistakes of the physical scientists see Prof. STEBBING: *Philosophy and Physicists*; and for an alternative analysis of the different aspects of human experience Prof. MacMurray: *Interpreting the Universe.*

1e conflicting economic interests benefited by them. Of course 1othing of the kind has been shown. As we have just seen, it 1ould be as sensible to argue that all experience is materially 1etermined because matter is present in it, or that we are solely 1fluenced by the state of the atmosphere because we have to 1reathe. It is obvious that in any great social conflict, like an 1ternational war or a religious reformation, the economic interests 1 groups will be affected by its outcome, and that some will 1enefit and others will suffer. It is obvious that the course of events 1ill be influenced at every point by a desire on the part of indi- 1iduals and groups to advance their rational self-interest. History 1ould be utterly different if this were not so. It is therefore certain 1hat economic motive is a *universal* element in the causation of all 1istorical events. But that does not, and cannot, prove that it is the 1ole or determining element. Exactly the same thing could be said 1f the other universal aspects of human behaviour — the intellec- 1ual aspect, the universal motive of altruism, or the universal forms 1f neurosis. In each and all of these cases it would be possible to 1how that these phenomena are always present, influencing the 1ourse of action — universal, but not solitary, determinants of the 1nfolding of events.[1]

Look for a moment at the precise form of Professor Laski's state- 1nent:

> . . . the admission of pluralism in historic causation is not the same thing as a denial of the primacy of the economic factor. *I am concerned only to insist that the part that any other factor will play depends on an environment the nature of which is determined by its system of economic relationships. . . .*[2]

Of course. The statement is obviously true. It is certain that the 1art that any other factor can play will depend upon the nature of 1he system of economic relationships. The result of a loss of faith in 1ranscendental religion will have a quite different influence in a 1rench peasant economy from that which it will exert in an 1merican capitalist economy. A great man of action arising 1mong the nomads of Arabia will lead a different life, and carry

[1] In fact all these universal attributes have been made the basis of such theories —idealist, religious and psychological theories of history.
[2] LASKI: *The State in Theory and Practice*, p. 121.

through very different changes in the social relationships of hi
people, from a man with the same capacities of leadership born int
nineteenth-century England. The influence of every other facto
in history will be conditioned by the state of the system of economi
relationships. But the vital point is this: *Exactly the same statemen
could be made about the effects of the economic factor itself.* The result
of economic changes will depend upon the state of intellectua
opinion, upon the state of religious belief, upon the state o
emotional neurosis, upon the form of political tradition, amon
any people within whose society the change occurs. The discover
of oil has radically different consequences in an ancient pre
capitalist economy like that of Persia, from those which it produce
in capitalist America. As we have already seen, the Industria
Revolution produces very different social changes if it occur
within a democratic society on the one hand, or a society governee
by a dictatorship on the other. It is not possible to say whicl
ingredient forms the loaf — the yeast or the flour.[1]

The mistake made by these thinkers, then, is that of fals

[1] The most deceptively convincing results of the economic interpretation o
history arise from the use to which it is put in the explanation of particular historica
events. Marxists take the great processes of historical change: the Reformation, th
English Civil War, or the French Revolution; crises in history that have bee
described and explained in the past chiefly in constitutional, ideological, or militar
terms, and show that economic interest, and group conflict based upon economi
interest, played an exceedingly important role throughout the story. It is com
paratively easy, and of the greatest possible interest, to show that certain classes wer
benefited by the Reformation, or by the defeat of the Crown in seventeenth-centur
England, or by the destruction of the *ancien régime* in eighteenth-century France
It is most illuminating to understand the part that acquisitiveness has played i
drawing men into groups and into struggle. But the Marxists use those analyses t
suggest that they explain away the other forces that are plainly at work and upo
which older historians concentrated. They say 'when we strip away the ideologica
fripperies of Protestantism we find *underneath, explaining the force of these ideas*, th
self-interest of the new landowners, or the new bourgeoisie or the rising tow
proletariat . . . ' or some such group. Because they find economic interest involve
in an ideological or emotional struggle, they assume that the economic interest i
real and the other forces are not. They assume that the doctrine of English freedon
from arbitrary authority is less real than the interests that happened to benefit fron
the outcome of the constitutional struggles of the seventeenth century. The
assume that the interests of the victorious bourgeoisie in France are more real tha
the frenzies of fear in the Terror, and of patriotism in the succeeding wars c
liberation. But why do they assume these things? It cannot be because they hav
demonstrated that rational acquisitiveness is the sole controlling motive in huma
life, because we know that it is not. It cannot be because they have demonstrate
that economic motives operate more frequently than any others, for no suc
psychological doctrine is anywhere sustained by them. The only possible explana
tion is the one which I respectfully suggest in the text.

implicity. They have discovered a universal element in the attern of life, and have assumed that the whole of its variety could e explained by their solitary clue. They have found one inter-veaving thread, and think that they grasp the pattern of the loth.

It is not so. We are more complicated than the Marxists would ave us believe. We are never free from acquisitive impulses, but ve are not wholly dominated by them. At every turn we must ranslate our ends into action through the medium of our rational iews as to how those ends can be attained. Thus the thread of nowledge, science and reason enters the pattern. We are not ven what we think ourselves to be. The thread of uncon-cious motive, ambivalence and emotional strain contributes a ark strand to the skein. We are deeply moved by a care for the ood of others and by loyalties to groups and ends that are larger han ourselves — to the family, to the nation, to mankind. And o the thread of community, brotherhood, co-operation and love nters in. Most of us cannot live at peace, or make terms with life, nless we possess, however dimly, some sense of unity in it, some ranscending idea that will give our hopes a goal and our suffering n interpretation. We cannot live as animals, blind to the end of ur struggle. And so philosophy and religion find a place in the reat pattern of action, thought and feeling that we call history — he written record of the life of humanity.

The idealist theory of history is not wrong — it is incomplete. he religious theory of history is not wrong — it is incomplete. The sychological theory of history, if ever we have it, will not be vrong, but it will be incomplete. The economic interpretation of istory is not wrong, but it is insufficient.

That is then my argument. Marxists cannot, and some of them o not, deny the plurality of the types of cause at work in history; ut they do not realize the radical consequences of this admission or their view of history. Little of it remains except the valuable nalysis of one element among a number of universal aspects of uman behaviour. In so far as their theory of politics is based pon a purely economic interpretation of history, it is insecurely ased.

B. *The Doctrine of Class Struggle*

We must now consider the second foundation of the Marxis analysis — the view that historical change and social developmen is always and everywhere due to the struggle of economic groups Witness the dogmatism of the *Manifesto*:

> The history of all hitherto existing society is the history c class struggles.

I believe that this second proposition is no more securel founded than the first. It will not, however, take so long t demonstrate why I think so.

To begin with, Marx's emphasis upon the exclusive loyalty c men to the economic group to which they happen to belong i difficult to sustain. Marx's prophecy about the future of national ism makes curious reading now. This is what he and Engels sai in the *Manifesto*:

> The Communists are further reproached with desiring t abolish countries and nationality.
> *The working men have no country.* We cannot take from ther what they have not got. Since the proletariat must first of a acquire political supremacy, must rise to be the leading clas of the nation, must constitute itself *the* nation, it is, so fa itself national, though not in the bourgeois sense of the wor
> *National antagonisms between peoples are daily more and mo vanishing, owing to the development of the bourgeoisie, to freedom c commerce, to the world market, to uniformity in the mode of productic and in the conditions of life corresponding thereto.*[1]

No prophecy could ring more false to-day. No part of th *Manifesto* seems more dusty. This passage was written almost century ago. During that time the history of the world has bee influenced profoundly by the struggles of *national* groups — : much as, or more than, by the conflict of economic classes.

In so far as conflict and fighting has been the key to the histor of the last hundred years, the conflict has arisen between natio states. The history of the period would be utterly unintelligible, suggest, if we had no notion that individuals were moved b passionate loyalty to the geographical and racial groups in whos

[1] *Communist Manifesto* (Lawrence and Wishart), p. 26.

culture they have been educated. An interpretation of these years that neglected the emotion of patriotism and the fevers of national-ism would resemble, if not *Hamlet* without the Prince of Denmark, at least *Othello* without Iago.

The prophecy of the *Manifesto* would have been no more absurd if it had read: 'The working men have no bowels. Hunger and sexual passion between persons are daily more and more vanishing . . .' Its relationship to reality would be scarcely more attenuated.

Of course it is perfectly open to Marxists to argue that these national passions are the epiphenomena of the underlying class struggle — that the common man is inflamed to excesses of nationalism by a bourgeois monopoly of the instruments of propaganda. I do not for a moment accept this view of the sources of patriotism; but whether that hypothesis is true or not, it does not yield the conclusion of the *Manifesto*, nor support the position that Marxists adopt. Even if their hypothesis explained the origin of national loyalty, it could not explain it *away*. The reality of the thing that has to be explained is the primary reality and more 'real' than the explanation. Hence the phenomenon effective in history, and the loyalty predominant in social life, is the nationalism of the working man — then and now.

But I am not deeply concerned, for the moment, with this subsidiary point. It is the broader thesis, the view that all historical change is due to group struggle, whether economic or national, that I wish to consider. Is the 'group struggle' theory of history valid?

I hardly think so. We saw that the Marxist theory arose from a line of thought parallel to Darwin's theory of Natural Selection, offered as an explanation of the origin of biological species, applied to the affairs of human society. It is supposed that, in the same way as new species arose, survived and multiplied in a struggle for exist-ence with other species, so economic classes arose and fought with each other. Biological evolution could be regarded as the record of such strife and the victories in it. Human history also could be regarded as a record of the victories in the class struggle. The dynamic power lies in the fighting. Change arises from victory.

Now, apart from the difficulty of accepting any theory of natural selection as a complete theory of the origin of species, there is a particular and certain fallacy in applying it to the life and history of human society. The fallacy lies in confusing a theory explaining the origin of a biological species with the explanation of the life of a social species after it has come into existence. Man, as a biological species, may have arisen by one law, and yet live by another. Indeed he may live by repudiating within the species the very principle by which the species came to exist.

Let me make this simple paradox clear. Man is a social animal. It may be the case, indeed it very probably is the case, that his sociability combined with his intelligence is the chief source of his survival value. Man, as an animal, is not a very impressive kind of animal — at least when he is compared with other mammals. His power of survival, on a basis of solitariness or even family isolation, is markedly inferior to that of a score of other animals. Yet he bestrides the animal creation and conquers the world. Why? Plainly because of the combination in him of a greater degree of intelligence and a greater power of co-operation with the other members of his species than any other mammal possesses.[1] Hence arising as he has done by a process of struggle with other species, man has survived and outstripped all his mammalian rivals by repudiating the law of struggle within his own kind and basing his life upon the principle of co-operation.

Of course much of his pre-human origin remains. Competition and struggle, hatred and cruelty, are still a recurrent theme, a never silent discord in the orchestration of human life. But if there is a principle of living more fundamental than another, or a form of behaviour more characteristic than another, of the human species—and therefore of history—it is the principle and practice of co-operation, and not that of destructive, or even creative, struggle. We have survived by the principle of society. We have conquered by the practice of community.

The point for which I am contending can be put in another and yet more obvious way. It is certain that struggle is an immensely important kind of behaviour in history. History would have been

[1] Intellectual intelligence and the power of co-operation act and react upon one another. Intellectual development is not only conditioned, but is largely created, by social life, and the intensity and complexity of our social relations is only made possible through the intellectual powers of *homo sapiens*.

utterly different without warfare. The political life of democracies is carried on by struggles of a peaceful type. Even between individuals, relations of a competitive and even combative character are common and important. All this has been stressed in the first Part of this book. But any interpretation of history, or theory, of society, that concentrates upon this phenomenon alone is worse than partial. It is blind. The part played by the habit of co-operation is obviously of equal or greater importance. We all live by co-operation — working together in peace. We get up in the morning and begin our day in the co-operative unit of the family. We leave it to work in a commercial or industrial concern, whose very existence consists in a complex pattern of intellectual and emotional co-operation between persons and groups of differing economic interest. We pass from it in the evening to play tennis or sing in a glee club — playing together with our fellow human beings in peace. On Sunday we attend a church, or the meeting of a political party — freely co-operating societies. And all these activities are conducted within a framework of social institutions that is, at least, partly voluntary and largely co-operative.

The economic life of an advanced society is peculiarly the sphere of the most complex and successful kinds of co-operation. Consider the organization of a modern large-scale enterprise. In it, shareholders, directors, managers and clerical workers, and thousands of workmen, must and do come together peacefully day by day, in order to operate a detailed pattern of activities, to arrange a vast number of rules to guide their connected activities, and subsequently to divide the fruit of their labours. There are, of course, recurrent break-downs, and much latent resentment of injustice in some of the groups concerned. Nevertheless they normally co-operate continuously, despite the conflicts between their group interests, without the immediate intervention of a single policeman, or the presence, except in the background, of any coercive authority. Could co-operation go further?

All this is peculiarly obvious. But what is not so obvious and yet of great importance for any theory of history, is the fact that changes and discoveries in the field of co-operation can be just as powerful as changes and discoveries in the field of struggle. The pattern of human co-operation is not a fixed and static thing.

New forms of co-operation are discovered. Old forms pass away.

These changes in the technique of co-operation are fundamental to the understanding of economic and political history. We have already seen examples of this fact in the development of capitalism. A collective bargain is an important form of co-operation. It is an arrangement whereby two groups of conflicting economic interests are enabled to work together for long periods in peace. Whether it is a good thing that such arrangements should be made is, no doubt, a matter open to question; but there can be no dispute that such arrangements are continuously made and observed; that the possibility of making them had to be discovered; and that a complex body of social traditions and emotional habits required to be built up before the structure of collective agreements could come into existence. As we have seen, the consequences of the growth of collective agreements are of the first order of importance. Without an understanding of them, the history of the labour market and of capitalism itself would be quite unintelligible. All these developments belong to the field of co-operation. A collective bargain is an instrument of co-operation, on the part of workers and employers amongst themselves, and between the workers and employers as separate parties to it. By it, a continuous state of struggle is avoided. It is, therefore clear that a development in the field of co-operation has been of radical importance in changing the course of economic history. Exactly the same thing is true of the discovery of the legal device of limited liability. By this legal invention the possibilities of co-operation between shareholders were greatly extended, and the number of persons brought into the field of co-operative investment was remarkably increased. The later historical development of capitalism has been profoundly influenced by this fact. There are still wider examples of the same principle. The discovery of the possibility of organizing and managing groups of workers in factories lies at the basis of the growth of all large-scale industry. The invention of exchange and specialization of economic function lies at the root of all post-primitive economic life. All these are discoveries in the field of co-operation. They are the foundation of all subsequent economic development.

It follows from this brief survey that changes in the field of co-operation are just as important for the understanding of history as events in the field of struggle. It is radically false, therefore, to suppose that the dynamic element in social life is solely that of warfare and struggle — especially that of class struggle and class warfare. Who is to say that changes in the powers of association among men are less important than changes in the technique of their conflicts? Indeed, to claim a fundamental character for either the one or the other type of interacting cause would be to fall into the same mistake as to the logic of multiple causation as we discussed at great length in the preceding Section of this Part.

We are therefore forced to abandon any exclusive 'Class War' interpretation of history.

The psychological analysis of the first Part of this book suggests two further points of interpretation arising out of the Class War theory of historical change:

1. It suggests that the true element in the theory lies in the certainty that group acquisitiveness, and the canalization of personal aggressiveness through group life, and particularly through group acquisitiveness, is a frequent source of conflict and change in history. The reality of group acquisitiveness or group conflict arising from it, and the central importance of this pheno-menon to the understanding of group history is denied by no one. As in the case of the economic interpretation of history, it is not the reality of the factors that is in dispute, but the unique importance attached to them. It is not the emphasis upon rational acquisitive-ness and internal group conflict that is at fault, but the neglect of other forces, the neglect of multiplicity in the effective causes of human behaviour; and in this particular case the patent neglect of co-operative relations and community of interest among men.

2. The second interpretation that psychological investigation would suggest is the equally obvious reflection that the balance of these forces is extremely likely to vary from group to group, and from nation to nation. Upon psychological grounds alone it is in the highest degree unlikely that the tradition of emotional educa-tion should be identical for all nations and all classes. It is, there-fore, almost inconceivable that the balance of emotions should be the same in all societies. The balance between love and hatred, the strength of the opposing wills to co-operate and to fight, are likely to be widely different as between one race and another, one

nation and another, one class and another; according to difference
in their history, their educational systems, their law and thei
philosophy. It would therefore accord with psychological ex
pectation that the history of nations with respect to interna
conflict should be very different. It is to be expected that civi
war and violence should be much more common in the history o
some peoples than in the history of others. It is to be expectec
that one nation could resolve a particular conflict of group
interest within itself, without the use of force, that would provoke
another nation to open civil war. It is obvious, as we shall see
that the historical evidence fits this expectation much more
closely than any other.

Finally, it may be worth while to say a word about the emotiona
character of those persons who hold blindly to the doctrine o
class struggle and a gospel of class hatred. It is, of course, no argu
ment to call one's intellectual opponent a cad. And yet it is necess
ary to remember, as I said at the beginning of this Part, that th
full significance of a doctrine can rarely be understood, until the
emotion that it justifies has been described. Let us apply this tes
to the theory which we are examining. What emotion is justifiec
by the doctrine that all historical change arises from class struggle
and that all desirable development in the future can only be
achieved through the destruction of a class enemy? The answer is
obvious. It justifies hatred and aggressiveness on the part of those
who hold such views towards their political opponents. This sug
gestion does not, let me repeat, prove that the 'class struggle
theory of history is wrong. But the reflection does suggest tha
those who concentrate blindly upon the existence of this pheno
menon, who deny hysterically the possibility of co-operation anc
good will among persons and groups of conflicting economic
interests, are conditioned to do so by the necessities of their
emotional life and by an overpowering desire to find a scapegoat
upon which to lay their own aggression. Fanatics, extremists and
persecutors of all ages are such as these — men of blood and men
of hate. Their underlying desire for suffering is not hidden by a
pair of spectacles or a high-pitched voice. Like the political thug
of Fascism or the criminal gangster, they edge the affairs of men
towards blood and elect themselves to be the enemies of social peace.

C. *The Inevitability of Civil War*

At the beginning of my analysis of the Marxist thesis I argued that the four fundamental principles in it are all separate propositions, and that they do not follow necessarily from each other. This earlier argument must guide us now. It must follow, if the propositions do not stand together, that they do not fall together. Hence to throw doubt upon the materialist interpretation of history or the class struggle theory of social change only weakens Marxism as a system of thought, and leaves the two more specific political theses, as yet, untouched.

Now it is in the political theses that I am particularly interested — that civil war is inevitable, and that a dictatorship of the proletariat can secure social justice.

Let us for the moment consider the first of them — that 'no class has given up nor will give up power without civil strife' — and by 'civil strife' is meant not merely political opposition of a peaceful kind, but the attempt to use force. It is important to be clear about this point. No one, of course, denies that the attempt to dispossess any vested interest will meet with determined opposition. This incontrovertible assumption is not, however, what the Marxists have in mind. As we have seen, they argue that no class can be dispossessed of political power and economic privilege without a resort to *force* — a development that is, they think, incompatible with the maintenance of democracy.[1]

This is a purely empirical issue. It can only be supported or refuted by historical evidence. I wish to suggest that the generalization is not borne out by our own recent political history.

Let us then consider the historical evidence. I must repeat that I am no historian. I have no new evidence to offer, and possess no more knowledge of English history than the average student of the social sciences. It may well be asked, then, by what right dare I trespass into the field of historical interpretation? My only defence is that the Marxists, although not Marx, trespass there also. That is to say, Marxist and Communist literature is full of new interpretations of familiar historical facts. The literature of Marxist history is far more occupied with new interpretation and with synthesis than with new research. They do not

[1] See footnote on p. 166.

seek to prove what they have to say by the discovery of new evidence. They ask us to look at perfectly familiar things in a new light. And it is entirely appropriate that they should do so. Many of the revolutionary advances in science have consisted in little else. Newton did not discover the fact that apples fall to the ground, or that the stars and planets move in the paths that they do — he simply applied a new hypothesis consistently to them. In the same way Darwin did not himself invent the classification of plants and animals according to their hereditary species. That work had been largely done by others before him. He suggested a consistent interpretation of the origin and relationships of species in that classification. Marx and his followers are, therefore, perfectly within their scientific rights when they begin by applying the simple hypothesis that he invented to the whole range of our historical knowledge without, in the first instance, seeking for new evidence. Exactly the same thing will have to be done in the next few years with the revolutionary hypotheses suggested by Freud, the social implications of which we are only on the very edge of exploring.

The fact remains, however, that much of Marxist history is simply a re-interpretation of familiar history, and it is with the interpretation that I am chiefly concerned. I wish to suggest that the facts — facts that are not in dispute — support a non-Marxist interpretation just as well as, and in my view better than, they do the Marxist interpretation of them.

In my view our own more recent history shakes to the foundation the doctrine that social classes cannot rise and fall, that privileged groups cannot be dispossessed of power, without an appeal to force. The history of the Reform Bill agitation, the broadening of the franchise in the nineteenth century, and finally the pre-war Irish struggle, all seem to me to point to this conclusion, rather than to any other. Let me take these examples in turn:

1. *The destruction of the power of the landed aristocracy and the Reform Bill struggle of the* 1830's. There can be no question, particularly from the Marxist point of view, that, somewhere between the fifteenth century and the nineteenth, a transfer of power took place between the medieval landed aristocracy on the one

hand, and the capitalist bourgeoisie on the other. At one end of the story is a relatively simple peasant economy, at the other an advanced capitalism. At the beginning of the period agriculture is dominant, at the end industry. Here, if anywhere, there is a change of class structure. Here, if anywhere, there is a transfer of power from one class to another — an example of class struggle to which the historical thesis of the Communists should directly apply.

This is what Marx himself said:

> *The bourgeoisie, historically, has played a most revolutionary part. The bourgeoisie,* wherever it has got the upper hand, *has put an end to all feudal, patriarchal, idyllic relations.* It has pitilessly torn asunder the motley feudal ties that bound man to his 'natural superiors', and has left no other nexus between man and man than naked self-interest, than callous 'cash nexus'. . . .

Resistance to such a class, rising to revolutionary power, must surely be as severe as any resistance can well be.

Now the period that is given by non-Marxist historians for the final and decisive stage of this class struggle is the Reform Bill agitation, culminating in the Act of 1832. It seems obvious to a non-Marxist that up to that time the political power of the landed interest had not been broken, and that the fate of agriculture as an industry, and as the basis of a political class, was decided then. Only a reformed House of Commons could have agreed to the Repeal of the Corn Laws twelve years later, and it was the Repeal that finally, though not immediately, sealed the doom of arable farming as a major foundation of our economy. In so far, therefore, as there has been a decisive transfer of power between one economic class and another in this country during recent times it occurred as a result of the successful struggle of the capitalist bourgeoisie for representation in Parliament.

It is also of the greatest interest to notice that, contrary to Marxist doctrine on this point, the issue at stake was interpreted in this sense by the opponents of the Reform Bill at the time. Marxists are inclined to suggest that the struggle over the Bill was a subsidiary and unimportant engagement between two sections of the governing class. That is not what the opponents of the Bill thought or felt. To typical representatives of the Tory opposition it appeared to be, what in the light of a larger historical perspective we now know it to have been, the end of one era and the beginning of a new one. It is true that they anticipated a more rapid and violent transition after the passage of the Bill than in fact occurred, but the degree of their opposition was determined by what they thought at the time, and not by what happened afterwards. The landed aristocracy thought the Bill a revolutionary measure, and they believed that their class privileges were put in danger by it. This is what the Duke of Wellington thought of the Reform Bill Government:

> *The gentlemen now in power* [the Whigs] *are committed to revolution* by the applause with which, as private persons, they greeted those in Paris and Brussels.

In 1831, after he had seen the Reform Bill, he said that the measure would 'by due course of law destroy the country' and that its provisions would *'give a . . . shake . . . to the property of every individual in the country'*, and in the Lords he said that Reform was synonymous with democracy — 'this fierce democracy, and . . . that *democracy involved an immediate onslaught on property'*.[1]

Wellington had betrayed the real grounds of his fears in an earlier speech in the House of Lords in which he had himself refused to introduce any measure of reform by saying:

> The representation of the people at present contains a large body of the property of the country, *and in which the landed interest has a preponderating influence*. Under these circumstances I am not prepared to bring forward any measure of the description alluded to by the noble lord.

These fears were shared by Tories of more moderate judgment than the elderly Duke. The same view was the considered opinion of John Wilson Croker, the editor of the *Political Quarterly* and a Tory M.P. He thought the Reform Bill would *'drag the country into the horrors of revolution'* and would lead 'to a vast subversion brought about by a succession of events, each encroaching on the monarchy, till at last all authority and therefore all security of persons *and property* will be lost'. In a letter to Sir Walter Scott he wrote:

---

[1] GUEDALLA: *Life of Wellington.*

I say nothing about the Revolutionary Reform, but I think of nothing else ... No king, no Lords, *no inequalities in the social system: all will be levelled to the place of petty shopkeepers and small farmers; this, perhaps, not without bloodshed, but certainly by confiscations and persecutions.*

The statement of the class issue is absolutely plain and emphatic. And these feelings continued to grow to the end of the battle. Lord Winchilsea said in the last debate that 'he suffered a pain of mind greater than he could express in thinking he had lived to that hour to witness the downfall of his country. *That night would close the first act of the fatal and bloody tragedy*'. Croker wrote to a friend at the same time:

> *Depend upon it, our revolution is a sure and not slow process;* and every legitimate government in Europe will feel its effects. *We have been for half-a-century the ark which preserved in the great democratic deluge the principles of social order and monarchical government. We are now become a fire-ship which will spread the conflagration.*

Quotations of this kind could be extended indefinitely. They show two things, first that the opponents of the Bill were still a self-conscious landed aristocracy; second, that their leaders really thought the end of their power, as a class, was at hand. It does not matter that they were wrong in their estimate of the time that the process of destruction would take. The degree of their resistance was determined, not by the nature of future events, but by their judgment of what the future would be like. There is strong evidence that they believed the future would mean, for them, a destruction of class privilege and class power. It was therefore, for them, a revolutionary situation of the Marxist type.

And of course revolution and civil war did nearly come. Bands were arming in the counties. It is the considered judgment of historians that, had the Bill not passed, civil war would have broken out. But the vital fact remains that the Bill was passed and that war did not break out. It is a critical fact that the Marxists cannot explain away. The landed interest, when faced by a crisis in which they felt their power and privilege to be at stake, *did not fight*. They accepted their fate, and the Bill became law. They did this, I suggest, not because they believed it to be safe to do so; but

DICTATORSHIP OF THE PROLETARIAT

either because a sufficient minority of them foresaw that the process of liquidation would be long and gradual, or because a substantial majority of them feared the alternative — civil war — more. Whatever the reason, the fact remains that here is a case where the final transfer of power from an older privileged class to a rising revolutionary group — in this case the capitalist bourgeoisie — was carried to a successful conclusion without the use of violence. This example shakes to the foundations the doctrine that the dispossession of a class, and the transfer of power from one class to another, *must* be accompanied by civil war.[1]

---

[1] 1. Marxist historians make some sort of reply to this obvious argument. Since they cannot deny that the Reform Bill struggle looked like a revolutionary situation and yet it did not eventuate in a civil war, they are forced to contend that it was not really a class struggle at all. The obvious line of defence is for them to argue that the Civil War of the seventeenth century was the period of real battle between the capitalist bourgeoisie and the landed aristocracy. This they do. MORTON in *A People's History of England*, for example, writes thus, trying to explain away the apparent religious character of the Civil War:

> Perhaps it was largely the absence of theory and of clear objectives which cast the political movement and thought of the seventeenth century so often into religious moulds.
> In spite of all that has been said to the contrary, it cannot be too strongly insisted upon that the civil war *was* a class struggle, *was* revolutionary, *was* progressive (p. 222).

It was then a class struggle – between the older, landed aristocracy on the one hand, and the bourgeoisie on the other.

> It was a struggle between the more advanced classes and areas, using Parliament as their instrument, and the most conservative, gathered round the crown (p. 222).

The Puritan party consisted of the Presbyterians, *the party of the upper middle class*, and of the

> Independents, the left wing drawn mainly from the yeoman farmers and the tradesmen and artisans of the country towns. They were the most democratic and revolutionary section. . . . (p. 230).

When the revolutionary struggle of the bourgeoisie has been identified with the Civil War of the seventeenth century, it is possible to explain away the conflict over the Reform Bill as non-revolutionary in character. It is commonly treated in this way by Marxists.

Now this is a plausible line of defence at first sight, but it will not stand a careful examination. It is based upon a notable confusion of thought. Let us consider it carefully. At some time between the fifteenth and the nineteenth centuries the decisive battle between the bourgeoisie and the landed aristocracy must have been fought. When was that battle? If it is contended that it was fought out in the Civil War, then the capitalist bourgeoisie must have emerged victorious from that war, since they were the victors at the end of the period. *But this is certainly not the case.* The immediate victory of the landed aristocracy in the seventeenth century, and their political dominance of the eighteenth century is admitted by everyone. Morton himself admits it:

2. *The Broadening of the Franchise.* It was only a very narrow circle of the bourgeoisie which was enfranchised by the Reform Act of 1832. Less than half a million of its richer members

> The urban middle class had proved too weak by themselves to afford a permanent basis for government (i.e. they were defeated) in the seventeenth century struggle, and the Restoration of 1660 was in effect a recombination of class forces more in harmony with the real distribution of strength . . . The character of the Restoration is most clearly shown in the land settlement that followed it. *The Church and Crown lands that had been confiscated during the Commonwealth were restored . . . By this action Marx says they 'vindicated for themselves the rights of modern private property in estates to which they had only a feudal title. . . .'*

Thus the essential point is that, in so far as the struggle was a class struggle, the capitalist bourgeoisie were *defeated* in the *Civil War* and the landed aristocracy emerged triumphant. Does anyone deny their class power in the eighteenth century? It was the Golden Age of the aristocratic landowner. Wellington is confident in 1830 that the 'landed interest' still holds the 'preponderating influence' in Parliament. The Civil War may or may not have been chiefly a class struggle, but it certainly ended in the victory of the landed interest.

Yet they were finally defeated. Again no one denies their ultimate loss of power as a class. When did that crucial event occur? It could only have occurred in the Reform Bill struggle of 1831 and 1832, if it had not taken place in the Civil War. That was the real end of their power, and Wellington and Croker knew it. So did Engels – for this is what he says summing up the struggle of 1832:

> *The Reform Bill of* 1832 *had been the victory of the whole capitalist class over the landed aristocracy,*

and again he says:

> *The Reform Bill had legally sanctioned the distinction between bourgeoisie and proletariat, and made the bourgeoisie the ruling classes.*

In this matter at least Engels's judgment seems clear and final.

There is then a certain confusion in the Marxist interpretation of English constitutional history. Let me briefly summarize it. They hold that transfers of power from class to class cannot take place without a civil war; this they must hold if their theory of political strategy is to stand. They further hold that one such transfer has been made, namely, that from the landed aristocracy to the capitalist bourgeoisie. When was that transfer made? There are two candidates for the honour of being the decisive event – the Civil War of the seventeenth century, and the peaceful struggle over the Reform Bill in the nineteenth. But this choice creates a dilemma for the orthodox Marxist. If he chooses the Civil War, then he must go on to maintain, if there is logic in him, that the landed interest was defeated then, since it was defeated at some time. This, as we have seen, no one can admit, since the evidence of the victory of the landed interest in the Civil War and of the domination of that interest in the eighteenth century is overwhelmingly strong and is admitted by Marxists. There is no consistent alternative except the view that the landed interest was victorious in the seventeenth century, and was finally defeated in the Reform struggle of the nineteenth. They were therefore ultimately beaten without civil strife. The power of the bourgeoisie won by violence in the Civil War was only a temporary success. The peaceful victory was the more stable, and there may well be a lesson for the proletariat here.

It is interesting to note that the Reform Movement was led by a group of landed aristocrats – 'traitors to their class'. This is a good example of the complexity of loyalties to be found in the real world.

197

were placed upon the electors' role. It was a decisive victory in the class struggle between landed aristocrat and capitalist entrepreneur, but it did not carry with it any considerable extension in the political power of the proletariat.

In the ninety years that followed — from 1832 to 1928 — the franchise was continuously extended, until it embraced the whole of the adult population. Only once during that period was there any violence or threat of violence — during the peak of the Chartist agitation in 1849 — arising out of this transfer of political power away from the upper bourgeoisie. There was, as we shall see, a most serious danger of civil strife, at least once subsequently — the Ulster Crisis of 1914 — but that did not arise from an electoral or class issue. Yet, as a result of these great extensions, the franchise came to include the whole of the proletariat. There was, in short, a transfer of legal political power to them without the loss of a single life (as far as I am aware), and certainly without any large-scale civil war. The successive Acts, by which this process was carried through, were, of course, the subject of prolonged political controversy and sustained party opposition. They were not achieved without struggle, nor conceded without resistance. But they were achieved without revolution, and they were conceded without a resort to force. At no time did the groups who felt their interests to be adversely affected by the progressive enfranchisement of the workers try to prevent the process by reactionary revolution. They may have wanted to do so, but they did not risk the hazard.

I am, of course, aware that orthodox Marxists would deny that any transfer of real or ultimate political power was involved in the broadening of the franchise. Marx's own description of the process is this: 'The population, every few years, is given an opportunity to decide which member of the ruling class is to represent them in Parliament.' It is implied by him that this choice is of no real significance. We shall discuss the justice of this verdict upon political democracy in the next Part of the book.

In any case, it is obviously no longer true that the persons chosen are necessarily of a class different from those who choose. Proletarian Members of Parliament are familiar enough by now, and the Marxist attack upon representative democracy must therefore be

ased upon different grounds. Marxists are not, however, at any
oss to find them.

The substance in the Marxist's refusal to accept this suggested
efutation of his position lies in the undoubted fact that the struggle
or the franchise was not associated with a direct or resolute
ttack upon social inequality. As we saw in the last Part, security,
ot equality, has been the foremost concern of the British proletar-
at.[1] It is in this sphere that the British people have been successful
n controlling institutional change in their own interest. Through-
ut the greater part of the struggle for electoral power, therefore,
he economic privileges of the bourgeoisie were not in question. It
nay well be that the history of our social peace would have been
ery different if they had.

It takes, however, a very fanatical Marxist to contend seriously
hat there has been *no* growth in the political power of the prole-
ariat in the last hundred years.

In that period, not only has the franchise been extended to
nclude the whole of the proletariat, but the economic, cultural
nd political status of the working class has been transformed. In
hat period, trade unions have grown to their present strength; a
ystem of national education has opened the flood gates of know-
edge; the standard of consumption has been nearly quadrupled;
ours have been shortened; unemployment insurance and health
ervices have been created; cultural and recreational activities and
ssociations of all kinds have sprung into active life. Is it really
ossible to contend that the oppressed and embittered working-
lass of a hundred years ago—freshly immigrant from the country-
ide, herded into insanitary hovels, riddled and weakened with
lisease, working ten or twelve hours a day, eating meat once a
veek, their minds darkened by ignorance and horrible superstition
levoid of trade unions, unemployment pay and the vote — was
eally comparable in political intelligence, unity and power with
he working class of to-day? It seems absurd to suppose so. How-
ver much we may lament the evils of the present time, the differ-
nce between the political character of the British working-class
o-day and that of the same class a hundred years ago is the differ-
nce between a horde of dispossessed and ignorant peasantry on

[1] As it is now becoming that of the American proletariat.

the one hand, and a lively and intelligent proletariat on the other
For purposes of political struggle, it is the difference between a
rabble and an army. And this great increase in wealth, this trans
formation of social status, this growth of political power consequen
upon other improvements have all been achieved and consolidate
without the use of force. That is the impressive thing. Two grea
changes in the balance of political power in this country have, as
see it, been carried through without the outbreak of civil war.

Now I am perfectly aware that neither of these two changes i
the particular alteration that the Marxists have in mind. The
are examples of the bourgeoisie wresting political power from, an
destroying the economic privilege of, the landed aristocracy in th
first case, and the conquest of *constitutional power* by the proletaria
in the second. There is, in these cases, no example of the proletaria
destroying the *economic privilege* of the bourgeoisie. We shall con
sider this question in the last Part of this volume.

But what has been done by this short survey of our constitutiona
development is, I believe, to shake to its foundations the doctrin
that the transfer of power from class to class, or the slow destruc
tion of the economic privileges of a class, must necessarily forc
every society, whatever its political tradition, into violence an
savagery.

3   *The Ulster Crisis of 1912-14.* We shall find this same conclusion
reinforced when we consider the attempt at political change tha
did bring us to the verge of civil war.

So far we have considered struggles that were resolved, an
changes that were made, without the use of force. But, just befor
the last war, a political battle was allowed to reach the point a
which a peaceful solution had become impossible. It is probabl
that civil war would have been avoided at the last moment by the
Liberal Government conceding the permanent exclusion of Ulste
from the operation of the Home Rule Bill.[1] But they would have
done this precisely because the only alternative had become war,
and for this they were not prepared. Change compatible with the

---

[1] 'What the Government (i.e. the Liberal Government) now proposed was, as
Asquith told the King, to proceed with county option, 'but with the *omission of
automatic inclusion after a term of years* and the *substitution of a fresh power of option*
as suggested by Sir Edward Carson at the Conference'. SPENDER and ASQUITH:
Life of Lord Oxford and Asquith, vol. II, p. 55.

maintenance of democratic government had become impossible. To maintain social peace the will of Parliament had to be set aside.

In the summer of 1914 the political situation was revolutionary. Two illegal armies were organized in Ireland. The British Government could not depend upon the British army.[1] The leaders of the opposition were in secret consultation with the servants of the Government and with the Director of Military Operations. Responsible [sic] Conservative politicians were making speeches in Ulster that were indistinguishable from sedition. The social peace of these islands, preserved since 1745, was more seriously in danger than it had been at any time since then, with the possible exception of the last few weeks of the struggle for the Reform Bill. *A change had been proposed by a British Government and carried through Parliament that could not be implemented without civil war.*

Now it is of vital interest for our present purpose to discover what kind of change it was that threatened our deep-seated democratic traditions. Here we must be careful, for there are *three* struggles entangled together in the events of these critical years, and they are of very different social significance. First, there is the ancient struggle of what is now Southern Ireland against the imperial dominion of the British nation. That was an ordinary, though tragic, example of a struggle for racial and national freedom. It can be paralleled all over Europe in the last three hundred years, and it is not in the least surprising that it should lead ultimately to war. It contains nothing of deep significance for us. Nor does the struggle between the South and the North within Ireland itself. Whatever the rights and the wrongs of the case, the difference of descent, the difference of religion, and the difference

---

[1] It is sometimes loosely said by Marxists (e.g. LENIN: *On Britain*, p. 57) that the British officers refused to execute the will of Parliament and of the Government. This is a travesty of what happened during the Curragh episode. All that the officers did was to accept one alternative of a choice that ought never to have been offered to them – i.e. the alternative of resigning their commissions, because of their political opinions, while on active service. Some mystery surrounds the exact circumstances in which this alternative came to be offered to them (see SPENDER and ASQUITH, vol. II, Chap. xxxi) but it clearly should never have been presented to Army officers at all. It therefore remains impossible to say whether they would have refused to carry out their orders, and have become guilty of treason, if this opportunity of resignation had not suddenly appeared. Nevertheless the fact remains that after the Curragh incident the Liberal Government was not in a position to coerce Ulster by moving the Army.

of economic structure, make it intelligible that Ulster should have
been willing to fight in order to preserve what she believed to be
her cultural existence, and natural too, that the Irish people
should so interpret their national unity that, standing upon the
principle of Lincoln, they would not allow the sovereignty of the
area to be divided without resistance. These conflicts raise no
critical points for the Marxist thesis — since in each of them
economic interests were at stake. I do not for a moment concede
that economic forces are a sufficient explanation of wars of liberation; but it is not necessary to go over that ground again, as I have
already discussed the point at some length.

But there was a third, and far more paradoxical struggle lying
beyond, and embracing the other two. *This was the struggle between
the Liberal and Conservative Parties in Great Britain.* It was by the
terms of this struggle that the other two were conditioned. It was
the Party position in Great Britain that produced the Home Rule
Bill. It was the balance of forces in the House of Commons that
made the resistance of Ulster possible. It was the leadership of the
English Conservative Party that produced the revolutionary
situation in Great Britain and Ireland alike. There is even good
reason for supposing that the English Conservative Party was more
'loyalist' than Carson, more 'Ulster' than Ulstermen, more
royalist than the King. This is what Mr. Spender says:

> *Seen in retrospect, the Irish controversy of these years looks like the
> climax of the long struggle between British parties which began with
> the Liberal victory of* 1906, and all but brought Parliament to a
> deadlock in 1909 and 1911. Pent up feelings of resentment
> at the defeat of the House of Lords in 1911 led men of con-
> servative temperament to condone the 'direct action' of
> Ulster as a means of redressing the Constitutional balance
> which they supposed to have been fatally upset by the Parlia-
> ment Act, and to do so without much thought of the example
> they were setting. *There were times when Sir Edward Carson
> seemed much more willing to settle than the Unionist Party were to
> let him settle,* and narrow as the gap was which divided parties
> at the end of their negotiations, it is possible that no appeal to
> reason would have prevented serious disorders.[1]

[1] SPENDER and ASQUITH: *Life of Lord Oxford and Asquith*, vol. II, p. 56.

If this judgment is correct, and it seems impossible to dispute it, the conclusion is of critical interest for the assessment of the Marxist thesis. It is true that the whole episode shows the kind of unconstitutional resistance of which the Conservative Party in opposition is capable. But it is obvious that it was not a class or economic interest of their own that stirred them to dangerous revolt. It was a symbolic issue and an issue of group pride and of personal domination. *As between the Liberal Party and Conservative Party in Britain there was no class issue, no serious question of economic privilege, at stake.* The economic position of the British Conservatives was simply not involved. Ulster could have been defeated and incorporated in a united self-governing Ireland, without the loss of a single penny or a vestige of privilege by the Conservatives in Great Britain. Yet it was this issue — without economic content, devoid of class significance — that brought this country to the verge of war less than a generation ago.[1]

Let me make my point absolutely clear. The Marxists cannot have their cake and eat it too — in the field of historical interpretation. They cannot contend both that the distinction between the Liberal and the Conservative Parties was not a class distinction and also that all civil war must arise between contending economic classes. They certainly maintain the first proposition. We have seen what Marx thought of the choice presented to the proletariat in a Liberal and Conservative election — 'the opportunity to

[1] I do not wish to argue that the whole blame for the descent into the danger of civil war rests with the Conservatives in the three years before the war. It is almost certain that the most important cause of the trouble lay in the Parliamentary position of the Liberals. They depended upon the support of a minority Party, not responsible for governing, which was extremist on the main question in dispute. It is probable that, if the Liberals had drawn up their proposals without reference to the demands of the Irish Nationalists, they would have granted the exclusion of Ulster from the beginning. They became committed to a policy in whose justice they did not believe. At the same time, even this fact does not excuse the seditious and violent activities of the leading Conservatives. I feel sure that the explanation for this shameful chapter in the history of that great Party lies in their growing anger at the series of defeats - over the House of Lords, over the Budget, over Ireland - that they were suffering at the hands of their political rivals. This emotion, though natural, was wrong and profoundly dangerous to democracy.

It is no doubt reasonable to suppose - as Mr. Spender points out - that the struggle over Ireland was embittered by the previous battles over the Budget of 1909 and the reform of the House of Lords. These controversies involved both economic and political privilege. But these matters had been decided and the heritage of bitterness was irrational. There was no current economic dispute or question of privilege at stake.

decide which member of the ruling class is to represent them in Parliament'. This kind of judgment on the democratic politics of the nineteenth century is passed again and again by Marxists. There is plainly a measure of truth in it. The leadership of the two Parties was a varying mixture of aristocratical and bourgeois capitalists, and the electoral support of both Parties was derived simultaneously from all classes.

All this may be conceded, but the Marxists cannot therefore maintain — or cannot consistently maintain — the second proposition. They cannot hold that all political and civil strife is economic in origin or grounded in the maintenance of class privilege. It is impossible upon this basis to explain a revolutionary crisis between Parties not based upon class divisions.

This rapid and crude survey of three incidents in the political development of Great Britain in the last hundred years appears to me to bear out the expectations of the earlier psychological analysis. I do not wish for a moment to contend that these simple interpretations of history would be of any final significance if they stood by themselves. As a purely amateur historian I only venture to offer these reflections because they seem to me to be alternative interpretations to those offered by the Marxists — interpretations that are just as consistent with the undisputed historical facts, and much more consistent with the psychological evidence about the causes of aggressiveness. These three events in our history seem to me to confirm in a striking and convincing way two common-sense psychological conclusions:

(a) The use of force is not primarily or exclusively involved in disputes over economic ends or class privilege. Men's primary loyalties, and therefore the things for which they will fight, are not at all times and in all places directed towards their social class or their economic interests. Men will sometimes fight for these things, but they will not always fight for them, and they do not fight for them alone. Consider the three cases before us.

The land-owning class was not prepared to *fight* against — as distinct from angrily opposing — the Reform Bill of 1832; although it believed its future as a class was at stake.

The bourgeoisie did not resist by force the growing political power of the proletariat throughout the nineteenth century.

But the English Conservatives *were* prepared to fight over the largely symbolic issue — for them — of the colour of the flag that should fly over Ulster. No doubt they were chiefly animated by political *amour propre* and by hatred of the Liberals as persons and usurping governors, rather than by high political principle. But the fact remains that they were prepared to fight *members of their own class* — to become guilty of treachery to democracy, and of sedition — in a cause that touched their interests far less directly than the changes they had seen take place and against which they had attempted nothing more formidable than protests in Parliament.

The truth is, I need hardly repeat, that men are prepared to fight for many things — for their country, for religion, for mere symbols. And they are often not prepared to fight for any of these things — nor for their economic interests even if these are threatened. The 'class struggle' is not therefore peculiarly the sphere of violence.

(*b*) The other reflection that follows from any psychologically enlightened survey of history is the obvious thought that the same institutional changes that can only be carried through by force in one society, are peacefully consummated in another; and are often more permanent in the latter. The extension of the franchise that cost hardly a drop of blood in this country is secured by civil war in Germany, Austria and Russia. Norway achieves her freedom from the Swedish domination without a single battle. Ireland can only struggle to hers through rivers of blood. To the psychologically minded nothing could be more likely than that, with different men, there should be different manners and different measures. Laws of history exist — otherwise human beings possess no ordered and intelligible character — but they are not as simple or as mechanical as the 'laws' of economic interpretation and of the class war would lead us to suppose.

Historical evidence, then, shakes to the foundation the doctrine that there must necessarily be bloodshed in the process of destroying economic privilege or in the transition from capitalism to socialism. The main reason for the 'dictatorship of the proletariat' is, therefore, gone. Further reflection will show that not only is this dictatorship unnecessary, but that it is wellnigh inconceivable that it could attain the end in view.

D. *The Dictatorship of the Proletariat*

The dictatorship of the proletariat is not a necessary instrument in the creation of social justice. Is it a possible instrument?

Even if such a dictatorship were not necessary, it might still be the best or quickest or, at least, a possible method of creating just society. Is it, in fact, any of these things? I think the only certain proposition in all these dubious matters is the answer that it is none of these things — neither the best nor the quickest nor even a possible road to the socialist goal.

I must begin by saying a word about the meaning of the phrase 'the dictatorship of the proletariat'. Since the Russian Revolution, at least until quite recent years, the phrase was used without ambiguity. It was used to denote a political programme, indistinguishable from the political strategy and political method used in Russia. It consisted in three processes: first the revolutionary conquest of the organs of government by the Communist Party; secondly, the suppression of all opposition Parties, both bourgeois and proletarian in origin (the Mensheviks and the Liberals); and thirdly, a subsequent period of indefinite duration in which the Communist Party governs with all the apparatus of judicial terror and in which no opposition is allowed legal existence.

The 'dictatorship of the proletariat' so defined is composed of two separable things — the dictatorship of the proletariat over all other classes (including the peasantry in Russia, who accounted for 80 % of the population) and the dictatorship of the Communist Party ('the enlightened vanguard of the proletariat') over the proletariat.

Now this clear and definite — if somewhat horrible — meaning stands in sharp contrast to the extraordinarily vague and confused definitions that are offered to us by English Communists to-day. This is what Mr. Strachey says in explaining what he means by the phrase:

> Now these institutions [trade unions and works' councils], when they have developed into institutions of government, will constitute a democracy for the workers. But at the same time these institutions will constitute a workers' dictatorship over the capitalist class. *This is what we mean when we say that, in order to get rid of capitalism, it is necessary to establish a workers'*

dictatorship. In order to establish a socialist economic system it is necessary, that is to say, for the working class to assume exactly that political relationship to the capitalist class which the capitalist class now assumes to the working class. Within the working class there will be effective democracy, just as to-day there is effective democracy within the capitalist class. Over the capitalist class there will be dictatorship, just as to-day there is dictatorship over the working class.[1]

This is an extraordinary passage. It is difficult at first sight to believe that a Communist can have written it. It has become, in Mr. Strachey's hands, so bowdlerized a conception that it is difficult to see that it means anything at all.

Let us look for a moment at this definition in its application to his country. The setting up of a workers' dictatorship in Great Britain will mean — according to Mr. Strachey — that 'the working class in Great Britain will assume *exactly* that political relationship to the British capitalist class which the British capitalist class now assumes to the British working class.' What does that imply? It implies that, under Mr. Strachey's working-class dictatorship, there will be exactly the same kind of political framework as exists to-day — there will only be a change in class power within it. The 'political relationship'· of the British capitalist class to the British working class permits the working class to exist as a class, to have political parties and political newspapers, to be elected to representative bodies and to form governments. Under Mr. Strachey's 'dictatorship of the proletariat' exactly the same 'political relationship' is to remain. That either means nothing at all (a possible interpretation) or it means that, under the dictatorship of the proletariat, there will be bourgeois Parties, bourgeois newspapers, bourgeois Members of Parliament, and bourgeois governments if the bourgeois Parties obtain majorities in the continuous free elections. The only change will be that there will be a dominantly proletarian House of Lords, and that proletarian parties will have more motor cars at general elections than bourgeois Parties possess. It sounds incredible that Mr. Strachey should mean this, but what else can he conceivably mean?

Exactly the same extraordinary obscurity cloaks Mr. Strachey's

[1] STRACHEY: *The Theory and Practice of Socialism*, p. 154 [The italics are mine].

view of the future relations between the Communist Party and
other working-class parties — such as the Labour Party. Accord
ing to Mr. Strachey 'within the working class there will be effectiv
democracy *just as to-day there is effective democracy within the capitalis
class*'. Extraordinary! To-day 'democracy within the capitalis
class' implies Liberal and Conservative Parties, radical and die
hard groups, controversy, free speech and freedom of politica
association; with a strife between the parties that can carr
us, as we have just seen, to the verge of civil war. All these thing
are then to remain? There are to be a number of free lega
proletarian parties, of which the Communist will only be one
and these parties are to alternate in power and dispute with eacl
other up to the point of civil war? What has become of the 'en
lightened vanguard of the proletariat'? — of the sacred missior
of the Communist Party to liquidate all opposition to Left or Righ
of itself? Are the Trotskyists and the poor, miserable Social Demo
crats, like myself, to be reprieved from the concentration cam
and the shooting squad after all? It seems too good to be true.

Fortunately the position is quite simple. Either Mr. Strache
means what he says, in which case the Communist Party has wholl
abandoned its traditional position, has become bourgeois an
liberal in philosophy, and there need be no more controversy be
tween us — or he has been led by the current hatred of all dictator
ships in this country, so to bowdlerize and hide the true Communis
conception that pure confusion reigns, if not in his mind, at leas
in his writings.

In any case the point need delay us no further. Plenty of peopl
and most Communists, believe in the 'dictatorship of the prole
tariat' as originally defined, and as practised in Russia durin
the last twenty years. They believe in the concentration cam
and the firing squad. Having made plain the meaning of th
terms and the implications of the strategy, we can proceed t
discuss this kindly doctrine in its clear-minded form.

The 'dictatorship of the proletariat' then means the dictatorshi
or authoritarian government of the society by the proletariat; an
what is of far greater importance, the authoritarian government o
the proletariat by the Communist Party. About this principl
there are two points that I wish to make.

1. It is surely obvious that any attempt to connect the justification of the dictatorship of the Communist Party with the preceding theory of the 'class struggle' or 'class war' is due to a fundamental confusion of thought. There is absolutely nothing in the view that the great changes of history are due to the struggle of social classes that justifies the authoritarian government of the proletariat by one group within itself. Even if it is held that the class struggle must lead to civil war, that does not justify the dictatorship of the Communist Party within the working class.

Let me make this point plainly, because it is of vital importance in judging the real nature of the Communist argument. Let us suppose that the Communist is right up to this point. Let us concede for a moment that the only motive in human life is acquisitiveness, that acquisitiveness must always manifest itself in group struggle, that class conflict will always lead to civil war. It still does not follow that the Communist Party must rule alone. The only step that would be justified by the truth of the Communists' argument up to this point would be the *disfranchisement of the bourgeoisie*. Upon the Communist assumptions the bourgeoisie is an inveterate and implacable enemy of the working class, but the only possible enemy. It is the bourgeoisie alone who can threaten the safety of the workers' state. It must therefore follow that the only thing that need be done is to remove the members of the bourgeois class from the electoral roll — to destroy their political power as well as to curtail their economic privilege.

I am not for a moment contending that this is a right thing to do. I am only showing that this is all that can be justified by the Marxist theory of class struggle.

The only state that is justified by a theory of the class war is a proletarian democracy — not a dictatorship of the Communist Party. All the logical requirements of the class struggle will be satisfied if the political power of the bourgeoisie is broken, and *the workers are left to organize as many political Parties as they choose, and these Parties are allowed to contend for power and to alternate in office.*

It is mere nonsense to argue that, in theory, there will be no such multiplicity of Parties within one class. *There has always been such a multiplicity, and there still is.* Even Marxist theory cannot make historical reality other than it is. In Russia the Communist Party had to destroy two other working-class Parties in order to establish its dictatorship — the Mensheviks and the Social Revolutionaries In France to-day there are three working-class Parties — the Trotskyists, the Communists and the Socialists. In England there are three, the Communists, the I.L.P. and the Labour Party. And so one could go on. At no time and in no country has the working class thrown up only one political party. There is always a competition for the political leadership of the working class, a multiplicity of views as to what that class really wants, alternative interpretations of the proletarian will. Why should not these parties compete for power? Why should not the proletariat be allowed to choose between them, after the bourgeoisie has been defeated? Why should the working class not control its political destiny? Who has the right to say which of the possible Parties represents the will of the proletariat except the proletariat?[1]

There is no answer to these questions. There is no conceivable reason why the Communist Party should deny to the working class a choice between working-class Parties. If the class struggle were the basic reality in history, the liquidation of the bourgeoisie would be justified, but nothing else would be justified. The liquidation of other working-class Parties is a crime against the liberty of the working class. It is the substitution of authority for freedom. It is the beginning of a new tyranny — at best the substitution of one tyranny for another.

Yet it is for this theory that the Communist Party stands. It is this policy that the Communist Party executed in Russia. To justify their action they invented the theory that the Communist Party is the 'enlightened vanguard of the proletariat'. But, if it is that, if it represents the highest common factor in the will of the proletariat, if it crystallizes in thought and realizes in action the unconscious wishes and purposes of ordinary men and women, *why cannot it endure political freedom among the working class*? Why cannot it tolerate opposition and offer to the Menshevik, the

[1] Indeed, it is open to doubt to what extent the Communist Party is really a proletarian or 'working-class' party at all. Where it has mass support, as in China, it depends upon a peasantry, hungry for land. In countries like Great Britain, where it has no mass support, it appears to be largely middle class in leadership, membership and mentality. It is obvious that in this country the proletarian poll of the *Conservative* Party is far in excess of that received by the Communist Party.

Social Democrat and the Social Revolutionary the opportunity to
criticize and the opportunity to govern? If a party really leads a
class in the direction that it wishes to go, why cannot it allow that
class to follow freely? Why must it coerce and crush, and ruthlessly
exterminate, the slightest trace of opposition?

The only possible answer to these questions must be that the
Communist knows in his heart that he does not represent the
workers, that they do not wish to follow where he wishes to lead —
that he could not command a majority of the class that he claims
to represent, if opposition within it were free. Of course the
leadership of a Communist dictatorship claims that it could command such a majority. Doubtless a large proportion of the lower
ranks of the Party believe in that claim. But all dictatorships make
the same claim. The members of all dictating Parties believe
in it. To them all the same acid test can be applied. If they
honestly think that they command a majority of the nations that
they govern, let them act as though they did. Let them permit
opposition Parties to organize freely and contend legally for power.
If the Communist Party in Russia is right in its claim that it commands the enthusiastic support of the great majority of the nation
— peasants and town workers alike — then an agrarian Party in
the country-side and a democratic Party in the towns could not
defeat the regime in a free election. If the National Socialist
Party in Germany really commands the support of an overwhelming majority of the German people, the Social Democrats or the
Communists could not defeat them in a free and legal contest.
The democrat challenges these dictatorships to put their bold
claims to the test. Let the Communist Party empty its prisons,
proclaim a political amnesty, allow a Peasants' Party to organize
freely in the country-side and argue its case in the towns. Let the
National Socialist regime close its concentration camps, restore
freedom of political organization to the Catholics, the workers and
the democrats. If the claims these Parties make bear even the
remotest resemblance to the truth they will be easily triumphant
and powerfully vindicated.

*Neither the dictatorship of the Right, nor the dictatorship of the Left,
dare do these things.* They dare not do them, because they know that
their claims are false. They have good reason to doubt whether

their regimes would endure if freedom of organization were granted to the opposition. If this is not so, why do they not grant it? There is no point in suppressing opposition, nothing is gained by doing so, unless you are afraid of it. The National Government in Great Britain or the Roosevelt Administration in America could gain little or nothing from such a persecution — just because they command a stable majority in the countries that they govern. The only people who gain from the suppression of political opposition are those who cannot retain power without suppressing it.

And so, in order to justify the ruthless dictatorship of a minority group within the proletariat, the Communists have invented the suspicious doctrine that it — the Communist Party — is the 'enlightened vanguard' of the proletariat.

We have discussed the mental process of rationalization elsewhere, and we need not repeat that discussion here.

It is only necessary to ask two questions — what authority admits persons to this 'vanguard'? Who decides that it is 'enlightened'? The answer to both questions is, curiously enough the Communist Party itself. The Party is a self-recruiting oligarchy the Party permits no criticism except the criticism that it has itself authorized. Not long ago a detective story was published with the title 'I'll be Judge, I'll be Jury'. It might be the motto of the Communist Party. High upon the Kremlin, and over the door of every office of the Party throughout the world, should be inscribed in letters of red, this inscription: 'This Party is on trial; it has been charged by itself; it is defended by itself; and it will return the verdict by itself.' Such has been the motto of all authoritarian regimes in all ages. The historians of justice will pass them by.

For that is really all there is to the matter. The dictatorship of the Communist Party within the proletariat betrays the cloven hoof of arbitrary government. The inability to tolerate opposition is the acid test of social evil. The doctrine of the 'enlightened vanguard of the proletariat' is a sorry, threadbare cloak of intellectual rationalization. A dictatorial Party must come to represent nothing but itself, and a Communist dictatorship must become what all dictatorships become, the dictatorship of the Party machine and the slavish cringing before a ruthless bureaucrat.

2. It will be obvious from all that has gone before that I shall

o on to argue that it is wellnigh inconceivable that a dictatorship
f the Communist Party could create social justice. I believe this
onclusion to follow from psychological reasoning and to be borne
ut by historical evidence.

We have seen that a deep current of destructive aggressiveness,
ie result of many causes, runs through the life of most persons
nd finds expression in the behaviour of social groups. It is prob-
ble that, for all sorts of reasons, such aggression exists to a smaller
egree in traditional democracies than in societies that have long
upported or endured authoritarian regimes. We shall enumerate
nd discuss the reasons for thinking this in the next Part.[1] But
hether this is the case or not, it is obvious that in the life of
emocracies, the internal group aggression that undoubtedly exists
verywhere is, in some degree, held in check. In no case is it
llowed to control without limit the course of government.

Democracy depends, as we shall see, upon toleration, and the
ecessity for toleration sets a limit to the expression of aggression
1 action. Political opponents may make very aggressive speeches
gainst each other upon platforms and in legislative chambers.
hey may lie about each other and denigrate each other in every
ay that mental ingenuity can suggest. But, as long as democracy
ists, they do not persecute or destroy each other. Mr. MacDonald
id not imprison Mr. Baldwin (as he then was); Mr. Baldwin did
ot have Mr. Attlee shot. Mr. Chamberlain does not commit the
hole Front Opposition Bench to prison or have them exiled to
abour camps in the Outer Hebrides. Aggression is not absent, but
t is strictly limited in the modes of its expression. Hatred is not
holly transcended, but it is muted to an important, yet subsidiary,
iscord in the life of the nation.

How different the emotional complexion of a dictatorship. It is
orn in hatred and it feeds upon cruelty. A dictatorship — of
whatever colour — usually, though not always, comes into
xistence after a period of bitter struggle. In any case, it always
epresents the complete and unconditional triumph of one partici-
ant in a struggle. That is the horrible thing about it. There is
othing to check the expression of the aggression by the victorious
roup. In a democracy the governors will one day be the governed,

[1] See below, Part IV §3.

the holders of power to-day will be the subjects of their present subjects to-morrow. It ill behoves them to persecute. They must, for the sheer safety of their own skins, 'do unto others as they would be done by'. But, in a dictatorship, the governed are completely at the mercy of their masters; the opponents of yesterday lie broken and powerless at the feet of the victors; and there is no reckoning day, no court of appeal, that the victorious need fear. This is a degree of power that no man is good enough to possess.

The results are horrible beyond my power to express — the torture chambers of the German concentration camp, the solitary confinement and sleepless agony of the Lubyanka, the senseless humiliation of the Jew, the dreary monotony of the timber camp in Siberia, torture by senseless questioning, torture by beating, torture by the threat of execution, torture by the punishment of innocent friends and relations, torture by starvation. Thousands are shot without trial every year — two thousand names were published in the Moscow papers during 1937 alone. Hundreds of thousands are thrown into prison. Over everyone there hangs the restless fear of the spy, the dread of the secret police. Friendship is dangerous. Family life is poisoned. Suicide is wisdom. What limit is there to the cruelty, the savage senseless cruelty, of man to man?

But how can these things be brought to an end? There can be no end to them; or at least, it is extremely difficult to end them. Therein lies the hideous dilemma of a dictatorship. How can it ever restore political liberty, when this has been the method of its government? It has driven opposition underground; it has made it illegal; it has persecuted and tortured its opponents. The only kind of opposition that is possible in Communist Russia or National Socialist Germany is secret opposition, illegal opposition, terrorist opposition. It can be organized only by persons and groups made savage by persecution, by men and women who carry the marks of torture on their bodies, who have known their friends and relations shot down without trial, who have been ruined and broken and degraded by cruelty. To such persons terror is natural; it is all but justifiable. Their first action would be, if ever they obtained power, to give back what they had received — to lash and torture the floggers and the torturers, to shoot down judicial murderers, to break and liquidate the liquidators. These societies are locked in death grapple of group hatred. The National Socialists in Germany and the Communists in Russia are fighting for their lives. They are fighting successfully, because their regimes are strong; but they are, nevertheless, fighting for their lives. If they give ground, if they lose in this savage battle for the command of the state, they will pay the penalty with their lives. Their lives are forfeit because they have governed by death. They have drawn the sword; if their hands tremble or their eyes grow dim, they will go down to death themselves. They must persecute to live. There will always be liberty to-morrow but never to-day.

This may seem an extreme judgment. But how can the vicious circle of hatred and persecution be broken?

How can social justice arise from such beginnings or in societies so governed? The answer surely is that it cannot. The minimum content of the idea of social justice is the combination in one society of political liberty — whose nature we shall investigate more fully in the next Part of the book — with economic equality. Now it is conceivable that dictatorships of either Right or Left can achieve great things, particularly in the technical sphere. They may be able to construct ambitious road systems, or drain the Pontine marshes, or drive canals across a continent, or afforest the central Asian deserts, or build an immense fleet of bombing aeroplanes. Even in this field of physical production there is little reason to believe that they prove, in the long run, to be superior to the established democracies. Judged by results, the democracies have established the most efficient productive systems in the world — is no accident that the ancient and traditional democracies are also the richest nations on earth. Nevertheless, it is obvious that a vigorous and authoritarian government can carry through great and spectacular programmes, just because the arguments and interests in opposition to such schemes can be crushed and ignored. But the one thing they cannot do, without which all the other achievements may become dust and ashes in the mouths of ordinary men and women, is to establish emotional security or social justice. They cannot do these things because they govern by terror and not by law, by force and not by consent.

Whatever political liberty may or may not mean, it is certain that it cannot exist without freedom of opposition to the govern-

ment. Without that essential institution, there is no political choic
before the people, and therefore no political liberty in society. It i
conceivable, yet again, that a dictatorship of the Left might achiev
a greater equality in the distribution of wealth. But it canno
achieve justice, because it cannot give freedom to those who do nc
like equality, and dare not put to the test its claim that the grea
majority of the governed really want equality at all. It can onl
substitute one kind of inequality for another — one kind of in
justice for another. It can only substitute political inequality fo
economic inequality, ruthless political injustice for injustice in th
distribution of wealth. The history of political agitation in Russi.
does not suggest that the peasants — who number four-fifths of th
population — prefer the fire to the frying-pan.

§ 5

Conclusion

I have argued that the Marxist system of thought is based upoi
four propositions of an ascending degree of particularity — firs
that the governing motive in human life is that of acquisitiveness
secondly that acquisitiveness must manifest itself in the form o
group struggle in so far as it produces historical change; thirdl·
that this group struggle must break out into civil war during an
period in which power is transferred from one class to another; anc
fourthly that a dictatorship of the proletariat and of the Communis
Party over the proletariat can achieve social justice or Socialism.

I have found it impossible to accept any one of these four pro
positions in an unamended form. While it is possible to conced·
that acquisitiveness is an important and universal motive ii
human behaviour — animating us all, present in every group con
test, deeply influencing the whole course of history — it is no
possible to accept the view that it is a sole determining cause, ;
solitary source of change, or the final or fundamental cause ii
history. The pattern of social causes is more complex, and th
causes at work in it are of many kinds. Nor was it possible t·
accept the view that even where rational acquisitiveness is present

t must take the form of group contest. It is obvious that co-operation plays just as important a role in the economic life of society, and that changes and discoveries in the field of co-operation are every bit as significant in the determination of historical change as are movements in the technique of struggle.

But the most important doctrines for my purpose are the two political theses — that civil war is inevitable, and that social justice can be secured by the dictatorship of the Communist Party. Neither of these doctrines, however, seems to bear the light of psychological or historical evidence particularly well. It appears from the history of our own country alone that classes have been defeated without violence, and that we were brought within measurable distance of civil war in a struggle between two parties of the same class. And we have just seen that the method of government implied by a dictatorship, and the release of un-bridled aggression made possible by the circumstances of a dic-tatorship, render it almost inconceivable that a dictatorship of any kind could create social justice, or restore political liberty without a further revolution.

It would perhaps be as well to say at this point that I do not wish for a moment to decry the importance or value of Marxist thought to the social sciences. After Marx and Engels had com-pleted their life work, all further historical reflection and political theory has of necessity been 'post-Marxian'. They accomplished an intellectual revolution in the historical and social sciences upon which all who come after them must build. Their emphasis upon the importance of acquisitiveness in history — Mr. Cole's 'realistic interpretation' of history — their analysis of the mechanics of group struggle, their picture of society as a mechanism of institu-tions, are ideas that may change and develop, but can never wholly disappear. They are part of our contemporary understanding of what we are.

It is only static Marxianism that is blind, and whose political implications are wrong. All that Marx said, and Lenin said, must be amended, re-interpreted and set in proper perspective by the greater knowledge of social institutions that we have now accum-ulated, the further historical experience through which we have passed since they wrote, and, most important of all, by the extraordinary increase in our knowledge of psychological motive and emotional process. Marxism must, like every body of thought, change and grow if it is to live.

For the purpose of this book the most important conclusion that I have tried to establish is the last. I have tried to show why I so profoundly believe that we cannot proceed by the Communist road to a better social order. Strong and violent men have always believed that they could build a new heaven and a new earth, if only they were allowed to override and destroy those who disagreed with them. It is not so. The problem of social life is the problem of reconciling the conflicting ends of different persons and different groups. Justice cannot be achieved, much less happiness, by the mere crushing of one party to a conflict. Injustice remains, hatred remains, the drawn sword cannot be sheathed, the machine gun cannot be put away. Monotonously and horribly the victims will continue to tramp down to death, their shoulders bowed by suffering, their eyes glazed with hatred and fear. It is twenty years since the Communist Party obtained undisputed political power in Russia. Still the victims tramp down to death. There is no end to the suffering, the river of blood flows on. For those of us who live in quieter and happier lands, this is not the way. To those who really seek a better social order — and are not merely seeking in political action relief from the explosive violence of their own natures — I would say with assurance: *This is not the road!*

Is there any other and better way to walk in?

ADDENDUM TO PART III

ADDENDUM TO PART III

Do the Communists still believe in the Dictatorship of the Proletariat and the Dictatorship of the Communist Party?

It may be thought that the remarkable change in front towards 'bourgeois democracy' initiated by the Seventh World Congress of the Third International in 1935 represented a real change of heart. In 1935 the Communist Party appeared to alter its attitude towards Social Democratic Parties and even towards the democratic institutions of the Liberal State. Up to that time, they had attacked these Parties and institutions with ruthless verbal savagery. The democracy of liberal regimes was an 'illusion'; it consisted of nothing better than the 'veiled dictatorship of the bourgeoisie'; the Liberal State was simply 'a committee for the management of the common affairs of the bourgeoisie'. The condemnation of Social Democracy, or democratic socialism, was, if possible, even more severe. Labour and Socialist Parties were the 'real enemy', because they deceived and misled the revolutionary proletariat. They were 'compromisers', 'social Fascists', 'traitors and assassins'. And then, in 1935, the tune was changed.

It would seem that the Communist dictatorship in Russia and the Third International had found by 1935, after two years' experience of Hitler, that they were able to distinguish between bourgeois democracies and bourgeois dictatorships. Until then they had claimed that no such distinction existed. Having — very late in the day as far as Germany was concerned — recognized the difference, they ranged themselves on the side of the bourgeois democrats, and joined hands, or tried to join hands, with democratic parties in all countries to form a United or Popular (anti-Fascist) Front. Apart from a slight smell of hypocrisy — Satan is never at his most convincing when rebuking sin — the change was carried through with remarkable efficiency and discipline. In every country the faces of Communist orators and organizers — faces previously contorted with contempt at the sight of a Social Democrat — became wreathed with smiles; voices recently hoarse

with denunciation became curiously muted and smooth; invitin
the class enemy to co-operation and comradeship. It is true tha
here and there, the old wolf emitted a snarl or two from behind th
sheep-skin, but in general the atmosphere became markedl
different. The 'defence of Democracy' is now a frequent phrase upo
the lips of Communist intellectuals, and everywhere the advocate
of United Fronts, Popular Fronts and Democratic Fronts plead th
cause of political liberty and representative institutions with muc
of the same violence with which they used to denounce them.[1]

Indeed, we are now frequently told that the only message tha
the Communists wish to carry to the democratic working cla
masses is the warning that they may have to resist — if necessar
by force — unconstitutional opposition from the Right. That is no
controversial. It is nothing more than sound democratic doctrine.

Does all this represent a real change of heart? Is my lament ove
the undemocratic doctrine of Communism old-fashioned? D
they really regret the continued ferocities of the Russian regime
Are they honest converts to the religion of political liberty an
compromise, and to the respect for social peace?

I wish I could think that they were!

Russian Communists were certainly converted to a fear of Hitle
They are plainly afraid to fight a European war with the loyalty of
the peasants in doubt. It is even possible that Communists i
Britain feel some interest in preserving the distinction between
society in which their letters are occasionally steamed open by th
police, and one in which they would be beaten to pulp with rubbe
truncheons and steel rods. But it is difficult to credit them wit
more than a change in tactics. They would still prefer, above every
thing, a society in which the Communist Party was a dictatorship
and they were in a position to do the beating and the shooting
They possess a different political programme, but the same goa
a new strategy, but the same enemy — democracy; a new method
but the same end — the dictatorship of the Communist Party.[2]

Let me substantiate these charges.

This is what Dimitrov said in his official reply to the debate i

---

[1] This policy is presumably a little obscured and confused by the agreement of
Russia with Germany, the invasion of Poland, and the support of German aggressio
by economic aid.

[2] For an excellent account of this position see PALME DUTT, pp. 33 and 38.

the Executive Committee of the Third International, after his speech explaining the necessity for the change of front:

> Our attitude towards bourgeois democracy is not the same under all conditions. For instance, at the time of the October Revolution, the Russian Bolsheviks engaged in a life and death struggle against all political parties which opposed the establishment of the proletariat dictatorship under the slogan of the defence of bourgeois democracy.
>
> *The Bolsheviks fought these parties because the banner of bourgeois democracy had at that time become the standard around which all counter-revolutionary forces mobilized to challenge the victory of the proletariat. The situation is quite different in the capitalist countries at present. Now the Fascist counter-revolution is attacking bourgeois democracy in an effort to establish a most barbaric regime of exploitation and suppression of the toiling masses. Now the toiling masses in a number of capitalist countries are faced with the necessity of making a definite choice, and of making it to-day, not between proletarian dictatorship and bourgeois democracy, but between bourgeois democracy and Fascism.*[1]

This passage makes two things obvious — as indeed does the whole course of the debate:

(*a*) that the change in policy is wholly dictated by a fear of Fascism — a fear of dictatorship on the other side instead of on your own side — and not at all by a love of democracy *per se*.

(*b*) that the dictatorship of the proletariat is still preferred — wholeheartedly and fanatically — to democracy. There can be no question about that — for this is what everyone said in the course of the discussion, and Pigck stated the position categorically in his official report on the work of the Committee:

> *As long as we cannot replace bourgeois democracy by the dictatorship of the proletariat, the proletariat is interested in retaining every scrap of bourgeois democracy in order to use it to prepare the masses for the overthrow of the power of capitalism, and to achieve proletarian democracy.*[2]

There is, therefore, no change in heart. The Communist stands where he did on the crucial matter of political freedom — he still

---

[1] Executive Committee of the Communist International – *Report of the Seventh World Congress*, p. 116. This debate makes amusing reading now!
[2] Op. cit., p. 28.

wishes to set up the 'dictatorship of the proletariat' and a dictatorship of the Communist Party within the proletariat.

What, then, is the nature of the change that has taken place in
the Communist view of political strategy? It is surely a change
in the way that they think a 'proletarian dictatorship' (i.e. a dictatorship of their own party) can be achieved. They have ceased
to hope that they can make a successful *coup* by armed rebellion.
They have lost their faith in the revolutionary will of the proletariat.[1] But they believe that what cannot be obtained by frontal
attack may be obtained by a stratagem — that the man who cannot
be knocked down from in front can be stabbed from behind. They
now believe that the right strategy *for the creation of a Communist
dictatorship* is to be found in this programme of political action:
(*a*) to conquer political power during a peaceful democratic
election, (*b*) to pursue a policy that forces a revolutionary situation
to arise as a result of it, and then (*c*) to use the power of the State to
crush the 'counter revolutionary' opposition and to establish the
dictatorship of the Communist Party. In short, they propose to
destroy democracy by pretending in the first instance to accept its
obligations — and then to use the power conferred upon them as
democrats to destroy the system upon which political liberty
depends.

It is interesting to note that this is an almost exact copy of the
political strategy pursued by Hitler in the period of high crisis
in Germany during 1932 and 1933.

The same strategy was recently suggested in this country, in an
excellent and revealing little book by Mr. Raymond Postgate —
How to Make a Revolution — a book that is not sufficiently widely read.
Much that has come afterwards in Communist thought — not that
Mr. Postgate is a Communist — is contained in it. Mr. Postgate
set himself to answer this interesting historical question — how, in
fact, have revolutions been made? What strategies have been
successful? Which have failed? He analyses various historical
revolutions and attempted revolutions and he comes to the conclusion that in peace time there is, broadly speaking, only one
method that offers any reasonable prospect of success. He ends

[1] We noted the same increasing lack of faith in the revolutionary will of the
proletariat in Professor Laski's views.

his book by appealing to the British Labour Party to adopt this one strategy as its general political programme.

Let us examine what he says. He begins with a moving confession of his democratic faith:

> I care only for a fundamentally democratic and libertarian change ... Because of this I am a Socialist and a member of the Labour Party. To those who agree with me in these opinions I wish to offer certain deductions from this study: others will not be interested in them.

This sounds excellent. But it goes on rather surprisingly:

> With this preface, I would like to offer the following entirely tentative suggestions. I think we might well concentrate upon inducing Socialists to abandon some of the subjects which are generally discussed at conferences, and endeavour to secure a collective agreement and will to some ends like the following:
>
> 1. *That the next Labour Government shall hold on to office as firmly as Stalin's or Mussolini's — that it shall not quit until it has founded a Socialist State so firmly that an appeal to the electorate is quite safe. It should not be jumped into an election by any campaign, however ingenious.* Its job should be to 'make Socialism', *it should fight one election on that issue, and not leave office until it has completed that job.*
>
> 2. *It should control radio broadcasting and other forms of propaganda, including the Press.* The existing Press is corrupt, as it depends upon the will of advertisers. Once the chief revenue-paying industries are in State hands, the Press will give no more trouble; for its proprietors and editors are not men with passionate convictions about freedom of speech, they are servants of money or owners of it.
>
> 3. It should secure forthwith, by the necessary reforms, the genuine support of the ranks of the services, including the police, *and it should remove swiftly any technical constitutional obstructions, such as the House of Lords in Great Britain.*
>
> 4. It should be prepared to offer an immediate palliative to existing sufferings; for example, a scheme of work for a million and a quarter unemployed [*sic*].
>
> 5. In a country such as England, where foreign intrigue might lead to a threat of starvation, it should accumulate food-stocks and grain in granaries.[1]

---

[1] POSTGATE: *How to Make a Revolution*, pp. 187-188.

Mr. Postgate goes on to argue that this strategy needs a particular kind of leadership — the 'enlightened vanguard of the proletariat' is about to make its appearance again — and so it does, three pages later. Here we learn that what is needed is '. . . *a society of men such as the Bolsheviks were in 1917, who can take the lead and direct a revolution*'.

That is Mr. Postgate's programme — a revolution without the blood — a nice, quick, decent libertarian little revolution, with kindness to all.

About Mr. Postgate's proposal two things are to be noticed. *First*, the revolution comes *after* the democratic election has been won. This not only saves the trouble of organizing armed rebellion, and avoids all the danger that goes with it; but it also gets round the practical difficulty that the oppressed proletariats of stable democracies show an extraordinary and inexplicable unwillingness to revolt against their oppressors. But *secondly*, the programme is to be a revolution. There is to be no half-hearted 'reformism' or 'compromise'. All constitutional obstacles are to be swept aside; the whole face of society is to be changed, the 'eggs are to be scrambled so that they cannot be unscrambled'; and all the rest of it.

It is scarcely surprising that Mr. Postgate — who, it will be remembered, is a 'fundamental democrat' — should feel in his bones that changes of this character can be carried through only by a political system and method indistinguishable from that of dictatorship. The Press and all forms of propaganda are to be controlled; the Government is to remain in office until it has 'made Socialism' (a beautifully indeterminate period = the 'transitional period' of the orthodox Communist) whatever anyone else may think; and the party completing these changes is to be led by 'a society of men such as the Bolsheviks were in 1917'. To underline the democratic nature of his proposals, Mr. Postgate, with a remarkable lack of humour, recommends that the next Labour Government '*holds on to office as firmly as Stalin or Mussolini*'. That is a good beginning for a 'fundamental democrat'.

Mr. Postgate, having in many ways a shrewd political judgment, perfectly appreciates, as we have seen, that his revolution can only be carried out by a regime that is not responsible to the people.

He is not prepared to fight for his revolution. He does not like blood, and he knows from his previous historical inquiries that an attempted rebellion is not likely to be successful. But he wants his revolution all the same; so he proposes the treacherous strategy of a Hitler. 'Pretend to accept democracy', says Mr. Postgate, win one election, remain in power until your revolutionary task is completed, and take all the steps necessary to protect yourself from popular opposition.' At this point the cloven hoof of the dictator hiding behind Mr. Postgate's 'democracy' appears. *Why is it necessary to retain power like a Mussolini? Why is it essential to refuse to fight an election like a Stalin? Why is it obligatory to wait until this mysterious time, when 'Socialism has been made', before the people can be consulted?*

The only possible answer to these questions is the obvious one — because Mr. Postgate's party would lose the election if an election were fought. But why would he lose it? Again there can be only one answer — because the majority of people do not like the programme that is implemented in their name.

It is irrelevant to say that they are wrong to dislike it, or that Mr. Postgate knows better than they do what they will ultimately like, or that they have been deceived by someone else. That is what every dictator has said throughout the ages — Caesar and Octavius, Henry VIII and Louis XIV, Charles I and Cromwell, Hitler and Stalin — all of them knew what people really wanted, or ought to want. They have all believed themselves to be the instruments of the 'real' will of the people; to be bringing 'true' liberty to the state; to be the architects and builders of a better social order. The essential point is that — like Mr. Postgate — they were not prepared to let anyone else have access to the ear of the people or to ask them whether they actually liked the things that were being done 'for their good'. That question is the first lesson in the primer of democracy, and it is that first lesson that Mr. Postgate has forgotten. He who wants uninterrupted power to carry through a transformation of society, without continuously consulting the people affected by this transformation — people who appreciated only in the dimmest possible way the implications of the slogans ('Socialism in our time') that were shouted at them in a single General Election — is still a dictator through and through. He will not submit his books of account to the auditors.

It is to this new strategy — the cowardly strategy of Hitler — that the Communist Party is converted. They have turned their backs on the barricades. They have no machine-guns and no bombs — now. But they still want their revolution, and they still want a dictatorship of their own Party. It is to be obtained through the stratagem of a General Election.

Let us look for a moment at an official pamphlet of the Communist Party (*What is the Communist Party?* — R. W. Robson, 1d., published by the Communist Party of Great Britain in 1936). It is in such a publication, addressed to the members of the Party and potential converts among the working class, that the real hopes of the Party will be contained. First there is the new found faith in democracy:

> The Communist Party says that the workers will never be able finally to end capitalism by resolutions in Parliament. This does not mean to say that the Party is against Parliamentary method. *The present Parliamentary democracy is a hundred times preferable to Fascism and the Communist Party will fight to the last to defend it.* Also, a Labour Government, pledged to action, is infinitely preferable to any 'National' Government, and the Party has made great sacrifices to assist the return of Labour members.[1]

So far so good — Parliamentary democracy is better than Fascism. The pamphlet continues at once, in a different vein:

> *But the overthrow of capitalism is a more serious matter. It means the seizure of* power *by the working class*, the taking away of the factories and land from the capitalists. This is a life and death matter for the financiers. *Threaten to touch their property and they will go the length of taking up arms to oppose you*, as they did over Ireland. Remember how they discredited the last Labour Government with the Savings Bank scare.

Power is therefore to be obtained in a peaceful general election, and then the revolution is to begin:

> What kind of a government will the British workers set up? The working class has always worked out its own form of government. The Paris Commune of 1871, the Councils of Action in Britain, the Soviets in Russia and in the Hungarian,

[1] R. W. ROBSON: *What is the Communist Party?*, p. 7.

228

Spanish, Chinese and South American revolutions, have all shown what sort of organization this will be.

Will the workers just walk into Whitehall and the Bank of England and the B.B.C. and take the seats the capitalists have vacated? No. They will not do this because *the present State is made in such a way as to hold down the people, not represent them.* The Government departments, the Police, the Army, and the B.B.C. are organized to take their orders from the few 'gentlemen' at the top. How can these snobs with soft jobs be expected to work for the working class when they have been scheming against the workers all their lives? We may use the same buildings, but *the corrupt organization inside them must go.* Similarly, *the antiquated Parliament will be of little use.* The people will need a government of a new kind, standing close to them, representing their interests all the time, a government capable of making decisions and carrying them out.

Does this mean that Democracy will disappear? Quite the opposite; it means that the men and women in our cities will be free, will be their own masters; for the first time in their lives they will have a real democracy of their own.

Workers' Councils, made up of delegates elected from every factory, mines and places where people earn their living, will control their own affairs. They will elect their own central powers. These delegates will be subject to instant recall. They will be answerable to the people at all times, just as the Soviet officials are. Among these delegates we shall probably find shopkeepers, doctors, students and writers. They will represent all except the capitalist class.

In all this difficult process the people must have a conscious leadership, it must have a General Staff. 'The working class cannot do without a General Staff unless it wishes to deliver itself, bound hand and foot, to its enemies' (Stalin). *Such a leadership can only be found in the revolutionary party, the Communist Party.*

The first job of the Workers' Government will be to take over, without compensation, the banks, factories, transport, mines, ships, etc. The unemployed will quickly be absorbed into the new expanding industries. The millions of pounds at present paid out in directors' fees, fat salaries, royalties, etc., will be released into production. Working hours will be shortened. All schools, academies and universities, and the

hospitals and clinics will be free for the use of the people
New houses will be built. The only limit on what the
factories and land can produce will be the needs of the people
Wages will immediately begin to rise to allow for this new
demand.

What will happen to the bankers and profiteers? At first
they will do everything in their power to smash the workers'
state. They will be doomed to failure. Workers will be in
possession of the arms. Their own Red Army will defend them
Capitalists will be denied any privileges. In the course of
time they will disappear as a class and production will have
been carried to such a level that men and women will work
only according to their abilities, and instead of wages they
will receive whatever they require.[1]

From this lengthy passage it becomes obvious that the Communist Party proposes exactly the same general political strategy
as that advocated by Mr. Postgate:

(a) Changes are to be rapid, revolutionary and so ruthless
against the minorities that are adversely affected by them that
these minorites will be driven into an attempt at armed opposition.
A revolutionary situation is to be deliberately created.

(b) Parliament — i.e. representative assemblies — and opposition to the Government are to be swept away.

(c) The Communist Party is to emerge victorious and
ferociously triumphant ('those snobs with soft jobs' has an emotional tone familiar to the psycho-analyst), and, above all, with
unchallenged power. 'The working class cannot do without a
General Staff . . .' (Stalin). 'Such leadership can *only* be found in
the revolutionary party, the Communist Party.'

So there is no change of heart. The Communists stand where
they have always stood. Their middle objective is what it has
always been — the dictatorship of the Communist Party. They
have only changed their view as to how that objective can best be
obtained. They no longer have any faith in a frontal attack upon
democratic institutions; they think it better to destroy them
from within. Of course, they will destroy them, and carry through
their revolution, in the name of 'true' democracy. Under their
guidance men and women will be 'truly free'. The only thing they

[1] R. W. ROBSON: *What is the Communist Party?*, pp. 10-11.

ill not be able to do is to unseat their leaders, as a Party, from
ower.

We have seen the horror and the futility of this method of
overnment — the hatred, the torture, the river of blood, the long
ory of pain and fear. There is no reason to believe that it would
e any better here. We are a liberty-loving people. We have
onceived and nurtured an ancient hatred of absolute govern-
ent. If ever we betrayed ourselves in a moment of weakness, or
lindness, or hysteria, into the hands of a Party dictatorship, we
ould react violently against the experience of its control. The
ictatorship, in order to maintain itself, in order to protect itself
om the rising hatred of the English people, would have to be
orrespondingly violent and ruthless.[1] More blood would have
o be spilt and, if that is conceivable, more suffering would have
o be endured.

Is there no alternative, no better way? Must we suffer these
hings in order to settle the problems of our future economic and
olitical development? Surely not. We must reconsider the
olitical method of dictatorship, and consider also the alternatives
o it. This is the subject of the next Part.

[1] Mr. Strachey, it will be remembered, made this point; see pp. 162-3.

SOCIALISM AND DEMOCRACY

An Examination of the Argument for the Method of Political Democracy

DEMOCRACY ... is essentially a matter of political *method* ... Democracy is not a particular kind of civilization: it is rather a civilized way of taking political action.

Democracy constitutes an attempt to reconcile freedom with the need for law and its enforcement. It may be defined as a political method by which every citizen has the opportunity of participating through discussion in an attempt to reach voluntary agreement as to what shall be done for the good of the community as a whole. It resolves itself, in practice, into a continuous search for agreement, through discussion and compromise, and action on the basis of the maximum measure of agreement obtainable.

... *Democracy, therefore, is based upon tolerance, and necessitates compromise.*

BASSETT: *Essentials of Parliamentary Democracy.* 1935

SOCIALISM AND DEMOCRACY[1]

§ I

Introduction — the Essence of Democracy

IF the method of dictatorship is an unlikely way to secure social justice, what alternative method is open to us?

I wish to argue that the only conceivable route to a better social order lies in the pathway of democracy, and that the political method of democratic government is an essential principle, not an accidental accompaniment, of any just society.

If by the 'socialist commonwealth' we mean a society in which a larger measure of social justice has been established through the instrumentality of a planned economy, then I believe that the democratic method is an inherent part of socialism, and cannot be separated from it — any more than batting can be separated from cricket or love from life. They are all necessary parts of a complex whole.

I am now concerned to argue the validity of this contention; but before I do so, it is necessary to make clear the sense in which I use the term 'democracy'.

Democracy is an ambiguous term in political discussion. Many people use it in such a way as to make it synonymous with the phrase 'the good society'. A community is a 'true' democracy only if all cause for sighing and weeping have passed away. Before such persons will call any society a democracy, it must be completely free from social inequalities and economic insecurity. J. A. Hobson uses the term in this sense when he says 'effective political democracy is unattainable without economic equality'.

---

[1] The contents of this Part owe so much to the published and unpublished work of Mr. Reginald Bassett that it can be considered as little more than my interpretation of the central argument of his *Essentials of Parliamentary Democracy*. At the same time Mr. Bassett is not responsible for my interpretation and is by no means in agreement with all I say. My debt to him is none the less for that.

In this use the term 'democracy' becomes identified with the conception of a social justice itself, and is therefore remote from the political practice of any present society.

By using the word in this way it is possible to say, quite rightly, that we have not got 'democracy' in Britain, or America, or France, or Sweden. In none of these countries has inequality, or insecurity, or class antagonism, passed wholly away. Democracy, in its Utopian sense, does not yet exist within these nations. They only possess 'capitalist democracy', or *political* democracy'. They do not possess 'economic democracy' or 'true democracy' or 'real democracy'.

Now it is perfectly open to anyone to use terms as they please. If some people choose to mean by 'democracy' what other people mean by 'Utopia' there is nothing to stop them doing so. The moon will still be the moon even if we call it the sun. Utopia by any other name will smell as sweet, and look as remote. But it is not in Utopia, nor in the perfect society, that I am, for the moment, interested. I wish to discuss a narrower thing, a single political habit, a method of taking political decisions, a practicable and actual condition of certain societies. In short, what I want to consider is the significance or value of what the Utopian 'democrats' would call 'mere political democracy'. In what does that consist? Of what value is it? By what arguments can it be justified or criticized?

It is obvious that the institution of 'mere political democracy' must exist in some real sense, even in a capitalist society, since it is possible to distinguish 'capitalist democracies' from 'capitalist dictatorships'. Even in his most fanatical moments the Communist has not denied the *possibility* of making the distinction, although he used to deny the *importance* of making it. There must be therefore some sense in which democracy is compatible with capitalism and consequently with economic inequality. It is with this limited form of political democracy, its meaning and value, that I am here concerned.

In what does 'democracy' in this sense consist?

I believe the correct answer to this question to be that political democracy consists in the possession by any society of *three* characteristic habits or institutions:

1. The *first* and most typical of these characteristics is the ability of the people to choose a government.

Disagreement between individuals is of the very essence of human personality. As long as we are different persons, there will be some of us who like one thing and some who do not, some who desire one order of society and some another, some who believe justice to be realized in one set of circumstances and some who disagree with that judgment.

Now the course of action taken at any moment, and the form of society thus brought slowly into existence, are determined largely by the decisions of the Government. The Government has its hands upon the controls of the 'apparatus of coercion', and is therefore the *immediate* authority determining social policy. The nature of the decisions taken by the Government will depend upon the character of the persons forming it. Consequently there can be no control of the form of society by us, the common people, unless it is possible to change the personnel of the Government and of the legislature. That is the first and most obvious characteristic of political democracy — the existence of a government responsible to the people, and the dependence of it and of the membership of the legislative assembly upon the free vote of the people.

In our own history we have found that the essential thing to attain and preserve is the power of the people to *dismiss* a government from office. This negative power is in reality an important positive power, because ordinary men and women are moved more deeply by the disapproval of measures they dislike in practice, than by their less definite conception of what they desire in the future. Political change in democracies is more frequently induced by a slow accumulation of resentment against an existing government or institution, than by the growth of a positive idea of new social forms. Experience is more real than imagination, to unimaginative people.

Every practising politician appreciates this fact. The enthusiasts composing the party machine through which he has to work may be animated by the clear vision of a new society; but they are, at the best, a small minority of the surrounding electoral masses, and the masses are rarely inspired by Christian's clear vision, from a great distance, of the Celestial City. This is not to

237

say that constructive social imagination is not powerful in the affairs of men, but only that democracies proceed to realize the prophets' vision by careful processes of empirical test. By the slow testing of ideas and of institutional experiments, by rejecting all those of which they disapprove and insisting upon the gradual extension of the things they find by experience that they like, an intelligent electorate unconsciously constructs a society that in large measure contents it. Little as we reformists of the Left may like it, the absence of a reforming or revolutionary zeal in our communities is a tribute to the fundamental, and often unrecognizable, ways in which society has been adapted to suit the unconscious, but essential, requirements of the people composing it

Of this I shall have more to say presently. For the moment I wish only to insist upon the importance of the negative power to destroy a government as part of the broader right to choose a government. It is the continuous retention of this power that I shall call the 'maintenance of democracy'.

2.   But the continued existence of this right implies and requires the existence of a *second*, and less obvious, political institution. If liberty is to exist, if the dependence of government upon the will of the people is to be real, there must always be a real choice before the people. This implies the steady maintenance of a critical and essential institution — that of *freedom to oppose the Government of the day*. Unless the electorate has more than one possible government before it; unless there is more than one party able to place its views before the country; unless, that is to say, the opposition is free to prepare itself to take over power, and the Government to surrender it peacefully after an electoral decision against it; there is no choice before the people. Their choice is Hobson's choice — they may walk or go upon their legs, they may die or cease to live, they may eat bread or bread. The range of choice is no greater.

This obvious reflection reveals at once the sharp absurdity of the electoral practices of modern dictatorships. Modern dictatorships pay to the institutions of democracy the sincerest form of flattery — that of imitation. They copy the device of the 'General Election'. But it is an empty and silly imitation — like that of an ape reading a newspaper or a baboon playing on a violin. I

eceives no one, except those who wish to be deceived. Of course,
o amount of electoral machinery, nor platform eloquence, nor
cret balloting, nor 'equal voting', has the slightest real significance
there is finally nothing to vote about, no choice before the voters.
he contemporary German and Russian elections, in which one
arty receives 98% or 99% of the votes polled, may be a tribute
 the efficiency of the terror by which these unfortunate peoples
re governed; but they have no more political significance than the
bbering of a school of marmosets or the senseless and uniform
issing of a gaggle of geese.

This we can see at once by asking the critical question: *What is
e choice before the German or Russian electorate?* There is only one
arty in the election. There is only one government that can be
rmed. There may be a choice of individuals, but there is no
hoice of party, no choice of government, no choice of policy.
he alternative before the German people is the choice between
ührer Hitler or Führer Hitler; before the Russian people Com-
ıde Stalin or Comrade Stalin. They may choose in the one
ountry, the National-Socialist Party or the National-Socialist
arty; in the other, the Communist Party or the Communist Party.
s Herr Goebbels said, 'All we National-Socialists are convinced
ıat we are right, and we cannot bear with anyone who maintains
ıat he is right. For either, if he is right, he must be a National-
ocialist, or, if he is not a National-Socialist, then he is not right'.[1]
:omrade Stalin thinks very much the same. It is only odd that
oth these self-righteous regimes consider it worth while to spend
 much time and money in marching the adult population
ıechanically and idiotically through the polling booths to affirm
 meaningless slogan.[2]

Here then is the acid test of democracy. Democracy may be
efined by the toleration of opposition. In so far as it is tolerated —

[1] Speech reported in *The Times*, October 6th, 1935.
[2] In point of fact, the external form and machinery of a General Election has been
nverted by both types of Dictatorship into a compulsory nation-wide class in
lult education and a compulsory exercise in the State religion. The campaign pre-
ding the Election is made an opportunity for lecturing – or rather shrieking –
out the political questions of the moment, and the actual farce of balloting is a
st of the efficiency and enthusiasm of the local parties. This horrible mimicry of
:mocratic institutions has become an important part of the modern apparatus of
ranny.

239

in so far as alternative governments are allowed to come int
existence and into office — democracy, in my sense, exists. In so fa
as opposition is persecuted, rendered illegal, or stamped out ‹
existence, democracy is not present, and either has never existe
or is in process of being destroyed.

Obviously this is not a simple test. There are varying degrees ‹
freedom permitted to those in opposition to the Government ‹
the day in the various political systems of the world. In the olde
democracies, like our own, there is complete legal freedom fc
parties in opposition to the Government. Their rights in respec
of political agitation are the *same* as those of the Governmen
From this extreme there is an almost infinite gradation of liberty
through the milder dictatorships of Poland and even Italy, to th
savage and ruthless insistence upon uniformity that characteriz‹
Germany and Russia. There is no precise line at which it
possible to say that all the communities on this side of it ar
democracies, and all on the other side of it are dictatorships. Bu
although the test is quantitative and complicated, it is neverth‹
less an acid test. The suppression of opposition, as distinct fror
sedition,[1] is the proof of dictatorial ambition. It is by our judg
ment of that condition in society that we shall judge democrac
itself.[2]

3. But there is a *third*, and still less obvious, characteristi
necessary to the existence of democracy. Both the previor
characteristics — those of responsible government and of leg‹
opposition — are the definitive properties of democracy, but the
are not the causes of democracy. When these conditions ar
present in a society, democracy in my sense is present also; whe
they are absent democracy in my sense is dead. But they do nc
cause democracy to become present; they simply define democracy
What then *causes* democracy to appear? What is the substanti‹
social condition guaranteeing its existence and continuance?

Now I shall go on to argue, before this Part is finished, that th
ultimate cause of stable democratic habits among a people is th
possession by them of a certain type of emotional character.

---

[1] The advocacy of the *violent* overthrow of the Government.
[2] Of course I am not arguing the proposition that 'the more Parties there are th
better'. The institutions of democracy clearly work best with a very small numb‹
of Parties.

shall argue that democracy is the epiphenomenon of a certain emotional balance in the individuals composing a nation, and I shall try to describe the kind of personality that, in my view, alone makes democracy possible. But there is a simpler and more immediate description of the *result* of the predominance of such persons in any society; and that is, in my submission, the most essential condition for the existence and maintenance of democracy. It is the existence of *an implicit undertaking between the Parties contending for power in the State not to persecute each other.*[1] It is upon that agreement that I believe democracy can alone be securely founded. Mutual toleration is the keystone of the arch and the cornerstone of the building.

It is obvious, upon a moment's reflection, why this should be so. Let us imagine for a moment that this condition is not fulfilled. Let us suppose that the Conservative Party now in power in Great Britain has reason to believe that the Labour opposition has never accepted, or does not now accept, the obligations of this informal compact of toleration. The Government has reason to think that, if and when the Labour Party comes to power, it will use that power not merely to carry out its programme, but to break up and destroy the Conservative Party as a political organization, and to stamp out, by persecution, conservatism as an idea. That is to say, it is the known intention of the Labour Party—as it is now the known intention of the Communist and Fascist Parties—to use the apparatus of coercion, control over which is vested in them as the Government, to 'liquidate' the Parties that will then be in opposition to them. What will then follow? I suggest that in these circumstances the continuance of democracy is inconceivable. It is not even necessary that one of the large Parties in the community should intend to resort to physical cruelty. It may be certain that they will be forced to do so by the attempt to liquidate their opponents; but even if this is not the case, the mere desire on their part to prevent the other Party, by force, from ever holding office again is sufficient to make the maintenance of democracy impossible. Why is this so? Because the Party so threatened will never surrender power peacefully. There is every reason why it should not do so. To

[1] Or any other minority – such as a racial or religious minority within the state.

241

hand over the reins of government to the victorious Opposition is to court political death, to put a noose around one's own neck to hand over the gun to a murderer. There would be no sense in such a procedure. Why should I present a knife to a man who is going to stab me in the back with it? Who would willingly hand over a machine-gun to a lunatic or a gangster?

Indeed, it may very well be the duty of a political leader not to hand over the control of government voluntarily to a persecutor. The leaders of the Conservative Party, in the case that we are imagining, are the responsible leaders of a certain section of the community. They have been entrusted with the guardianship of certain interests and certain ideas. It may be their duty not to step aside, even in the face of the popular will, to give places of power to persecutors and tormentors. By so doing they sell the men and women they represent into slavery. They betray the ideas, for which they stood trustee, to destruction. It may be their duty to fight, to meet force with force, and not to yield. Only the extreme pacifist contends that it is our certain duty to allow ourselves to be tortured and persecuted and killed. In any case it is certain that most people will not do it — even were it their duty to do so.[1]

These moral dilemmas need not delay us now, as we shall return to them before the end of this Part. I am merely trying to elucidate the conditions necessary for the existence of democracy as have defined it. Democracy requires the peaceful alternation of Parties in government. This is impossible if the Government believes that the Opposition intends to liquidate them if and when they, the Opposition, attain power. The Government is not likely in these circumstances to surrender power peacefully. Even if they did, democracy would nevertheless cease to exist, since the victorious Opposition would then proceed, by the persecution of those who disagreed with them, to the destruction of democracy itself. Political liberty or democracy, in my sense, depends then

---

[1] It may reasonably be contended that this judgment applies to Germany in 1932 and 1933. In the November Election of 1932 the Parties that ultimately combined to support Hitler's Chancellorship obtained 44.3% of the votes cast. The Communists obtained 17.2%. I am not sure that the leaders of the democratic minority, or of the anti-Hitler majority, should have permitted him to obtain power peacefully. It might have been better for them, and for the world, if they had attempted to retain or secure power by force.

rst and last, now and in the future, upon mutual toleration
etween opposing Parties.[1]

It will be noticed that, in my description of democracy, there is
o reference to social equality or distributive justice, or to any
haracteristic of the ideal society. It is therefore perfectly open to
nyone to suggest that it is not a valuable institution. It is possible
o say: 'If that is all you mean by democracy, I am not interested
a it. It does not appear to me to be a particularly important
r valuable political habit. I see no necessity to trouble myself
reatly over its preservation.' We are therefore brought, at once,
o a consideration of the advantages and disadvantages of this
aethod of government. What are the arguments for democracy?
Vhat are the arguments against it? What are the forces that sup-
ort or undermine it?

§ 2

The Assessment of the Democratic Method

Let us begin with the oldest and most familiar of these matters —
he arguments for democracy. What advantages are claimed for the
lemocratic method? What are the superiorities over irresponsible
overnment that can be attributed to it?

In answer to this question, I have little or nothing to add to the
raditional arguments in favour of democracy. They have been
tated over and over again in the course of political discussion in

[1] It is perhaps worth saying one further word in explanation of what I have
alled 'the implicit agreement between the main Parties in the state not to persecute
ach other'. I do not mean by this that the political conflict between them is unreal.
'hey may disagree about everything else under the sun – the right form for the
tate, the proper distribution of wealth, the appropriate economic policy to pursue –
s long as they agree upon this one single point, that they will not use the opportunity
f office to persecute one another. That is the fundamental question. With agree-
nent about that, democracy is possible. Without it, democracy cannot survive.
Jor do I in the very least intend to suggest that a democratic government must
overn with the willing consent of the Opposition. It is the duty of a duly and
reely elected democratic government to execute the will of the people, and to
verride unconstitutional opposition, if necessary, by force. But what it must not
lo, if democracy is to continue, is to use force to liquidate the Opposition just
ecause it is in opposition, or to refuse the electorate the recurring opportunity
o vote it out of power. Toleration is the essence of the contract. Freedom of
ccess to the people is the first principle of continuity.

this country. They were elaborated in something like a final form in the writings of the democratic Utilitarians — especially Mill.

Summarizing them very briefly — there were *two* main argu ments advanced by the Utilitarians in favour of democracy: tha responsible government is the only certain method of securing th society that ordinary men and women desire; and, paradoxical a it may seem, that the toleration of opposition within the nation i the only method by which real national unity can be secured. I is further possible in these days to advance a third argument - that the only alternative to responsible government is governmen by terror.

I propose to say a word about each of these arguments in turn The *first* argument for democracy is the most familiar argumen of all. We have found again and again in our own history tha no person or group can be trusted to execute the popular will unless they are responsible to it. However noble the principles o the regime may be — whether that of Stuart monarchy, or Purita theocracy, or landed aristocracy — the story is still the same. Th moment that the country is able to express its opinion — in Civi War, or Restoration, or Reform Bill agitation — the irresponsibl group in power find themselves with a majority of the peopl against them.

I have already emphasized the logical dilemma of any dictator ship that claims to be a popular dictatorship. If it is popular, wh cannot opposition be tolerated? If opposition could be victoriou in a free general election, in what sense is the absolute governmen popular? There can be no validity in the claim that a regime in capable of permitting its fate to be decided by free voting is really executing the will of the voters.

It is therefore certain that only responsible governments car be trusted to do what the great majority of the governed wisl them to do. The only logical defences for dictatorship are to be found in the arguments advanced by the more honest of the ol absolute monarchies; either that the greatest happiness of the greatest number is not the purpose of social organization, or tha common men and women do not know what will make them happy. We need not concern ourselves with either of these broac ethical and psychological judgments at this point, because we all return to them before this book is finished. In any case, most people in this country, for whom primarily I am writing, will be content to accept the quality of executing their common will as an advantage in any political system or method.

It is therefore safe to conclude that historical evidence proves that, and logical and psychological reasoning shows why, an absolute government cannot permanently, or even long, retain the positive support, as distinct from the fearful acquiescence, of the great majority of the governed.

The *second* argument is more paradoxical. It has always been argued, and in my view correctly argued, that democracy in any sense is the only institutional framework within which the spontaneous emotional unity of a nation is possible. That this should be the case is paradoxical, since one of the basic principles of the democratic method lies in the toleration and protection, and in some cases the positive encouragement, of disagreement and division within the nation. As we have seen, democracy is based upon the toleration of opposition. Every dissident minority is allowed to raise its voice in protest against public policy. Nor is the toleration merely passive. The law actively protects the right to disagree — it is the business of the police to preserve order at the meetings of parties opposed to the Government just as much as at those supporting it. Mr. Lloyd George and others who opposed the South African War were protected from the fury of the pro-government masses even during the period of the war itself.

We have, in this country, carried the principle to its logical conclusion. We now *pay* people to criticize and denounce, and in certain instances to misrepresent, the policies of His Majesty's Government. And, if the Labour Party were victorious at the next General Election, Mr. Chamberlain or his successor will be paid the same sum for the discharge of the same duty. 'Toleration' could scarcely be carried further. In fact it is more than toleration — it is the recognition, by now almost explicit amongst us, that our political life is founded upon the principle of duality in politics, upon the principle of discussion between organized parties to the debate — parties that have equal rights to be heard, and who trust each other not to persecute or liquidate each other

as they alternate in power. The existence and peculiar functio
of His Majesty's Opposition have become recognized ai
honoured in our constitution.

Those of us who believe, as I do, in the necessity of this princip
to the life of a just society will delight in the consummation
the paradox peculiar to it. They will see in the payment by F
Majesty of one of his subjects to oppose another of his subjec
a neat and illuminating parable of our genius as a nation. B
the fact remains that such a practice would seem, at first sigl
to be the very last to secure agreement or unity within the natio
If the quarrelsomeness and factiousness of human beings
tolerated, and protected, and positively encouraged by the acti
of the State, will not chaos result? Men seem prone enough,
all conscience, to disagree. Will not the protection of their fa
tiousness lead to the dissolution of the State in bitterness ai
hatred?

Yet what are the facts? If we look for a moment at the bro:
division of the nations of the world into democratic and authoi
tarian states — Britain and France on the one side, Germany ai
Russia on the other — it is surely obvious that the deeply divide
nations are the dictatorships, and not the democracies. It
possible to apply a few practical tests. In which type of natic
is opposition so deep-rooted, so bitter and so dangerous th
it is not even possible to govern by due process of law? In wh
country is it necessary to imprison harmless clergymen by tl
score because they wish to preach the Christian religion? Wh
country is so afraid of opposition that more than three-quarters
the original revolutionary government have been exiled or shc
and more than three-quarters of the Presidents of the associate
republics have been executed in the last few years? In wh
countries are divisions so deep that the nation can only I
governed by secret police, by punishment without trial, t
imprisoning, torturing, exiling and killing hundreds and thousanc
of persons — in order to hold the people in restless subjection?

Everyone knows the answers to these questions. The deep
divided peoples of the world are not the democracies of Gre
Britain, France, the United States, Sweden, Belgium and Ne
Zealand, but the dictatorships of Germany, Italy, Russia, Polan

ASSESSMENT OF DEMOCRATIC METHOD

oumania, Japan and Latin America. In the former group of
ations no one is in prison without trial by jury and due process
f law; judicial murder is almost unknown; free associations are
·gal; men have rights and dignity and freedom. And yet they
ave unity. Each of them lives and acts as one people. The
1ajor decisions necessary for their life as a nation are arrived at
·ith a high degree of general consent, and its members can resolve
·eir political disputes, not without bitterness, but normally with-
ut force.¹ Among the latter group of peoples freedom is unknown.
.ll political organizations except one are illegal. Open dis-
greement is suicide. And yet they are divided, so deeply divided,
1at the secret police must be strengthened every year, the
)ncentration camps for ever enlarged, the instrument of judicial
1urder used with unremitting ruthlessness. The governments of
ictatorships are afraid of their oppositions. They are surrounded
y armed men, and by the humiliating paraphernalia of armoured
1rs and armoured trains. They walk, like Macbeth, starting at
1adows; the ghosts of the murdered standing at their elbows.
'hey know only too well the hatred that surrounds them as
ersons and as regimes. Meanwhile, the Governments of demo-
·acies pay salaries to the leaders of their Oppositions. They walk
narmed in the streets of their capital cities. The British Chan-
:llor of the Exchequer walks down to the House of Commons,
·llowed by one plain clothes detective. The Prime Minister
alks every morning in St. James's Park, followed by one private
etective. The President of the United States entertains at
ıncheon the candidate who opposed him at the last Presidential
lection. Which of these two types of people are more deeply
ivided against themselves?
Nor is the unity of democratic peoples and the disunity of
ictatorial peoples a matter of the class or party in power. Upper
ass and landed classes are in power in Bulgaria and Hungary.
ower middle class and bourgeois groups are in power in Italy
1d Germany. Proletarian groups are in power in Russia.
evertheless, the terror and lack of unity are everywhere the

¹ A number of these statements are not true of all parts of the United States.
. many of the backward States judicial murder, the persecution of minorities,
d the use of force on a large scale, still take place.

247

same. In democracies every sort of democratic party is in power. A democratic and conservative party is in power in Great Britain. A radical party is in control of the White House. A socialist and liberal block is in a majority in France. Labour governs New Zealand. A Socialist government rules Sweden. Everywhere the degree of toleration and unity is roughly the same. The distinction between the two groups of nations can scarcely be denied.[1]

From this brief survey of the distribution of democracy and authoritarian government in the contemporary world on the one hand, and of social peace on the other, it would seem to follow that the arguments in favour of democracy are substantiated by historical evidence.

Supposing for the moment that this interpretation is correct we are clearly faced by a second question. Why does not this beneficial institution spread slowly over the whole area of human society, bringing peace and contentment wherever it grows? Why is it, at the moment, in retreat in some of the most civilized

[1] It is now possible to understand why this distinction has always existed. The work of modern psychology has rendered more fully intelligible facts that could only be partially understood on purely institutional grounds. The institutional reason why dictatorship is associated with internal violence we have already discussed – the driving of opposition into secret, violent and terrorist channels because no legitimate method of expressing criticism is allowed to exist. The psychological reasons for this process should be obvious from what I have written in the first Part. There is no way of destroying or mitigating human aggression by restraint. If it is disciplined or punished, or crushed, it is only driven underground and made more bitter, more savage, more cruel. It may be necessary to restrain it from active destruction. No society has ever been governed or kept peaceful without the use of force – for reasons we shall see in a moment. Nevertheless, restraint is no cure. The only cure is some form of expression. Personal aggressiveness, and the political opposition that springs from it can be mitigated only in a social environment that allows to it some relatively harmless outlet. The physical analogy of a steam boiler under pressure is not wholly inaccurate. If steam is being generated, the stronger the container the more destructive the final explosion. The only solution of the problem, the only path to safety, is a safety valve. So, in the political life of a nation, the only way to overcome the aggressiveness arising between the smaller groups within the nation, the only way to lower the emotional temperature and generate goodwill and friendliness between these groups, including political parties and economic classes, lies in the provision of opportunities for the expression of disagreement and dislike. In discussion, in superficial hostility and quarrelsomeness, lies the sole hope for deeper understanding and the slow growth of a common purpose. No man is your friend until you have quarrelled with him and the quarrel has been forgiven and forgotten. Trust is founded upon a freedom to disagree – not upon an imposed and unwelcome uniformity. It is therefore easy to understand why toleration and deeper unity grows up, and can only survive, in a nation that appears at first sight to be divided and weakened by party strife.

We shall see in a moment how the dictatorships have been confused and misled on this point.

reas of the earth? This question again divides itself at once into two problems — the *arguments* used against democracy, and the *forces* that, argument or no argument, operate against democracy. To these points we must now return.

What then are *the arguments against the democratic method?*

In recent times *three* main reasons have been offered by dictatorial parties to persuade people to abandon government by consent. One of these arguments is peculiar to the authoritarian Party on the Left, the Communist Party; one peculiar to that on the Right, the Fascist Party; and one reason is given in different ways by both of them. The argument peculiar to the Communist Party is the argument that political democracy cannot secure economic equality. The Fascist argument is that political democracy is incompatible with national unity. The argument common to them both is the view that common people are not competent to rule the modern world, or to obtain what they want from its complicated machinery. We must examine these arguments in turn, although it will not be necessary to say a great deal more about two of them.

1. I have already dealt with the *Communist argument* that the institutions of political democracy must necessarily break down in the attempt to establish social equality (See Part III). There is little that need be added here. I argued, it will be remembered, that Marxist reasoning is wholly unconvincing on the point. The basis for their view is supposed to lie in the materialist theory of history and the class-struggle interpretation of historical change; but, as I tried to show, these theories form no basis for the view that civil war is inevitable, or for the belief that a just society could arise from a Communist dictatorship. These arguments may be right or wrong, but there is no point in repeating them here. If they are accepted, the Communist argument against democracy is deeply shaken. It will finally be brought to the ground, if it can be shown in a more positive way that a political strategy compatible with democracy and leading towards equality is conceivable. To this task I shall turn in the next and last Part of the book.

2. I have also considered, at least by implication, the *Fascist argument* against the democratic method during the earlier part

of the present Part. The Fascist is misled by the appearance of inherent division in democracy. The Fascist says, and says rightly that national unity is one of the first necessities of political life Rightly or wrongly, our social life is organized upon a national basis. Rightly or wrongly, our primary loyalties are directed towards, and some of our deepest passions stirred by, the life and character of the geographical and racial group to which we belong. We grew up in its culture. It has entered into our bone and made us what we are. In a very real sense it is part of us As a consequence, much of the wealth, security and derivative well-being of the individual depend objectively upon the unified and successful administration of the nation state, and subjectively the happiness of the individual may be bound up with the unity of the nation.[1]

It is this necessary unity that the Fascist believes to be threatened by the party strife of democracy. To tolerate disagreement, and to permit alternative governments to contend for power with every appearance of mutual antagonism, is, to the Fascist, to divide the nation. *Wir müssen Einheit haben* — 'we *must* have unity — shrieks Herr Hitler in a real agony of spirit. Tempestuous personalities — torn by ambivalence, their peace of mind destroyed by internal conflict — cannot bear to see their conflicts made objective outside themselves, in the life of the societies to which they belong. They feel that such conflict will paralyse the will of a nation. How can a house, divided against itself, stand? Party bitterness will destroy the love of the common good. Faction is social suicide. These are the questions that genuinely trouble the Fascist in opposition to democracy — the dogmas in which he genuinely believes.

No doubt these disinterested views are combined with all sort

---

[1] I should perhaps make plain here that I am speaking of facts rather than of moral judgments. It appears to me to be obvious (*a*) that the happiness of the individual must always depend, objectively and subjectively, upon the unity and health of some social group, (*b*) that the dominant group of the historical period in which we live is the nation state. Hence it is essential, for the continuation of individual well-being, that national unity should be preserved. In saying this I am not contending that these things are desirable. Loyalty to the nation is not in my view the greatest or finest loyalty. Unless it becomes the channel through which a greater loyalty to mankind can flow, national patriotism is exclusive and dangerous. But we have to deal with people as they are, and to admit the power and contemporary importance of loyalty to the national group.

f less honourable motives — with a crude love of power, with
he selfish desire to protect old, or acquire new, privileges; with
simpler and more horrible compulsions to be cruel. But we
are complex personalities, and these intellectual arguments and
judgments are not the less genuinely held because they are inter-
woven and corrupted with more shameful motives.

In any case, what are we to make of the Fascist argument on
its own merits?

It would obviously be absurd to contend that there is nothing
in it. It is certain that Party strife; faction, mutual distrust and
fear; can be carried to such a point that the will of a people and
the unity of the nation are destroyed. It is at least arguable
that this had occurred in Germany before the conquest of power
by the National Socialists, and in Italy before the victory of the
Fascists. It had become difficult to form stable governments in
those countries. Party strife had rendered the maintenance of
parliamentary majorities impossible. In contemporary France
the parties are so fragmented, and the coalitions between
them so unstable, that the Parliamentary situation is often
chaotic, and the conduct of affairs sometimes lacking in continuity
and power. Even in Great Britain we were not far removed from
this position in the period immediately preceding the last war, and
again during the life of the second Labour Government. It is no
accident that we were brought to the edge of civil war in the first
period, and to a breakdown of financial confidence in the second.
Democracy can therefore plainly divide a nation and paralyse
its will.

There is an important lesson for democrats in all this.
Democracy is possible only if party strife is strictly limited in
method and scope. We have discussed at length the agreement
between the parties that is essential if democracy is to survive —
an agreement not to use the methods of persecution against one
another. But now we must add a second essential requirement
to the first. *It must be possible — continuously — to form stable governments.* The obligation is complex. The electorate must elect
parties with substantial majorities to the legislative chamber.
If majorities cannot be formed otherwise, democratic parties
must enter coalitions to obtain them. 'The King's Government

must be carried on' — that is a vital principle of survival for democracy. Any constitutional device that weakens Government - such as proportional representation, or the alternative vote, (uncompromising party programmes — must be sacrificed, by thos who believe in the democratic method, to the overriding necessit of maintaining a powerful executive government. Nations mu: act. To act they must have governments. Even tradition; democracies will not survive the paralysis of a partisan deac lock.

Nevertheless, the Fascist argument and the Fascist conclusio are fundamentally false. It is true that democracy can divide nation. It is fundamentally untrue that it must divide it. A we have seen, precisely the opposite is the truth. It is only demc cracy that can unite a free people. Unity is founded upon tru: and is nourished by compromise. Unity follows after the expre: sion of aggression in harmless forms. Unity springs from goodwi and the recognition of a common good. Unity is good fellowshi and the rudiment of love.

Uniformity is possible to a dictatorship but never unity Repression and persecution, oppression and cruelty, can and d create uniformity, but they destroy, perhaps for ever, the hope (unity. Behind the drilled enthusiasm, the endless repetition c common slogans, and the monotonous tramping of militar reviews, there lies a deeper reality of hatred, division and fear Every now and then dissension boils up in blood — the massacre of June 30th in Germany, the shooting of the Russian peasantry i 1932, the loathsome trials of 1937 and 1938. The uniformity i sham and superficial, the enthusiasm partial and partisan. Lif the curtain for a moment, and the horror shows within.[1]

Let no one be deceived. When a Hitler, or a Mussolini, or Stalin, stands up before shouting crowds, to make a speech tha is cheered, hysterically, to the last syllable; to review an endles stream of armoured cars and mounted troops; to greet a hundred thousand men or women or children dressed in the same uniform shouting the same slogans, their arms raised in the same salute scarcely more distinguishable from one another than the member

---

[1] For a powerful description of this process see LYONS: *Assignment in Utopia passim.*

of a flock of sheep; *there is still no unity in that people.* Do not let me be misunderstood. I am not saying that there is no real enthusiasm in the immediate crowd before the Dictator. Of course there is. These are the supporters of the regime, the beneficiaries under its will, the privileged minority in power — whether it is the young and the middle class in Germany, or the industrial proletariat in Russia. Those who benefit and those who conform sit down at the feast. But where are the absent faces? — those who did not benefit and those who will not conform. Where are the Socialists and the Catholic Democrats, the pacifists and the Jews, in Germany? Where are the Socialists, and the bourgeois Liberals and the Social Revolutionaries and peasants in Soviet Russia? They do not appear to be in the crowd or to be shouting, or to be raising their hands in senseless uniformity. They are not there — because they are in jail or concentration camp, in Dachau or Siberia, or in the grave. This is odd, since between them these groups account for more than half the population in each country — or did before the terror began.

Uniformity is merely the empty and ugly imitation of unity, and social unity cannot be obtained by those means. There is more unity expressed in the sharpest and angriest debate in the House of Commons, than in all the marching and counter-marching and shouting enthusiasm of a National Socialist Rally or an All-Soviet Party Conference in Moscow. There is more unity in a querulous House *because the opposition is present*, because men of different opinions may meet and argue and quarrel, and yet appreciate the common good and live to serve it.

Dictatorship may be necessary to secure action, democracy alone can secure unity in action.

3. We come to the last of the three arguments against democracy that I am examining — the argument common to both Fascism and Communism in different forms. It need not delay us long. The argument consists in little more than a misinterpretation of the democratic process. It begins with an emphasis upon the change that legislation has undergone in this country, for example, over the period of the last generation. In the nineteenth and early twentieth centuries the questions before the nation were largely those of constitutional and political importance — the

extension of the franchise, the disestablishment of the Church c
Wales, the constitutional relations between Great Britain an
Ireland, the constitutional position of the House of Lords. Thes
matters involved broad and simple judgments of principle. The
were no more easy to solve for that — one of them indeed, brough
us to the edge of civil war. Nevertheless, there was and is, a sens
in which these questions were easier of solution and less hard upo
the pure intelligence than the questions that have recently bee
debated in Parliament. Since the war our problems have bee
predominantly economic — control of the price level, control o
the foreign exchanges, the reorganization of the coal industr
commercial policy, industrial policy, the endless discussion c
unemployment.[1]

Now, says the Fascist, since this is the case — and likely to remai
the case for as far ahead as we can see — it can be argued that th
institutions of democracy have outlived their usefulness. It wa
sensible, or at least it was not obviously absurd, to consul
ordinary people about those earlier problems. It is conceivabl
that every man should have some opinion on 'Home Rule fo
Ireland' or 'the Lords versus the People'; but it is quite incon
ceivable to suppose that he, the man in the street, can have an
valuable opinion on the Gold Standard, or the advantage
of tariffs, or the terms of a Trade Agreement with America
or the right way to cure the Trade Cycle. Ordinary person
simply cannot deal with these difficult technical matters. I
capable and intelligent men are paid to devote their lives to th
study of these problems, and still cannot come to any intelligibl
verdict or simple opinion about them, how is it possible to expec
ignorant and uneducated men and women to pronounce fina
judgment upon them? The trouble with democracy, conclude
the Fascist, is not that it is wrong or evil in principle, but simpl
that it is old-fashioned. It cannot deal with the increasing com
plexity of our economic and institutional life. Men do not expec
to ride in dogcarts for ever, or indeed in horse-drawn vehicle
at all. Why should they expect to be governed always by th

[1] Of course there was much economic legislation in the nineteenth century
the Free Trade controversy, the control of hours of labour, the control of th
railways. It is easy to exaggerate the difference between the two periods, but ther
is clearly something in the suggested contrast.

ame political method and never to be obliged to try a new
one?

Stated in this form, the Fascist argument possesses a certain
degree of superficial plausibility. But the plausibility is very
superficial. There is, in fact, no substance whatever in it. To start
with, the institutions of democracy and the instruments of the
political method are not static. The constitutional machinery of
this country is radically different now from what it was a hundred
years, or even a generation, ago. The machinery of our government: legislature, executive, civil service and local authorities
have all been continuously altered and adapted to meet the
changing need of our social development.

The real fallacy, however, lies deeper than this. Apart
altogether from the continuous change that the institutions of
democracy undergo, it would be absurd, let us admit at once,
to suppose that the electorate could itself decide the complicated
technical questions that must be answered by the nation. It
would be a *reductio ad absurdum* of the democratic method to
suppose that ordinary men and women are to be asked whether
we ought to return to the Gold Standard or stay off it, whether
we should inflate the currency by 5% or 10%, whether the
owners of mining royalties should receive £100 millions
or £50 millions, whether oil should be extracted from coal,
and where every new aeroplane factory should be located.
Interested parties in all these questions should, no doubt, be
allowed to state their cases to as wide a public as they can persuade
or bully into taking an interest in them, but the electorate will
decide none of these questions directly for itself. Even to state the
possibility is to emphasize the absurdity of such a procedure,
and to expose the elementary fallacy from which the absurdity
follows. It is only the system of *direct* democracy to which such a
criticism would apply.

Let me make this simple point plainly. As every schoolboy
knows, the type of democracy that we enjoy, the only type of
democracy in the least applicable to the immense aggregates of
population composing the modern nation state, is that of *representative* democracy. That is to say, the electorate — the ultimate
source of sovereignty in the state — decides directly no more and no

less than who shall represent it in the legislature — the persona
composition of the House of Commons or Chamber of Deputies
Hence the question that has to be settled by the ordinary man and
woman in the act of voting is not the value of the Gold Standard
or the proper height of tariffs, or the correct strategy for the aeria
defence of London; but much more general and simple question
represented to them by local candidates and national party leader.
It is true that in the curious and meandering life of a democrac
much more will be decided indirectly by making these simpl
decisions — but the immediate decision that the elector is calle
upon to make is that between one local candidate and another
between one Prime Minister and another, between one part
principle and another. These are decisions different in kind from
the complex technical problems that have to be resolved by thes
representative Prime Ministers and Party Governments after the
have been chosen.

Hence it follows that the change in the nature of our legislation
and the growth in the technical complexity of the question
before the nation, impose no real strain upon democracy. Th
change may require some, and will certainly be very greatly aide
by any, increase in the knowledge and intelligence of the people
Adult educational services and associations perform an invaluabl
service for democracy by spreading far and wide even the simple
elements of historical, psychological and political information
But that is not the essential adaptation that is required for th
health of democracy. The important thing to do is to change th
character and intellectual capacity of the *representative*. If
democratic nation has to face a period of difficult and comple
economic legislation, what it needs most — next to the spirit
tolerance and charity — is a legislature that knows what it
talking about. Charity, intelligence, and knowledge — thes
three — and no one of them is enough without the other two.

The need, then, is not to abandon the vital principle of respon
sible and representative government, but to obtain, in this country
a technically competent House of Commons. There is ampl
evidence to convince those who read the debates in the Hous
that, quite unconsciously, a healthy democracy like our own ha
appreciated the need, and is carrying out the necessary process

ASSESSMENT OF DEMOCRATIC METHOD

election.[1] Discussion in the House is not conducted by men wholly ignorant of the business of the nation.

I am left therefore with the conclusion that no one of these arguments against democracy will bear examination.[2] The Communist argument we have discussed at length. It leaves us with a question on the political strategy of equality to be answered in the next Part, but with no reason to suppose that the democratic method is inherently incapable of securing equality. The Fascist argument about the necessity for social unity leaves us with an unshaken faith in democracy but with a second essential condition for the health of democracy — the continuous maintenance of a strong government — to bear in mind. The last argument against democracy is founded wholly upon a misunderstanding of its nature. Hence, as far as I understand the intellectual arguments in the case, the democratic method emerges unshaken from criticism — the one hope of social peace, the sole foundation for a growing and deepening civilization.

Once more the insistent question returns to me — if these things are true, why is democracy even temporarily in retreat? If the arguments for democracy are so strong, and the arguments against democracy are so weak, why does it not conquer the earth? To answer this question I am brought to the last and most important matter in this Section — a discussion, not of the arguments, but of the *forces* that prevent the establishment, and undermine the stability, of the democratic method of government.

I believe the clue to the mystery lies in the fact that democracy demands a certain kind of *emotional* life and character in individuals before it can exist or survive in society. The forces that endanger

[1] An interesting comment on this point was made to me by an ex-Cabinet Minister in the Labour Party who has had long experience of Parliament – he was first elected in 1906, sat continuously until 1931, and was re-elected in 1935. He therefore entered the House for the first time in 1906, and re-entered it, after a temporary absence for the second time, thirty years later. He was thus able to compare his first impressions of two new Houses separated by a generation. I asked him what was his chief impression in the comparison. He replied that he was chiefly impressed 'by the lower level of speaking and the *higher level of technical information*' exhibited by the Members. Less rhetoric and more knowledge. This was precisely the adjustment needed in the modern world.
[2] I do not mean by this that there are no good arguments against democracies, or that democratic nations are incapable of stupidity and wickedness. Democratic countries have often been very aggressive and intolerant at home and abroad, and they are usually most tragically short-sighted in the field of foreign policy.

257

democracy and prevent it from coming into existence are emotional forces. The things that destroy democracy are human passions, and in the light of historical and anthropological evidence — natural and normal passions. Democracy is a difficult system to set up and maintain, because the emotional characteristics that must be preserved in a great majority of the persons that make up the nation are not easy to create or preserve.

The qualities of character that are necessary for the survival of democracy are two in number — a tolerant disposition, and a willingness to undertake responsibility. Without the coexistence of both of these qualities in the people at large, democracy can never be created, or, once created, successfully continued. Let us look at each of them in turn.

1. I have emphasized again and again that political toleration, the absence of political persecution, is the foundation of the democratic method. If it is present in society, democracy is at least possible. If it is absent from society, democracy is plainly impossible. Political toleration and democracy are related in the way that sun is related to light, fire to heat, desire to life. The one is the first necessary condition for the other — not the sufficient ground, but the first requirement.

Now it is obvious from the simplest survey of history and the records of anthropology that a tolerant habit of mind is an exceedingly difficult characteristic to establish in any people. The substance of the first Part of this book emphasized that point. History is full of the records of persecution — savage, ruthless, senseless persecution — for the most slender differences of thought and interest. Men have killed and tortured each other, not only for the dominion of the earth and the good things contained therein, but for the slightest divergences of political, or religious, or ethical judgment. Men and women have been burned for believing in the 'transubstantiation of the elements in the sacrament' in one part of Europe, and for not believing in this obscure doctrine in another part of Europe, at the same time. Men and women have been hanged and drowned for adultery, or even for disbelieving in the theory of absolute monogamy, all over the world at different times. Men and women are shot and imprisoned to-day for the most subtle and obscure differences of political doctrine — in Germany because they preach the service of God through the state, instead of the service of God in the state, although no one could distinguish the practical consequences of either doctrine — in Russia for refusing to accept the Stalin-Leninist form of the theory of the 'proletarian dictatorship'.

All this persecution of ideas is in addition to the more substantial reasons for intolerance — disputes over property, or status, or political power. The hatred exhibited by men over differences of opinion would be in the highest degree ridiculous, if it were not already in the highest degree horrible. Men will mutilate and destroy the delicate and living fabric of our flesh for the difference of a comma, or the accent on a diphthong. They will burn down a temple to destroy one grain of sand, and yet it will not be destroyed.

It is no wonder, then, that democracy is difficult to establish. It requires toleration over the whole range of possible disagreement. It is not surprising that it is unstable, once it has been established. Men of blood, with loud voices and with thin voices, we have always with us. They hate the structure of understanding and good will.

2. It is not only the strong who become the enemies of democracy. The weak also may destroy it. The strong hate it; the weak fear it. For democracy is not possible unless ordinary men and women are prepared to bear the responsibility of *self* government.

This they must do, since in the last resort they alone are responsible for social action. They have chosen the agents by which that action has been decided. The people under an authoritarian government carry no weight of responsibility. The government has not been elected by them; it does not submit its record to them. 'Theirs not to reason why — theirs but to vote aye.' But this is not the case with a democratic people. Theirs, in the last resort, is the sole responsibility. If the Government does wrong, the people elected it. If there is a deadlock in the legislature and no stable government can be formed, it is the people that returned the parties to the legislature in those proportions. Indeed, it is only by a false abstraction that it is possible to speak or think of 'the government' as standing in opposition to the people — for they are really aspects of the same unity — the nation in action. It is true, of course, that particular governments can transgress, or fail to fulfil, their mandate or their promises, but in the long run the government of the people is self government by the people. Theirs is the will and theirs the deed.

Again, it is obvious that this is a responsibility that ordinary people often find it hard to bear. For reasons we have discussed the individual may project his personal guilt into the social life of the nation. If this process takes place on a wide enough scale, the burden of public responsibility, always heavy, may become intolerable. Particularly this is the case when things go wrong. It is then that people cry out for a political 'saviour', not only to resolve the real problems before the nation, but also to lift from their shoulders the burden of decision and the terrible weight of guilt for having done wrong. Again and again in history, democracy has been swept aside in periods of national disaster; and even peoples who survived as democracies have temporarily chosen more authoritarian forms of government.

There can be no question but that this consideration throws a great deal of light upon the recent history of Europe. It is no accident that democracy in many countries disappeared during a period of universal, though temporary, economic depression. It is no accident that democracy in Germany was relatively stable in the late '20's when unemployment was low, capital flowing in from America, and the national life recovering from the war and the inflation. Democracy was tolerable to the German people while things were going well. The depression of 1929 not only plunged Germany into real economic and commercial difficulties, but it also swept away the faith of the people in the democratic method. By the August of 1932, 60% of the German electorate (7% Nationalists, 38% National Socialists, and 15% Communists) had been converted to a desire for authoritarian government in one form or another. It is impossible not to believe that the fear of responsibility as such, no doubt aided by the tradition of monarchical government, played some part in this sharp reversal of fundamental political faith.

These then are the real difficulties that democracies have to ace — the difficulty of maintaining a reasonable and tolerant temper in face of disagreement between persons and groups within the state, and the difficulty of keeping ordinary people willing and able to support their responsibility for public policy when things go wrong. Tolerance and responsibility — on the part of common men and women — those are the necessary conditions for stable democracy.

They are not the only conditions for the maintenance of democracy. As we shall see before this book is finished, it is also essential that democrats should realize the necessity of defending, and if necessary be prepared to defend by force, the basic instruments of the democratic method.[1] But the psychological requirements are the first essential conditions for the maintenance of a stable democracy, and we must turn aside for a moment to discuss the source of their development.

§ 3

The Psychological Origins of the Democratic Method

It has always seemed to me that the discussion of the origins of democracy in the past has been infected with a considerable lack of realism. It is no doubt important to discuss the legal framework of democratic constitutions. It is certainly desirable to understand the consequences of certain methods of election, representation and legislation. Constitutions can vary very greatly in the degree of their efficiency, and we shall always need experts in constitutional law and political organization. Nevertheless, the secret of democracy cannot lie here, for the most carefully prepared constitutions cannot protect democracy; and the most clumsy constitutions, like that of the United States, can be made the basis of vigorous democratic life. Democracy is more than a matter of law. It is a method of living peacefully together within a framework of law.

It is also beside the point, in my view, to concentrate upon the

[1] See below, § 6 of Part IV.

analysis or defence of the privileges that result from democracy
The worthy and excitable persons who are always agitating about
'freedom of speech' and 'civil liberties'; and who carry their
obsession over these things to the point of opposing Acts of
Parliament that forbid the wearing of political uniforms and the
organization of deliberately provocative public demonstrations
are simply confusing cause and effect.[1] Freedom of speech and
freedom of political agitation are not the causes of democracy
they are the results of it. They are the privileges that flow from
and are alone made possible by, the self-denying ordinance of
mutual toleration between the parties. The sources of life for
tree are its roots, not its fruits; and the roots of democracy lie
deeply buried in the attitude to each other of people who disagree
with one another, not in the benefits arising from social peace
The proper understanding of this point will lead us to important
conclusions in the last Section of this Part.

Nor is an exclusive emphasis upon intelligence or intellectual
education appropriate. These things are, of course, invaluable to
democracy. The higher the general level of intelligence, the
better the system of public education, the greater the extent of
political understanding among the people; the easier the tasks of
self-government become. Effort expended in raising the educational level of the people in, or spreading throughout the country
an understanding of, the democratic method, is effort well directed

By itself, intellectual education is not enough. Intelligence is not
sufficient, and knowledge is not sufficient, to preserve democracy
The German people were among the most intelligent and best
educated people (intellectually speaking) in Europe. Yet they
proved utterly incapable of maintaining the democratic method
of government. Intelligence can be made to serve any emotional
end or to achieve the purposes of any type of character. Men must
wish to agree and to live in peace, before intelligence will lead them
to do so.

[1] Compare, in this context, the extraordinarily confused position adopted by the
Council for Civil Liberties when it opposed an Act that was clearly intended to
weaken the power of Fascist and Communist parties in this country. This they did
despite the knowledge that in other countries similar Acts had greatly weakened
authoritarian parties. The Council for Civil Liberties appeared to think that they
could best serve the cause of civil liberty in this country by protecting the 'rights' of
Fascists and Communists to grow more powerful!

Democracy is much more a result of character in a people than of law or learning. Its roots are emotional rather than intellectual. It is fundamentally a consequence of psychological health and the absence of neurosis.

This matter brings us back to the kind of consideration that we discussed at the beginning of this book. We traced there the origins of aggression to acquisitiveness, to frustration, and to the animism of the primitive mind; and followed it through its later modifications by the mechanisms of displacement and projection in the life of society. We also discussed, more briefly, the origins and consequences of a sense of guilt. Now these emotions are the ultimate enemies of democracy: aggression is the enemy of tolerance and guilt of the willingness to accept political responsibility. Democracy cannot long survive the dominance, among a people, of either emotion.

Situations requiring tolerance and demanding the willingness to bear responsibility are bound to arise in any advanced society. Consider the first of these probabilities. Differences over judgments of value are of the very essence of personality. It is therefore certain that, quite apart from disputes over the distribution of wealth, disagreement and divergence of interest are bound to arise within any group. No doubt the sources of dispute are increased, and the anger arising from them exacerbated, by great differences of wealth; but quite apart from this important question, there are bound to be different views about a hundred things: the efficiency of constitutions; the appropriate relations with other states; the forms of education; the cultural, and architectural, and ethical, and technical policies of the nation. Opportunities for disagreement are as numerous as the categories of question to be decided. It is, further, certain that groups possessing a common judgment upon these questions will come together and seek to impress their will upon the legislature. Total abstainers will form 'temperance' societies, and try to secure prohibition. The brewers and drinkers will organize societies to oppose them. Lovers of the country-side will form National Trusts and Councils for the Preservation of Rural England, to restrain and limit the destructive vandalism of the speculative builder. The building trade will reply in kind. Those who dislike class divisions will form

egalitarian parties. Those who like them will form snob partie:
There is no end to the sectional disputes of a free people.

Now, in all these disputes, it is impossible for both sides to hav
their own way completely. It is impossible for the sale of alcohol
liquor to be wholly forbidden and wholly free from legal restrair
in the same area at one time. It is impossible to cover the countr\
side with squat and glaring pink bungalows, and to leave it lookir
as it did before they were built. Hence the mutual frustration o
groups is inevitable. Everybody cannot secure precisely tł
society in which they would like to live. Disputes are unavoidabl
and frustration is certain. There therefore arises this critical an
central question — *how are these disputes to be resolved?*

Broadly speaking, there are two methods, and two methoc
only, for resolving differences between groups. They can figł
them out — submit the disputes to the arbitrament of force — o
they can compromise with one another. There is no thir
possibility.

It is not necessary to repeat at length the overwhelmin
disadvantages of the first alternative. We have already discusse
the horror, the cruelty, the misery; and, in some cases, the sel
frustrating futility of international or civil warfare. The apes o
Monkey Hill, unable to compromise their conflicting interes
in the distribution of females, fought and in the course of fightin
they destroyed the very females over whose possession the conflic
had arisen. That is a sad parable for all of us. It is easy to destro
the very thing desired in the attempt to obtain it by force.[1]

The only solution that is compatible with the maintenance o
social peace and the growth of mutual respect between contendin
groups is that of open and honest compromise. As betwee
individuals, so between groups, social peace can only be pre
served if both sides to the argument are determined to agree;
they both recognize that the worst outcome of the dispute is
rupture of social equilibrium in which all may be lost for each o
them individually. A free society is only possible if they are bot
prepared to recognize the right of other people to their ow

[1] This obvious reflection does not lead me, personally, to a pacifist conclusion o
to a religion of non-violence. I have discussed this point in the last Section o
Part I and I shall revert to it in the last Section of this Part.

pinions, and to an interest in their own rights. From this attitude
lone will spring a willingness to come to terms, a respect for that
plendid tribute to reason, that great constructive activity in
ociety, the activity of compromise.

The democratic method involves the determination of
political principles as a result of discussion. The person or
party formulating political principles or policies in advance
of discussion and refusing to compromise under any circumstances; or settling such principles or policies before the
process of discussion is completed, and refusing to compromise
further; renders discussion a farce in the first case, and in the
second limits its usefulness ... A compromise, of course, is
only a settlement by mutual concessions, and, in practice,
any aggreement involves a measure of compromise ...
*Compromise, therefore, far from being the source of political immo-
rality, is, from the democratic standpoint, one of the cardinal virtues.*[1]

It is obvious that this attitude of mind and heart — the respect
or the rights of other persons, the desire to seek agreement through
liscussion, the willingness to compromise rather than destroy — is
endered impossible by a high degree of internal aggressive ten-
ion. Men who are holding aggressive impulses in check with
lifficulty; who are struggling with guilt, and fear, and hatred; or
nen who have displaced these emotions into the parties to which
hey belong, or upon the parties to which they are opposed; are
not 'good compromisers'. They are intransigent and ruthless and
pure'. They cannot sit down with the enemy in peace, because
they hate their political opponents — not necessarily as individuals, but as groups. The willingness and ability to enter into
discussion and to compromise with those with whom one dis-
agrees — the characteristic of 'reasonableness' in disputes — is a
critical sign of a relatively free and healthy emotional life.

Exactly the same relationship could be established between
the willingness to carry responsibility in action and the internal
neuroses of guilt and fear. The fearful and the guilt-burdened
will find political responsibility intolerable, because it will only
increase the amount of evil that they believe they have done

---

[1] BASSETT: *Essentials of Parliamentary Democracy*, p. 149. He goes on to explain
on p. 153 the relations between 'compromise' and 'agreement', and discusses
briefly the limits that must be set to 'compromise'.

and will do to the world. Aggression, as I have said, is the enemy of toleration, and guilt of political responsibility.

Democracy, on this view, is not due to intellectual education, nor to law. It is not the result of one particular phase of economic development, or of the growth of one particular school of thought. It is caused by the appearance in a people of a certain emotional temperament, so widely distributed that it becomes typical of them — a compromising, tolerant and moderate temperament, a fundamental reasonableness in action and a hatred of violence. The origin of such a temperament is not far to seek. It must lie in a particular form of emotional education, and we must consider this matter briefly.

The theory of psycho-analysis would suggest two possible methods by which a reasonable temper in social relations could be produced.

1. It is first possible that political moderation and goodwill may be part of the whole character of the individual. The ordinary man may be reasonable in politics because he is reasonable in all things. Characters of this type can only be produced, if the theory of education compatible with the findings of psycho-analysis is true,[1] by the existence of a free, or relatively free, emotional environment in early childhood. The friendly and co-operative adult can be produced only from an early environment in which he or she has been free to express the hatred and aggression that follow naturally after the frustration involved in family and social life. The free or unpunished expression of aggression in the early years is, upon this theory of character formation, the only method of diminishing aggression in the later and socially more important years of adult life.

2. There is, however, a less probable alternative. It is at least conceivable that reasonableness in political and social relations could be secured at the expense of peacefulness and friendliness in the other relationships of life. It is, theoretically, possible that a society might be composed of personally violent men and women who displaced and projected, and so expressed, their aggressiveness upon and through entities other than political parties. Their violence, that is to say, might be canalized and relieved through non-political channels — in the life of religious institutions, or in

---

[1] See Part I, § 6.

thletic and personal activity. It is conceivable that a nation might enjoy relatively peaceful politics, and suffer from violent religious disputes. There are periods of English social history in the nineteenth century that bear some resemblance to this distribution of behaviour. And it is further possible that political life should be quiet, and industrial or personal relations be governed by violence. It might be suggested that America is an example of the first case; and some more primitive peoples, among whom personal violence is common but civil strife unknown, of the second.

But in general, it is surely improbable that a people will be peaceful in one set of social relations and violent in another. If the persons composing a social group suffer from a high degree of internal tension and have to dispose, speaking in physical metaphors, of a large quantity of aggressiveness, it is likely to appear, and find expression, in all their relations with the external world. Violent religious conflict is likely to be associated with violent politics, and both with a high proportion of violent crime.

My conclusion is, therefore, that the immediate cause of the growth of democratic political institutions in any society is the appearance in that society of certain widely distributed emotional characteristics; and that the establishment and maintenance of democracy is a sign of growing psychological health in any people.

I have stated this view shortly, because this is not primarily a book on social psychology — a subject that I should be profoundly incompetent to discuss — but a book on social policy. I must turn now to other things.[1]

---

[1] All these propositions and suggestions are here offered in the most tentative spirit. They require immense elaboration, and, above all, they call for empirical evidence and convincing proof. It needs to be shown by some psychiatrical or psychological inquiry, that the people of democracies do in fact exhibit the characteristics of psychological normality in greater proportions than those of dictatorial societies; that the practice of free emotional education is more frequent among them. Unless this is the case, the theory advanced here is false. Until it can be shown that it is the case, the theory remains unproven.

Nor do I wish to suggest in the very least that there are no historical or institutional forces at work in producing the character of a people, or that these institutions are less worthy of study in the attempt to explain historical and social behaviour. Quite the contrary. For two clear and final reasons the study of history and institutions must always remain the equal partner of psychological hypothesis and explanation:

In the *first* place, the characters of individuals, whose statistically normal features

§4

The Social Importance of the Democratic Method

Up to this point I have discussed the definition of democracy
the intellectual arguments for and against the democratic metho
as I have defined it, and the emotional origins of democracy
It is time that I discussed the importance of democracy as a
institution. What is its value to us?

It will be obvious that I think its value is immense. I thin
its continuous preservation is essential to the achievement of th
'just society'. I believe this for three reasons:

1. In the first place, I have argued that the only alternativ
method of government is that of terror — prison without tria
mental and physical torture, ruthless execution and the universa
vigilance of the secret police.

In this country it is extremely probable — for the reasons t
which Mr. Strachey has pointed — that the necessary degree o
ruthlessness would be as great as, or even greater than, in any othe
country. We have been accustomed to political liberty, freedon
of association, security from arbitrary arrest, and the absence o
household spying, for so long that we should react to the absenc
of these things with astonishing force. The screw would have t

determine, in my view, the immediate course of social behaviour, are themselves th
product of the reaction between the hereditary traits of children and the socia
environment in which those children were educated. Adult characters do no
materialize out of the air. It is the nature of human experience, human behaviou
and human character to be the result of a reaction between two things – inherite
potentiality and environmental stimulus. The nature of the environment active i
the formation of 'national character' is social and institutional through and through
Hence the study of social institutions and the historical development of particula
societies will always be necessary to the understanding of those societies and to th
formation of any judgment about their future behaviour. It would be absurd in th
highest degree to imagine that we could understand this country without a
knowledge of the development and significance of Parliament, or the Crown, o
the Syndicated Press, or organized athletics, or the distribution of property. In th
same way it would be ridiculous to study America without understanding th
significance of 'the frontier', or Germany without a knowledge of the part playe
in the development of that nation by the prosecution of a series of successful wars
And, in the broader understanding of society as a whole, it would be fantastic t
suppose that we shall not need as much information as we can gather about th
basic social institutions of the family, the structure of authority, the forms o
property, the system of education and ethical opinion. All these investigations ar
just as important for the understanding of history and society as any past or presen
study of individual psychology. I hope that, after my attempt in the second Par

e applied with immense pressure to this people, and the bonds
f their oppression drawn exceedingly tight, in order to break their
pirit. If there is to be a terror in this country it will have to be
particularly efficient one.

It is hardly conceivable to me that anyone can seriously contend
1at a country so governed possesses a good society. Freedom of
ssociation, freedom from arbitrary arrest, power to count with
thers in the government of the nation — these are essential
roperties of any social order that can be described as good.
"hey are fundamental requirements for any society claiming
o provide an opportunity for the free development, and growing
1appiness, of the individuals composing it. An opposition
1etween 'socialism' and 'the democratic method', if 'socialism'
ontains any reference to 'social justice', is meaningless to me.
The relationship between these two things appears to me to be
he relationship between the whole and the part. The democratic
nethod, and the absence of terror, are an indispensable part of my
:onception of social justice.

2. It might, however, be suggested that while the method of
1olitical democracy, as defined by me, was one necessary charac-
eristic of a just social order, it was not the only characteristic of it,
1nd therefore no more fundamental than any other: for example,
he existence of a just distribution of wealth. In that case it might

f this book to trace out a number of significant trends in our institutional arrange-
nents, no one will accuse me of any faith in individual psychology divorced from
he measurement of environmental change, as a basis for a positive social science.

In the *second* place, it is obvious, in this particular instance, that the institutional
1nd historical study is absolutely essential. Suppose that it is conceded to me for a
noment, that democracy is immediately caused by the presence in a people of a
1igh proportion of persons with a particular type of emotional life, and further that
his predominance of certain emotional characteristics is due to the presence in the
:ociety of a particular type of emotional education. The next question that
mmediately arises in tracing the causal sequence is this — how did that type of educa-
ion arise in this people? The form of emotional education is itself a social institu-
:ion of the greatest possible importance. How did that institution arise? What is
ts history as an institution? Why did it come into existence among this people and
not among that? All these questions can only be answered by historical and
institutional inquiry.

Nevertheless, my first point remains. It is the sole methodological contention of
this book. Historical studies are vital. Institutional studies are vital. But so also
are psychological studies. History and institutions are made by individuals. Social
behaviour consists in the reactions of individuals to social and institutional stimuli.
The study of the mechanism of those reactions, the task of individual psychology,
is essential to the work of social study, to synthetic sociology or the science of social
causes.

be reasonable to sacrifice one of these characteristics — liberty — in order to obtain the other — equality.

Now it is perfectly possible for persons to prefer equality in the distribution of wealth to political liberty. They are then perfectly consistent — though in my view morally mistaken — to advocate a political terror in order to make the distribution of income less unequal. My point is not that such a position is untenable — since it is plainly logical — but simply that such a programme and such a strategy does not touch the problem of constructing a just society. Economic equality can be fully achieved, and social justice remain as far away as ever, because one kind of injustice has replaced another — because one type of privilege (political) has been substituted for another (economic). The problem of a just society is not the single problem of economic equality, but the much more difficult problem of achieving simultaneously in one society both liberty and equality.

It is precisely here that my argument about the inherent permanence of dictatorship — apart from further civil war — becomes relevant. In discussing the Communist strategy I argued at length, and I need not repeat the argument, that a dictatorship of any kind, including that of the Communist Party, is almost certainly incapable of restoring the essential institution of political liberty — freedom of opposition. A dictatorship has governed by terror, and has denied, for as long as it has been in power, the access of all other parties and groups to the ear of the people. It is certain, human aggressiveness being what it is, that the opposition called forth by such methods of oppression will be of a certain kind. It will be of a like kind. It will be ruthless and savage, terrorist and cruel. One great evil of cruelty is that it begets cruelty — of dictatorship that it makes it increasingly difficult to establish, or re-establish, democracy. The opposition within a dictatorship will desire to give back as much as they have received. They will bully and torture and kill their opponents as they have been bullied and tortured and killed.

That is the supreme importance of preserving a *continuous* democracy. One break with democracy is a break with it for an indefinite period. A dictatorship once seated in power is likely to continue in that seat, until it is forcibly ejected by a further

SOCIAL IMPORTANCE

volution. A single departure from government by consent is
most certain to initiate a prolonged period of government by
rce, or recurrent civil war, or of permanent servitude.[1]
We reach then this final position — that the democratic method
not only essential for the achievement of socialism, but that it is
rt of that achievement. In so far as we are democratic we are
ready, in some degree, socialist; and to betray democracy is to
tray socialism.

There is a complex and important sense in which socialism is
cessary to democracy — the sense in which capitalism is in-
mpatible with democracy.[2] But there is a very simple and much
ore obvious sense in which democracy is necessary to socialism.
is not that democracy is the pleasantest, or most efficacious,
most certain method of achieving socialism, but that it is the
ly method; that all other hopes and all other programmes
e mistaken and illusory. Democracy is not related to socialism
gilt to the gingerbread, or cream to coffee — a decorative
ldition or a great improvement; but as air to breathing, as
al to fire, as love to life — the indispensable means, the *fons et
go* of all our social hopes.

And so I am brought to the final statement of my central point
this Part of the book.

3. Democracy is a *method* of taking political decisions, of
mpromising and reconciling conflicting interests. The method
more important, more formative of the resulting social order,
an the disputes so resolved.

*When individuals or groups disagree — including nations and classes and
rties within the state — the most important question is not what they disagree
out, but the method or methods by which their disputes are to be resolved.*[3]
force is to be the arbiter between them, international war, civil
ar, cruelty and persecution are the inevitable consequences.

[1] There are clearly exceptions to this generalization. France in the nineteenth
ntury, for example, alternated between Bourbon and Buonapartist dictatorships
the one hand, and democratic constitutions on the other. It is at least conceivable
at Germany may pass through the same process in the twentieth century. But it
nevertheless clear: (*a*) that a dictatorship can only be replaced by force, (*b*) that
most probable outcome of further force is a different kind of dictatorship. There
many more countries that exhibit a prolonged alternation of dictatorial regimes.
[2] See Part II *passim* and Appendix II.
[3] This is merely a short statement of the central thesis of MR. BASSETT's *Essentials
Parliamentary Democracy*, Chap. IV.

Civilization cannot be built upon these crises of destruction

There are two great principles at struggle in the hearts of men – friendliness and aggressiveness, co-operation and struggle. The lives of us all, and the slow growth of reason and kindliness between us, depend upon the victory of the first principle over the second It is only if men will agree at least in this, that their disputes shall not be resolved by force, that culture and justice can slowly develop in our midst. The vital question is the question of method The method will determine the end.

This is not a pacifist conclusion — not in the very least. I am not contending that it is the duty of any man to surrender his own purposes simply because other persons or groups use force, or threaten to use force, against him. That appears to me to be nonsensical, and to offer prizes to the unreasonable and to the aggressive. It may very well be our duty to repel force with force, and to see that — once the peace is broken — the group to which we owe our loyalty is victorious in the struggle that ensues.[1]

My point, then, is not that we should be pacifist or believe in non-resistance, but that we should be pacific and believe in compromise. It is our supreme social duty to aid contending groups to agree not to use force in the settlement of their disputes. I set the maintenance of such agreements first in the sequence of our social values.[2]

It is of the first importance to notice that the principle of pacific settlement and of mutual compromise must be accepted by all the parties within a democracy. The obligation not to use force and the obligation to compromise, is not restricted to one party. No party within the state is called upon to contemplate its own liquidation or to surrender its own objectives, simply because it

[1] In most wars, international or civil, that come to my mind, it appears to me to have been important that one side, rather than the other, should have won.

[2] It must, of course, be remembered that at all times, and in all parts of the world there are minority groups within the nation, and a minority of nations within the society of nations, who will not accept the agreement to use peaceful methods who advertise and act upon the intention to alter the world in the direction of their desires, and to pursue what they regard as their rights, by the use of the whole of the force at their command. As a consequence, the agreement not to use force must be protected by force; the aggressive and recalcitrant minority must be restrained by force; law must be enforced by the police, and international order protected by measures of collective coercion. Here we have, in my view, the unassailable elements of the case against the pacifist and of the case for the metropolitan and international police force.

ponents threaten to use force against it. I shall consider this
atter in the next Section.

With these further explanations of it, my central point now
ands. I wish to maintain that the question of method is prior
the substance of the dispute between any pair of groups,
cluding economic classes. If the method is to be that of warfare,
en the hope of justice must be indefinitely postponed. Terror
ad cruelty must rule the affairs of men, and we must walk
r ever in the shadow of fear. It may be that as individuals we
all belong to the group that is victorious in the struggle, or it
ay be that we shall be with those who are defeated. In victory
defeat we shall live in fear and see blood upon our hands. The
ctorious will live in fear of the oppressed, and the defeated in
rror of the victors. And all those who fight must carry the guilt
destruction in their hearts. It may be our duty to join in such
battle — for it is often impossible to be indifferent to the
utcome of a fight, however savage or irrational its origins
ay have been. But the basis of social justice, of friendliness
etween persons, of happiness and security in society, cannot be
unded upon a regime of warfare. It can only be founded
pon the principles of compromise and peace, and upon the
striction of force to the single task of coercing the aggressive
inorities who will not accept the rule of law.

The authoritarian architects of Utopia all start by building the
pper floors of their buildings. They try to build insubstantial
astles in the air'. Social justice is the spire and the crown of the
uman habitation. But there is only one foundation for it.
ommon security and common happiness can only be founded
pon common consent — men must come freely to their own
alvation — justice can only spring from liberty. Democracy is
he foundation and corner-stone of the temple.

§ 5

The Defence of Democracy

I am brought to the last point that it is necessary to discuss in
his Part. I have already raised it briefly in the last Section. It is

this problem: What is the duty of a democrat belonging to society in which the faith in democracy is declining, and the fai in dictatorship growing?

Democracy in Western Europe has, in some sense, been retreat in recent years. It is very easy to exaggerate the extent which this historical judgment is true. If we compare the prese geographical distribution of constitutional forms in Europe to-d with that of 1913, the most obvious point about it is the degree continuity in national differences and national character. Rough speaking, and with the exception of Italy, the territorial distrib tion of responsible government and authoritarian government precisely the same now as it was then. The nations that we traditional democracies before the last war — Great Britai France, Belgium, Sweden, Switzerland, Denmark — are d mocracies still; while those who were living under absolu governments or authoritarian regimes — Germany, Russia, Austri Hungary, Bulgaria — are living under them still. Only Italy h been lost, in this wider historical perspective, to the democrati fold; and democracy was never a very glorious, or a very stabl thing in Italy. To offset that loss, there is a certain gain of toler tion in the new nation states temporarily emancipated by th Treaty of Versailles from foreign domination — like Czech Slovakia and the Baltic States. All in all, speaking geographically it is not possible to say that democracy has lost much ground i the last thirty years.

But it has clearly lost ground in the last ten years. I opene this book with a dreary account of the wave of revolution, wa dictatorship and cruelty that has swept over Europe and th world since 1930. Democratic constitutions have been swep away in Germany and Austria after a decade of trial. A demo cratic constitution has been destroyed in Spain. In numerou other countries the hand of authoritarian government has bee laid more heavily upon the life of the nation. Unfortunately, there fore, we must consider the problems raised by the growth o authoritarian parties — Communist and Fascist — within de mocracies.

What is the position of a democrat in face of such a development

About this problem, I have two things to say:

In the *first* place, I think it important to realize that Fascists
and Communists cannot claim, as their right, the privileges of a
democratic society.

There is much confusion on this point among those of liberal
opinion. They regard the privileges of democracy as the cause
of democracy, and wish to preserve these privileges to all members
of the state, regardless of their attitude to the obligations
of democracy. We have seen the extraordinary attitude of the
Council for Civil Liberties, who wished to prevent the weakening
of Fascist and Communist organizations, *in the name of civil
liberty*.

Now this attitude, however expedient it may be, contains in my
submission a confusion of thought. Freedom of speech, freedom
of association, freedom of opposition to the government — the
precious privileges of a free society — are the *fruits* of a continued
use of the democratic method. They are not that method itself,
nor the basis of it. The method of democracy is that of government by discussion and choice. The basis of democracy is the
contract between the parties in the state not to persecute each
other. It is by this method, and upon this basis, that the privileges of democracy are alone made possible.

In what way, then, can Communists or Fascists claim, as a
right, the privileges of free speech and free association? They do
not accept the obligations by which those privileges have been
created. They are not parties to the contract that alone creates
the possibility of political liberty. Why then should they enjoy it?
Why should they be allowed to play the game when they advertise
openly their intention not to play according to the rules?[1]

To put this simple point in another way — why should we, as
democrats, hand over the weapons of destruction to those who
openly advertise their intention to destroy us with them? There is
no reasonable doubt about the matter. Fascists and Communists
are perfectly open and definite in the statement of their intentions.
They advocate, unashamedly, the establishment of dictatorships of
their parties, and the suppression and liquidation of all groups and

---

[1] Cf. BASSETT, pp. 249-250: 'Faced by such attempts the democratic State is fully
justified in excluding partisans of dictatorship from parliamentary representation,
and in taking any ancillary measures'.

organizations in opposition to them. Those policies have neve
been carried through in any country without the use of force an
the employment of terror. The knuckleduster, the whip, th
rubber truncheon, the sleepless cell, forced labour and the shootin
squad, are the weapons of every dictatorship in the world.[1] Thes
rods are in pickle for us if either the British Fascists or Communis
obtain power. Whether we are Democratic Socialists, or Liberal
or Conservatives, or Christians, or Jews, or pacifists, or Co
operators, or Trade Unionists, we shall come under the flai
Dictatorships are jealous gods and will tolerate 'none other besid
them'. For books like this, for far less controversial writings; fc
the slightest deviation of thought or speech; we shall be brough
to trial and punishment.

It may be said that it would never be like that in this country
But why should that be believed? The tradition of liberty i
older and stronger here. It would die less easily. As we hav
seen, a more brutal persecution and a wider espionage would b
necessary to stamp out the love and practice of political libert
among us.

Why should we suffer these things? The power is still ours. We ar
not called upon to lie down before our tormentors and give our
selves over to their cruelty. Only the pacifist believes that it i
wrong to resist force with force. We need not, and we ought not, t
surrender our liberties without a fight. The happiness of those wh
come after us depends upon our resistance.

What exactly do I mean by these bold words? I mean tha
we should continuously remind ourselves that the enemies o
democracy have no moral right to the privileges of democracy
and that a time may come when, to defend ourselves, it will b
necessary to suppress their political organizations. It is obviousl
not *expedient*, at the moment, to proceed to any extreme measures
In Great Britain the Communist Party and the Fascist Part
are both so small that they constitute no serious threat t
our liberties. Between them they can only claim one mem
ber of Parliament. It is not necessary, and it would greatl
confuse the public mind, to proceed against them as politica
organizations.

[1] See Appendix I.

But it is perfectly proper to prevent either the Communist or
: Fascist Party from forming military or quasi-military troops,
·m disturbing the peace by provocative demonstrations or
llies, from wearing uniforms. It is proper to do this because the
·vileges of liberty can only be extended to minority groups
·thin a society upon the understanding that the power acquired
· exercising them will not be used to deny those privileges to
·ers. The Fascists and Communists alike will not sign this
·al contract. It is this refusal that binds them together as the
·mmon enemies of liberty and peace. It is only the intolerant
·o cannot be tolerated, and those who deny freedom to others
·ve lost the right to freedom for themselves.

Further than this, it may become essential to limit, and even
·ppress altogether, the political activities of the authoritarian
·rties. If the Fascists and Communists between them grow to a
·bstantial proportion of the electorate, the basic principles of
·litical activity are changed. If, between them, the two revolu-
·nary wings command as much as 40 per cent of the electorate
· of the seats in Parliament, the contract to tolerate differences of
·inion is in danger. A peaceful society, in which so substantial
·minority were prepared to coerce and persecute their fellow-
·untrymen, could not long endure.

In such circumstances, the conditions and methods of political
·uggle are radically altered. When any important group
·thdraws from the undertaking not to use force in the settlement
·disputes, a regime of coercion or of 'power politics' is substituted
· that of government by discussion and consent. In these new
·cumstances, it is both the right and the duty of the democratic
·ups and parties to protect themselves from destruction by the
·ly method open to them — that of force. There is no reply to
·ce except pure pacifism, or resistance in kind.

This brings me to the *second* point that I wish to make. If all
·at I have argued in this Part of the book is true, it follows that it
· of the greatest importance for democrats in different parties to
·alize the importance of the convictions they hold in common.
·ave tried to demonstrate that convictions about the method of
·olving disputes are more important, far more important, than
· substance of the disputes themselves. Political method

277

determines the form of society. Political method makes broth
or murderers, peaceful citizens or ruthless criminals, of us a
Hence, however deep our party differences, we must recogni
the overriding strength of the common bond.

In British political life there are democrats in all parties a
Fascists at both wings. There are men and women of reason a
compromise in Labour, Liberal and Conservative Parties. The
are men and women of violence and cruelty at both extremes
the political stage. Political opinion, at least on method,
arranged on a horseshoe curve and not in a straight line. T
psychological character and basic ideas of the two types
extremist are nearer together than they are to the modera
opinion that appears to lie between them. Fascists and Co
munists have more in common, even though they will willing
kill each other, than Fascists and Conservatives or Communi
and Socialists — just because they will kill each other. *A*
murderers have much in common.

It therefore follows, that in any acute constitutional crisis,
which the democratic method itself was at stake, it might easi
be the duty of Socialists and Conservatives to combine again
Communists and Fascists for the protection and the preservati
of democracy amongst themselves. This was the real positio
when the Labour Party voted for the 'political uniforms' B
introduced by the National Government. It is essential for a
democrats to realize that this is a type of political alignme
of the greatest importance for the preservation of democrac
There must be collective security amongst all democrats
resist the aggression of all authoritarian minorities.

Those who feel that there is a logical inconsistency in a democr
advocating the suppression of any opinion or party organizatio
are guilty, in my opinion, of confusing cause and effect. Toleran
and political liberty are not the cause or definitive property
democracy, but the consequence or desirable result of it. The cau
of democracy, the thing that alone makes it possible, is the mutu
agreement not to persecute. Only those who renounce persecuti
can be tolerated. Only those who accept the rules can play t
game. Only the tolerant can be free.

The sole alternative to this view is the doctrine of the pacifist

mplete non-resistance to aggression, force and persecution. No
mocrat is called upon to accept the doctrine of non-resistance.
personally, do not.

§6

Conclusion

I have tried in this Part to explain what I mean by political
mocracy and the democratic method. I have tried to show that
e arguments in its favour are overwhelmingly strong, and that,
on examination, it proves to be the only secure basis for the
w growth of our national civilization.
But that does not mean that it will last. Our civilization is not
rtain to grow. It may pass into decline and eclipse. We cannot
retell these things. They depend upon complex historical events
d psychological factors, and upon the will of men. We have no
cial science capable of prophesying the outcome of these compli-
ted forces. We face the unknown.

This island of social peace is surrounded by the fierce sea of
uropean hatred and fear. We cannot cut ourselves adrift from
e continent whose races and ideas have peopled and inspired us.
e may be overwhelmed by the rising tides of cruelty and destruc-
on that have swept unchecked over those beautiful but unhappy
nds, our nearest neighbours. But come what may, we have con-
ibuted a great idea and a great example to the turbulent flood
human experience. We have lived in peace with one another
r nearly three hundred years, despite the existence in our midst
racial, religious, and class differences that have torn apart less
ppy peoples. Out of our common happiness we have made
ociety rich in peace and good will. And whether we go down to
cial disaster, or whether we survive the more terrible days that
em now to lie ahead of us, we have set on record a discovery
at cannot be forgotten — the secret of social peace. We
ve to fight to preserve ourselves as persons and as a nation
the days that are now to come. In the ferocity of that struggle,

our calmer habits and our deeper community may perish for a time, or from this land for ever. But our comradeship will have been, and will remain in history, a peak of human achievement, a shadow in a dry land, a sunny interlude in storm. Let us value it for what it is, and keep it for as long as we can.

THE STRATEGY OF DEMOCRATIC SOCIALISM

A Discussion of the Political Programme of a Democratic Socialist Party

OCIALISM, as a means to the emancipation of the proletariat, with-
ut democracy is unthinkable ... We understand by modern
ocialism not merely social organization of production, but demo-
ratic organization of society as well. Accordingly, socialism is for
is inseparably connected with democracy. No socialism without
lemocracy.

KAUTSKY: *The Dictatorship of the Proletariat.* 1918

Once upon a time, socialism in any of its varieties was automatically associated with the whole heritage of mankind in terms of
liberty and human dignity ... Socialism, in short, was not
merely an economic formula but an ethical system of ideals.

LYONS: *Assignment in Utopia.* 1938

THE STRATEGY OF DEMOCRATIC SOCIALISM

§ 1

Introduction — the Problem

AM left with a practical problem to face. If the economic ystem is in urgent need of reform, and if the maintenance of lemocracy is an essential condition of social justice, how can the ne be used to secure the other? How can expansionist and galitarian policies be secured through the practice of the democratic method? The democratic socialist must discover such a trategy.

§ 2

The Formal Conditions of the Problem

The preservation of democracy consists in the maintenance of government by consent, and in the toleration of all opposition to he government, in so far as it accepts the primary and fundamental obligation of democracy — the contract of mutual toleration between the Parties. The problem of strategy facing the lemocratic socialist is therefore to find a policy that makes an advance towards socialism, and yet does not render the continuation of democracy impossible. It is consequently easy to state the ormal conditions for the solution of the problem. A programme must be found that fulfils these three conditions:

(1) It must not be so extreme that it drives the opposition to it into *armed* resistance, or rebellion.

(2) It must not be so emasculated that it fails to retain the active and loyal support of the reforming democratic party that is asked to advocate it.

283

(3) It must lie in the relevant sphere of policy — the sphere of economic and social measures.

Let me say a word about each of these purely formal conditions in turn:

(1) The *first* essential condition for a successful democratic strategy is that it should not force the opposition into armed rebellion. This is plainly a condition of success, since rebellion means civil warfare, and it is morally certain that peaceful and democratic conditions will not be restored for a generation afterwards — until the memory of the hatred and savagery of the civil strife has passed away.

But there are a number of points that are worth noticing about the nature of this formal condition:

The only thing that has to be avoided is *armed* resistance. This does not mean that the Socialist programme must be approved by the future Conservative opposition, or that the conflict between the political parties during the struggle will be in the least unreal. Nor does it even imply that the opposition to the programme must necessarily be of the orthodox political type.

We have heard a great deal in recent times about the danger of the 'economic sabotage' in which the opponents of a constitutional Socialist Government might indulge. We are told that the advent to power of a Labour Government in this country will provoke a 'crisis in confidence', or a 'financial panic', and that these crises and panics cripple a Government unprepared to set up a dictatorship. This has been the main contention of recent Communist theory.[1] While it is difficult to explain, on this view, the quiet history of New Zealand and Sweden after the accession to power of Labour and Socialist Governments in those countries, it is not unreasonable, after the experience of the Popular Front Governments in France, to expect some substantial and unfavourable reactions in the foreign exchange and capital markets of this country in similar circumstances.

But it is a long step from supposing that there will be a 'crisis in financial confidence' to the view that such a crisis must provoke an armed rebellion. Let me repeat that it is only armed

[1] See Addendum to Part III.

esistance that endangers the maintenance of democracy. The
onservative Press may fulminate; the political orators may grow
urple in the face; the prophets of doom may shriek in chorus;
vithout the stable foundations of our political order becoming
eriously shaken. These things have happened often before, and
he heavens have not fallen. On the other hand, with a determined
eople like the British, a serious outbreak of civil strife is likely to
e fought out to the bitter end. It is therefore only if there is good
eason to believe that a 'crisis in confidence' must lead to civil war
hat we need be greatly afraid of it.

Again it is reasonable to admit that, if a financial panic is allowed
o become uncontrolled so that the exchanges fall catastrophically,
r the volume of employment is allowed to decline steadily, the
eople as a whole will insist, and insist rightly, through the
sual channels of political agitation, that some more competent
overnment takes control of the nation's business. A General
lection in such a case could be properly requested, and if a
abour Government were sufficiently unwise to refuse the popular
lemand, rioting against it and a slow degeneration of public
rder into civil war might conceivably take place.

But why should the crisis in confidence be allowed to get out of
and in this way? I have never been able to accept the views of
hose who see nothing but crisis and gloom ahead, because I have
never been able to see why these 'crises' and 'panics' should not
be confidently encountered and overcome. Why should our
ancient liberties perish because the financial houses in the City are
frightened, and elderly ladies in Bournemouth are excited?

I must turn aside for a moment to consider the results of a
decline in financial confidence.

The rising fears of the propertied class can lead to three, but
only three, important types of unfavourable reaction. The foreign
exchanges can fall. There may be an internal cash drain. The
prices of securities might decline and unemployment rise. I am
not aware of any other serious forms that 'economic sabotage',
conscious or unconscious, can take. But no one of these possibilities
is a fatal possibility. Each one of them can be rendered innocuous
by appropriate measures.

A decline in the level of the foreign exchanges is the least serious danger. There is not a country in Europe that has not met, fought and survived this unfavourable development in its economi position. The problems and methods of exchange control are wel understood and largely perfected by now. We have already create in this country a powerful agent for the control of precisely th weak point in our financial armoury — the Exchange Equalization Fund — and there is not the slightest reason for supposing that resolute government could not in a few days, if it wished, bring the Foreign Exchange Market under effective governance, and prevent an organized minority from frustrating the chosen pur poses of a majority of the nation.

Indeed, this has already been done to meet the demands of war and there is no reason why the same thing should not be done again — if, indeed, freedom is ever restored to this particular market

Nor does the less likely chance of serious cash withdrawals from the banking system present any greater difficulty. If the depositing public became very frightened, they might conceivably attempt to draw heavily upon their balances. *It is only necessary, in such circumstances, to provide them with the form of money they wish to hold.* The Government need only print the number of notes required by the banks, and undertake to help them to keep open as the quantity of their earning assets contracts, in order to survive the crisis successfully. The printing of notes is not inflationary since every note issued to the public has been preceded by an equal reduction of bank deposits. The withdrawal cannot last for long, since the public cannot for long endure the nuisance of keeping any substantial sums of money in the form of legal tender, and therefore thievable assets. After a few days of holding large quantities of notes, and in face of the continued stability of the banks, the public will have no choice except quietly to deposit their notes with the banks once again. The abnormal issue of notes can then be safely returned to the note-issuing authority and the 'crisis' is over. The history of the American banking crisis exhibits this process in its simplest form.

The most difficult, and therefore the most serious, possibility is the third — that the 'crisis in confidence' will result in a decline of investment, a rise in the market rate of interest, and a fall in employment. In this case the theory of policy is simple, but the ractice of it may prove more difficult. To maintain employment is only necessary to maintain the level of investment, and this the Government can do, in theory, by replacing the fall in private investment by an increase of public investment — by an extended programme of public works.

But there are certain practical difficulties. The Government has only just been formed. It may lack adequate plans for capital expenditure. In any case, it will take time to get the investment started. Nevertheless, if the volume of public investment is raised, the third difficulty can be overcome. To this point we shall return.

For these reasons it is difficult for me to accept the view that the advent to power of a democratic Socialist Party, committed to the policy of increasing the social control of business, is bound to lead to civil war via the outbreak of an uncontrollable crisis in confidence. Crisis in confidence there may be; but there is no good reason for believing that it need become, in the least degree, uncontrollable. Resolution and intelligence in government, exhibited in other countries and in our own in the past, are all that is required to surmount this first hurdle in the race for social justice.

But let me go on to say at once that this first condition for a successful democratic and socialist strategy — that the capitalist opposition should not be driven to armed resistance — is not a negligible limitation upon the choice of programme. It sets an essential limit — a limit upon the *pace* of change — beyond which the programme must not go. I do not think that there is any competent judge of the British political tradition, and of the distribution of power between classes, who doubts that a programme of action aiming at the rapid destruction of economic inequality — in, say, the lifetime of a single Parliament — would provoke civil war. If any party sought to carry through a revolution of this type by 'constitutional' means it would have to fight. If it sought to pass confiscatory legislation, or take general powers to govern by decree or Order in Council, armed resistance would in my view be certain.

It would be certain in the first place because the working class itself would not approve of such measures. With the possible exception of the periods immediately before and immediately after the last war, the working class has not been in a revolutionary mood for nearly a hundred years. They have not armed them selves. They have not contributed to an 'underground' or seditious organization. Every society and institution that they have evolved or controlled — whether industrial, co-operative or political — has been in the highest degree careful and evolutionary, moderate and constitutional, in its programme, method and mood. It would be difficult to conceive a more stable, a more respectable, a more responsible mass movement than the British Labour Movement to-day. Extremists of all classes, and particularly intellectuals of the middle class, hate to recognize this historical fact. They struggle to avoid its political implications. But the generalization remains obstinately true, and any Labour Government that was foolish enough to commit itself to revolutionary action would lose the electoral support upon which it had been formed, would have to fight without an army to lead, and would become a sorry company of deluded Jacobins, fighting a people. There is, of course no danger whatever that the existing leadership of the Labour Party would make such a crass mistake; but if ever a body of men obtained control of it, who were misled by the noisy persistence of the small extremist minority within it, and embarked upon measures involving very rapid social change, there could only be one of two outcomes to the resulting struggle — either the constitutional defeat of the would-be revolutionary government at a second General Election, or a popular dictatorship of the Right. Apart from defeat in war, we are not such stuff as social revolutions are made on.

This very fact constitutes a problem in political action and a great difficulty in the choice of policy. A programme must be found that does not outrage the conservative sections of all classes in this country, but which at the same time does not discourage too deeply the militant elements in the Party of the Left. This brings me to the second essential condition that a true solution of the strategic problem must satisfy.

(2)   One central problem of action in a democracy is to reconcile the enthusiastic aspirations of the active minority within each party in the state with the slower moving and less radical requirements of the great mass of the electorate. The battles upon which the future of democracy depend must be fought within, and not

between, the parties contending for power. The continuous defeat of the extremist minority on the right of the Conservative Party, and the continuous defeat of the extremist minority on the Left of the Labour Party, is the price that must be paid for democracy itself. That much is clear.

But nevertheless a great difficulty remains. Political action is only possible in a democracy through the active work and vigorous life of a party machine. The Labour Party and the Conservative Party alike must depend, for the maintenance of active political propaganda, upon the 'rank and file' of its party workers. It would be impossible for either party to obtain power or to govern without its army of unpaid canvassers, ward secretaries, municipal councillors, aldermen and mayors; its constituency committeemen, secretaries, chairmen and agents; its parliamentary candidates; its subscribers and advisers. These are the troops, the steady infantry and the gallant cavalry, of our peaceful political warfare. With them rests victory or defeat.

Yet, for obvious reasons, some of these very people tend to become the purists of any movement, the main core of party intolerance and unwisdom and intransigence; upon whose resistance many a wise policy of compromise and moderation has foundered. Because they are the enthusiasts, they are also the diehards. Because they have given so much thought and devotion to one party, they naturally tend to exaggerate the significance of party differences and the importance of party doctrine. Because they are sound party men, they see all things as either black or white, imparting into their politics the transferred aggressiveness, and the dangerous simplicity of mind, whose origins we traced in the first Part of this book.[1]

Nevertheless the support of these people must be retained, if democratic Socialism is to be achieved. The party machine must be maintained. The activities of explaining policy to the country

---

[1] I do not mean to suggest either that the rank and file of local party organizations are wholly manned by unreasonable people, or that the rank and file are necessarily extreme in their political views. There are many well-balanced men and women of goodwill in all party machines. And the local leaders are often people of very moderate views. But the party machine as a whole is usually highly partisan and doctrinally orthodox.

The party machine at the centre is often the opposite of all this – and may decline into an excess of caution and inactivity.

suading the electorate to support it must be continued.
 chinery of local and central government must be manned.
     his requirement of a successful strategy sets a limit to the
degree of moderation that is practicable. Just as the first requirement sets an upper limit, so the need to maintain party enthusiasm
sets a lower limit, to the pace of change consistent with ultimate
success. If the engine runs too fast it will run off the rails, but if it
goes too slowly, it will lose momentum altogether.[1]

Fortunately in his country the problem has, in recent years,
proved comparatively easy of solution. The machinery of both the
main Parties in the state has contained sufficient men of moderation and goodwill to make the promulgation and advocacy of compromise programmes possible. But this condition may not be
permanent; and in any case the programmes must not be too
moderate, or even the sober British trade unionist and Labour
'back bencher' will become restless and disillusioned. A programme must be found that is too moderate to drive the retired
colonel and the City merchant to arms, and too positive to cause
the engine driver and the miner to lose all interest in politics.

(3) Finally, the programme must be in the relevant sphere
of social action. It must, that is to say, be concerned with the
transfer of economic control and the redistribution of real income.

This, oddly enough, is an important point to stress in the period
in which I write (1939). Many persons are eager to broaden the
basis of opposition to a Conservative and capitalist government.
They propose to do this in the name of Socialism and Democracy.
But they intend to do so upon a programme from which all the
'socialism' has been quietly deleted. The policies suggested for
such United or Popular Fronts, as they are called, are various.

[1] It is my view that a failure to give correct emphasis to this point is one of the few
weaknesses of MR. BASSETT's *Essentials of Parliamentary Democracy*. Mr. Bassett i
excellent in his explanation of the first of my 'principles of strategy', and hi
emphasis upon the necessity for moderation, compromise, and mutual understand
ing between the parties. He is brilliant in his revealing analysis of the betrayal o
democracy implied in the programmes of the extreme Left in this country. But he
does not seem prepared to admit that in the normal course of events parties must be
held together, and that the problem of party Leadership is not merely that o
defeating the extreme wing but also of placating it. It is this necessity of combining
resolution with moderation, of satisfying friends without outraging 'enemies', that
makes the work of the professional politician so difficult, and makes him sometime
appear hypocritical to those who bear no responsibility, and can therefore afford th
luxury of pure categories of thought and simple judgments.

mixtures of proposals almost entirely restricted to the field of social service legislation and of foreign policy.[1]

Now I am not saying that such programmes are mistaken. It may be very wise to seek to unite and broaden the basis of the opposition to the government of the day; we certainly live at a time when it is difficult to sustain for long an interest in anything far removed from foreign policy.[2] But the fact remains that such programmes are no solution to the problem before us. It may be possible to win an election upon the basis of a programme composed wholly of social service and foreign policy measures; but the execution of such a programme, though it may protect the conditions of working-class culture within which alone socialism can be secured, would not of itself constitute any advance whatever towards the socialist goal. In order to solve the strategic problems of democratic Socialism, the measures proposed must deal with the control of industry and the distribution of income — the final socialist objectives.

We return therefore to the question with which this Section began. Is it possible to find a programme of political action that will neither drive the opposition to armed resistance, nor discourage the reforming party, and that nevertheless constitutes a step towards the socialist goal? Only if such a programme can be constructed will the strategic problem of democratic Socialism stand resolved. Is there such a programme?

The first and most obvious answer to this question is that 'nobody knows'. Future political development depends upon so many factors — historical tradition, the international situation, the

---

[1] In, for example, the programme announced for the United Front in the *Daily Worker* for January 18th, 1937, there were 13 points. Of these no less than 10 were purely ameliorative extensions of the social services, 2 were extremely vague ('Power to get back the land for the people' and 'Effective *control* of the Banks, the Stock Exchanges . . .') and only one ('Nationalization of the Mining Industry') was clearly in what I have called the 'relevant sphere'.

[2] I have already explained in the Addendum to Part III that I believe the participation of the Communist Party in such Fronts and their support of 'reformist' programmes to be purely tactical. These things are regarded by them as a step towards the creation of a revolutionary situation, and the subsequent exploitation of it to obtain absolute power. It has been explained to me in private conversation that the 'demands' in the sphere of the social services are deliberately made extravagant in order to make them 'revolutionary'. I have, in any case, little enthusiasm for joining with a Party that advocates the 'dictatorship of the proletariat' with a view to 'defending democracy'.

hidden and unconscious movement of emotional forces and th
inscrutable will of men and groups — that no one can be sure wha
will, in fact, occur. The exponents of the social sciences have no
yet become, and are not likely to become, for many years ahead
prophetic seers.

'We know not what awaits us . . .'

But this lack of certainty does not remove all obligation from us
We must not refuse to look ahead because we cannot see clearly
We must not refuse to think about the future because we lack th
gift of prophecy. We must·do the best we can with the facultie
and judgment that we possess. It clearly behoves those of us whc
believe in democracy and socialism to seek to combine the tw
articles of our faith, and to search for the policy most likely to fulf
the three conditions I have laid down.

This I propose to do; but, before I describe the policy that I
believe to approach most nearly to the ideal, it is necessary to say
a word about the various components of what I have termed the
'relevant sphere of social action'.

§3

The Contents of the 'Relevant Sphere'

If we consider the field of economic and social legislation from
which measures must be selected to compose any internal political
programme there are, I suggest, four different types of measure
that it will be wise to distinguish from each other. They are:

1. *Ameliorative Measures.* By ameliorative legislation and administration I mean the use of the power of the State to ameliorate
the condition of the relatively poor. Of this type of measure the
social services are the most important example. By them education, the care of the ill, the unemployed, and the old, is financed
out of the proceeds of general taxation. In addition to the transfer
of real income thus secured, there is a great deal of regulative
legislation, the object of which is to secure a reasonable degree of
safety in the conditions of employment.

The distinguishing feature of the purely ameliorative legislation
is that it deals with the consequences of inequality, and brings
about a substantial redistribution of income, without changing
the basic principle of administration in the capitalist system, or
the distribution of executive power between the classes in it. That
is to say, property remains the source of authority and administrative decision in the sphere of industry, finance and trade. The
financing of the social services transfers income without transferring power over industry, and we have seen some of the unwelcome consequences of such an arrangement in the second
part of this book.

The main historical feature of these measures is the enthusiasm
with which they have been received by the electorate, and the
widespread support that they now enjoy from all classes in the
community. The period of their establishment and subsequent
extension constitutes what I have called the 'second liberal
revolution'.[1]

There is no part of our social structure and cultural achievement that is more valued by the great bulk of our citizens. The
preservation and extension of the social services is the one matter
that is fully understood by the electorate, and the one political
question about which there is real constructive enthusiasm among
our people.

Nevertheless, the further extension of these services is not all
plain sailing. As we have seen, their maintenance involves a
constant pressure upon the Budget. Their further extension can
be financed only by further increases in the burden of taxation, and
this will have the consequence, in the future as in the past, of still
further reducing the volume of our national savings. The process
of taxation has already halved our Rate of Saving and reduced

[1] The first 'revolution' consists in the comprehensive set of changes that occurred
in this country during the first half of the nineteenth century, and had as their object
the emancipation of industrial management from the 'dead hand of the past', and
the freeing of the immense productive power of the intelligence and constructive will
of human beings. The second set of changes, scarcely less comprehensive and
important, have as their object the protection of the employed, who constitute the
great bulk of the population, from the evil consequences of the unregulated
emancipation of the employing individual and corporation. The second process
began with the educational legislation of the 1870s, and passed through a critical
period during the budgetary and constitutional struggles of the 1910s. The victory
then secured by the Left has proved amazingly popular.

the collective saving of the very rich to nothing. If it goes muc
further, the increase of taxation will wipe out social savin
altogether, and leave us with a relatively stagnant econom
dependent on a certain type of invention — that which reduces th
need for capital — for the whole of our economic progress.
development dependent on this type of invention alone would b
slow. There is therefore a serious danger lurking in the enthusias:
of the public for the social services, and a conflict betwee
the various types of social betterment that they desire —
conflict of which they are not even aware. To this point we sha
return.[1]

2. *Socialization Measures.* By measures of socialization I unde
stand the acquisition by the State of the power to decide the outpu
investment and employment policy of any economic undertak
ing. The classical method for acquiring such power, advocate
by the European Socialist Movement (as distinct from th
Syndicalist Movement) is that of 'nationalization' — or th
compulsory purchase by the State of the controlling propert
rights in economic enterprises. But it is obvious that this
not the only possible method of obtaining control. It is th
most forthright and comprehensive; but there •may be usefu
'half-way houses' that will give substantial control withou
ownership.[2]

Whether the control is obtained by ownership or somethin
short of ownership, need not concern us for the moment, since
shall assume, for the sake of simplicity, that control is obtained i
every case by the outright purchase from their present owners o
the undertakings said to be 'nationalized' or 'socialized'.

Now the most important consequences of measures such a
these are precisely the opposite of those that I have called amelior
ative. The ameliorative measures transfer income without tran:

[1] This conclusion may seem to be in conflict with the evidence I offered in Part
that the poor are now saving rapidly and contributing a large proportion of ou
total Rate of Saving. There is, however, no contradiction. As the level of taxatio
rises, especially if it takes an increasing proportion of estates as they are inherited
the rich tend positively to decumulate. As a class they sell securities (cf. Coli
Clark, quoted in Part II) and so absorb the savings of the other sections of th
community. By an acceleration of this process they could, as I have said, reduce th
rate of social accumulation to nothing.

[2] This is another of the questions I shall hope to consider in my projected book
The Economics of Democratic Socialism.

rring power. The socialization measures transfer power to the tate before they transfer income. The power over industry and ade acquired by the State may be used at a later time to change he distribution of income, or to finance the increase or maintennce of any given Rate of Saving within the economy, but the ower is acquired *before* the transfer is made. It is therefore proper) call measures of this kind a programme for the acquisition of conomic power by the State — or the 'power programme' of the)cialist strategy.

Whatever the difficulties or disadvantages of the socialization of idustry, and although it does little in the first instance to increase he wealth of society, it is clear that this part of the socialist proramme is not subject to the same criticisms as the proposal to xtend the Social Services indefinitely.[1]

3. *Prosperity Measures.* Quite different in kind from either of he foregoing groups of measures are legislative acts and, more nportant, administrative acts the purpose of which is to maintain nd increase the volume of industrial activity.

These measures, which I would call 'prosperity measures', have een, in my view, unduly neglected by socialist thought. Obsessed y the determination to prove the proposition, doubtless true, hat recurrent depressions are due to the capitalist system, socialist hinkers and economists have been too ready to ignore the overiding necessity of maintaining production and life in the transiional period — a period likely to be long — during which the ransfer of economic power to the State is being effected. Yet this s a fundamental problem, taking precedence in time and import.nce over all other matters. We must be assured of life, wealth and mployment as individuals and as nations, before we can concern urselves with the more distant and less urgent tasks of revolution r reform. A starving man cannot fully enjoy the beauty of the tars, and a depressed society cannot concern itself primarily with n egalitarian Utopia.

The capitalist system suffers from recurrent depressions of

[1] It is perhaps worth pointing out here, as I have done elsewhere (see Part IIIC), hat any services that increase the personal force of the workers – such as educational nd health measures – will result in a transference of political power to them. The istinction between *ameliorative* and *power* programmes is therefore not hard and ast. But the main distinction is obvious.

varying degrees of intensity. The major depressions that occur during every generation are one of the most potent reasons for the rising discontent of the democratic electorate with the institutions of the system, and are therefore one of the most frequent causes of a change in government. The last depression swept away every democratic government that was ruling in 1929 — bringing new Parties or new Party combinations into power in Great Britain, France, America, Sweden, Denmark, New Zealand; while it destroyed democracy in Austria, Germany and Japan. It is therefore highly probable, though not of course certain, that the Labour Party in this country will be brought to power by a major depression. Its first task and most urgent duty would then certainly lie in the field of industrial activity. Even if it comes into power on the top of a Trade Cycle boom, as it did in 1929, the maintenance of prosperity will still be an acid test of its success. It will be a precedent condition for its retention of power at the next election, and for the gradual achievement of its ultimate objectives. Prosperity measures are therefore a vital part of the equipment of a democratic and socialist Party.

It is not possible to discuss at this point the reasons for the recurrence, under the capitalist system, of periodic depressions. Fortunately it is not necessary to do so, in the first place because I shall revert to this subject elsewhere, and in the second because there is a wide measure of agreement among economists, if not about the nature of the causal processes at work in the cycle, at least about the practical measures necessary to mitigate and overcome the depression. There is a wide agreement, that is to say, that a vigorous programme of public investment, combined with the power to control the lending operations of the commercial banks, would go a long way towards mitigating, and carried out on a large enough scale towards reversing, any tendency to contraction on the part of independent capitalist enterprise.[1] Moreover, it is obvious that adequate control over the lending policy of the joint stock banks could be obtained in this country by measures far short of full social ownership.

[1] Cf. the published works of Messrs. Keynes, Harrod, Robertson, Meade, Kaldor, etc. and the periodical manifestos sent to the Press and signed by representative lists of economists.

If this argument is correct it is difficult to exaggerate the political importance of it.[1]

4. *Egalitarian Measures*. Finally there are the measures, primarily of taxation, that aim directly at changing the inequality in the distribution of income and wealth.

Such measures resemble the ameliorative measures in so far as they redistribute income between persons. They differ from them in that egalitarian measures, unlike the taxation of large incomes to finance the social services, destroy the large incomes themselves. They leave a permanent mark upon the distribution of income and power. They consist in the levying of particular sorts of taxes, of which the most obvious and typical are inheritance taxes and capital levies.

Fortunately it is not necessary to say much of a controversial character about egalitarian measures, since it is so largely agreed among socialists now, that the most expeditious and most equitable policy to pursue consists in the imposition of a certain form of inheritance taxation. Some form of the Rignano Plan — whereby the rate of taxation at each inheritance varies, not only with the size of the estate, but also with the number of inheritances since the tax was first imposed — would enable society to rid itself of large fortunes, and to attenuate property as a source of unearned income to vanishing point, without at any time bearing harshly upon particular persons or generations. It is an admirable method of causing the objectionable parts of this fundamental institution to wither slowly and painlessly away'.

These, then, are the elements from which a successful programme must be constructed. Is it possible to choose a combination of them that will fulfil, simultaneously, the three conditions that are necessary for a democratic and socialist strategy of political action?

To this vital question I now turn.

---

[1] For those who are interested in the more technical aspects of the causes and cure of Trade Cycle depressions I might refer to Chap. iv of HARROD: *Trade Cycle*, or to my own account of the arguments by which I think the creation of a Central Financial Authority can be justified, and the type of policy that it might pursue in final liquidation of cyclical movements. This account is contained in Chap. viii of my *Problem of Credit Policy*.

§ 4

The Suggested Solution of the Strategic Problem — a Programme for a Democratic Socialist Party

Very tentatively I would suggest that the correct general line of policy can only be found by the observation of *four* broad principles of action. I write in humble mood because at least one of these principles is very repugnant to the present temper of the British electorate, and a democrat should respect, and ultimately trust, common opinion. I·write tentatively, because the political scene shifts rapidly and the future is therefore uncertain. What is written on policy to-day often seems absurdly out of date by to-morrow. This is especially true in time of war. But, with these limitations clearly in mind, I would like to suggest that problems of political strategy can be resolved if democratic socialist parties can be persuaded to base their legislative and administrative programmes upon four general principles:

(1) The first of these is a self-denying ordinance: that they should be willing *to place further ameliorative measures in their order of priority after, and not before, the socialization of industry* — or, to put the same point in a more extreme form, that they should be willing to reduce their social service proposals to the minimum consistent with the retention of political power in order to pursue more actively the transfer of industrial ownership.

To take this principle seriously, and to act upon it, will require considerable courage and self-denial on the part of the Left wing electorate and the working class as a whole. It means abandoning the hope of rapid social betterment for some considerable time. It means placing power before benefits — the pill before the jam, of social legislation. It means preaching an unpopular gospel to an electorate that, as a whole, is deeply stirred by the hope of, and instinctively determined to possess, further substantial benefits from the public chest. The legislative trend of a generation must be reversed, and the people at large must be made to think about, and care for, something less immediate than better housing and family allowances. It may well be that practical politicians will feel that this is an impossible task, and that the 'man in the street' too determined in his intention to be diverted from his perfectly roper appetite for minimum standards of safety and comfort. .nd many influential groups of wise persons, particularly the becialized advocates of this or that social need — the educational becialists, the family allowance experts, those who care for the nemployed — will claim that the immediate needs for which they beak are so urgent that all more distant aims and more Utopian rojects must wait upon the relief of shameful and urgent distress.

Indeed it is certain that a political Party like the Labour Party, rounded in the life of the people and financed by the coppers of ie poor, will always be committed to certain improvements in ie social services on which it would be political suicide to default.[1]

Yet I feel sure that the price of socialism is the reduction of these dvances to the necessary minimum, and a determination on the art of the party and the electorate that it represents, to concen- rate its main energies upon other fields of policy and achievement.

I feel sure of this for two reasons. The *first* of these is the one hat I have already mentioned. The continuous extension of the bcial services, and the steady rise in the proportion of the national icome that is taken in taxation, imposes a strain upon the capi- alist system that has already reduced its potential pace of .evelopment and will reduce it still further. Despite the plausible rguments of the apologists for the social services, and of the older ype of socialist, there must be some limit to the height that taxa- ion can wisely be allowed to reach. We may not have come up to hat level yet, only there must be such a level somewhere ahead of s; and I feel sure that it is far short of one that would produce, by tself, substantial social equality or even finance the major ameli- rative provisions that the enthusiast for the social services always ias in mind. It is not sensible, in the last resort, to tax property ncomes to the limit and at the same time to leave the decisions bout investment, employment, the rate of social accumulation .nd the volume of production in the hands of persons who look rimarily to that source of revenue for their maintenance and

[1] At the moment at which I write the Labour Party is so deeply committed to mproving the regulations under which assistance is given to the unemployed, to ome modest increase in the expenditure on education and to the enlargement of the ension system, that it would be impossible for a Labour Government to remain ong in power if it attempted none of these things.

guidance. It is not wise in the long run to expect to live upon golden eggs and slowly to strangle the goose that lays them. At certain point economic power must be placed before social betterment if social betterment is to be secured.[1]

The *second* reason is even simpler — though scarcely less important. The time and energies of any party or any Government are limited, and there is a low maximum to the amount of legislation that any group of men can press through Parliament or subsequently administer. They cannot concentrate all their forces on all fronts at once. The laws of arithmetic, let alone those of psychology, make it impossible to proceed equally rapidly and forcibly in all directions at the same time. Particularly this true of a large Party whose machinery for taking decisions, even in its Parliamentary section, has become too 'democratic' and cumbersome to permit of great speed in legislation. If therefore the energies of Party and Government are concentrated too exclusively upon the improvement of the social services, all other types of action will fall into the background, and in the end cease altogether. It is only if the main enthusiasm of the Party, the main determination of the Government, and the clearest mandate from the electorate, all lie in other fields, that any substantial advance in the reorganization of the national economy will, in fact, be completed. Only if the 'power programme' is put first in the priorities of Government, Party, and electorate alike, will the slow-moving and easily bored mind of elector and elected ever put itself out of the well-worn rut of social service legislation. The Government will relapse into the comfortable and valuable, but in the last resort self-limiting, course of spending more money for the benefit of the relatively poor. There is nothing more conservative than an old reforming party, and particularly one that has repeatedly achieved political success by pressing for a programme of social improvement.

---

[1] I should perhaps mention that, in so far as there is a considerable volume of unemployment, it is possible to increase the funds available for the social services or for social accumulation, by raising the total money income of the community. There may, therefore, be no conflict in the short period between these two desirable purposes. Over a longer period, however, the conflict is inevitable, and the maintenance of social accumulation essential. In practice certain extensions of the social services are inevitable, but they must not be achieved at a pace that is incompatible with a substantial level of new investment.

I therefore feel clear that, unless this first and difficult denying ordinance is accepted willingly and enthusiastically by the people, all other precepts of policy are likely to be empty and formal.[1] But if we may suppose, for the moment, that this extremely difficult barrier to socialism has been surmounted, it is worth discussing the remaining three.

(2)   The second guiding principle that I would suggest is *the proposal to nationalize, during the first completed period of office, some considerable, but limited, section of the industrial system* — the transfer of ownership to be accompanied by *full compensation* to the existing owners of the common stock.[2]

About this principle it is, perhaps, worth noting three things. The *first* is that the proposal for 'fair compensation to existing owners' is technically complex but politically fundamental.[3]

[1] It is always supposed by extremists that the chief barriers to socialism lie in the vested power of the capitalist class and the cowardly treachery of the democratic socialist leaders. They assume that the working class is an active and determined revolutionary force, held in check and betrayed by those in control of it. My own experience is quite different. I have always found the real difficulty of political organization and political action to lie in the apathy, the lack of imagination, and the fundamentally conservative outlook of the democratic electorate. I have never encountered seething discontent or revolutionary energy anywhere outside the narrow circle of extremists, who proclaim its existence everywhere. It is, I believe, largely a creation of their own uncomfortable ardours. No doubt, the condition of the workers varies from time to time, and we may at some time in the future pass into another and potentially revolutionary epoch – but it is not with us yet.

[2] This principle, as we shall see, was embodied in the programme of policy, *For Socialism and Peace* (published by the Labour Publications Department, Transport House, Smith Square, S.W.1), p. 15, upon which the British Labour Party fought the General Election of 1935. They proposed the socialization of six or eight major industries: of which coal, electricity supply, transport, iron and steel and agriculture were, as far as size is concerned, the most important. Together these industries employ something like one-third of the wage-earning population, and a considerably larger proportion of the unionized workers. Such a programme would not prove impracticably large, if the Labour Party enjoys an uninterrupted period of office; since it is possible to dispose of at least two major measures in each Session of Parliament; and Acts for the socialization of industries should become easier to draft, debate and amend as Parliament becomes accustomed to this type of legislation.

[3] Only a lawyer could discuss the technical aspects of the matter. 'The suggested basis of compensation', continues the paragraph in *For Socialism and Peace*, from which I am quoting, 'is, broadly, the *net reasonable maintainable revenue* of the industry.' The general idea is clear enough, and the details of it are further discussed in the Report of the Annual Conference for 1934 (*Public Ownership and Compensation*, published by the Labour Publications Department, Transport House, Smith Square, S.W.1), but doubtless there will be an infinite number of doubtful points and particular cases to be decided in the case of each industry, and ultimately, no doubt, these complex matters will have to be submitted to some court or special tribunal. We need not concern ourselves with these details here.

The importance of the compensation proposals is obvious and I shall revert to a discussion of it when I come to consider the assessment of the programme as a whole. But there is one further point about the principle of 'full' or 'fair' compensation that is perhaps worth making. It is often assumed that the payment of 'full' compensation will leave no net gain, no surplus revenue for the State or society, available as an immediate result of socialization for redistribution or other purposes. This is, in fact, not the case. There are at least two reasons why such surplus may be realized. To start with the payment of 'full' compensation does not mean that the State is required to provide the same money income to the erstwhile owner, plus an added degree of security in the receipt of that income. If the compensation arrangements contain, as they probably will, some kind of State guarantee, then there is no reason to pay as large a sum in annual income to the original shareholders. The State can make out of the bargain, perfectly justly, the average difference between the rate of interest earned upon relatively risky industrial investments and the market rate on gilt-edged securities during the base period. The surplus funds so released may be considerable. And further than this, if economies can be reaped as all students of the particular industries believe that they can from a centralized organization of them, still larger funds can be obtained immediately from the process of socialization. But, at the same time, it is clear that the funds available and the benefit obtainable are only a fraction of the present income and benefit accruing to the owners of property.[1]

In the *second* place, I should like to state at this point my conviction that it will be highly desirable to set up at an early stage some central control, or Supreme Economic Authority, for the 'socialized sector' of industry. A consideration of the administrative machinery of a Planned Economy is not appropriate in this Part,[2] concerned as it is with the principles of 'programme

---

[1] In a longer period there is a third possible source of gain for the State – the additional capital value and profit resulting from the growth of an industry. These gains would be very great in certain industries – the electrical and aircraft industries, for example. But they would not accrue to the State in the short period.

[2] Another subject with which I shall hope to deal at length, in my projected work *The Economics of Democratic Socialism*.

ilding', but it may be as well to say a word about the principle
at is, in my opinion, involved.

Little good will be done, and the purposes of planning will not be
ved, if we merely replace a growing number of State organized
tier monopolies by a larger number of autonomous 'socialized'
nopolistic Corporations. Doubtless the form of 'public corpor-
on' is a desirable, and increasingly familiar, form of economic
terprise; but one of the main purposes of economic planning, and
leed of all rational economic activity, is the pursuit of expansion-
production policies beyond the point, far beyond the point in
any cases, of the output that would bring to a maximum the
urns to particular industries. Now the temptation in any mono-
listic organization to make a partial use of its monopoly power
extremely great. The only way of becoming even reasonably
re that this power is not exerted at all — to the detriment of
cial welfare — is to take all final responsibility for output policy
t of the hands of those who could benefit in any way from
triction. Responsibility in the socialized sector must, from the
ginning, be *upwards* and not downwards — upwards to bodies
ncerned primarily with the interests of the consumer, with
ciety as a whole, with the rational end and common good of
alth and production. This is a vital principle of economic life
d of social reason, not a detail of administrative organization.

In any case, a co-ordinating authority for the socialized sector is
und to be brought into existence early in the process of its
owth, if only in order to deal with the great number and variety
questions that will call for settlement between the sections of it.
e most obvious of these, and economically the most important,
the question of *transfer prices*. If the socialized mining industry is
ling coal to the socialized railway industry, and the socialized
ctrical supply industry is selling electrical power to a socialized
ine, some competent body will have to decide the appropriate
ices at which these sales are to take place. There will be number-
s other questions of the same kind. Since some co-ordinating
thority must be brought into existence to decide them, it is far
tter that it should be created consciously and openly given the
ponsibility, from the beginning, of seeing that costs are properly
essed, prices wisely determined, and that the vital social purpose

of increasing production is set foremost in the order of priorit within the socialized sector of industry.

Finally, it may be worth saying a word about the relationsh between the argument of the second Part of this book and th of the present Part. In Part II we saw that one of the mo obvious and important of the autonomous trends in the instit tional development of democratic capitalism is the trend towar State sanctioned private monopoly. The monopoly is usua created at the selling stage, and the monopoly stops short of Sta ownership. The results are therefore almost wholly bad. T existence of this trend lends overwhelming historical and soc support to this part of the democratic and socialist programn In advocating the extension of social control over indust we are merely taking further steps in a course that society is alrea actively pursuing. The movement of history is with us, and with it. But, in suggesting that the form of social control should more radical and that the principle of responsibility to socie should be introduced into it, we are proposing to remedy the ma faults of the present trend, and so to convert what has been dangerous movement towards restriction and economic frustr tion into a new engine of economic expansion and social progre It is given to us to repeat in different institutional circumstanc and with a different social order in mind, the same fundamen proposition that the Classical economists propounded over century ago — that the economic end of man is production and t increase of wealth, and that no vested interest, no powerf minority, and above all no outworn tradition, should be allow to frustrate that eminently sensible activity. It is our duty n to turn back, but to divert to useful ends the slow, but immens powerful, movements of democratic history.

(3) It is not easy in this predominantly political section of t book to say anything particularly useful about the third princip that I should like to propose. I believe that it is of fundament importance to include in the programme some measures, large administrative in nature, whose purpose is to restore prosperi if the democratic socialist Party comes into office during a peri of depression, and to maintain prosperity if they are elected duri a boom. The measures that I have in mind include a considerab

ogramme of public investment, a centrally directed expansion
 bank credit, the use of its influence by the Government to
ntrol the Rate of Saving, and, if necessary, the intention to
1-balance the Budget. Most of these steps could be taken without
1y new legislation, and they imply, as I have already pointed
1t, the control but not necessarily the ownership of the joint
ock banks. If the policy that I have in mind were pursued
ith sufficient vigour it should prove possible to control the
olume of business activity, and to use that control to prevent all
rge-scale fluctuations in it — or, to put the same thing in another
ay, it should prove possible to reduce general unemployment
zero and to maintain it there indefinitely.

The further elaboration of the technical aspects of this item in
y programme is contained in Chap. viii of my *Problem of Credit
licy*, and it is unnecessary to repeat the technical argument here.
he political importance of it is obvious.

(4) Finally we come to the last essential proposal in the pro-
amme, and this again need not delay us long. Somewhere to-
ards the end of the first period of office — or early in the second —
ter the process of extending the socialized sector of industry is
ell under way, it should be possible to proceed to *an instalment
' purely egalitarian taxation*. There are a number of variants of the
ignano principle. One suggestion is made by Hugh Dalton[1] that
1 estates over a certain figure should pay a Supplementary Duty:

> ... This Supplementary Duty, equal to this excess (over
> £50,000) or to some proportion of it, say one half, should be
> payable in cash or land or appropriate securities. But the
> taxpayer should receive from the State in exchange a termin-
> able annuity, say for twenty years, of equal annual value to
> that of the property handed over in payment of the Supple-
> mentary Duty ... By this means a steadily increasing
> quantity of private property rights now running in perpetuity
> would be transformed into terminable annuities, running off
> within a comparatively short period.[2]

y this, or some such method, a beginning could be made with a
ow but systematic destruction of all large fortunes; a withering

[1] HUGH DALTON: *Practical Socialism for Britain*, Chap. xxxiii, *passim*.
[2] Op. cit. p. 342.

away of the institution and consequences of inheritance — to mal a beginning for the equal distribution of the national income.

But it would be disastrous, in my view, to start such pure egalitarian legislation until some substitute for the institution property had been found — in the shape of the growth of Sta authority in the industrial sphere — to provide the saving, an secure the efficiency, that are both necessary for economi progress.

§ 5

The Assessment of the Strategy

These then are my four principles to guide the task of pro gramme building — the reduction of ameliorative proposals to minimum consistent with the maintenance of political power; th socialization of a considerable, but limited, section of the industria system during the first period of office; the execution of a comple monetary policy aimed at securing and maintaining a high leve of prosperity throughout the 'transitional period'; and the initiatio of egalitarian taxation towards the end of the first period of office after the growth in the economic power of the State has proceede far enough to enable it — the State — to offset the evil consequence of trenching still further upon the present sources of saving an authority in the economic · sphere. A programme, constructe upon these lines, would be: poor in social service measures, rich i socialization proposals, active in financial administration, and careful, but determined, in the sphere of egalitarian taxation. I would place the acquisition of power before the abolition o privilege, control before benefits, the pill before the jam, in socia legislation.

About such a programme two things are to be noticed. In th *first* place, it is very different from the purely social service pro grammes that have been emanating, curiously enough, from the extreme Left in recent years. I have already called attention to the programme produced early in 1937 by the United Front o the Communist Party, the Independent Labour Party and the cialist League (since deceased). It consisted almost exclusively ameliorative proposals and only touched, most unconvincingly, on what I have called the 'power programme'. The programme at would result from the application of my four principles would much more 'socialist' than that. It would set in the forefront the stage, not in the back row of the pit, the proposal to extend e economic power of the State; and it would relegate to secondary portance the immensely expensive proposals that flow in an er-rising tide of optimistic ink from our 'revolutionary' contem- raries.[1] It will be obvious from all that has gone before, that I lieve this point of difference to be one of essential principle, and at the prior acquisition of economic power is a vital part of y sound political strategy. In the *second* place, however, it will obvious that this programme is not revolutionary. On the ntrary, it is an attempt to substitute a sound evolutionary ogramme for an unsound one. The unsound evolutionary pro- amme is precisely the programme recommended by our tremist comrades — that of promising and expecting immense aterial benefits out of the old game of taxing the rich — the lusory hope than an egalitarian society and a progressive onomy can be produced by the strategy of increased taxation for e social services.[2]

But does the programme that I have suggested meet our litical needs? Does it make possible the progressive realization the time-honoured socialist objectives without leading to a eak-down of democracy?

I can best proceed to what I have to say on this question of timate judgment by referring to the three formal conditions of ccess, by which I defined the problem of strategy — the necessity avoiding counter revolution, the preservation of the enthusiasm the democratic socialist Party, and the determination to find easures in the relevant sphere.

[1] One proposal alone – that to pay pensions at 60 of £1 a week – contained in e social service programme of the United Front would have cost between £200- 00 million in a year!
[2] It is one of the extraordinary phenomena of the history of political thought that e very people who attacked this programme most bitterly a few years ago – mediately after the crisis of 1931 – are its most active supporters now. I have ggested a possible explanation of this peculiar fact in my Note appended to rt III.

The relationship of my suggested programme to two of the conditions seems to me to be clear and certain, but its relationsh to the third is not so simple.

(1) It seems to me inconceivable that the execution of this pr gramme will drive the Conservative and capitalist opposition in *armed* resistance. Rebellion is not only a very dangerous proceedin it is also a very difficult one. Men must take their careers ar their lives in their hands, before they embark upon it. Ancier habits of discipline and loyalty must be broken, and a ne machinery of political and social action must be created. A these things can be accomplished, particularly in a quiet, cor tented, and law-abiding country like our own, only under th pressure of great fear or the thought of great injustice.

Undoubtedly the fear of social revolution or the expectation of sudden cessation of the payment of income from property — eith to the whole rentier class or to selected minorities in it — could pr voke fury, hatred and armed rebellion. And there is little doub I am very much afraid, as to who would win such a battle. Britis Conservatism and not British Communism would emerge triun phant from an armed encounter.

But it seems to me inconceivable that these would be the resul of the programme that I am proposing. The compensation pr posals alone guarantee that the opposition to the programm will stop short of the risk to employment, and life itself, implie by armed resistance. 'Full compensation' means that no perso or arbitrarily selected minority, will be expropriated. Indeed n single generation will be called upon to bear the whole cost transferring economic power to the State. The adoption of th principle that large fortunes are to be destroyed by the steep grading of *death* duties means that no group of living persons ca be reduced from great riches to complete poverty, and that th burden of transition for any one age group will not be sever There is therefore no desperation, no overwhelming fear, fror which revolutionary courage in this country alone could quickl spring.

No doubt, there will be fierce *political* opposition to this pr gramme. Such opposition may very easily pass into consciou and unconscious economic 'sabotage'. There may be a genuin

ıock to confidence'. There may be an honest conviction in the
ınds of the investing and employing classes that the commercial
ospects are not good, and that the removal of part or all of their
operty to safer places is wise. It is possible that these opinions
ay arise without any conscious desire to embarrass or destroy
democratically elected government, much less to produce a
volutionary situation. 'Flights from sterling' and a depression
ıe to loss of the internal 'will to invest' might be the result — in
me sense the 'natural' result — of the attempt to carry through
e programme that I have described. But what, from our present
ınt of view, do those things matter? They are highly undesirable
velopments, and the utmost efforts should be made to avoid or
ıtigate them; but they are not, in the last resort, at all fatal to
aceful progress. As we have already seen, every one of these
ıfavourable reactions in confidence can be overcome, and over-
me without great difficulty, if the appropriate administrative
ıion is taken. The exchanges can be controlled if they tend to
1 heavily. The notes can be printed if there is substantial cash
arding. Public investment can be increased to offset a decline
the activity of private ventures. There is really nothing, short
armed rebellion, that should prove impossible to control within
e framework, and by the instruments, of popular government.

Hence it seems morally certain that the programme constructed
on these four basic principles will fulfil the first of the criteria of
ccess. It is unlikely that it will injure private interests so deeply,
provoke such fear, as to make armed rebellion likely. I can
ırcely believe that any responsible political opinion will judge
herwise.

(2) Nor can there be the slightest doubt that the programme
mpletely fulfils the last of my three criteria. It is unquestionably
ntred in the relevant field of economic and social legislation.
ıe completion of the programme would constitute, without the
ghtest possible doubt, a marked and impressive step towards the
cialist goal. The members of a government that succeeded in
ınging something like another 30 per cent of the employed
pulation into the socialized sector of industry[1] (raising it, shall
: say, from something like 10 per cent to approximately 40 per

---

[1] See footnote 2 on p. 301.

cent), and began a type of taxation that would slowly undermin
the basis of inequality, in the course of one period of office, migh
be legitimately proud of the service that they had rendered to th
cause of economic planning and social equality. If, at the sam
time, they maintained the general level of prosperity, or onl
allowed it to decline a little, they would have completed a remark
able service to the cause of democracy and popular governmen
If these things can be done there cannot surely exist a socialist s
extreme, or so lost to the meaning of words, as to deny that th
successful fulfilment of these tasks would constitute a step in th
building of the socialist commonwealth?

There is therefore no question but that this programme li
within the relevant sphere.

(3) *Will it satisfy the members of the democratic and socialist Part*
That is the one remaining question, my sole ground of doubt, an
in my view, the only possible source of weakness in the strateg

Here it is necessary to distinguish two periods of time, and tw
different types of emotional reaction likely to occur within each
them. I think that there can be little doubt that the Labo
Movement of this country, discouraged by a shattering defe
in 1931 and a disappointing recovery in 1935, after nearly t
years in the political wilderness and in face of a persistent failu
in the by-election results to suggest any substantial change in th
balance of political opinion; would be more than satisfied now b
the thought of political achievements half as considerable as tho
contained in my suggested programme. It is said by those wh
ought to know that the 'rank and file' of the Party organizati
would be well pleased if a Labour Government succeeded
nationalizing a single industry, however small, in the first peri
of office. This may be an exaggeration, but it is merely illustrati
of the undoubted fact that in this period of defeat and discourag
ment the political ambitions and hopes of the reforming Par
are modest. A man with a wooden leg does not hope to win a ra
or a bird with a broken wing to reach the top of the mountain.

This attitude may be greatly changed by the war, but the
is little reason at the moment to suppose that it will be.

But political hopes are notoriously buoyant. I am not so certa
that in the future — if and when the Labour Party is success.

ace more, after the tide of opinion has swung for long in its favour,
nd when it has passed through the supreme spiritual exhilaration
winning an openly contested election — its ambitions will
main as modest as they are at present, or that the 'rank and file'
the Party will be easily contented. It is conceivable that in this,
in other things, the will to power will 'grow by what it feeds on',
nd that, as the Party feels the strengthening of the ground be-
eath its feet and a growing authority coming to it from the dele-
ated will of the people, it will become impatient and intolerant
compromise.

I do not feel certain that this will happen. I do not even think
at it will. The tradition of common sense and moderation is
rong in us. But I cannot feel certain that it will not. There are
rtain unreasoning, violent and simple-minded elements in the
arty who will do their utmost to press it to the Left, and to trap
into uncongenial and disastrous games of bluff and bluster.
here are too many arm-chair Stalins and platform Lenins in our
nks for either our own good or the good of the nation. They
ve the sound of revolution in the distance, and they trumpet the
csins of hatred and intolerance, without understanding con-
iously the meaning of the words they use, or foreseeing plainly the
orrible consequences of the courses that they advocate. Unconscious
their own motives, they press us towards the abyss of civil war.
Will these people, in the first flush of victory, have their way?
hat is my only fear. It is the only danger, in my view, that could
reaten the success of the programme that we are discussing.
Let me repeat that I am not sure that this danger will material-
e. In fact I do not expect it to do so. But if it does, it will be
lely because of the unreasonable demands made by a minority of
tremists. Their demands are unreasonable, because they are
ot consistently pursued by their authors, and because the means
oposed are not consistent with the ends proclaimed.
Let me explain what I mean. The ends are not consistently
rsued because the revolutionaries of the British Labour Move-
ent — the Communists, the leaders of the Independent Labour
arty and the persons associated with the old Socialist League —
each revolution without preparing for it. They are inflammatory,
t irresponsible. Such people plead for violence, denounce

311

STRATEGY OF DEMOCRATIC SOCIALIS

compromise and hate moderation. But they do nothing, absolute
nothing of significance, to meet the real crisis that they do the
best to produce. Revolutions are not made by words in the
days — or at any other time for that matter — but by machin
guns. Civil war, if it comes, will be decided by aeroplane an
tank, bombs and artillery. Yet these people, who press upon th
working class the necessity for shedding blood, have none of the
things in their possession — nor dare to possess them. They hold r
secret stores of arms. They have no bombs in their cellars, machin
guns in their back gardens, or aeroplane parts in their air rai
shelters, to be assembled for the contest of force that they do the
best to precipitate. They could not use them if they had. Most
them would be more dangerous to themselves in charge of
machine-gun than to any fortunate enemy who might be on th
other side of the 'barricades'. These persons do not seem
realize that revolutions are made by men of blood, that Lenin an
Trotsky and Stalin dealt in weightier weapons than words, an
that even Hitler, who had an easier passage to power than th
Russian revolutionaries, was something more formidable than a
excitable don. Our extremist leaders are revolutionaries wit
gloves on, academic and journalistic gentlemen whose natur
weapon is the pen — 'sheep in wolves' clothing' as Mr. Low
cruelly but truly satirized them.

Yet these revolutionaries of ours, men of words though they b
are not innocuous. Words are not weapons, but they are drug
They will not kill men, but they will make them mad. That is th
shocking thing about the irresponsible revolutionary. He incit
men — usually poorer and less educated than himself — an
then betrays them; not perhaps by the cruder steps of flight an
desertion; but by a subtler treachery of unforeseen consequence
the blind leading the blind. These men talk of blood, but the
do not consciously desire blood. If and when it comes, as part
the fruit of their labour, they will be horrified and ashamed. An
the unfortunate people who have been deluded by their gre
words and their impressive 'systems' of thought will find then
selves trapped in a civil war that they cannot win, left to pay th
price of a hopeless, horrible and unnecessary defeat.

Worst of all, the battle will always have been a battle for a fal

ope, since we have seen again and again throughout this book
hat the method of revolution against a democratic government
an never lead to the creation of a free and equal society.[1]

The fear that the Labour Party, excited by political success,
vill listen to its irresponsible revolutionary minority is, then, the
nly danger, and that a remote one, that qualifies the wisdom of
he political strategy that I propose. Its existence does not, how-
ver, make it unwise to pursue this course of action. All policies
nvolve some danger. It is impossible to devise a strategy against
vhich nothing can be said. The risks of this policy are much
ess than those of any other and more extreme proposals. It
herefore seems clear to me that it is the nearest possible approach
o the strategy that fulfils the three crucial conditions of success,
nd, as such, is the strategy and programme that should be adopted
nd advocated by all democratic socialists in the national parties
o which they belong.

§ 6

The Domestic Policy of the British Labour Party

A practical question at once arises — what is the relationship be-
ween the programme I have here proposed and that which has
)een adopted in recent years by the British Labour Party?

It will be obvious to those who have studied the domestic pro-
:ramme of the Labour Party that the resemblance between it
nd the kind of policy that I have described is very close. Let us
ook at the relationship.

The most recent official and comprehensive statement of the

[1] I am not, of course, arguing that the real danger to democracy comes, in this
ountry, from the Left. A formidable threat to free government is much more
ikely to be offered by the extreme Right, or by the Conservative Party turning again
o unconstitutional opposition, as they did in the last stage of the Irish dispute. Any
letermination on the part of the rich to maintain their privileges against the will
f the people, if and when the electorate desire to reduce the benefits accruing to
roperty, is incompatible with the maintenance of political freedom. British
Conservatism is more likely to become intransigent and revolutionarily re-
ictionary, than is the Labour Party to be captured by the Communists or to
ecome revolutionarily reformist. It is precisely this historical probability that
nakes irresponsible revolutionary propaganda by, or within, the Labour Party,
nighly dangerous.

programme of internal policy proposed by the Labour Party
contained in the document *For Socialism and Peace*[1] upon which the
Labour Party fought the last General Election.

The first third of the document deals with foreign policy and
does not concern us here.[2]

The remainder contains a variety of proposals that may be
summarized, from our point of view, in this way:

(1)   *A limited number of improvements in the social services* — in the
fields of housing, health, education and unemployment — whose
total cost would not be heavy.[3]

(2)   *A number of changes in the Standing Orders of the House of
Commons, and in the relation between the two Houses of Parliament* that
would have the effect of increasing very greatly the potential output of legislation.[4]

(3)   *A programme of industrial socialization* that is the most serious
and the most controversial part of the programme.

The socialization programme is described in two different ways
in the central section of the pamphlet.[5]

The section opens with a comprehensive list:

> Banking and Credit, transport, water, coal, electricity,
> gas, agriculture, iron and steel, shipping, shipbuilding,
> engineering, textiles, chemicals, insurance — in all these the
> time has come for drastic reorganization, and for the most
> part nothing short of immediate public ownership and control
> will be effective.

This list sounds rather Utopian in its comprehensiveness, but in
the paragraphs that follow a shorter list of more immediate importance is appended. It reads as follows:[6]

Banking and Credit
Transport
Coal
Electricity Supply Industry

[1] Published by the Labour Publications Department in 1934, price 2d.
[2] *For Socialism and Peace*, pp. 1-14.   [3] Ibid., pp. 25-28.
[4] Ibid., pp. 31-32.   These proposals are further elaborated in another official
publication of the Party entitled *Parliamentary Problems and Procedure*.
[5] Ibid., pp. 15-22.
[6] Ibid., pp. 16-22. The actual list of paragraph headings includes 'The Land'
but as this is not an industry, and as the proposal is only that of an 'Enabling Act'
I have omitted it from the list of immediate socialization proposals.

Iron and Steel
Agriculture
Water Supply

'ith the probable exception of the joint stock banks under the rst item in this list, and the possible addition of the 'armaments dustry', we may take it as a description of the contents of the first art of the industrial system that a Labour Government would ttempt to bring within the socialized sector.[1]

About the technique of socialization two points are worth oting:

(a) The participation of the workers in the government of the ndustries in which they are employed is to be guaranteed by gislation, but is to be very limited in form:

> The Labour Party also believes that the employees in a socialized industry should have a right, which should be acknowledged by law, to an effective share in the control and direction of the industry.[2]

'Workers' Control' is, in fact, to be reduced, as it should be in he view of everyone except a syndicalist, to 'Workers' *represent-tion*' on the board of the industry, and to nothing more. Indus-ries must be controlled by, and operated in the interests of, the community; and not by and for the minority of workers employed n it.

(b) The compensation policy is clearly stated:

> The public acquisition of industries and services will involve the payment of *fair compensation* to existing owners; but there-after the former owners as such should have no further part of any kind in the control or management or policy or finances of the publicly owned concern. *The suggested basis of com-pensation, broadly, is the net reasonable maintainable revenue of the industry concerned.*[3]

---

[1] A still further process of selection and concentration of the Party's proposals has produced the Short Term Programme. I have, however, concentrated my attention on *For Socialism and Peace*: (a) because it is a clearer and fuller statement of the Party's position; (b) because the Short Term Programme is very short, and may be exhausted before the end of a single Parliament.

[2] *For Socialism and Peace*, p. 15.

[3] Ibid., p. 15. The problem of compensation is further discussed in a separate publication – *Public Ownership and Compensation*. Labour Party Publications, 1934.

We have just discussed the implications of this proposal (see p. 308).

(4) The document contains a less precise account of *a programme of Public Works*[1], by which it is hoped to:

> diminish unemployment substantially, (and), by increasing public revenue and reducing expenditure on unemployment benefit, will relieve Budgetary stringency and make possible further programmes of social development and extension of social services . . .

i.e. that will raise the national money income.

(5) Finally there is one reference to the imposition of taxation with a primarily egalitarian purpose.

> . . . it (the Labour Party) proposes to revise the system of death duties, not only as just in itself, but as a step toward breaking that tradition which binds poverty in one generation to poverty in the next, and towards preventing the perpetuation of great fortunes by unearned inheritance.[2]

The remarkable similarity between these proposals and the contents of the programme I attempted to build up from first principles will be obvious at a glance.[3] The socialization programme of the Labour Party is identical in size, content, and technique of transfer to that which I believe to be required by the correct political strategy. The attitude to the social services is, in my view, just the right one; and the proposals for their extension are suitably limited. The suggestions for raising the volume of the national income are along lines that I consider to be technically correct; those for the improvement in the potential output of legislation are new to me, but are obviously admirable.

If criticism is to be offered of this practical programme it would centre, in my opinion, around the lack of clarity in the expansionist scheme, and subsequent monetary policy, proposed by the Party; and in the details of egalitarian taxation which are referred to somewhat vaguely at the end of the document. Both

---

[1] *For Socialism and Peace*, pp. 28-30. These matters are also discussed in *Socialism and the Condition of the People*.

[2] Ibid., p. 30.

[3] The two programmes were in fact worked out quite independently of each other and the degree of their convergence came as a surprise to me.

316

ese suggestions need much more consideration, research and
ιboration.

The latter of these two requirements is supplied, together with a
uch more detailed discussion of almost all the proposals contained
For Socialism and Peace, in a work by Mr. Dalton, *Practical
cialism for Britain*.[1] Mr. Dalton's book is an invaluable compan-
n work to *For Socialism and Peace*. All those who are interested in
e administrative detail of the various items in the programme
at we have here discussed in principle, and who would like to study
e particular arguments in favour of each separate proposal, cannot
better than to read this lucid guide-book to Labour policy.

Details apart — and we are nor primarily concerned with details
this book — the political programme thrashed out in the slow and
parently unorganized discussions of Party Conferences, National
ecutive and Policy Committees, *ad hoc* sub-committees and
official groups, has emerged with a remarkable and compre-
nsive resemblance to the very policy that can be built up syste-
atically from the first principles of Socialism and democracy.
ree discussion has, in this matter, again 'produced the goods'.
ithout thinking consciously in strategic terms, or even in all
obability setting down upon paper the logical categories that
have here employed, the Labour Party has evolved another
atement of its purposes that is internally consistent, ethically
nourable, and a powerful expression of its continued devotion
the principle of government by consent. Whatever may lie in
e future, for the Labour Party as for Britain, the domestic pro-
amme stated in this document will remain, fulfilled or unful-
led, another fitting testimony to the reasonable moderation, the
nstructive will, and the political genius of our people.

§ 7

Conclusion

Certain important matters have been omitted from this Part.
I have not discussed the political tactics, as distinct from the

[1] Routledge, 1935.

strategy, of democratic Socialism in this country. In particular, have not considered the central matter of the House of Lord There can be little reasonable doubt, I imagine, that this hoa constitutional anachronism will, in the future as in the past, off an unfair and one-sided impediment to the legislation a government of the Left. I have not discussed this matter for number of reasons. In the first place this book is chiefly concern with the broader aspects of social change, and it would not I wise to pass on to a discussion of detailed party tactics.[1]

Nor have I been able to discuss, and this is the more serio omission, the administrative details of the programme I ha defended. In practical politics detail is the essence of succes Nationalization measures will stand or fall by the contents of su clauses. Monetary policy can be correct only if the minutiae method, as well as of consequence, have been foreseen and dete mined wisely. In the fields of ameliorative, egalitarian and co stitutional legislation, the proposals must be precise, as well comprehensive. Intellectual socialists would serve the cause th profess to love more truly if they gave their minds to the concre detail of good government instead of to the advocacy of extremis and violence.

The Party of the Left needs to be better prepared for the respo sibilities of office, not because they are certain to meet unconstit tional opposition from their opponents or administrative sabota from their civil servants, but for the more obvious reason th they wish to carry through extensive and less familiar changes the economic and social structure of the country than a conserv tive administration would wish to do. Although they work with a broad stream of change, they wish to divert the stream; and th task will raise new problems and call for fresh minds to resol

---

[1] I abstain from a discussion of this matter, not because I believe the problem political tactics to be particularly difficult, but because it is undesirable to write book that never ends. In the second place, there are certain parts of the tacti problem, particularly the relative merits of the various methods available overcoming the House of Lords, that are not yet ripe for public discussion. T only thing that it is necessary to do is to remind the Labour Movement that t British people has always been able, when it was united and serious in any purpo to override the will of the privileged minority, apparently entrenched in the Upp House. What has been done before can be done again, and the Lords can be ma to bow once more to the People – if the government of the day really represe 'the people', and not merely an embittered faction.

CONCLUSION

.em. Hence the great need of the democratic socialist Party is
resight. 'Forewarned is fore-armed.' We must be forewarned —
rewarned of difficulties and obstacles.

It is necessary to mix a ton of detail with every ounce of general
·inciple before the result is administratively edible. We need,
democratic socialists, a clarion call, a religious conversion to, and
rising passion for, detail. We are sometimes in danger of for-
:tting the lesson that the Fabians so successfully taught the
oneers of our Movement — that the parents of political wisdom
·e mastery of detail and moderation of statement.

Fortunately, in the British Labour Party as a whole, there are
ʒns that the lesson is remembered; and that some preparation,
 least, is being made for the responsibilities of office. The
ıblications of the Labour Party itself are increasingly complex
ıd technical — and increasingly dull to the general reader for
ıat reason. A comparison between *Labour and the Nation* (the
arty Manifesto approved in 1928 for the Election of 1929) and
ιe later publication of the same general character, *For Socialism
ıd Peace* (1934) will demonstrate the reality and character of the
ιange. The later publication is far more complex, and con-
quently far duller, than the fine enthusiasm but rather elusive
ɔctrine of the earlier gospel. In the same way the 'policy
ımphlets' of the Labour Party[1] do not make exciting reading,
ıt they exhibit a respect for detail that is greatly encouraging.

Nor are the official Party and the official Research Department
ιe only bodies that have concerned themselves with this task.
·nder the guidance and leadership of Douglas and Margaret
ole, an independent society, devoted wholly to research into
ιe problems of socialist government, was formed and has been
:tively at work since 1933.[2] Its steady stream of publications
:ars witness to the work of a small body of persons competent
ıd willing to give their services freely to the task of understanding

[1] Reference has already been made to a number of these: *Socialism and the
ındition of the People; Currency, Banking and Finance; The National Planning of
ansport; The Reorganization of the Electricity Supply Industry; The Socialization
the Iron and Steel Industry;* etc. etc. See Official Labour Party Publications.
[2] The New Fabian Research Bureau was formed in conjunction with another body
ociety for Socialist Information and Propaganda) in 1932, but its independent
istence and period of active work began with the disappearance of its twin (in a
sion to form the Socialist League) at the later date.

319

and preparing for the problems of transition.[1] The success of th
venture is one of the most encouraging signs of the times.[2]

I have not been primarily concerned with these matters [
detail in this Part of the book, for the reasons that I have alread
given, and because I propose to reserve my own contribution [
this constructive work for the second volume. I have written th
Part, and indeed the whole of this volume, with a different pu[
pose in mind. I have tried to set forth the analysis of societ
and the systems of ethical and scientific principles, upon which
defence of moderate democratic socialism can, in my view, [
based.

Reflecting upon the last century of our political experience,
colleague of mine once remarked 'the Left Centre has alwa[
been right'. I have written in the belief that his aphorism [
near to the truth.

The extremists in the Labour Party often succeed in creatin
the impression that their views are derived from a more compr[
hensive analysis of history, and a longer tradition of scientif[
thought, than that available to their moderate opponents. Th
moderates too often appear to be offering uncoordinated and u[
systematic 'practical objections' to the dangerous proposals mad
by the extremists. To those who have not studied these matter
for themselves the appearance of greater system and greater pro
fundity on the part of the intransigent revolutionaries is impressiv
and disturbing.

Now it is perfectly true that the revolutionaries are entrenche
in a citadel of thought — the wide and deep stream of reflectio
contained in the Marxist sociological tradition. But it is the co[
tention of this book that the moderates are in no sense inferior i
this matter, but that, on the contrary, their position is more firml
grounded in the evidence of history, psychology and economic

[1] See the long list of N.F.R.B. publications in book pamphlet and book form
The New Fabian Research Bureau has now amalgamated with the older Fabi[
Society, and from the union there is every reason to expect a larger, more efficie[
and more productive research organization.

[2] Of course much remains to be done. The various departments of sociali[
policy are in very different stages of development. In all of them there is still wo[
to do, in some of them the stage of preparation is still primitive. Everyone who c[
help should do so. The research worker is still the architect and builder of o[
future society.

CONCLUSION

he first Part of this book was directed to the task of showing that
e Marxist citadel has become a prison for those who inhabit it
nd that the Marxists, and those who think with them, are chained
its dungeons, unable to see the light, or the movement of the
niverse about them — chained by their fidelity to an outworn
tellectual tradition.

The purpose of this Part has been to complete the task — to show
at the position of the moderates can be stated systematically and
erived from first principles. I believe that the policy of modera-
on is derived logically, and therefore inexorably, from the evidence
f the first two Parts.

Those of us who believe in democracy, have faith in moderation,
nd search for agreement in the field of politics, have behind us
he long and splendid tradition of British political thought and
ractice. We can add to our armoury in these days the new dis-
overies of psychology and economic history. We can face the
orld and our critics to Right and to Left; not indeed with a new
logmatism or with closed minds, since it is part of our faith that
o system of thought is final nor the whole truth revealed to any
ne generation; but certain that we embrace within our inter-
retation of society more evidence and more enlightenment than
hey. The slowly conquering mind of man has shed new light
pon our faith — light to which they are blind. Theirs the twilight
f the dawn; ours the fuller light of the growing day.

CONCLUSION

have seen that movements for economic change are worthless,
ven dangerous, as soon as they throw off respect for life, for
berty, for justice . . . Our epoch is gangrened by a contempt for
e protoplasm of society: the individual human being.

. . . I know also that through changing systems, through con-
icting programmes, those undefined values have survived and
ill survive as the ultimate tests of all systems and all programmes.

No set-back can end the adventure in idealism. That adventure
egan with the dawn of the race and will continue when the
ogans and phobias of our own day will have been forgotten.

LYONS: *Assignment in Utopia.* 1938

CONCLUSION

§ I

Summary

HAVE tried to establish two important, though simple, propositions in the course of this book — one relating to the desirable purpose of social action in the contemporary world, and one concerned with the method necessary to that purpose. I propose to summarize very briefly — and for the last time — the course of my argument, before I set it in the broader perspective of human purpose.

(1) In the second Part of this book I tried to analyse, by means of historical evidence and economic statistics, the trends of development in the capitalist system. From that analysis two conclusions appeared clear — *first*, that the reactions of public opinion to the insecurity, inequality and wide fluctuations of prosperity springing from the institutions of free enterprise and property have imposed upon those institutions, at least in political democracies, such a comprehensive system of regulations and burdens that the economic order can no longer be described as a *laisser-faire* system or a 'free economy'. It is an organized economy; and it is a monopolistic and restrictive economy. It has become, in the clumsy phrase that I coined, a 'State organized private monopoly capitalism'. But at the same time, and in the *second* place, the historical evidence clearly demonstrates that this economy is not in a state of collapse, or even of decay. On the contrary it is still an expanding economy with a rising standard of living, a broadening ownership of property and an important set of regulations — the social services and factory legislation — that are protective in their origin and consequences. It is a system unlikely, except in the event of defeat in war, to move into a crisis of economic or political dissolution.

At the same time it is a profoundly unsatisfactory economy, and

325

it calls insistently for reform. Capitalism is a system that can only be justified by a spectacular rate of expansion. Property in industrial capital, and the inequality to which it leads, can be tolerated only if it is the main agent of rapid economic progress. Neither of these conditions is fulfilled to-day. Extreme inequality remains, but the incomes accruing to property no longer make any substantial contribution to social welfare. Moreover the intervention of the State has destroyed freedom of enterprise, but has replaced it by monopolistic restrictions that reduce, irrationally and unnecessarily, the productive capacity of the nation. We are actively reducing, without knowing it, the standard of living and the degree of wealth that we could enjoy. And finally our lives are dominated, and our political purposes frustrated, by the continuance of violent oscillations in the quantity of industrial activity.

From these empirical judgments of Part II I derived my first main conclusion — that the case for a planned economy, centrally controlled in order to pursue expansionist and egalitarian policies was urgent and· overwhelming; and I was then left with the problem of method — by what political method should this reorganization of the economic system be achieved, if it is ever attempted?

(2) In Part IV of the book I have tried to state the reasons - established, in my view, from historical and psychological evidence — for believing that the only possible basis for a healthy and just society is the continuous maintenance of a tolerant party democracy. This is the recurrent theme of the whole book. In the first Part I tried to show, from the evidence of modern psychology, that the social life of adult human groups can be largely understood as a conflict within their minds between repressed impulses to violence and cruelty on the one hand, and their love for each other, for constructive achievement and for the common good, on the other. In Part III I attempted to prove two propositions, first that the Marxist and Communist defence of the 'dictatorship of the proletariat', propounded by them as a refutation of the foregoing argument, was based upon faulty logic and inadequate empirical evidence; and secondly, that it represented in our day the series of false religions by which the impulses to cruelty and destruction have been rationalized into an appearance of reforming zeal and

love for justice and freedom.[1] The only hope for the future
appears therefore, to me, to lie in the preservation, if necessary by
force, of the system of political democracy from all assaults upon it.
In the last Part of the book I have tried to describe the programme by which I believe these various ends can be reconciled.

§ 2

The Two Greater Excluded Questions

I have written this book during a period of tense international
crisis. We have all lived through a decade in the last two years.
The expansion of dictatorial Germany has continued throughout
the period at an extraordinary pace. We were brought within
sight of a general European war in the autumn of last year, and we
all felt the cold wind of death in our nostrils. The grave was
closely boarded over for a time, and I am glad that it was, both
because we thus demonstrated our will to peace beyond all
reasonable doubt, and also because we increased our relative
strength in the meantime. But German imperialism has not been
restrained by persuasion or threats, and war has been thrust upon
us. Another generation is called upon to march, without cheering
this time,[2] into the silence of the unremembered grave. We live
precariously upon the edge of life, and death is in the midst of us.

[1] It is scarcely necessary to repeat that I regard Fascism as the psychological and
intellectual counterpart on the political Right, of Communism on the political Left.
It is the rationalization of hatred and destructive impulses as a reforming and
constructive national conservatism. Both schools of thought are animated by
the same emotions, use the same methods, and, in my view, arrive at the same goal –
a cruel and tyrannical society.
External observers are often misled by the selfless devotion of the extremists into
supposing that the differences between them and more moderate persons is wholly
one of opinion. I do not share this view. People who are violent, intolerant and
severe in politics, having expressed the aggressive side of their characters in this part
of their life, are free to be friendly, kindly and unselfish in their personal relations.
The temperamental differences are just as real as the intellectual. By their fruits
they must be known — and in this case the fruit of their counsel would be violence
and cruelty.
[2] It is interesting to notice that when Europe was brought to the edge of war in
the last week of September 1938, there were no cheering crowds in the capital
cities of London, Paris and Berlin, as there had been in the last week of July 1914.
There were, instead, silent and strained crowds, and women praying.

CONCLUSION

I am not therefore inclined to exaggerate the importance or the relevance of the matters I have just been discussing. All questions of economic organization and policy are overshadowed by two greater matters — the preservation of peace, and the therapy of guilt and aggression in the individual mind. Without international peace we cannot live, and without peace of heart we cannot be happy. It is impossible for me to close this book without attempting briefly to set what I have tried to say in the perspective of these two larger questions.

On the first of them I have little to say. I have not dealt with the problem of foreign policy and international relations in the course of this book, except by implication. It would require another work of this length to deal with the causes and prevention of war, and I am not competent to write it. It will, however, be obvious that I am not a pacifist. I find no warrant in the evidence of psychology, or of history, for believing that aggressive groups of adult human beings can be restrained by kindness, or cured of aggression by submission to their will. On the contrary, I believe that social justice and international justice can be founded only upon peace and law; and that peace and law, in their turn, can be based only, in the last resort, upon the use of force. Aggressive individuals and minorities within the state and within the growing comity of nations must be restrained by force, if they cannot be persuaded by reason. We cannot hand over the world to the law-breaker, simply because he is armed with machine-guns and bombing aeroplanes. Nor would ordinary men and women permit it to be done. They are prepared to pay the heavy price that is necessary to prevent it.

It therefore seems to me to be right to advocate the use of war as an instrument of collective security, and to give all necessary power to some instrument of collective authority — such as the Council of the League of Nations or an executive meeting of the signatories of the Kellogg Pact.

More than this, I believe it to be our duty to fight, in this country, for the preservation of our national existence. I should not feel such an obligation if I were the citizen of a dictatorially governed nation — whether Fascist or Communist. But, living in a community that has slowly built up a system of responsible

328

overnment, I believe that it is worth our while to die in order to
preserve the way of life that has become natural to us. I think it
our duty to do this; even if the hope of collective security is now
dead; and even if we fear, as I fear, that democracy itself may
be modified and endangered by the remorseless exigencies of
modern warfare. It is our unwelcome duty to die because the
danger to democracy will be greater if this war is lost than if
is won.

But let me hasten to add that I am not one of those persons who
prepared to die in order to extend the principle of self-government to other nations; or to destroy the dictatorial principles in
those countries that have accepted it. I have no stomach for new
wars of religion'; and I refuse to be led on from the defence of
democracy, or the maintenance by force of an instrument of collective authority, to an aggressive attack upon dictatorship or the
sacrifice of British lives in anti-Communist or anti-Fascist crusades.
I am not even willing to die in order to preserve democracy in
other countries, unless it is necessary to do so in order to preserve
ourselves. Collective security and national existence seem to me to
be the only pair of causes for which it is worth while, collectively,
to lay down our lives.

There is a second matter that I have not here considered.

To those of us who were brought up in the liberal and democratic traditions of British political life a certain form of utilitarianism is bred in our bones, and will not pass from us until we are
dead. It is not the utilitarianism that degenerated into the personal hedonism of the 1920's. We do not believe that personal
pleasure, narrowly defined, is the object of life. We respect the
importance of the common good, and we recognize the obvious
biological and psychological fact that 'we are members one of
another', and that the good of those for whom we care is essential
to our happiness. We are prepared to offer to all mankind the
sentiment and responsibility of unity with us. We will do our
trifling best to be citizens of the world.

But we shall always be utilitarians in the sense that we put the
happiness of men above the vainglory of institutions. We shall
always believe that the State was made for man, and not man for
the State. In the service of the State great happiness may be

329

found, but only because the State can be used to preserve the li[f]
and secure the happiness, of its humblest members. That, in o[ur]
view, will always be the desirable end of social action — the hap[pi]
ness of ordinary men and women. Beside that end, the splendo[ur]
of empire, the trappings of power and even the creative artist[ry]
of privileged minorities, fall into insignificance and pass awa[y]
It is, in our view, the supreme social duty, the one enduring achiev[e]
ment, so to think and so to act that men and women may sing
their work and children laugh as they play.

Many things can contribute to the happiness of us all. Weal[th]
can contribute to it. A rising standard of living will increa[se]
leisure, reduce the physical fatigue of labour, bring comfort an[d]
health to a growing proportion of our fellow human being[s].
Wealth, properly distributed, can tear down the slums, drive bac[k]
the diseases of malnutrition, open the country-side to our peop[le]
and bring fresh air, sunlight, and safety, to those who now lac[k]
these elementary necessities. It is the honourable task of th[e]
economist, the industrial scientist, and the technician to serve tha[t]
'not ignoble end'. Physical health can also increase men's joy i[n]
living. Wealth is useless to a diseased or over-tired populatio[n]
Strength and vitality are the salt and wine of life; and the medic[al]
and biological scientist, the doctor and the dentist, the institution[s]
of health service and public games, contribute worthily to commo[n]
enjoyment. Social equality could certainly increase our joy i[n]
living. It would rob wealth of its guilt, and take away the sense [of]
shame that must haunt those of us who are rich enough to enjo[y]
life in the present social order — the shame that arises from th[e]
thought that so many are denied, through poverty, an access t[o]
the means of happiness that we possess. A sense of justice is th[e]
necessary savour to all our happiness in society. For this end th[e]
socialist politician honourably strives.

But although wealth, physical health and social equality ma[y]
all make their contributions to human happiness, they can all d[o]
little and cannot themselves be secured, without health in th[e]
individual mind. We are our own kingdoms and make for our
selves, in large measure, the world in which we live. We may b[e]
rich, and healthy, and liberal; but unless we are free from secre[t]
guilt, the agonies of inferiority and frustration, and the fire of un[

pressed aggression, all other things are added to our lives in vain. The cruelty and irrationality of human society spring from these secret sources. The savagery of a Hitler, the brutality of a Stalin, the ruthlessness and refined bestiality that is rampant in the world to-day — persecution, cruelty and war — are nothing but the external expression, the institutional and rationalized form, of these dark forces in the human heart.

The only hope for the creation of firm and lasting happiness in society lies in the greater emotional health of the persons composing it.

Men do not not gather grapes of thorns, or figs of thistles.

We are brought back, in full circle, to where we began. The greatest achievement of the scientific method in this century, and the greatest hope for the future benefit of mankind, lies in the therapy for mind and spirit discovered by modern psychological science. In the light of those discoveries, and by means of its curative practices and above all by its preventative techniques, humanity may hope in the future to conquer the neuroses of fear and hatred from which the most horrible things in society now spring. It is the next chapter in man's slow conquest of pain and disease. To the psychologist and psycho-analyst belong the honour and responsibility of struggling, foremost in the vanguard, for the supreme goal of common happiness.

Nevertheless these hopes are not for us. New generations must grow up in future years, with greater emotional freedom and deeper understanding for the needs of the developing human spirit before a better people will make a better age and a better society. We must live in the world as we know it, racked with the fear of strife, many of its great people in the hands of ruthless and savage minorities, with injustice and cruelty before our eyes. We must do the best that we can with people as they are. There is no easy road to social salvation, no gate around the corner that we may simply unlatch, and walk into a garden of peace. We can only deal with each social problem as it arises, and try to preserve the circumstances within which democracy may survive, and the slow but curative processes of a new emotional education bring men nearer to the full stature of their rational humanity.

CONCLUSION

§ 3

Great Britain

I value the social tradition in which we live. The services o
this country to the cause of human happiness cannot be lightl
dismissed. We have, for centuries now, led the world in the art
of government and in the discovery of the springs of social peace
We first applied the principles of reason to the tasks of economi
organization and industrial production. By so doing we mad
possible, for all men, levels of prosperity and wealth that woul
have appeared Utopian, even fantastic, to generations that live
before the onset of the English Industrial Revolution. We have
from the beginning, made invaluable contributions to the advance
ment of science and learning. To-day through the generosity an
long-sighted wisdom of one group of our scientists — the practisin
psycho-analysts — standing in marked and honourable contras
to the behaviour of most other professions, we have gathered int
our society the most distinguished group of psychologists in th
world, working in the forefront of contemporary science. We shal
continue, in many fields of human endeavour, to lead and not t
follow the generality of mankind.

We have, in this country, much of which to be ashamed. Th
distribution of income is nowhere less equal. The grip of a clas
system that frustrates the search for comradeship between us, an
wastes a monstrously high proportion of our natural talent, i
extraordinarily strong, and is not the less strong, nor the les
destructive, because it is so little resented. In this generatio
moreover, we have been guilty of the most terrible crimes o
popular vandalism. We have torn down some of our finest build
ings, and we have permitted the speculative builder and th
profiteering landlord to drive hideous scars across our country-side
straggling in promiscuous rape over the lovely body of our ancien
agricultural civilization. We have revealed ourselves to the worl
as ruthlessly uncultured, and our generation will go down t
posterity as one of the most aesthetically destructive in ou
history — a rival in the popular demonology of the future to th

332

forgettable excesses of the Reformation and the Civil War.
though we have reason to be proud of our social tradition we
ve, therefore, no occasion to be contented with its chequered
ttern.

The future of the British tradition is not secure. It is threatened
om within and from without. There are dictatorial parties at
me and there is the ever-present threat of attack from abroad.
e could no longer walk quietly in our traditional paths of
erty if either of our violent parties grew to power, or if we were
the losing side in the present European war. Even victory in
will endanger the stability of our society. Hence peace was and
one, though not the sole or the first, of our vital interests.

When the peace of Europe is restored, and in so far as we have
eserved the institutions of a free government, we have still a
eat service to perform for ourselves and for the world.

Every generation is in part united, and in part inspired, by some
nception of a better and a more just society. The conception
ries from age to age, and reflects in large measure the peculiar
eds and the dominant philosophy of the time in which it
livens men to hope. There is a rough law of compensation in
form. The deeper the distress of the world in which they live,
e more Utopian is likely to be the hope by which men sustain
emselves in their daily labour. Despite the fear of aerial
mbardment, ours is predominantly an age of quietness and
mfort. The standard of living continuously rises about us, and
ir social life is not torn by deep religious or political conflicts,
oving men to violent solutions. We can therefore afford modest
eams and practicable aspirations. We do not need the soothing
sion of a perfect society to reconcile us to a bitter distress.

The conception of a better society, by which the broad trends of
ir policy can best be instructed, is therefore of a specific kind.
e need not be content with anything less, nor need we ask for
ore, than a society in which property as a source of social
equality is made to wither slowly away, in which the establish-
ent of a rational central control has restored expansion and
eated economic stability, in which political democracy is
reserved and perfected as a method of government, and in which
ildren may grow, free from secret fear, into a sociable and

CONCLUSION

happy maturity. This is what I mean by a more just societ
An important, indeed an essential, part of it is the constituei
principle of Socialism. Within it the common happiness of mar
kind can be, for a long season, safely established.

Nor need we fear that this society is far away, or difficult
achieve. There is nothing in it that could not be established in
single generation, if we had the eyes to see, and the hearts to wi
this reasonable programme of social betterment. We have on
to open our eyes and stretch out our hands to pluck this precio
fruit from the tree of knowledge.

I feel the conviction, ever more strongly as I grow older, th
it is in this land, rather than in any other, that these hopes a
likely to find their first fulfilment. We shall not be conscious of tl
birth in our midst of a new society, because we do not exerci
our minds in self-analysis, or construct systematic social philos
phies. But as I move about this island, in its quiet lanes and in i
crowded streets, meeting people of all classes and persuasions,
feel the life of a strong and quiet people about me; more deep
united than they realize, more creative than they ever suspec
Here, if anywhere, the will for the common good is strong. Fro
it and from the common friendliness we bear to one anoth
we can continue to make, if we will, a society of which all men w
be glad.

APPENDICES

CRUELTY UNDER DICTATORSHIPS

By Jane Samuel

Note: The following Appendix is a summary by Miss Jane
muel of the evidence published in this country on the nature of
: 'terrors' in Germany and Russia. It should be noted that the
dence is derived, in almost all cases, from unfriendly sources. In
: case of Russia it comes from papers, like *The Times*, and from
illusioned newspaper correspondents, like Mr. Eugene Lyons. In
: case of Germany it comes from the British Press, and from
ugee publications. Each reader must judge the evidence
· himself. Personally I believe that the terrors are, in both cases,
rse than the evidence suggests. It is difficult and dangerous to
·e evidence. I think it is also obvious that the two regimes differ
tle in the degree of their cruelty.

E. F. M. D.

§ I

'*The Enemy of the State*'

HERE are certain notable similarities in the general attitude
wards 'enemies of the State', and their treatment, in the two
ctatorships, Germany and Russia. Being 'the enemy of the
ate' is a condition which rests largely upon status rather than
on personal action. To be a kulak or a bourgeois in Russia, or a
w in Germany, is to be of a caste apart; all one's actions are
spect and one can be arrested merely for being oneself. These
·e the permanent scapegoats; but also any other section may
me in, at different periods, for a share in the blame. Social
mocrats, trade unionists and Protestants have their turn in
ermany; while engineers, generals and diplomats seem to be the
shion in Russia.

Liberty for the individual is out of the question; men are too
One of the accompaniments of dictatorships is the withdraw
of passports for foreign countries and the institution of interr
passports so that mobility is stopped, and every phase of a mai
life is in the hands of the Government. This restriction of
man's personal liberty makes him an easier victim for cruelt
The loss of individual freedom entails the loss of individual respo
sibility — the sins of the father are visited upon the children; wi
this attitude goes collective responsibility, and the maltreatme
of all members of a family for the faults of a single member of
Also, in each country, the punishment given to a political offend
is very much more severe than that of the ordinary criminal.
the Russian timber camps, the criminals act as guards over t
ordinary political offenders, thus showing that they have a high
status. The brutality exhibited in the treatment of the politic
prisoner is much greater than in that of the criminal, who
regarded in the same way as in any other country.

The enemy, or the potential enemy, of the State, is not allow
the benefit of impersonal justice, but is invariably treated in eith
country with the most prejudiced brutality.

§ 2

Arrest

Methods of arrest in Germany are said to be brutal; the suspec
are threatened with revolvers; storm-troopers invade their hom
and probably confiscate their wages, while their family has to loo
on; usually the prisoner is beaten up and generally maltreate
The *Brown Book* describes many such arrests. In Russia, arrest
also brutal, but there is far less evidence than for Germany. The
is no book for Russia equivalent to the *Brown Book*; but Lyons
Assignment in Utopia quotes the evidence of eye-witnesses.

§ 3

'Trials'

The German prisoner is hustled straight to his trial. Th
courts look militant; there are daggers and bayonets on the tabl

338

d, in front of the judge, a uniformed Nazi official. The prisoner
ay have to run the gauntlet through a crowd of storm-troopers.
ustice' is largely administered by storm-troopers, who are almost
variably far more brutal than the army or the police. This
parate army of hooligans has no parallel in Russia. During
ial, the prisoner is not listened to, and beaten up, or so it is
leged. Each country moreover gives almost limitless power to
e Secret Police. Proceedings at trials are generally not published,
d there is no appeal from the sentences of their courts.

§ 4

Mass 'Trials'

The demonstration trial is a feature of the Russian regime.
 has not been so successful in Germany. The Reichstag Fire
rial was the one big attempt, but the effect of that was spoilt
 the prisoners refusing to confess. In Russia, the mass demon-
ration trials elicit mass confessions. Last year in Germany the
ial of Pastor Niemöller was something of a demonstration
nce the great gesture was made of acquitting him. That was
ounteracted, however, by his being immediately placed under
rotective arrest', and he has not yet been released. But this was
thing to the great Russian mass demonstration trials. The first
 these was the Schakhty sabotage trial in 1928; Lyons gives an
e-witness's account of it.
The accused were thirty Russians and three Germans, and it was
ade into a public spectacle.
The charges were not proved in court — presumably this had
een done by preliminary investigation — but a sheaf of partial or
ll-length confessions was produced.
Lyons had the impression that the confessions had been
xtracted by torture. One man went mad during the trial.
he accusation was of a huge international plot; the fact that
itnesses were brought in who were in prison proved that those
ho were in court were only a small section of the prisoners;
e others never came to trial. Every one confessed in court,
ough one or two rescinded their confessions one day, and

then made them again the next. They were all sentenced, thoug not all to death. They had virtually been prejudged.

This was a typical trial, but still more astonishing was the tri in 1938 of 'Rights and Trotskyists' in which every single accuse made full and circumstantial confessions in court. A namele Russian, writing in the *Sunday Express*, on March 6th, 1938, allege that prisoners were tortured; being kept for months in the dar then taken up suddenly to the light, which nearly drove them ma and being prevented for months at a time from sleeping by guard threatening them with a revolver through the door of the cell, till they were worn to a state in which they would sign ar confession.

But does this account for these full confessions in court? It ca only be a subject for speculation how these are elicited. Possib under hope of release — or more likely by the threat to execu friends and relatives. Without having seen the trial, it is impo sible to gauge the bearing and mental condition of the accuse but on close perusal of their confessions it looks as if these we true. Even then, if, however, they acted according to their lights, is impossible to understand how each one in his last plea accus himself, not only of his crimes, but also of being a traitor. Th allegation of torture scarcely accounts for the whole behaviour the accused.

The Nazis also have mass trials, though they do not give the the same publicity. The *News Chronicle* of June 17th, 1937, giv the following list derived from the statistics of the Nazi Terror the *Labour International Service* of the previous day.

Wuppertal Trial, 600 accused of illegal trade union activitie
Dusseldorf Trial, 600- accused of underground politic activities;
Hamburg Trial, 570 accused of terrorist activities of th 'Red Front Fighting Society';
Zeits Trial, 150 accused of 'high treason' by distributin pamphlets calling attention to low wages;
Other Trials: Elmshorn, 270 accused;
Stuttgart, 60 youths;
Kiel, 60 accused.

§ 5

Torture

The *Brown Book* is full of evidence of torture more brutal than
btle. After a prisoner is tried, he is taken to the cellars and
aten with steel rods by Nazis, often until he is nearly dying; then,
ter this, quite often he is told, 'You will be shot', and turned with
s face to the wall. They shoot, but not at him; meanwhile the
her prisoners have to look on. The threat of death — not carried
t — is quite common. This seems to be the only form of purely
ental torture practised in Germany. There are much more
btle physical tortures, such as pressing burning cigarettes into
e feet of prisoners and beating them up while they are being
terrogated; there is the torture as a rule reserved, on the whole,
r intellectuals, of administering castor-oil and then, after a little,
ating the victim with steel rods. Medical aid is called only
hen the prisoner is dying. Schumann, in *The Nazi Dictatorship*,
ints out that the tortures practised are mainly those which will
ford the Nazis themselves prolonged physical exertion. By read-
g accounts from victims and witnesses, one gets the impression
at they take great pleasure in brutality, and seem to cherish a
rsonal hatred for their victims.

It is much more difficult to discover whether the Russians treat
l their prisoners brutally, but Lyons claims to have first-hand
idence of the 'valuta' tortures.

People were tortured to give up their gold, and it is unlikely,
these methods were used quite indiscriminately for that purpose,
at the G.P.U. would abstain from using them with political
isoners.

Mainly the torture consisted of the *parilka* or sweat-room. Hun-
eds of people are packed in a very small room, leaning up against
e another, covered with sweat and lice. Quite a few die.
hen there is the 'conveyor'. Examiners sit at desks in a long
ries of rooms strung out over corridors and stairways. The
isoners have to trot from one to the other, abused, bullied and
reatened by the hour. From *parilka* to conveyor and back, they

go for weeks, being demoralized at last into telling where the valuables are. If the prisoner will not talk, his family is brought and tortured before his eyes. He may be induced to turn inform by a promise to let him off more torture. If he confesses t soon, they will continue to torture him in case he still has mo hidden treasure. Sometimes a prisoner is forced to write to rich relative abroad, asking for money on a matter of 'life death', in order to escape more torture.

It seems on the whole that Russian torture is not much mo subtle or mental in character than in Germany. The habit, whi started in Russia, of implicating the families of accused or suspe persons, has spread to Germany. One Russian method of co trolling the activities of their officials abroad, who are oft reluctant to return home, is to arrest the family of an offic: who refuses to return when sent for.

There are no available figures with regard to Russi brutality, but many with regard to Nazi brutality and sadis in the *Brown Book*, necessarily incomplete since it was writt in 1934. Moreover it seems indisputable that Nazis act und orders. There is a document (reproduced in the *Brown Bo* p. 226) from Goering's Ministry to Kurt Haas, who had co plained of unjustifiable maltreatment, saying that the stor troopers were entirely in the right. There is also evidence, collected from victims (p. 205). There are 536 declarations fro persons severely ill-treated, all checked and found correct.

There are 137 certificates showing that the victims were sever injured, 375 declarations saying that prisoners had to sign sta ments that they had been well treated before leaving the tortu chamber. There is evidence that during 1933 about 60,000 peop were subject to violence, and many individual cases are describ in the *Brown Book*.

§ 6

Mass Persecution

In both Germany and Russia there is a professional sca goat — in Germany the Jew, in Russia the kulak. There is

rtain amount of anti-Semitism in Russia; but, except in the
kraine, where Jews form a considerable proportion of the
•pulation, it is not an official political attitude, though there is
;ood deal of it among State servants and other Russians. Many
those subjected to the 'valuta' tortures happened to be Jews,
d were ill-treated with added gusto. Evidence with regard to
:rman anti-Semitism is in the *Brown Book*. More recent attacks
e as yet without record.

In 1933, or before, 43 people were shot or beaten to death .for
ing Jews. There were 301 recorded cases of severe bodily injury,
d the actual number was probably well over 10,000.

There were numberless disappearances and suicides.

For one day, in April 1933, there was a Jewish boycott. There
s no official Jew-baiting or violence, but there had been incite-
nts to Jew-baiting before that day. The open boycott of shops
s only on April 1st, but since then there has been a general
ycott of Jews from all professions and qualifications and trades —
iiversities admit few Jews. Non-Aryans are disfranchised;
is confirms the attitude that all men are not equal before the
v and justifies cruelty.

In Russia, the equivalent — the disfranchised class or scape-
at — is the person with the wrong social origin, the kulak and
son, the nepman (small trader) and his son. These again
e an inferior race and subject to constant persecution.

The liquidation of the kulaks took place from December 27th,
29, to March 2nd, 1930. Then, when Stalin called a halt, he
amed his subordinates and dismissed wholesale many respon-
•le officials. According to official figures, about 4 million kulaks
ve been liquidated. The *News Chronicle*, November 14th, 1937,
ves 5 million as the figure, of which at least 10 per cent are dead.
vernment officials had a free hand to turn them out of their
mes completely destitute, and there was practically no check
on their treatment of them. They could kill them, or else hav-
; stirred up the hatred of the village people against them, could
rn them over to their mercy; they could let them wander forth
ne, which usually meant death, or transport them in cattle-
icks to distant parts of the country, usually the timber forests of
: north. Thousands died on the way of epidemics, of starvation.

343

or of exposure, and uncounted numbers died when at their desti
ation. They are disfranchised and treated like cattle, and the
whole treatment amounts to mass murder.

§7

Concentration Camps

Concentration camps for political enemies are another comme
feature of the two regimes.

In Germany, 'guilty' people are not in the camps, but
prison. In the camps are only the suspects. There is no tria
merely 'protective detention'. According to the *Brown Boo*
prisoners in the camps are under very strict guards and escape
are machine-gunned. There are no official figures, but in Ju
1933 it was deduced that there must be 45 camps and fro
35,000 to 40,000 prisoners.

Prisons, such as Fuhlsbüttel and Sonnenburg, which had be
closed as unhygienic, were used as camps. Nazis are forbidd
to talk to prisoners, for fear of being influenced by them. Lette
are supervised and only allowed at long intervals.

There are three grades of prisoner:

Easily reformable (German Nationals, guards and politic
followers)
Not easily reformable
Unreformable

and their treatment is graded accordingly. The treatment of t
unreformable is brutal, and despite official denials there is go
reason to believe that they are often tortured. There is evidence
prisoners to this effect. They all have to do compulsory labou
usually of a quite useless kind, and hours of exhausting drill. T
camps are more dreaded than the prisons, as camp prisoners a
entirely in the hands of storm-troopers, whereas in prisons warde
act as a protective barrier. Storm-troopers have lately taken
baring the chests of prisoners coming into camps and smeari
them with hot pitch. Then, when it is dry, they come along a
tear it off. Intellectuals are made to wash latrines out with aci

d sometimes they are made to attempt to do this after the storm-
oopers have cut off their hands.

In the *Monthly Report of the Social Democratic Party*, June 1937,
ese conditions are confirmed by reports of prisoners from Fuhls-
ittel and other camps, laying stress on the starved condition of
e prisoners. There are many suicides, especially among the
ws, who are particularly maltreated.

There is no sentence; prisoners never know when they will be
ee. A favourite device, borrowed from Russia, is to tell them
ey are released, then to shoot them as they go, and report that
ey were 'shot while trying to escape'. In 1934, the number of
mps was reduced, and less brutal treatment enforced. In Sep-
mber political prisoners were to be tried in the ordinary courts,
ut these were completely reconstituted and Nazified and more-
ver political prisoners could still be put into 'protective custody'.
ut, with each new annexation, the number of State prisoners
vells. There are no figures, but old and new camps have been
pened, and obviously there must be many thousands of new
ictims. The Gestapo is always in the van of the German occu-
ation.

In Russia, according to Tiltman's *The Terror in Europe*, the
ussian timber industry is conducted almost entirely by forced
bour. There are three classes: native or indentured workers im-
orted from elsewhere (about 1¼ million); the enforced labour of
anished kulaks without other means of support; and convicts or
olitical prisoners in concentration camps.

The conditions for all these classes are naturally bad, since the
mes are so hard and food is scarce. In the camps, 99 % are
entenced by the G.P.U., by administrative courts with no appeal,
ut at least they have a defined sentence, whereas in Germany
hey have neither trial nor sentence. Accounts as to hours of work
iffer. Often a man has to work until he has completed a given
ask. There are also different kinds of sentence; a man committed
o simple exile may find himself a job. Mostly they go to camps.
here are various accounts by ex-prisoners in Tiltman's book.
onditions are frightful, a starvation diet and the food is very often
utrid; Spartan barracks to live in; inhumanly hard work and
rutal guards, who are often criminal convicts. There are many

suicides, prisoners die like flies from overwork, and their gener
health is appalling. 'Shot while trying to escape' is a phrase
useful in Russia, where it originated, as in Germany, though escap
to the Siberian forests is not very practicable, and the risks suc
that there is no need for such strict supervision as in Germany. O
the whole, these camps, bad as they are, do not seem as bad as tl
German camps; but in 1932 they contained about a quarter of
million prisoners, and in 1938 the *News Chronicle* of November 14t
estimated that the Russian camps and prisons held about two millio
prisoners.

Kulaks, transported in cattle trucks to the north, received ver
harsh treatment too, and lived in conditions almost as bad a
political prisoners, though they are accused of nothing but the
origin.

§ 8

Mass Murder

There has not been much large-scale murder in Germany. Bu
in the *Brown Book* there is a list of 500 murders between 1933 an
1934. 250 are specified — verified by official documents or wit
nesses (p. 341). For example, of non-prisoners murdered:

> On March 7th, 1933, Bernhard Krause, Communist worke
> of Weisenau, Frankfurt an der Oder, was shot by storm
> troopers
> Two unnamed workers were killed in a Nazi raid in Ham
> burg
> On March 6th, Hanns Bauer, a worker of no party, neve
> returned from the Nazi barracks in the Hedermanstrasse
> Berlin
> Grete Messing, a working woman, was shot in the street
> While in prison, on March 18th, Walter Schutz, a Com
> munist worker from Wittstock, was murdered
> Sigbert Kindermann of Charlottenburg, Berlin, was take
> to the Hedermanstrasse, beaten to death and thrown fron
> the window

An unnamed worker from Wedding was beaten to death at
   Nazi headquarters
On March 27th, Max Bilecki of Schoneberg was tortured in
   Nazi barracks and died in hospital
On April 3rd, A. Wertheimer of Kehl had an alleged stroke
   before arrest
On April 4th, Hans Beassler of Dusseldorf was shot while
   trying to escape —

ιd many more such. These are only examples.
Schumann, in the *Nazi Dictatorship*, gave some figures (p. 298):

   Jan. 1st to Oct. 1st 1933:
      67 prisoners officially executed
      3000 murdered
      119,000 wounded
      174,000 gaoled
      (These were denounced in Germany as senseless and useless,
   and it was said that no reply was necessary, but they were
   not actually denied)

Besides the careless slaughter of the kulaks in 1930, there have
εen many death sentences in Russia.
Citrine in *I Seek Truth in Russia* (p. 361) quotes the *Daily Herald's*
ιsualty list of July 10th, 1937. In the previous five months there
εre 167 death sentences (for wrecking, sabotage, etc.).
And in the eleven and a half weeks from July 10th to September
ιth, there were a further 501 people executed. In October, the
ily Telegraph reported 496 death sentences. To take a small
ιlection from all the newspapers from 1925 as representing a frac-
ιn of all the executions reported:

   Morning Post, Oct. 26th, 1925, quoted the Special Corre-
      spondent of *Dni* (Kerensky's paper) reporting 300 political
      prisoners who had been deported from Moscow to Siberia
      in connection with strikes in the Moscow district in June
      and July, for since Stalin came into power, strikes have
      become illegal in Russia
   The Times, Oct. 24th, 1925, 167 persons shot without trial
      in the second half of September
   Daily Telegraph, June 16th, 1927, more than 200 executions
      since the Voikoff murder on June 7th

CRUELTY UNDER DICTATORSHIPS

Manchester Guardian, Jan. 1st, 1930, reported that in Oct. ar
    Nov., 1929, there were 247 executions, mostly kulaks
Morning Post, Sept. 9th, 1930, 300 executions in two days
Daily Telegraph, Sept. 6th, 1932, in the first three days
    September, 20 death sentences were reported in the Mosco
    press
Daily Herald, Sept. 29th, 1937, 466 deaths since July

In fact, there were mass executions all through 1937. *The Tim*
of March 2nd, 1938, gives 4000 executions for 1937. Estimates
the number of people killed for political reasons since the revol
tion vary from one to twenty million, so that it is impossible 1
arrive at any even approximate figure. Following up the histor
of the Russian revolution since Lenin's death in the newspaper
there are perpetual reports of executions and mass trials almo
every day. As the *Manchester Guardian*, June 11th, 1930, says: 'Th
Russian newspapers record death sentences in much the sam
way as ours record road accidents.'

Apart from this, there have been, since 1928, several mass tria
of anything up to a hundred people at a time. Nearly all ar
executed after sentence, and the occasional calling of a witne:
from the prison cell proves that these are only a fraction of thos
who are arrested and executed. Many Communists are arreste
and imprisoned.

Ammend in *Human Life in Russia* blames the regime, not onl
for the death of the kulaks, but also for the death of many millior
of the peasants from famine. After they were collectivized, in th
resulting terror, they killed off a huge portion of their stock. Th
result of this, and of the neglect of their agriculture, was a terribl
famine in subsequent years and the death of millions of people. Th
responsibility, he contends, lay with the Government, not only fc
liquidating the kulaks and collectivizing the peasants, but also be
cause they would not sacrifice prestige and devote any resourc
from the Five-Year Plan to food production, nor would the
import food.

Instead they hushed up the famine.

COMPARISON

§ 8

Comparison

Although in principle there is so much in common in the treatment of the enemy of the State in the two countries, there are
certain differences of a dynamic nature which are very marked.
The Russian regime has had a series of supplementary scapegoats
which it has pushed into the ranks of the old class enemy. There
have been fashions in these scapegoats; during the first few years
of Stalin's power, they were mostly people responsible for the
working of the Five-Year Plan. The general inefficiency of Russia
was blamed upon thousands of engineers, technicians, foremen
and professors, who were executed or exiled. These were usually
called 'Wreckers' or 'Intellectuals'. The Russian regime started
as a socialist democracy, and the idea of a dictatorship was foreign
to it, while the German, on the other hand, was always frankly
authoritarian. It has always been a dictatorship, if not of Hitler
alone, at any rate of a very few men. At the outset, Hitler helped
to kill with his own hands thirty of his associates for whom he had
no more use, but since then there has until now been no great
change in the regime. It is possible of course, that if Hitler remains in power without war for another twenty years, a similar
shifting of guilt may happen in Germany, with its attendant
punishment. He has only been in power five years and the character of the future can only be surmised. There have been immense
changes in Russia. Lenin's Russia was governed by a Polit-bureau
of nine men. They were nine 'Old Bolsheviks', steeled in Imperial
prisons, hardened and unscrupulous. And this was the type of man
who held the important places all over Russia. They continued
after Stalin had begun his rise to power in 1927, and had disgraced
Trotsky and his associates. They remained until 1934. The break-
ing-up of the society of Old Bolsheviks in June was a sign of the
times, and the Kiroff murder was the signal for the beginning of a
new epoch. Linked up with it were the series of arrests and trials,
till in 1938 there were practically no Old Guard Bolsheviks left in
Russia, and Stalin was left unquestioned dictator with no man of
his own metal to oppose him.

The following lists give a rough idea of the immense chang
there has been in the last four years:

Of the members of Lenin's Polit-bureau, Lenin died naturally
Tomsky committed suicide on August 27th, 1936; Trotsky wa
exiled; Kameneff was executed in 1936; Zinovieff executed 193(
Rykoff executed 1938; Bukharin executed in 1938; Sokolniko
executed 1937. Stalin alone survives.

Directly connected with the Kirov murder were eight demor
stration trials, and in these years there were countless othe
trials and executions. In the second of these trials, Zinovieff an
Kameneff were executed — the first Old Bolsheviks to have tha
fate. Later they were followed by Pyatakov, Sokolnikoff, Rade
Karakhan, Yenukidze, Bukharin, Rykoff and many others.

The Times, March 23rd, 1938, gives a fairly comprehensiv
summary of the fate of many Soviet officials:

> To estimate the real effect which the executions and tria
> since 1935 have had on the country, it is important first t
> study the list of victims and the offices they held. Among th
> men near the top of the central Government, two deput
> Prime Ministers (Rudzutak and Mezhlauk) have bee
> 'removed'; the Ministry of Defence has thus by suicide an
> the executioner lost three deputy ministers (Gamarin
> Tukhachevsky, Orloff) who were unmasked as 'traitors', an
> three others (Yegeroff, Alksnis, Viktoroff) have disappeare
> to unknown fates, the Ministry of Defence Industry has lo
> both its minister and deputy minister (Ruhkimovicl
> Muklevich). Posts and Telegraphs has been for many
> kind of condemned cell; Smirnoff, Rykoff, Yagoda, held th
> post for brief periods before going to the dungeons of th
> G.P.U., their successor Khalepsky and his deputy (Prokofief
> friend and assistant of Yagoda) have followed them. Stalin
> police have shot, removed, and otherwise handled or mi
> handled so many officials that their names make a lon
> weary list, in fact they have been the chiefs in almost ever
> Ministry including Envoys to almost every country. Th
> purge of the eleven constituent Republican Governments o
> the Soviet Union has been even more thorough than at th
> centre. To mention a few the R.S.F.R., or Russia prope
> has this way lost its ministers of Education, Finance an

Justice; the Ukraine, its Premier, its Minister of Education; White Russia its Premier and Minister of Agriculture; Tajikistan, its President and 7 Ministers; Turkmenistan, its President and 4 Ministers; Georgia, its Premier and 6 Ministers; Armenia, its President and 5 Ministers; and Kirghizia, its President (Shamurzin). Some 40 chairmen of territorial oblast (executive committees), the mayors of Kieff, Kharkoff and Rostoff. More than 500 directors of trusts, factories and big industrial undertakings have also recently paid the penalty of the 'enemies of the people'.

Havoc among Communists engaged more particularly in high party posts than in the administration has been on a similar scale. They include Bukharin, Zinovieff, Kameneff, Rudzutak, all former members of the politbureau, the highest organ of the party, and many of the highest officials in the constituent republics.

The blow delivered to the Red Army last June, when Marshal Tukhachevsky, and Generals Yakov, Uborevitch, Kork, Eideman, Feldman, Primakoff and Putna were shot without the formality of an open trial, has been followed by the wholesale 'removal' and disappearance of senior officers. In most cases they are taken by an unknown hand and no announcement is made. Nothing definite was known about Admiral Orloff, Deputy Minister of Defence and Commander in Chief of the Red Navy, who represented the Soviet Union at the Coronation in London last year, until Voroshiloff in his speech on February 22nd mentioned that Orloff had been 'wiped off the face of the earth as a traitor and a spy'.

Among others who have disappeared from the highest posts in the fighting services are deputy political chiefs of the Army, generals, commanders, deputy commanders of the Kharkoff, North Caucasus, Ural, Transbaikal, Leningrad and Moscow military districts, and the tank corps; Tkacheff, commander of the civil air force; Tupoleff, the famous head of Soviet aeroplane construction; Admiral Sirkoff, Commander of the Baltic Fleet; and nearly all the political chiefs of all the military districts and the Red Fleet. In 1938 the newly organized commissariat or military council attached to the Ministry of Defence consisted of 80 men: of these 51 have since been proclaimed traitors.

ut the similarities under the two dictatorships are much more

marked than the differences. In Germany, it is striking wh
pleasure the Nazis seem to take in torture, especially in beating
and in that calling for physical exertion — this may exist in Rus
too, but less evidence is obtainable. In Russia, the striki
feature is the entirely callous attitude towards human life — t
liquidation of one class after another — four million kulaks liq
dated — millions more people dying of famine — not one but fi
persons tried at a time, and countless executions.

But these are only differences of degree. What is so remarka!
is that dictatorship should produce such insensate cruelty. Is
some psychological reason that leads those having absolute pov
to abuse it? It may be fear of revolution that leads to both countr
being run by the secret police. Where there can be no inter-pa
friction, which can work itself out in a democracy, there is
means of protest, but plotting and revolution. The Governme
having no powerful opponents to blame for the country's misf
tune, has to find a scapegoat — be he Jew or kulak.

In each country, persecution, secret police methods and t
scapegoat seem so far to be a continuous feature, and not jus
phase, and the powerless minority is essential to this purpose. T
Government is above the State in both countries, and not only l
it arbitrary powers, but what is vital is that all men are not eq
before the law. The State avenges itself upon all its 'enemies', l
the scapegoat class start with an insurmountable initial handic;
The democratic attitude — that Justice is an end in itself and t
an instrument, and that no accused person is guilty until the c
is proved against him — is dead in dictatorship countries. 'Justi
is the vengeance of the insane.

J. M. P

THE 'CLASSICAL' DEFENCE OF THE CAPITALIST SYSTEM

§ I

The Classical Position

It is well known to the students of economics and economic history that one school of economists has constructed an explanation of the internal mechanics of *laisser-faire* capitalism, and that this explanation is often interpreted by them as a *rationale* and a defence of it. Classical economics began as an intellectually revolutionary movement — as a plea for the beneficent power of 'rationalism' and acquisitiveness — and consequently as a defence of the emerging capitalist system. Modern representatives of this school of thought have, however, continued to defend the system long after it emerged, and in recent years they have restated the traditional argument in a new form.

The substance of this assessment consists in the attempt to show that the *laisser-faire* form of capitalism is the best practicable type of economic order. The reasons given for this belief are numerous, and have varied from time to time; but they can be summarized under four heads:

1. There is first the famous argument, derived from the traditional theory of value, that freedom of enterprise *in a state of perfect competition* will resolve one of the central problems facing any society able to produce some, but not all, of the commodities the consumers within the society desire to consume. The theory of value purports to show that under these conditions the most urgent wants of the owners of income will be satisfied. And it used to be argued that any other system, not based on private property and competition, could not resolve this problem at all.

It has been shown over and over again by economists, in different forms and with increasing degrees of generality, that under the

conditions of perfect competition the search for maximum moneta
reward by the owners of labour and capital will bring all the fact
of production into positions where they make the greatest possib
contribution to the satisfaction of the owners of final income.[1]

I think that no one who has studied the logic of the theory
value carefully now disputes the validity of this formal conclusic

It is necessary, however, to be clear as to the precise nature
the conclusion thus established. It does not imply that any prac
cal policy of *laisser-faire* has, in any sense, been justified. It is
purely hypothetical proposition. It only shows that if a numb
of highly complex conditions are assumed — scarcity, perfe
competition, and a certain type of foresight — the distributi
of real economic resources will possess one rational characterist
It will satisfy the most urgent desires of the existing owners
income. If any of these conditions is not fulfilled no such co
clusion follows. Moreover the argument can only demonstra
that *laisser-faire* is *one* logically possible method of solving t
problem. It does not show that it is socially practicable. Much l
does it prove that it is the best method or solution.

2. Realizing this or something like it, the defenders of capitalis
have gone on to argue that, *in fact*, no other system will make t
rational adjustments of means to ends, rendered necessary by t
changing condition of demand and production.[2] The argume
underlying this doctrine appears to arise from the view that t
vested interests opposing socially necessary change will becon
stronger in any framework of institutions that does not establish
system of atomistic competition in the economic sphere. Adjus
ments will be made, according to this view, only if the individua
whose interests are adversely affected by them, are quite powerle
to influence the course of events, and this condition will obta
only if there are so many of them determining each particul
decision that they are all impotent to influence the nature of it.

[1] See any standard text on the Theory of Value – MARSHALL: *Principles
Economics*; WICKSELL: *Lectures on Political Economy*, vol. I; PIGOU: *Economics
Welfare*; or CASSELL: *Theory of Social Economy*. For more recent statements of t
broad thesis see BROWN: *Framework of the Pricing System*, *passim*, or MEAD
Introduction to Economic Analysis and Policy, Part II.
[2] See HAYEK: *Collectivist Economic Planning*, Chap. viii, the present stage of t
Debate, *passim*; ROBBINS: *The Great Depression*, Chaps. vii and viii, and *Econom
Planning and International Order*, *passim*.

I shall attempt to examine this doctrine of perfect competition
detail in a future book. All that it is necessary to say now is that
e modern form of the argument is not based upon logical reason-
g, but upon psychological presumptions. It does not expose by
gical reasoning the meaning implicit in assumptions — as does
e theory of value — but it seeks to establish the high probability,
moral certainty, of certain objective forms of social behaviour.
opositions of this kind are more interesting and more valuable
an systems of abstract logic, but they are also more difficult to
tablish, and it is not easy to discover the historical evidence and
ychological analysis upon which alone views of this kind can be
curely based. They savour more of assumption than of induction
sed upon evidence.[1]

3. The third type of proposition upon which the defence of
pitalism has been based is another set of psychological pre-
mptions. It has been argued that the economic incentive to
rsonal gain is an emotional incentive necessary to promote and
aintain personal efficiency. There is some obscurity in connect-
g this doctrine of 'necessary incentive' with the institutions of
pitalism, since it is obvious that the retention of the economic
centive is perfectly compatible with the disappearance of certain
stitutions that are basic to capitalism. A centrally controlled
onomy could easily make use of differential incomes to secure a
gh degree of effect and output, and social equality is quite content with the retention of significant differences of earned income.
deed the whole argument fails signally as a defence of any social
der in which unearned income is an important part of the
stributive arrangements, since this type of income cannot con-
ibute in any way to the maintenance of personal efficiency just
cause it is unearned. It has never been argued that the dis-
ibution of large sums of money through the chance good fortune

---

[1] The economists who hold these views believe that there is historical evidence
support their assumption (cf. ROBBINS: *The Great Depression*, Chap. vii). But the
idence upon which they depend is derived wholly from the existence of State
ganized monopolies whose origins we discussed in Part II. It is pure assumption
transfer this type of behaviour to the circumstances of a planned economy.
o do so it is necessary to ignore all the evidence derived from the experience of
ussia and Germany. Whatever the faults of the economic administrations of these
untries, *restriction* has not been one of them.
These countries are, however, political dictatorships. The argument must
erefore remain in the field of speculation as far as democracies are concerned.

of lotteries or horse-racing was necessary to the preservation
industry and vigour in the working population. Why then shou
it be argued that the distribution of even larger sums of mon
through the grand lottery of birth and inheritance is necessary
the same end?[1]

4. The only justification of an economic sort that has ever be
offered for the preservation of the institution of inheritance, a
the economic and social inequality that flows from it, is the arg
ment that the very rich will be able to meet the expenses of gover
ment and of social accumulation with a minimum of conscio
suffering. Thus political stability and economic progress are ma
socially possible. It is contended that the very rich can be made
contribute heavily to the public exchequer, and that they w
automatically save a large proportion of their relatively enormo
incomes. If the distribution of income were made more equal t
conscious burden of public expenditure and of capital accumulatic
would be made much greater, and their volume would cons
quently be forced down. Inequality and a high rate of econom
progress are, therefore, according to this argument, inextricab
bound up with each other.

The difficulty in accepting this series of propositions as a defen
of capitalism lies partly in their logical nature and partly in t
historical evidence that I have examined in Part II of the prese
book. As I have already pointed out, the presumption that t
vested interests opposed to industrial adaptation will become ove
whelmingly strong in a socially controlled economy implies a
assumption about social behaviour for which little evidence
offered. It may be so, or it may not be so. It is difficult to do
matize, and impossible to do so upon the basis of the existi
theory of value. To this point I propose to return in detail in n
projected book upon the *Economics of Democratic Socialism.*

But whatever the answer to this question may be, it seems certa
that the consideration of social practicability throws the grave
doubts on the validity of the 'Classical' argument. We ha

[1] I am not supposing that this consideration disposes of the case for proper
as a major social institution. The case for property is derived directly from t
general case for capitalism considered in the previous paragraph. But the relatio
ship between the institution of property (and inheritance) on the one hand and of t
incentive to labour and efficiency on the other, is quite inconsequential, in my vie

lready seen that several of the necessary presumptions of the
classical position are destroyed by recent historical change
nitiated by democratic pressure:

(*a*)   The institutions of *laisser-faire* and of competition have not
roved historically stable. They have passed away into voluntary
nd compulsory monopoly. The distribution of resources under
he guidance of private enterprise is becoming increasingly un-
conomic (see Part II, § 4 A (*c*)).

(*b*)   The growth of taxation has reduced the saving of the rich
 nothing, and may convert the group of wealthy rentiers into a
ositive danger to the growth of capital (see Part II, § 4 B, *passim*).
It is therefore extremely difficult to argue that the socially
efensible form of capitalism has proved stable.

The members of this school of thought do not adopt this inde-
nsible position. They lament the growing rigidity and restrictive-
ss of the system as much as anyone else. They contend, however,
at these trends are not inevitable, and that they can be reversed
 the future. This brings us to the subject of economic *policy* (the
bject of Part II, § 6).

§ 2

The Restoration of Capitalism

The modern representatives of the Classical School — Pro-
sors Mises,[1] Hayek,[2] Robbins[3] — wish to use the power of the
ate to free enterprise, to protect competition and so to restore
 capitalism its earlier elasticity and power of spectacular ex-
nsion.

The positive policy that they propose consists in restoring
asticity to the economic system by the destruction of monopoly
d the preservation of competition. It is the internal consistency,
d particularly the political consistency of this programme, that
vish to examine.

MISES: *Gemeinwirtschaft*, published in translation as *Socialism* in 1937, *passim*.
VON HAYEK: *Collectivist Economic Planning*, Essays I and VIII, *passim*.
ROBBINS: *The Great Depression*, Chaps. vii and viii. *Economic Planning and
ernational Order*, *passim*.

Now it is extremely difficult to see how such a policy is compatible with the maintenance of political democracy. As we have seen, the main sources of rigidity and lessened vitality in the system are:

Trade Union restrictions
Social Services
the measures that I have called 'depression or monopoly planning'
the principle of progressive taxation, and certain consequences for the capital market of the institution of limited liability and the growth of providential saving

Of these sources of growing rigidity only the last does not spring directly from the political pressure and democratic power of the common people. Consider them in turn. The right to form trade unions and the principle of collective bargaining is one of the earliest and one of the most strenuously defended democratic privileges. The movement to form such protective organizations began with the growth of factory labour and was uninterruptedly sustained through persecution and legal frustration; the right once conceded, has been defended with obstinate pertinacity from every kind of attack. It would surely be unwise to deny the inherence of this demand in the nature of democracy and responsible government. Precisely the same is true of the growth of the social services. The demand that the taxing power of the State should be used to support the common people during the periods of necessity is a demand that arises later in the history of capitalism than the demand for the right to bargain collectively but it is equally insistent and more widespread when it comes. The internal questions about which the British people now really care are chiefly those of the social services. This is, no doubt, a conservative tendency in the mind of the ordinary voter not without its dangers; but it is a real one. No one, contemplating the immense growth of the social services in the last twenty years and the continuous success of the agitation to extend them, can honestly deny that their origin lies in the virtually unanimous wish of ordinary men and women for greater economic security and social well being. The same is true of the more recent increase in the progressiveness of taxation, and of the most recent change of all — the

e of the legislative function of the State to create sellers' and pro-
ucers' monopolies.

Again, can the popularity of the principle that the rich should
e taxed more than proportionately be denied by anyone? Does
nyone suppose that the principle could be reversed without over-
helming popular opposition? And, although it is early yet to speak
 the permanent popularity of the restrictionist policies of recent
overnments, it must be admitted at the same time that no
dministrations in Great Britain and America have ever been
ccorded such huge majorities and such universal support as the
 ational' governments of Messrs. MacDonald and Baldwin in
 is country and the two administrations of Mr. Roosevelt in
merica. Yet these are the governments of restriction and
 onopoly. It would seem that it is only the institution of limited
 bility that is not deeply entrenched in the affections of the
 ople.

Yet it is only by sweeping away these things that elasticity and
 ee movement can be restored to the capitalist system. How can
 e unchecked movement of wages and the mobility of labour be
 eatly increased, unless the power of the trade unions is broken?
ow can the volume of saving be restored, unless the rich are made
 cher by a limitation or reduction of public expenditure, and a
 odification of the progressiveness of taxation? How can expan-
 onist movements be resumed until the apparatus of restriction has
 en swept away? It is clear that in each case there is no alternative
 cept the positive uprooting of the defensive institutions of the
 ople.[1]

Do the advocates of this policy face its real political implications?
 hey must go to the people with these proposals upon their lips.
 et us liquidate the trade unions! We must reduce the social

[1] It is scarcely necessary to point out that those who hold these views do not
 lieve these steps to be implied by their policy. They believe that weakening the
 wers of collective bargaining, the protection of competition by the State, and
 tailed changes in the administration of the social services will be sufficient to
 store elasticity to the system. I am unable to accept this view for two reasons:
) because I believe that the trends of change deplored by this school of thought
 ring from much deeper levels of the popular will than they suppose (see Part II,
 ssim); (b) because the practical steps that would have to be taken – the weakening
  trade unions for example – can only be justified by the belief that the capitalist
 stem is the sole economic order that is both practicable and desirable. To this
 int I propose to return in a future publication.

services! Progressive taxes must go! Commodity taxes must
raised! Profits must be increased — or, in general — the rich mu
be raised and the poor must be degraded! It is difficult to suppo
that these are *popular* cries. The measures aimed at restoring
free enterprise economy do not seem consistent with the mai
tenance of responsible government. Freedom of enterprise seem
incompatible with freedom.

Let us consider the matter a little further. There are only tw
ways in which such measures can be carried — either the peop
must be persuaded of their necessity, or they must be impose
against the popular will. I am not seeking to deny the possibility
the first method. I believe that rational argument and intellectu
ideas play an important part in the causation of political event

Nevertheless it is obvious, I think, that intellectuals, and parti
ularly economists, exaggerate their importance. Mr. Keynes co
cludes his work on the abstract theory of money with this dogmat
passage:

> ... the ideas of economists and political philosophers, bo
> when they are right and when they are wrong, are mo
> powerful than is commonly understood. *Indeed the world
> ruled by little else.*[1]

Professor Robbins, disagreeing with Mr. Keynes over so mar
things, agrees with him at least in this, for Professor Robbins hir
self writes:

> The measures of the last decade have been the result, n
> of spontaneous pressure by the electorate, but of the influen
> of a number of men whose names could be counted on t
> fingers of two hands ... In the short run, it is true, ideas a
> unimportant and ineffective, *but in the long run they rule t
> world.*[2]

These statements seem to me to be exaggerated. They appear
spring from one form of the idealist theory of history, and to
suggested by no credible theory of human psychology.[3]

---

[1] *General Theory of Employment, Interest and Money*, p. 383.

[2] *The Great Depression*, p. 20.

[3] Such theories of history depend, I would suggest, upon the same logi
fallacy as the materialist interpretation of history. They confuse the universal
of an element in social life and history with its solitary causality. Ideas are eve
where present, but they are not the sole causes of social behaviour.

But, these high matters apart, it is probable that a quiet and
asonable electorate like the British could be persuaded to forego
e things for which it most cares if it could be shown that such
sires were incompatible with the common good. The sense of
sponsibility and the discipline of the British people have resulted
the adoption of most remarkable measures of self-sacrifice in
e past. No doubt in this, as in other features of our national
aracter, virtue has not yet departed from us. It is, therefore,
t wholly inconceivable that the politician of the future, inspired
the persuasive reasonings of these economists, should persuade
e trade unions voluntarily to disband, and the people to accept
permanent reduction of the social services, with the kind of
thusiasm that greeted the sharp deflationary budget of 1931. It
not impossible that the British working class could be persuaded,
the compelling force of ideas, to abandon with cheerful courage
e social hopes that they have entertained for generations; and
us to acquiesce in a mournful return to the world that they be-
ved they had left behind them for ever. It is not impossible to
nceive this; but such a change is, surely, in the highest degree
probable. Social systems have rarely developed backwards
less they have been in process of retrogression and disintegration.
here seems little reason to suppose that this generalization will be
lsified in the immediate future. Unless it can be shown that
ery other type of economy is inherently unworkable, and that
llectivist economies, in particular, are certain to produce chaos
d poverty, the hope of voluntary reaction to a simpler and
eer capitalism is illusory.[1]

If my political judgment is correct the policy of the 'liberal'
onomists is internally inconsistent. Their political theory is
compatible with their economic policy. They must abandon the
ne or the other. They must choose between capitalism and
berty. In so far as these thinkers are liberal, they must give their
inds and intellectual gifts to the solution of the problems of a
lanned economy. They must distinguish 'freedom of enterprise'
om 'economic freedom' and make up their minds to follow and

[1] The validity of the argument for capitalism here briefly criticised will be fully
scussed, as I have already said, at the opening of the second volume of this book.
r myself, I believe that it is wrong, and I shall there state my reasons for rejecting

aid the slow, but inevitable, search of a free people for happine. In so far as they are capitalist, they must either abandon tl struggle in despair, or reconsider their democratic faith. The would seem to be no other choice before them.

APPENDIX III

STATISTICS

§ 1

Ossification of Labour Market

(a)   Professor HENRY CLAY: *Public Regulation of Wages*, 1929,
p. 323-324.

Trade Union Membership	4,900,000
Trade Boards	1,500,000
Joint Industrial Councils	1,000,000
Agricultural Wages Board	1,100,000

'. . . if we add together the numbers covered by Trade Boards,
Agricultural Wages Boards, Joint Industrial Councils, and Unions
in certain industries, which, like coal and cotton, have adopted
one of these forms of organization, we get a total of *eight millions*
out of a wage-earning population, which excluding domestic
service, numbers *something under fourteen millions*. When we remember that the influence of an agreement or a determination reached
by a representative body tends to go beyond the limits of the membership of the organizations, and even trades, directly represented,
we may safely conclude that there are few important gaps left in
the provision for the settlement of wages by collective bargaining
in Great Britain.'

(b)   Relation of Money Wages and Prices.
           (ISLES: *Wages Policy and the Price Level*)

i. Tables, p. 247

	Index of Wage Rates with trend removed	Index of Wholesale Prices with trend removed
1870	173	104
1	177	109
2	184	121
3	192	124
4	192	114

STATISTICS

	Index of Wage Rates with trend removed	Index of Wholesale Pri[ces] with trend removed
1875	189	107
6	186	107
7	184	106
8	180	98
9	177	94
80	177	101
1	176	98
2	175	98
3	176	96
4	176	89
5	174	85
6	172	82
7	172	82
8	173	85
9	177	89
90	183	90
1	182	91
2	180	87
3	179	88
4	178	82
5	177	82
6	177	81
7	179	82
8	179	83
9	183	88
1900	189	96
1	188	88
2	184	86
3	181	85
4	179	85
5	179	87
6	180	93
7	185	96
8	183	85
9	180	86
1910	179.5	90

ii. Tables, p. 243

		Index of Money Wages (Bowley)	Index of Wholesale Prices (Bd. of Trade)
1922	4	100.5	94.0
1923	1	100.0	
	2	100.0	95.2
	3	98.3	96.4
	4	97.7	94.5
			97.0
1924	1	98.3	100.0
	2	100.0	98.8
	3	101.1	99.4
	4	101.1	102.4

		Index of Money Wages (Bowley)	Index of Wholesale Prices (Bd. of Trade)
1925	1	100.5	101.6
	2	101.0	96.0
	3	100.5	93.9
	4	100.5	92.0
1926	1	100.5	88.6
	2	100.5	87.2
	3	100.0	90.2
	4	100.5	90.4
1927	1	100.5	85.6
	2	101.0	84.8
	3	101.0	85.1
	4	101.0	84.8
1928	1	100.5	84.6
	2	100.0	86.1
	3	100.0	83.8
	4	99.7	83.1
1929	1	99.5	83.6
	2	99.5	82.2
	3	99.3	82.1
	4	99.0	80.7
1930	1	98.7	76.9
	2	98.3	73.4
	3	98.2	70.7
	4	98.2	67.0
1931	1	97.9	64.0
	2	97.0	62.8

iii. Graphs

(See Graphs on pp. 366 and 367).

ᴏᴛᴇ: An inspection of these two pairs of curves will show a ᴐugh correspondence between the movements of money wage ᴀtes and of wholesale prices in the earlier period, *and no such ᴏrrespondence in the later period.*

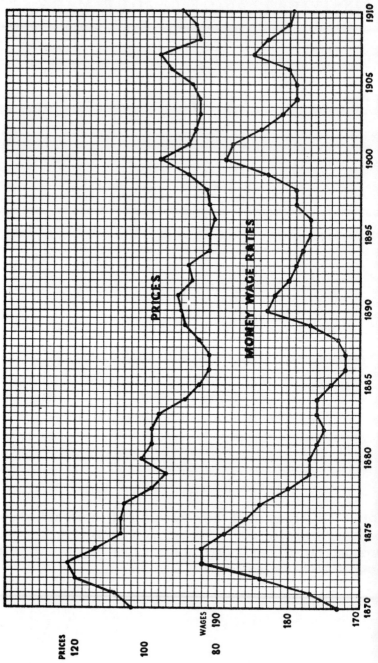

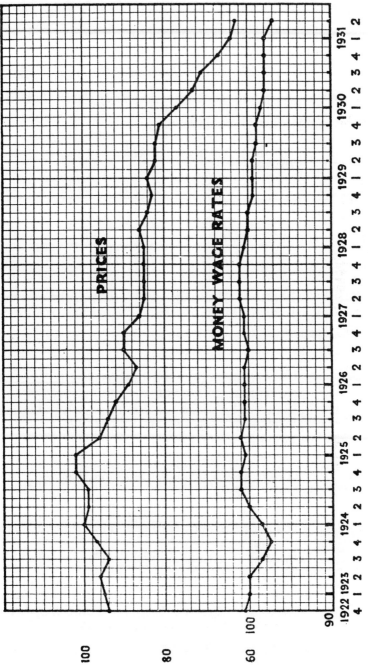

§ 2

Growth and Changing Incidence of Taxation

(a)   *Proportion of National Income Absorbed by Public Authorities*

Table compiled by Jane Samuel:

	National Income £ millions	Budget £ millions	Rates £ millions	Total £ millions	Percentage
	(a)	(b)	(c)		
1860-1 [1]	760	68.4	14.9	83	10.9
1868-9 [2]	814	71.7	25.3	97	11.9
1882-3 [3]	1,274	83.6	38.1	122	9.5
1884-5 [4]	1,274	72	44.1	116	9.1
1889-90 [5]	1,285	91.2	48.1	139	10.8
1913-4 [6]	2,300	197	93	290	12.6
1923-4 [7]	3,800	690	162	852	22
1929-30 [8]	4,384	748	185	933	21.2
1933-4 [9]	3,962	778	179	957	24

NOTE: It will be seen that from the 1880's (1884-5) the percentage of the National Income taken in rates and taxes has risen without interruption from 9.1 % to 24.0 %.

Sources of Tables:

Column (a) — *National Income*

1, 5	MULHALL: *Dictionary of Statistics*, p. 320
2	BAXTER: *National Income for United Kingdom – Gross Estimate* (in *Tracts on Trade*, p. 7)
3, 4	SIR LOUIS MALLET: *National Income and Taxation*
6	*MacMillan Report*, p. 176
7, 8, 9	COLIN CLARK: *National Income and Outlay*, p. 88

Column (b) — *Budget*

1, 2	Finance Account, Parliamentary Papers, 1861 and 1869
3	Statistical Abstract, 1892
4	SIR LOUIS MALLET: *National Income and Taxation*
5	MALLET and GEORGE: *A Century of British Budgets*
6, 7	BOWLEY: *Wages and Incomes in United Kingdom*
8	*Economist*, April 1937: Supplement, p. 2
9	Finance Account, 1936

CHANGES IN THE RATE OF SAVING

Column (c) — *Rates*

MULHALL: *Dictionary of Statistics*
Statistical Abstract, 1883-1893-1903
SIR GWILYM GIBBON: *Expenditure and Revenue of Local Authorities*
Parliamentary Papers, Local Expenditure Account, 1890
Statistical Abstract, 1915
BOWLEY: *Wages and Incomes in United Kingdom*, p. 116
Statistical Abstract, 1935

(b) *Distribution of Burden of Taxation between Income Groups*
Table from the Report of the Colwyn Committee on National Debt and Taxation: Percentage of Income paid in Taxation.

| Income £ a year | Wholly Earned | | Income Half Un-earned | |
	1913-14	1925-26	1913-14	1925-26
	%	%	%	%
100	5.4	11.9	6.6	13.0
200	4.0	10.2	5.3	11.3
500	4.4	6.2	7.1	8.4
1,000	5.2	11.0	8.3	14.4
2,000	4.9	15.2	8.4	19.3
5,000	6.7	23.2	9.6	29.5
10,000	8.0	31.2	11.8	40.1
50,000	8.4	44.4	13.6	57.7

NOTE. An inspection of these figures shows an increase in the progressiveness of taxation.

§ 3

Changes in the Rate of Saving

i. Table compiled from BOWLEY, *Economic Consequences of the War*, p. 136, and COLIN CLARK's *National Income 1924-1931*, pp. 70 and 138.

	Total Income £ millions	Net Savings £ millions	Rate of Saving Percentage %	
1911	2,160	350	16.3	} 17.25
1913	2,200	400	18.2	
1924	4,165	475	11.4	
1926	3,680	247	6.7	
1927	3,890	381	9.8	
1928	3,850	380	9.9	} 7.75
1929	4,000	335	8.4	
1930	3,940	250	6.3	
1931	3,500	190	5.4	

ii. COLIN CLARK, *National Income and Outlay*, p. 185: '. . . In
vestment as a percentage of the national income was as follows.

	%
1907	12.2
1924	8.1
1929	7.2
1935	6.9

NOTE: Both these tables show a marked decline in the Rate of
Saving and Investment measured as a proportion of the National
Income.

§4

Growth of the Middle Class

i. BOWLEY and STAMP, *The National Income*, p. 78, estimate of
the numbers included in the Middle Class — and their percentage
of the occupied population:

	Numbers	*Percentage of occupied population*
1881	1,600,000	19.0
1921	4,600,000	26.9
1931	4,483,000	29.1

ii. KLINGENDER: *Conditions of Clerical Labour in England*, p. xx
Estimate of professional classes as a percentage of the number in
employment:

	Higher Professions	*Lower Professions*	*Total*
1851	1.0	1.6	2.6
1881	1.2	2.6	3.8
1901	1.3	2.5	3.8
1931	1.5	2.9	4.4

iii. COLIN CLARK: *National Income and Outlay*, p. 32.

Table 10
Occupied Population in Work 1931 (in thousands)

	Males	*Females*
Managerial	1028	152
Working on own account	921	351
Clerical, Commercial and Professional	2207	1491
Agricultural and Fishing Operative	892	44
Other manual workers	7445	3454
Unemployed	2508	781
Total	15001	6273

iv. COLIN CLARK: *National Income and Outlay*, p. 94. Figures compiled from Table 39 — Distribution of Income between Factors of Production:

	Wages	Salaries	Property
1911	39.5	15.6	45.9
1924	42.1	25.4	32.5
1925	40.0	24.8	35.2
1930	40.5	25.3	34.2
1935	40.5	25.0	34.5

v. CARR-SAUNDERS: *Social Structure of England and Wales*, p. 43. Salaries as a percentage of National Income:

	Percentage
1911	12
1924	22
1931	24
1935	26

NOTES: (1) Tables i and ii show an increase in the proportional importance of the middle class, and the professional class respectively, over a period of fifty years.

(2) Tables iv and v show a growth in the fraction of the National Income taken by these classes.

(3) Table iii shows the present distribution of the population between occupational classes.

§ 5

Growth of Small Property

All the figures in this section were compiled from the United Kingdom Statistical Abstract.

(a) *Proportion of Estates over £100 Gross to Deaths*

	Number of Estates	Number of Deaths over 35 in average about Tax Year	Percentage
1901–2	61,393	318,000	19.3
1911–2	70,222	329,000	21.3
1921–2	106,000	353,000	28.6
1931–2	130,000	414,000	31.4

STATISTICS

(b) *Members and Funds in the Various Types of Society*

(i) Savings Banks

	Post Office Savings Banks		Trustee Savings Bank	
	Sums Due (£ millions)	Members (millions)	Members (millions)	Sums L (£ milli
1846				31.7
1850				28.9
1855				34.2
1860				41.2
1865	6.52			38.7
1870	15.09			37.9
1875	25.19			42.3
1880	33.74			43.9
1885	47.70		1.59	47.0
1890	67.63	5.78	1.53	44.9
1895	97.87	6.45	1.51	46.5
1900	135.55	8.43	1.62	52.8
1905	152.11	9.96	1.73	55 0.
1910	168.89	8.37	1.82	54.8
1915	186.32	9.97	1.96	54.7
1920	226.35	12.74	2.33	91.3
1925	285.49	10.67	2.50	110.4.
1930	290.23	9.85	2.58	133.19
1935	390.33	9.71	2.19	197.4

(ii) Building Societies

	Members (millions)	Funds (£ millions)
1877		25.72
1880		39.39
1890		52.28
1900		45.75
1910		61.62
1920	.75	82.18
1930	1.45	353.54
1925	1.93	571.41

(iii) Industrial and Provident Societies

1877	.53	6.56
1880	.60	7.57
1890	1.05	14.79
1900	1.78	23.25
1910	2.69	35.81
1920	5.34	178.17
1930	7.51	236.76
1935	8.61	302.97

(iv) Friendly Societies

1920	7.16	67.50
1925	7.24	91.24
1930	7.52	108.41
1934	7.60	118.77

(v) Retail Co-operative Societies

1913	2.88	45.76
1920	4.44	91.39
1925	4.86	106.68
1930	6.37	142.90
1935	7.44	175.70

(c) *Conspectus of Small Property*

(i) *Great Britain* 1935

Adult Population 1931   31,000,000
No. of Census Dwellings   12,000,000 approx.

	Members	Funds £	Average £
Building Societies	1,930,000	571,400,000	296.0
Retail Co-operative	7,440,000	175,700,000	23.5
Industrial and Provident	8,610,000	302,900,000	35.2
Friendly Societies	7,600,000	118,700,000	15.6
Savings Banks	11,900,000	587,730,000	49.9
National Savings Certificates (approx.)	8,500,000	500,000,000	58.8

(ii) *Change in the Conspectus in the Quinquennium* 1930-35

	1930 Members thousands	1930 Funds £ millions	1935 Members thousands	1935 Funds £ millions
Building Societies	1,450	353.54	1,930	571.41
Retail Co-operative	6,370	142.90	7,440	175.70
Industrial and Provident	7,500	263.76	8,600	230.97
Friendly	7,520	108.41	7,600	118.77
Savings Banks	12,430	423.41	11,900	587.73
Totals	35,270,000		37,470,000	
	£1,265,020,000		£1,756,580,000	

e. increases: 6.25% in Total Memberships; 38.8% increase in Total Funds.

(d) *Rate of Small Savings* (Publication of S. Maguire & Son, November 1936)

	Total Funds
1925	£1670 millions
1934	£2480 millions
1936	£2800 millions

§ 6

Growth of Limited Liability

(a) *Domination of Business*

(i) Great Britain (Sombart, *L'Apogée du Capitalisme*, Chap. xiv)

	Number of Companies in Existence	Nominal Capital £ millions
1885	8,692	475.5
1890	13,323	775.1
1900	29,730	1,622.6
1905	39,616	1,954.3
1910	51,787	2,178.6
1913	60,754	2,425.7

(ii) *America.* (Berle and Means, Chap. ii)

	Proportion of Manufacturing Labour Employed by Joint Stock Enterprise
1904	73.7
1909	79.0
1914	83.3
1919	87.9
1929	92.0

(b) *Dispersion of Stock Holding — Great Britain*

Figures collected from recent Company reports (random selections—not largest)

Horlicks, Ltd.	May	'37	20,258
Central Argentine Railway	Nov.	'36	38,934
Bradford Dyers Association	Aug.	'36	22,780
Bleachers Association	June	'36	21,734
Calico Printers Association	May	'36	18,200
London & North Eastern Rly.	March	'36	172,950
Great Western Railway	March	'36	93,000
Shell Transport & Trading	March	'36	75,420
Vickers, Ltd.	July	'35	32,777
Guest, Keen & Nettlefolds	June	'35	20,148
Courtaulds, Ltd.	April	'35	41,726
Imperial Chemical Industries	Sept.	'35	76,400(Defrd
Home & Colonial Stores	April	'34	22,750

(c) *Increase of Dispersion — America*

BERLE and MEANS: *Modern Corporation and Private Property*, p. 55

	Number of Stock Holders		
	American Telephone & Telegraph Co. Ltd.	*Pennsylvania Railroad*	*United States Steel Corporation*
1902	12,000	28,408	25,636
1905	18,000	40,385	20,075
1910	41,000	65,283	28,850
1915	66,000	93,768	45,767
1920	139,448	133,068	95,776
1925	362,179	140,578	90,576
1930	567,694	207,188	145,566
1931	642,180	241,391	174,507

§ 7

Recent Movements in the Standard of Living

(i) LAYTON and CROWTHER: *Introduction to the Study of Prices,* p. 266.

Table I

	Money Wages	*Money Prices*	*Percentage Unemployment*	*Real Wages Full Work*	*Real Wages Less Unemployment*
1850	100	100	0	100	100
1900	179	89	2.5	183	179
1913	188.5	103	2.1	172	169

	Money Wages	Money Prices	Percentage Unemployment	Real Wages Full Work	Real Wages Less Unemployment
1922	398	198	14.3	201	184
1925	371.5	190	11.3	195	180
1929	367	178	10.4	206	192
1933	347	149	19.9	233	202

(ii) COLIN CLARK: *National Income and Outlay*, p. 208.

Table 194

	Net National Income at 1930 Prices	Real Income Per Person in Work at Consumption Prices	Real Income Per Occupied Person including Unemployment
1924	3679	202.4	185.0
1925	3947	214.2	194.3
1928	4117	214.0	195.2
1929	4337	221.9	203.4
1932	3995	220.4	183.4
1933	4160	228.8	194.2
1934	4445	235.2	204.8
1935	4735	240.8	211.8
1936	4960	251.2	221.8

§ 8

Production Trends in Great Britain

(a) *Absolute Physical Productions — Great Britain.* Compiled by iss Nadine Hambourg from: *British Foreign Trade and Industry* port to Parliament in 1908; *League of Nations Statistical Year Books* for ter figures; *Vierteljahrshefter zur Konjuncturforschung.*

Quinquennial Annual Averages – Million Tons

	Pig Iron	Steel	Coal	General Production Index
1855–9	3.5		66.1	
1860–4	4.1		84.9	34
1865–9	4.9	.2	103.0	
1870–4	6.4	.5	120.7	44
1875–9	6.4	.9	133.3	
1880–4	8.1	1.8	156.4	53
1885–9	7.7	3.0	165.2	
1890–4	7.3	3.2	180.3	62
1895–9	8.6	4.2	201.9	

	Pig Iron	Steel	Coal	General Production Index
1900–4	8.6	4.9	226.8	79
1905–8	9.8	6.0	254.1	
1910				85
1913				100
1919–23				90
1924–28				
1929–33				98

(b) *Per Capita Productions*:

(i) The same figures as in (*a*) divided by the total populati
in the same period.

Tons per Capita

	Pig Iron	Steel	Coal	Production Index Divided by Population
1855–9	.12		2.34	
1860–4	.14		2.91	.61
1865–9	.16	.01	3.41	
1870–4	.20	.02	3.79	.70
1875–9	.19	.03	3.99	
1880–4	.23	.05	4.44	.74
1885–9	.21	.08	4.52	
1890–4	.19	.08	4.72	.78
1895–9	.22	.11	5.05	
1900–4	.20	.12	5.40	.88
1905–9	.22	.14	5.79	
1910				.89
1913				
1919–23	.12	.15	5.05	1.11
1924–28	.13	.16	5.06	
1929–33	.11	.15	5.01	1.05

NOTES: 1. There is no continuity in these figures between the earli
period and the later as they are derived from different sources.

2. The *per capita* figures for the later period have no absolu
productions shown in these tables for the same dates as the *p
capita* figures are given in the League of Nations Statistical Ye
Book.

3. In all cases the General Production Index refers either to t
year at the beginning of the period or to a three-year averag
about it.

INDEX

377

INDEX

INDEX

INDEX

INDEX

INDEX

Staple industries, fate of, 142

State, 57, 63, 136; Communist view of, 229; made for man, 330

State control, 148

State-controlled capitalism, *see* Capitalism

State-organized monopoly capitalism, 100, 133, 137, 325

State-sanctioned monopolies, 304

States, 52

Stationery Office, 97

Stebbing, Prof. Susan, 180

Stock Exchange, New York, 125

Stock Holding, dispersion of, 374

Strachey, John, 156-9, 162, 168, 172-3, 175, 206-8, 231, 268

Strangeness, 62

Strangers, resentment of, 46

Strategy of Socialism, 283 ff.

Struggle, 186; and force, relation of, 164

Stuarts, 244

Sudetenland, 24

Super-ego, 56

Sweat-room, *see* Parilka

Sweden, 236, 246, 248, 274, 284, 296

Switzerland, 274

Syndicalist movement, 294

Tawney, Prof. R. H., 13

Taxation, 104, 293-4, 296-7, 299, 309 ff., 316, 368-9; growth of, 138, 357, 368; progressive, *see* Progressive taxation

Terror, 276, 337 ff.

Textile trades, 97, 314

Third International, 221, 223

Thomas Aquinas, St., 167

Tiltman, 345

Toleration, 258

Tomsky, 350

Torture, 24-5, 49, 214, 339, 341-2

Trade Boards, 89, 363

Trade Boards Acts, 98

Trade cycle, 23, 85-6, 90-1, 99-100, 119, 137, 296

Trade Union membership, 89, 363

Trade Unions, 89, 199, 358, 359, 363

Traditionalism, 78

Transfer prices, 303

Transport industry, 301, 314

Transport, Ministry of, *see* Ministry

Treasury Bills, 97

Trials, in Germany and Russia, 338-9; mass, 339-40

Trotsky, 312, 350

Trotskyists, 60, 208, 210, 340

Trustee Savings Banks, 114

Tukhachevsky, 350

Tupoleff, 351

Uborevich, 351

Ukraine, 343

Ulster crisis of 1914, 197, 200 ff.

Unconscious, 70; importance of, 70

Under-consumption theories, 137

Unemployed, 299

Unemployment, 22, 137, 314, 316

Unemployment assistance, 94

Unemployment insurance, 94, 199

Uniformity, 252

Uniforms, political, 278

United Front, 221-2, 290-1, 306-7

United States, *see* America

United States Steel Corporation, 12[.]

Unity, 252; National, 247

Universal and solitary causes, rela[.] of, 179, 181-2

Upper Bourgeoisie, *see* Bourgeoisie

Utilitarianism, 329-30

Utilitarians, 244

Value, Theory of, 353 ff.

'Valuta' Tortures, 341

Versailles, Treaty of, 22, 274

Vickers Ltd., 374

Viktoroff, 350

Voroshiloff, 351

Wage Rigidity, 91

Wages Boards, 145

Wages, Money and Prices, 363-4

Wages, real, 106; history of, 142

War, 24, 29, 39, 222, 272, 327; *see* [.] Civil War; Religion, Wars of

War, International, 62

Water supply, 314-15

Watt, James, 79

Wealth, 330

Wellington, Duke of, 194, 197

Wicksell, 354

Widows' Pensions, 94

Will, human, 51

Winchilsea, Lord, 195

Workers' control, 315

Workers' councils, 229

Working class, British, not revoluti[.] ary, 288

Yagoda, 350

Yakov, 351

Yegeroff, 350

Yenukidze, 350

Zinovieff, 350-1

Zoology, 28

Zuckerman, Dr., 39, 44